The Waging War Within
A Devotional For Winning
The Daily War

GREGG JOSEPH KRETSCHMER AND

JASON CHRISTIAN RAVIZZA

To Terry

I pray that the Words God has used in this Devotional Put a Light on your Heart. God Bless You and Your Walk.

Wayne.

Copyright 2011
Library of Congress Number   TX0007780274
ISBN 9780988729025

Publisher:
Media 14:36, Inc.

PO Box 447
Agawam, MA 01001

Media1436.com

Acknowledgements

I wish to thank God for all of His blessings. I wish to thank my Brother in Christ, Gregg Kretschmer for his dedication, devotion, focus and friendship in working with me on The Waging War Within. My friendship with Gregg and this combined effort in writing The Waging War Within has truly been a blessing from God in my life. I also wish to thank all of my brothers and sisters in the Body of Christ that have touched my life throughout the years. I would especially like to thank my family; my wife Kimberly, my son Jared, and my two daughters Kaitlyn and Meredith for all of their love and encouragement while writing this book.

I would like to thank God for finding me worthy to be called a son of The Most High. I would also like to thank Jason for the invitation to work with him on this endeavor. Writing this book with Jason allowed me a great opportunity to delve deeper in the Word, all the while growing closer to God. Working with Jason was a great pleasure as it allowed us to get to know each other on a totally different level. I wish to thank my wife Maria for understanding my devotion not only to her but also to the Word and God. This book took both Jason and I away from our families for a considerable amount of time, but our families understood the passion of our hearts.

Dedications

First and foremost, I dedicate this book to God and His Son, Jesus Christ. May He, by the power inherent within the Holy Spirit, use this book to bless lives all over the world. I dedicate this book to my wife Kimberly, to my son Jared and to my two daughters, Kaitlyn and Meredith. I am eternally grateful to God for blessing me with such a wonderful family. Let us always keep in sight our relationship with and our faith in God. I love you all.

I wish to dedicate this book to God and His Son, Jesus Christ. I pray it blesses all who read it as much as it blessed me in writing it. I also dedicate this book to my wife Maria and my son Kyle, two gifts from God given to a man who doesn't deserve them but who is glad he has them. You are both a light in my life. I wish to also dedicate this book to the late Leo LeBlanc, a man who showed me what a real Christian man was. Leo was a Godly man and a man's man all in one. I miss him dearly, but I will see him again, praise God. This is also dedicated to Miss Janet Desrosiers, my spiritual mother. She is the one who will tie a knot when one is needed. I love her dearly. This is also dedicated to Pastor Jim Grove, a friend when I needed one. Pastor Jim had the patience of a saint. He was the one who took me under his wing when I first came to Christ. I thank you brother.

Foreword

Gregg and Jason bring a wonderful blend of the "counselor warrior" dynamics that explain and evaluate the raging war that we fight daily. Their insights and biblical truths found in this book will serve us well in the battle that will ensue in the end of days. I know both of these men personally and know that as God gives them the platform and freedom to express their full God given potential, you will be hearing more from them.

Richard E. Adams
Senior Pastor, Bethany Assembly of God, Agawam, MA

Fighting the war within requires constant focus and a daily commitment to God. This devotional will accomplish both.

Reverend Chuck Brewster
President and Founder of "Champions of Honor",
A World Wide Men's Ministry

The scripture-based and life experienced wisdom that lies within the book you now hold is worth the investment of your time and understanding. As a man pursuing God's best, I am grateful to learn from authors who have personally proven the principles communicated in this volume.

Tom Greene
National Director of Men's Ministries and Light For
The Lost, General Council, Assemblies of God

Benediction

Lord, we offer up this book to you as a testimony of all that you have done for Jason and I. We thank you for your continued love, guidance, and continued protection over us and our loved ones. Lord we ask that you go out with each copy of this tome and bless whoever picks it up and reads it. Lord we ask that you will enlighten their minds and hearts and give them the ability to see the truths written within these pages. Lord, please have them take the words and have them apply them to their walks and lives so that they will be able to fight off the fiery darts flung at them by the dark one. Lord, we ask that you have them give application to the words and allow them to enhance their walks and lives through the words put forth. Lord we thank you in advance for all that you will do with and through this book. The blessings of researching this book was a delight that we hope all who read it will share in. Lord, we wish for you to have this book as an offering for all the grace that you have shown to us and for all that you have brought us through. We thank you for pulling us out of our pasts and for putting us on the pathway of righteousness. This book is an offering of thanks and praise being offered up to you, Lord. Thank you for all that you have done and continue to do for each and every one of us, your children. We, your humble servants ask these things in and through the glorious name of your Son, Jesus Christ. Amen.

Jude 1:24-25; **"To Him who is able to keep you from falling and to present you before His glorious presence without fault and with great joy-- to the only God our Savior be glory, majesty, power and authority, through Jesus Christ our Lord, before all ages, now and forevermore! Amen."**

The Whole Armor of God Ephesians 6:10-18

10Finally, be strong in the Lord and in the strength of his might. 11 Put on the whole armor of God, that you may be able to stand against the schemes of the devil. 12 For we do not wrestle against flesh and blood, but against the rulers, against the authorities, against the cosmic powers over this present darkness, against the spiritual forces of evil in the heavenly places. 13 Therefore take up the whole armor of God, that you may be able to withstand in the evil day, and having done all, to stand firm. 14Stand therefore, having fastened on the belt of truth, and having put on the breastplate of righteousness, 15and, as shoes for your feet, having put on the readiness given by the gospel of peace. 16In all circumstances take up the shield of faith, with which you can extinguish all the flaming darts of the evil one; 17and take the helmet of salvation, and the sword of the Spirit, which is the word of God, 18praying at all times in the Spirit, with all prayer and supplication. To that end keep alert with all perseverance, making supplication for all the saints.

5~ The Waging War Within

INTRODUCTION

Since 911, Americans have been awakened to the ever changing era of warfare. Americans not even enlisted in the armed forces confronted an attack from a distant land that paralyzed, traumatized, and opened our eyes to the very act of war. An enemy penetrated the infrastructure of the United States of America and killed thousands of people. This enemy had many Americans come face to face with a violent attack. Other than Pearl Harbor, like never before in history, many Americans came face to face with their humanity, fragility, and mortality, while on American soil.

Unlike 911, which was able to be seen by the eyes, heard with the ears, and literally experienced by all five senses by those who witnessed the 911 attacks, this book focuses not on warfare that is seen, but on the warfare that is unseen and spiritual in nature. The purpose of this book is to create an awareness of the spiritual attack and the onslaught of the enemy (Satan) that is **Waging a War Within** the confines of our families, our hearts, our minds, and our communities.

Never before in history has there been such an attack on the lives of Christian Americans as we are witnessing today! With the advent of the collapse of the American family and the anti-life campaign, (abortion), American Christian values, morals, and ethics throughout our land have gone topsy-turvy. We should be hearing a public outcry from Americans that hold to Christian values!

Hollywood has inundated American Culture with sexually explicit and often violent movies and television shows. These movies depict Christian men and fathers as spineless dim witted oafs, incapable of thinking straight. The video game industry is thriving similarly on this practice. The entertainment industries have found that violence and sex sells. An ever present **Waging War** exists within the hearts, minds, and souls of Americans. Many researchers within the realm of counseling & clinical psychology have and continue to research the effects of violent and sexual images on the human psyche. Can you imagine the impact of violent movies, television shows, and video games on the minds, hearts, and souls of our youth? How is this impacting our society, culture, churches, and families? Just turn on the evening news and you will see the effects of these mediums.

Currently the major political issues are border control and the wars in Iraq and Afghanistan. What about **The Waging War Within** and the onslaught of the enemy against the minds and hearts of our youth within our borders? How do we counterattack the assault being advocated by the counterculture? How do we aid those in crisis from the; devastation of divorce, substance abuse, alcoholism, mental illness, suicide, abortion, murder, adultery, sex before marriage, single parent homes, teen pregnancy, domestic violence, child abuse and neglect and the brokenness and devastating consequences associated with sin? How can we impart to our youth the truth within the Bible? **The Waging War Within** will bridge the gap between these issues and the hope that rests in the awesome Word of God. Our hope in writing this book is that the power of the Holy Spirit would ignite you the Christian believer and that the captive would be set free and the unsaved would come to know Jesus Christ as their Lord and Savior.

PREFACE

The Waging War Within will expound upon Scripture from the Book of Matthew, New Testament NIV version of the Bible with the primary emphasis being on Spiritual Warfare. This book will examine specific Scriptures that we can draw from to help us confront and combat spiritual warfare taking place within our lives. This book will examine the strategies, perspectives, attitudes, and behaviors needed to counterattack **Spiritual Warfare.**

Ephesians 6:10-20; The Full Armor of God; "[10] Finally, be strong in the Lord and in his mighty power. [11] Put on the full armor of God so that you can take your stand against the devil's schemes. [12] For our struggle is not against flesh and blood, but against the rulers, against the authorities, against the powers of this dark world and against the spiritual forces of evil in the heavenly realms. [13] Therefore put on the full armor of God, so that when the day of evil comes, you may be able to stand your ground, and after you have done everything, to stand. [14] Stand firm then, with the belt of truth buckled around your waist, with the breastplate of righteousness in place, [15] and with your feet fitted with the readiness that comes from the gospel of peace. [16] In addition to all this, take up the shield of faith, with which you can extinguish all the flaming arrows of the evil one. [17] Take the helmet of salvation and the sword of the Spirit, which is the word of God. [18] And pray in the Spirit on all occasions with all kinds of prayers and requests. With this in mind, be alert and always keep on praying for all the saints. [19] Pray also for me, that whenever I open my mouth, words may be given me so that I will fearlessly make known the mystery of the gospel, [20] for which I am an ambassador in chains. Pray that I may declare it fearlessly, as I should."

The emphasis on **The Waging War Within** will be on creating an awareness for the believer in Christ as to the power inherent within the Word of God (The Sword of the Spirit), Scripture (which is God breathed), and the Person and Work of the Holy Spirit. We will explore how to put on the **Full Armor of God** so we can stand against the devils schemes, allowing us to live out a full and more abundant and fulfilling life without fear and trepidation. We will discover that everything that God wanted us to know within the Bible is sufficient for us to be set free from any and every bondage that may have us shackled.

The Waging War Within will bring us face to face with an actual map, or blueprint, that will deliver us from anything that may hinder us from living freely in Jesus Christ. You the reader will experience the inherent power within the Word of God. Your relationship with Christ will be enriched, abounding in power and assurance found in our Heavenly Father, who loves us beyond worldly belief. The reader will begin to see how high, deep, and unfathomable the love of Jesus Christ is. His love exists within each and every believer! The key to a healthy and full life in and through Jesus Christ is to unlock the ever present reality of the Holy Spirit's power and anointing that exists within us and to be the soldier for Christ that God has called for us to be. No longer will you be intimidated by unbelievers and this worlds system, but living in the absolute power, anointing, and authority of God! This is what Jesus intended for His church to be; fully empowered by the Holy Spirit and performing miracles and healings far greater than He did. John 14:12; "**I tell you the truth, anyone who has faith in me will do what I have been doing. He will do even greater things than these, because I am**

going to the Father."

God desires for us to live in the unbridled power and love that exists within Him. This power flows from nowhere else except from within the Trinity; the Father, the Son, and the Holy Spirit. Truth, power and love belong to and flows from Jesus Christ and His followers. God has called each Christian in such a time as this, to be an **anointed warrior and soldier.** He has called us to march to the beat of a different drummer, no longer allowing the prince of this dark world to have any power in our lives. We as Christians need to start acknowledging, understanding, accepting, and living in the power of the divine destiny that we have in Jesus Christ our Lord and Savior.

We have been called to actively participate in life, but a life that honors God. We are surrounded by temptations, worldly friends and acquaintances, and pitfalls that are trying to trip us up. We need to don the Full Armor of God as in Ephesians 6:10-20. Once we have put it on we can stand with the assurance that God has given us a way to win the battle. There is only one piece of the Armor that is offensive, the Sword of the Spirit, the Bible, The Holy Word of God. We have to know our battle plan my friends. We have to know the Word. If we study the Word and really get to know it, we stand a much better chance of living a life that will bring honor and joy to our Lord and Savior Jesus Christ. I pray that this devotional will benefit you in your daily walk. It was a pleasure writing it and I pray you use it to the fullest intent in which it was written, that in getting to know Jesus Christ better and taking His Word and placing it as a treasure within our hearts. Thank you for purchasing this work and I pray God's blessings on you and yours. Happy reading.

JANUARY

January 1st

Matthew 1:21- "She (Mary) will give birth to a son, and you are to give him the name Jesus, because he will save his people from their sins." –NIV

Imagine the birth of Jesus Christ! God the Father, God the Son and God the Holy Spirit is born into the world to save humankind from their sins. The most incomparably significant and captivating event in history had evoked **The Waging War Within**. In the book of Matthew, Jesus is born, and through Him is the key and passage to eternal life, where humanity can now escape the clutches of the evil one (the devil) and hell. We now have the power in Jesus to escape the power of death, hell and the grave through God sending His Son in human form, as a little baby.

At the onset of time, a **Waging War Within** was being strategically initiated by Satan himself. The ever-present war between the forces of good and evil was manifested within the realm of the supernatural and natural worlds! In Matthew we observe John the Baptist preparing the way of the Lord (Matthew 3:1-12)

John, in Matthew 3, is calling for the repentance of sins and heralding in the calling of Jesus. He was the herald for Christ. The message was that rewards come to those who will believe and repent but there will be a terrible time for those who choose not to listen. Christ came first as a servant to be sacrificed on the cross for our sins but will come again as our Lord and soon coming King. John the Baptist knew this and was desperate to prepare for the coming of Jesus so that He could start His ministry which would live to this day and all the days to come.

We are also called to bring people to repentance. We are to be like John the Baptist in that we are given a commission in Matthew 28:18-20 to go and spread the Good News into all the world. God has placed a calling on our lives just as John the Baptist had on his. The difference between John the Baptist and us is that John the Baptist readily accepted his calling. There are many today who are shying away from their God given calling. God has entrusted us with a task to spread the message of Jesus Christ to all those that we come into contact with. It is a rather simple task. We are the ones that complicate it. We need to mimic the ultimate herald, John the Baptist. We can read a profile of John the Baptist in John 1.

Repent!

January 2nd

Matthew 3:2- "Repent, for the kingdom of heaven is near."-NIV

God has entrusted John the Baptist with ushering sinners into sainthood through water baptism. Religious leaders of the day were outraged by this event. A man (John the Baptist) claiming with such purpose and power that he's baptizing in the name of the One called Jesus for the repentance of sins Matthew 3:11, **"I indeed baptize you in (with) water because of repentance [that is, because of your changing your minds for the better, heartily amending your ways, with abhorrence of your past sins]. But He who is coming after me is mightier than I, whose sandals I am not worthy *or* fit to take off *or* carry; He will baptize you with the Holy Spirit and with fire."**

John the Baptist was a bold man. He went head to head with the religious leaders of his day regardless of the outcome to himself. There are accounts where he called the religious leaders a brood of vipers and where he told the king that he, the king, was an adulterer because he was sleeping with his brother's wife (Matthew 14:1-12, Mark 6:14-29, Luke 9:7-9). John was a bold man who spoke the truth regardless of the cost. He took a stand for his faith and it cost him his life. Are we willing to do that? Are you willing to lay down your life for Jesus Christ? He did it for you.

Look at some Christians today; they get upset when someone calls them a Jesus freak. Honestly people, how can you expect to stand on and for the truth if you can't even take a little name calling. There is going to come a day where Christians are going to have to make a choice between living for the world and dying for Jesus. Think about that. That choice may have to be made soon the way things are going today.

There are Christians the world over who are laying down their lives for the name of Jesus Christ. Young girls are being raped and brutalized to dissuade their faith in Jesus. There are people who are being butchered on account of their faith in Jesus Christ. These atrocities are happening all over the world and we have people here in the U.S. who cry and complain because someone called them a name, shame on us. What are we going to do when the heat really gets turned up?

Living in sin
vs.
Repentance

Matthew 3:6 (people) were confessing their sins, they were baptized by him in the Jordan River."-NIV

We need to get back to the basics with us having a repentant heart before the Lord. God works through a humble and contrite heart. When is the last time you asked for forgiveness for your daily sins? When is the last time you got down on your knees and asked God to forgive you of the wrong words that you've said, or the wrong things that you've done? God lifts up and delivers those who fall down and cry out to Him. He delivers those who ask that His grace be poured out in their lives. God answers those who are sincere in their walk with Him.

Once we acknowledge and grasp the forgiveness that God has for us and how much we're in need of His forgiveness to blanket our lives, God will lift us up. His love will be poured out in our lives, giving us hope, power and love. Psalm 107:1 says, **"Oh give thanks to the LORD, for he is good, for his steadfast love endures forever!"** God will pour out His love abundantly in your life if you just call out to Him and honestly ask for His forgiveness. He loves you with a love you couldn't begin to imagine. You will win **The Waging War Within** once you drop to your knees and cry out to God in full and utter humility! Genesis 1:27, **"So God created man in his own image, in the image of God He created him; male and female he created them."** God wants a relationship with us. That is what we were created for, relationship with Him. Our sinful nature blocks that relationship. We need to eliminate sin from our lives. If we sin, we need to call out to God for forgiveness as soon as possible. It is a good practice to ask for total forgiveness each night when we get ready to retire for the evening and we say our prayers. I hope you do this. If you don't, try to make it a daily routine. God wants to hear from you.

Let's agree not to willfully sin. Let's agree to do everything we can to live a life which is pleasing to the Lord. Let's pray daily for the strength to stand strong when faced with adversity. Prayer is our lifeline to God. There are no other mediators needed to communicate with God. All we have to do is pray and He will be there for us. Remember, God is a gentleman and He only goes where He is invited.

Talk to God daily

January 4th

Matthew 3:7- "You brood of vipers! Who warned you to flee from the coming wrath? -Matthew 3:10- The ax is already at the root of the trees, and every tree that does not produce good fruit will be cut down and thrown into the fire.-NIV Again in Matthew 3:11,12- He will baptize you with the Holy Spirit and with fire. His winnowing fork is in his hand, and he will clear his threshing floor, gathering his wheat into the barn and burning up the chaff with unquenchable fire."-NIV

Can you imagine the reaction, indignation and confusion amidst the religious leaders when John the Baptist called them a brood of vipers? They had probably never been spoken to in that manner before. They thought they were so high and mighty. Their religiosity was getting the better of them and their thoughts were precipitating a **Waging War Within** their very beings. John the Baptist was rocking their world, and all he did was call it like it was! Don't you wish that you would have guts to do something like that? It takes nerve to speak to a high ranking official like John did.

My friends when you become a son, or a daughter of God, you will receive a gift from the Holy Spirit. Boldness from the Holy Spirit will come upon you. This boldness will most likely surprise you. You will find yourself saying and doing things you never thought you would say or do. John 16:13 informs us of how this power comes to us, **"When the Spirit of truth comes, he will guide you into all the truth, for he will not speak on his own authority, but whatever he hears he will speak, and he will declare to you the things that are to come."** You will find yourself quoting Scripture that you never knew you knew. It is truly amazing. You will be witnessing to friends and strangers and you will surprise yourself with what you say. God is awesome in what He does when we allow Him and His Spirit to work in and through us. Just look at what John the Baptist did. Don't you wish you could have been there to witness how boldly he spoke to the Pharisees? I sure do.

Good fruit
vs.
Bad fruit

Matthew 4:1-5-"Then Jesus was led by the Spirit into the desert to be tempted by the devil. After fasting forty days and forty nights, he was hungry. The tempter came to him and said, "If you are the Son of God, tell these stones to become bread." Jesus answered, "It is written: 'Man does not live on bread alone, but on every word that comes from the mouth of God.' Then the devil took him to the holy city and had him stand on the highest point of the temple. "If you are the Son of God," he said, "Throw yourself down. For it is written: "He will command His angels concerning you, and they will lift you up in their hands, so that you will not strike your foot against stone."-NIV

The temptation of Jesus was a **Waging War Within** GOD Himself. This was the devil attempting to disrupt the plans of God Himself. How often do we see this taking place in our own lives? If we look hard enough we can see the spiritual battles raging in our lives. Are you prepared for them? You need to be. Perhaps you need to get back to the basics, just like a person entering the military.

Have you ever wondered why a new recruit entering the military has to go through Basic Training? It is so that they can be reprogrammed. The military, whichever branch it is, has to retrain the recruit's way of thinking so that they will learn a new mindset and understand the military way of life. The military has a very short period of time in which they need to undo what civilization has done over a period of years, 18 plus years. We need to do the same thing in our new walk, we need to learn to trust and rely on God our Father. How do we do this? We do it by reading His Word daily and praying earnestly for His will to be done in our lives. We do it by training our minds and bodies. We cannot rely on someone else to read and interpret the Word for us.

If you are reading this right now you have just proven that you are intelligent and able to understand the words, so why would you expect someone else to do that for you? Don't be lazy. Do your own work. We all need to read the Word in order to keep our minds and our walks fresh. It doesn't matter if you have been a Christian for a matter of days or a number of years; you still need to read the Word daily. Acts 17:11 has the Apostle Paul visiting Berea, look what he found with the people there once they grasped their calling. **"Now these Jews were nobler than those in Thessalonica; they received the word with all eagerness, examining the Scriptures daily to see if these things were so."** Did you catch what they did? They searched and studied the Scriptures daily. Are you following their lead?

Read daily and show yourself approved.

January 6th

Matthew 4:7-11- "Jesus answered him, "It is also written: 'Do not put the Lord your God to the test.' Again, the devil took him to a very high mountain and showed him all the kingdoms of the world and their splendor. "All this I will give you," he said, "If you will bow down and worship me." Jesus said to him, "Away from me, Satan! For it is written: 'Worship the Lord your God, and serve him only.' Then the devil left him, and angels came and attended him."-NIV

Here is GOD and Satan going head to head in combat in the ultimate **Waging War Within** tag team bout that the world has ever witnessed! Imagine GOD and Satan dueling it out! Here we have Satan pushing and shoving God with all his manipulation and seduction, but God not budging, not moving, and ultimately prevailing! What an example for us as Christian believers to emulate. Here God didn't combat the warfare of Satan by hitting him below the belt or even stooping down in any way, shape or form to the devil's schemes. God just resisted the lure of the devil. He didn't fall into the devil's trap set before Him.

Many Christians, when confronted with a **Waging War Within,** would be smart to follow the example set by Christ Himself. Don't give in to temptation. When tempted, quote scripture in your head, speak scripture with your mouth, and denounce the devil in his tracks. Don't give the enemy a foothold in your life. Scripture clearly and simply shows us the power of avoidance and the importance of setting smart boundaries when it comes to the tempter and his sinful accusations. You can only do this if you know scripture, so learn it! You defeat Satan by knowledgeable use of scripture. Battles are won one day at a time, and over time you will eventually win the war if you just persevere.

If we read our Bible daily we will have a foolproof plan to defeat Satan at his own game. We need to crack the covers of our Bible's and get to really know His Word in order for it to work. All Scripture comes from God and it is our weapon to win the **Waging War Within,** the battle for our souls. 2 Timothy 3:16; **"All Scripture is breathed out by God and profitable for teaching, for reproof, for correction, and for training in righteousness"**

After taking a stand for righteousness and acting under our own volition toward the things of God, God is able to act on our behalf. Remember, we're not puppets; we have a mind of our own. The devil will flee from our presence, due to our embracing whole heartedly the very things of Christ. God will send His angels to protect us if we call on Him! (Psalms 91:11-12, Daniel 6:21-22)

Matthew 4:16,17-"the people living in darkness have seen a great light; on those living in the land of the shadow of death a light has dawned. From that time on Jesus began to preach, "Repent, for the kingdom of heaven is near."-NIV

Radical & revolutionary is the act of repentance. We must humble ourselves with the realization and ever present awareness that as Christians, we're not the ultimate authority. We're the created, not the creator. In submission we must humble ourselves, die to self, and allow Jesus Christ to operate in our hearts as the skillful surgeon He is with humility. We must surrender and sacrifice our will, for the ultimate will of God. This is accomplished by being born again. John 3:5-9, **"Jesus answered, "Truly, truly, I say to you, unless one is born of water and the Spirit, he cannot enter the kingdom of God. That which is born of the flesh is flesh, and that which is born of the Spirit is spirit. Do not marvel that I said to you, 'You must be born again.' The wind blows where it wishes, and you hear its sound, but you do not know where it comes from or where it goes. So it is with everyone who is born of the Spirit."**

Humility is reverence to God in the acknowledgement of His sacrifice for us with His death on Calvary and His glorious ascension into Heaven three days later. We must remember what He did on our behalf in order for us to spend eternity with Him. We must surrender and sacrifice our will to Him; this gives us the revelation of the abundant and overflowing grace and salvation that is ours through our Lord Jesus Christ. We need to swallow our pride and place our egos on the shelf if we plan on being truly effective workers for the Kingdom of God.

My friends, when we get into the mindset where we know that we can't but He can, then we are in a place where God can work in and through us. We have to remember that ego is **E**dging **G**od **O**ut. I know that I have made plenty of mistakes when I tried to take over and get in the driver's seat. I know today that God is much better equipped to handle all of the things that life throws at me than I am. I pray that I don't forget that. I can't but He can. I don't want to **E**dge **G**od **O**ut and I pray that you don't either.

Light
vs.
Darkness

January 8th

Matthew 4:16,17-"**the people living in darkness have seen a great light; on those living in the land of the shadow of death a light has dawned. From that time on Jesus began to preach, "Repent, for the kingdom of heaven is near."**-NIV**

Humanity wrestles within both the supernatural and natural realms of our existence. By nature we like to control things and think that we're the center of the universe. We like to be in control and ultimately take charge of our lives. Surrender isn't even an option! What, surrender? Surrender to whom? I don't think so! We in our human existential thinking associate surrender with giving up and failure. Failure to lift ourselves up by our proverbial boot straps and make something of our lives is not looked upon favorably in today's society. The world consists of me myself and I, yes it's a trinity, but not the Trinity.

Pride can come into our lives and manifest itself in any number of ways. Another name for pride is ego and as we have said earlier, ego is edging God out. If we're not careful, pride can pervade our lives and permeate us to the depths of our soul. Pride is a major part of the human condition which Christ speaks about in His Word. Pride can lead to devastation and is often synonymous with arrogance. Pride can ease in as a cancer, affecting us at the very core of our being. Pride can bring about apathy, and apathy discontentment, and discontent anger, and anger eventually spiritual death and destruction. Proverbs 16:18 is a warning we all need to heed. **"Pride goes before destruction and a haughty spirit before a fall."** Let's take this to heart. Ego is dangerous; in its place let's use wisdom. After all, pride and ego are protective shields we use when we don't want to face the facts that we don't know everything there is to know. Wisdom teaches us to be wise in our decision making. Proverbs 16:16 gives us the value of wisdom. **"How much better it is to get skillful *and* godly Wisdom than gold! And to get understanding is to be chosen rather than silver."**

A Waging War Within transpires within when we allow pride, selfishness and unforgiveness to reign in our mortal beings. We must, through a choice of surrender, let go and let God. He must work on us from the inside out. Spiritual surgery begins with prayer and with us surrendering our will to God. His aid and intervention in our lives is of critical importance. No matter the issue, He has already paid the price to set us free.

We need to surrender

January 9th

Matthew 5:11-12-"Blessed are you when people insult you, persecute you and falsely say all kinds of evil against you because of me. Rejoice and be glad, because great is your reward in heaven, for in the same way they persecuted the prophets who were before you." –NIV

Just as Jesus was persecuted in His time, we can expect the same. I think we can draw from this. How relevant this is to today's litigious society. Slander, slander, and more slander. Rape, murder, beatings, and such are an everyday occurrence, all we have to do is turn on the television or read the newspapers.

Everywhere you look, people are slandering each other both within the church and outside of the church. People are constantly making false accusations about others. It may start off as talk in the rumor mill and then gradually it becomes slanderous. God speaks to this all throughout His written Word. Scripture reveals over and over the importance of pure thoughts, pure speech and pure living. How many are compromising within the church of Jesus Christ today? If many are living as if there is no God, than certainly their speech will reflect their worldly lifestyle. Luke 6:45 states **"The upright (honorable, intrinsically good) man out of the good treasure stored in his heart produces what is upright (honorable and intrinsically good), and the evil man out of the evil storehouse brings forth that which is depraved (wicked and intrinsically evil); for out of the abundance (overflow) of the heart his mouth speaks."**

My friends, we must guard what comes out of our hearts and out of our mouths for we can speak life or death. Proverbs 18:21 tells us **"Death and life are in the power of the tongue, and those who love it will eat its fruits."** Proverbs 12:13-14 says **"An evil man is ensnared by the transgression of his lips, but the righteous escapes from trouble. From the fruit of his mouth a man is satisfied with good, and the work of a man's hand comes back to him."** Matthew 12:36-37 states **"I tell you, on the day of judgment people will give account for every careless word they speak, for by your words you will be justified, and by your words you will be condemned."** We need to watch our tongue my friend. The tongue is a very small muscle, but it also happens to be tremendously strong.

We need to choose our words wisely and think before we speak. James 3:8-10 says emphatically **"No human being can tame the tongue. It is a restless evil, full of deadly poison. With it we bless our Lord and Father, and with it we curse people who are made in the likeness of God. From the same mouth come blessing and cursing. My brothers, these things ought not to be so."**

January 10th

A **Waging War Within** exists within friendships, marriages, churches, businesses, schools, and relationships of any kind when insulting comments are spoken. Sticks and stones break my bones and names never hurt me. My friends, we all know that this is far from true. Names, accusations and slanderous hurtful comments do hurt and are also unnecessary. I am sure that we can all recall times when we were young and someone said something that hurt us to the core. Am I right? I thought so. Why fuel the fire and allow the enemy to continue to operate through you? Let's pray that we would each be cleansed by the blood of the lamb and be filled with the Holy Spirit continuously.

In a day and age where church splits are happening all around us we need to use caution. Christian homes are disintegrating, Christian leaders are backsliding, and Christians themselves are being plagued with innumerable addictions. We're in great need of God's love and grace for each other and ourselves more than ever. I've seen church board meetings where pastors have been lambasted and ridiculed by board members; it reminded me more of a secular talk show rather than a church board meeting with so called and mature Christians. As Christians, we need to hold ourselves to a higher standard of moral living for ourselves. We need also to remember that God's love and grace should be at the forefront of all of our relationships both with Christians and also the unsaved.

My friends, we need to not only watch out for each other's well-being, we need to offer up prayers of thanks, protection and guidance. 2 Thessalonians 1:3 plainly tells us **"We ought always to give thanks to God for you, brothers, as is right, because your faith is growing abundantly, and the love of every one of you for one another is increasing."** If we are doing this with all of our heart we will not have time to speak ill or maliciously or even malign one another. We are our brother's keeper people.

Here are some examples of **how we are to show our love for one another**...

1. We are to "receive one another"–Romans 15:7
2. We are to "edify another"–Romans 14:19
3. We are to "serve one another"–Galatians 5:13
4. We are to "bear one another's burdens"–Galatians 6:1-2
5. We are to be "forgiving one another"–Ephesians 4:32
6. We are to be "submitting to one another"–Ephesians 5:21
7. We are to "exhort one another"–Hebrews 3:12-13
8. We are to "consider one another"–Hebrews 10:24-25
9. We are to be "hospitable to one another"–1 Peter 4:8-10

January 11th

Matthew 5:21, 28-30-"You have heard that it was said to the people long ago, 'Do not murder, and anyone who murders will be subject to judgment.' 'Do not commit adultery.' But I tell you that anyone who looks at a woman lustfully has already committed adultery with her is his heart. If your right eye causes you to sin, gouge it out and throw it away. It is better for you to lose one part of your body than for your whole body to be thrown into hell. And if your right hand causes you to sin, cut it off and throw it away. It is better for you to lose one part of your body than for your whole body to go into hell."-NIV

The Bible speaks of murder, adultery, sin and hell. We witness on the news, within the papers and other sources of media, murderous and adulterous things happening within our world that even the ungodly are shaking their heads at in disbelief. Hell has become an elusive term not even mentioned or preached upon within the realm of the church. We need to stop preaching the warm fuzzy messages from our pulpits and start preaching the hard truth! The truth of the matter is that people are destined to an eternity in hell if they don't turn from their sinful ways and get their hearts and lives right with God.

The Word of God enlightens us to the realities of Hell. It is a place where you don't even remotely want any part of. Matthew 11:20-24 **"Then he began to denounce the cities where most of his mighty works had been done, because they did not repent. "Woe to you, Chorazin! Woe to you, Bethsaida! For if the mighty works done in you had been done in Tyre and Sidon, they would have repented long ago in sackcloth and ashes. But I tell you, it will be more bearable on the day of judgment for Tyre and Sidon than for you. And you, Capernaum, will you be exalted to heaven? You will be brought down to Hades. For if the mighty works done in you had been done in Sodom, it would have remained until this day. But I tell you that it will be more tolerable on the day of judgment for the land of Sodom than for you."** How about this? Here is some more for you, Revelation 20:10-15 **"And the devil who had deceived them was thrown into the lake of fire and sulfur where the beast and the false prophet were, and they will be tormented day and night forever and ever.**

Then I saw a great white throne and him who was seated on it. From his presence earth and sky fled away, and no place was found for them. And I saw the dead, great and small, standing before the throne, and books were opened. Then another book was opened, which is the book of life. And the dead were judged by what was written in the books, according to what they had done. And the sea gave up the dead who were in it, Death and Hades gave up the dead who were in them, and they were judged, each one of them, according to what they had done. Then Death and Hades were thrown into the lake of fire. This is the second death, the lake of fire. And if anyone's name was not found written in the book of life, he was thrown into the lake of fire." These are pretty convincing facts that Hell is indeed real.

Are you living a life that is right and pleasing to God? If not, why not? Now is a good time to square up with God. Time is running out my friend. Don't put off until tomorrow what needs to be done today. God wants a relationship with you; after all, that is why He created you and me. I still find it amazing that people can say that they will get with God later. My friends there may not be a tomorrow. Mark 13:32 **"But concerning that day or that hour, no one knows, not even the angels in heaven, nor the Son, but only the**

Father." No one but God knows when our number is being called. Why put off tomorrow what you can do today?

1 John 5:11-13 **"And this is the testimony: God has given us eternal life, and this life is in his Son. He who has the Son has life; he who does not have the Son of God does not have life. I write these things to you who believe in the name of the Son of God so that you may know that you have eternal life."** Life with God is great. I wouldn't trade my life today for anything. I have a peace today that I never had before. My worst day today is far better than my best day before I came to know the Lord. Philippians 4:7 explains that peace. **"And the peace of God, which surpasses all understanding, will guard your hearts and your minds in Christ Jesus."** Peace which surpasses all understanding, now wouldn't you like some of that? Get right with God while you still have the chance. Please.

The Ten Commandments
vs.
The Ten Suggestions

A Godly life
vs.
Selfishness

January 12th

People are more concerned with church attendance then with people understanding that lives are hanging in the balance between Heaven and Hell. We cannot forget that even God has become an elusive term for many portions of our society today. People have become very complacent and matter of fact in relation to the things of God. The media and movies in particular, are relegating God, Heaven, the devil and hell as unreal, fictitious entities. The world would redefine who we are and they would ultimately separate us from God if they had their way.

God's Word is emphatic about **The Waging War Within** which is taking place within our souls, spirits, minds, hearts and lives. Let's open the Word of God and take a closer look for ourselves, shall we? Genesis 4:7 **"If you do well, will you not be accepted? And if you do not do well, sin is crouching at the door. Its desire is for you, but you must rule over it."** This tells us that sin is crouching at your door. It desires to have you and your very soul. You need to master your sin life and bring it under control. Can you control this all on your own? How has that been going for you? You can't control it on your own and you know it. The Bible and Jesus Christ can and will show you how. You have to surrender to Jesus and you can bring it under control with His help.

1 Corinthians 15:31 says **"I die every day!"** My dear brothers and sisters, we must do as the Apostle Paul tells us, we must die to ourselves daily so that we might live in Jesus Christ. If we do this and surrender our will for God's will, we will have life, and have life more abundantly. This is the only way we have any chance at life. Complete and total surrender, not 10% or 25% but 100% complete and total surrender.

Once you give Him your life and things start to go good once again, don't take back control of your life. I have seen people do this and it breaks my heart. People see that things are going good and that life is on an even keel and they decide that they don't need God any longer. It was God who had their life on that even plain not them. When you decide to accept control once again He will allow you to take it knowing that you were going to totally mess it up all over again. God allows this because He is a gentleman. He only goes where He is invited and He is not going to be a rude guest and argue over who ought to be in charge. I pray you relinquish control of your life to the One who is better equipped to run it than you are.

Let go and Let God

January 13th

Can't we see the blurring of reality with unreality as we live our life? Can't we see with the mind of Christ or are we walking the streets blindly? Are we allowing the unreality of Hollywood and television to infiltrate our minds to such an extent that God's Word is taking second place in our thought life?

As Christians, when we witness the murders and rapes and the other atrocities that are taking place today, shouldn't we be getting down on our knees, mourning and crying out to God for Him to heal our land? We must be careful that our hearts do not become hardened with the onslaught of the enemy. Psalm 95:8 **"Today, if you hear his voice, do not harden your hearts"**. To "harden the heart" is to make the heart dull and unresponsive to God, and ultimately it strengthens the heart in disbelief. Satan will triumph within the lives of Christians and the Church of Jesus Christ if we allow him to harden our hearts. Let's not give the devil a foothold in our lives.

The church can combat these false notions of God, Heaven, the devil and hell by taking a serious stand in our lives as true Believers. If we stand on the Word of God and live it out daily we will be giving the devil a heart attack. We need clear and poignant preaching, teaching, and evangelism to flow forth to all parts of the world and in order for this to happen we as Christians need to hunker down and study the Word, speak the Word, and believe the Word. We need it to flow **without compromise!**

2 Chronicles 7:14 shares **"If my people who are called by my name humble themselves, and pray and seek my face and turn from their wicked ways, then I will hear from Heaven and will forgive their sin and heal their land."** Let's get busy in our walks. Let's speak positive affirmations to others and let's make a change in this chaotic world. Are you with me? Let's get going.

Reality
vs.
Unreality

January 14th

Matthew 5:31 & 32- **"It has been said, 'Anyone who divorces his wife must give her a certificate of divorce.' But I tell you that anyone who divorces his wife, except for marital unfaithfulness, causes her to become an adulteress, and anyone who marries the divorced woman commits adultery."-NIV**

It cannot be denied that a **Waging War Within** exists within the confines of marriages all across the United States. Some statistics say the divorce rate is increasing for Americans. Why? What's causing divorce? Obviously there are multiple factors that are interfering with heterosexual couples maintaining a happy and healthy traditional marriage. The scariness of these statistics becomes apparent when you understand that children from divorced homes have a much greater chance of being divorced themselves and the pattern can and often does continue for several generations. Broken homes are becoming the rule rather than the exception. God in His written Word specifically states that marital unfaithfulness is the only ground whereby someone who is married can even contemplate divorce.

What's this communicate to you about the standard that the world and even some in our churches hold? Do they hold to a Biblical standard, obviously no? People seem to be getting divorced for multiple reasons, not just adultery. If God was at the center of their lives this wouldn't happen. The fact of the matter is there exists a proportionally smaller incidence of divorce among those that attend church on a consistent basis and follow His precepts than that of their counterparts that have only a nominal church attendance. When anything is affecting such a large population, it can definitely be considered to be in epidemic proportion.

Let's be sensitive to those that have divorced, especially to the many whose fault it wasn't. Many divorced people have wanted and seriously tried to reconcile, obtain mediation, counseling and renew their vows for each other. Many have even mustered up enough forgiveness toward the culprit who sabotaged their vows. The reasons why Christians divorce are complex and come with a myriad of precipitating factors. Many of our Christian brothers and sisters have experienced the devastation of broken homes, broken promises, broken dreams, hurting children, and the overall terrible hurts often associated with this permanent separation within a family. Never forget that the church is made up of people that are hurting and that the church is a spiritual hospital. Let's be a part of the healing process not the destructive force associated with hurting others. Let the restoring power of God flow through you (Joshua 24:15). Let's be a shining light. Be vigilant, persistent and diligent in not allowing **The Waging War Within** the world culture, your family history, or the attacks of the enemy to permeate your household.

January 15th

Matthew 5:33- "Do not break your oath, but keep the oaths you have made to the Lord."-NIV

People have to turn to God and humble themselves in the sight of the Lord and He will lift them up from wherever they are. An oath is an oath. Oaths are being broken all across the board. Not many people keep their word today. We must be careful of this because the worldly culture in which we live is frequently placing images in our minds of what it means to break an oath or a covenant relationship.

Have you ever loaned money or perhaps a tool to someone only to have them never pay it or return it? Did you get frustrated about it and perhaps talk ill of them behind their back? The Bible says this regarding that situation, Luke 6:30-31 says **"Give to everyone who begs from you, and from one who takes away your goods do not demand them back. And as you wish that others would do to you, do so to them."** In other words, if you can't afford to lose it, don't lend it. If you get it back, great, if you don't, so be it. When I loan someone money or whatever, I do it as if I won't get it back, that way I don't have a burden on my mind wondering if or when I will be paid back. Life is easier for me this way.

The culture of today is frequently inundating believers in Jesus Christ with its worldly ways. We're in denial if we think that we can completely live in this world and not have it negatively impact our thinking. We can impact the world for Christ even though the world is frequently attempting to program our minds both in subtle and profound ways. Whatever we allow to come into our lives can interfere with our relationship with Jesus Christ if it is not from God. 2 Corinthians 10:5 says to **"Take every thought captive in order to obey Christ"**. We need to control our thoughts, and in order to do this we have to be walking with a Christ like mind. This is the bottom line. It is where the rubber meets the road.

We must believe and keep at the forefront of our minds that heaven versus hell, life versus death, good versus evil, light versus darkness and God overcoming Satan all exemplify **The Waging War Within.** Let's be over-comers. These truths need to be foundational for the Christian believer. If we don't believe that we're in an all-out war for our soul, then we are grossly deceived. We are in a battle each and every day my friends. It is waging all around us 24/7, 365 days a year and 366 on leap year.

John 10:10 says that **"The thief comes only to steal and kill and destroy. I came that they may have life and have it abundantly."** Whose team are you playing on? I choose life with Jesus Christ.

January 16th

An oath isn't just something you say because you're feeling it at the time. An oath represents an extension of who you are in Christ Jesus. An oath represents that you're acknowledging before the Lord Jesus Christ, family and friends, that you're committed, steadfast and determined to accomplish the things that you're saying you're going to do. Before you take an oath you should really take time and pray things through in order to obtain the wisdom needed to make the decision to take an oath. Are you ready to take this particular oath to heart and see it through to completion? Are you able to carry it out? Do you possess the characteristic traits and the relationship with the Lord that will allow you to work toward maintaining and accomplishing the very oath you set out to take? Taking an oath is not something to be taken lightly. Let's be careful that we're completely prepared before making a commitment to something that we might not follow through on. As a Christian you're representing the most high God, Jesus Christ. God doesn't appreciate the breaking of an oath or a covenant.

James 5:12 has been falsely interpreted over the years to mean that we are not to take oaths, here it is; **"But above all, my brothers, do not swear, either by heaven or by earth or by any other oath, but let your "yes" be yes and your "no" be no, so that you may not fall under condemnation."** What this really means is that we are not to take unlawful or unbiblical oaths. We are to be people of our word. We have taken vows in our marriages which we are to obey. If you have ever been on a witness stand you took a vow to tell the truth and the whole truth. If we do not hold to our words my friends we are just giving the secular arena more fodder to use against Christians as a whole. We have enough of a challenge dealing with that already that we don't need more fuel heaped onto the fire.

God honors those that withstand the fiery darts of the enemy and those who persevere through the storm to accomplish an oath. God honors those who honor Him. God is all for character building!

Are you committed?

January 17th

Matthew 5:38- 39-"Eye for eye, and tooth for tooth. But I tell you, do not resist an evil person. If someone strikes you on the right cheek, turn to him the other also."- NIV

We have to remember that our fight as Christians isn't against flesh and blood. Our fight is a spiritual battle that is won on our knees before the God of the universe. Ephesians 6:10-20 is the Armor of God verses where He shows us how He has equipped us. **"Finally, be strong in the Lord and in the strength of his might. Put on the whole armor of God, that you may be able to stand against the schemes of the devil. For we do not wrestle against flesh and blood, but against the rulers, against the authorities, against the cosmic powers over this present darkness, against the spiritual forces of evil in the heavenly places. Therefore take up the whole armor of God, that you may be able to withstand in the evil day, and having done all, to stand firm. Stand therefore, having fastened on the belt of truth, and having put on the breastplate of righteousness, and, as shoes for your feet, having put on the readiness given by the gospel of peace. In all circumstances take up the shield of faith, with which you can extinguish all the flaming darts of the evil one; and take the helmet of salvation, and the sword of the Spirit, which is the word of God, praying at all times in the Spirit, with all prayer and supplication. To that end keep alert with all perseverance, making supplication for all the saints, and also for me, that words may be given to me in opening my mouth boldly to proclaim the mystery of the gospel, for which I am an ambassador in chains, that I may declare it boldly, as I ought to speak."**

God has our back in our battles against the evil one. There is no need for us to retaliate, be vengeful, spiteful and vindictive. God is quite able to fight **The Waging War Within** our souls for us. Romans 12:19 shows us **"Beloved, never avenge yourselves, but leave it to the wrath of God, for it is written, "Vengeance is mine, I will repay, says the Lord."** All He requires us to do is to lay down our lives, our issues, our insecurities, our fears, and our humanity before Him. He will repay anyone who tries to do evil against us. We don't need to repay evil for evil as God will do it for us. God gets paid to stay up nights and worry about this stuff. He will battle for us against whatever and whoever opposes us. God longs to work in our lives this side of heaven. He longs to become real to us, to guide us, to lead us and most importantly to help us work out the salvation that He has so freely given us.

January 18th

Matthew 5:44- 45- "But I tell you: Love your enemies and pray for those who persecute you, that you may be sons of your Father in heaven. He causes His sun to rise on the evil and the good, and sends rain on the righteous and the unrighteous."- NIV

God's Word makes reference of evil people, enemies and those that persecute Christians. **A Waging War Within** can exist within our relationships with others. A battle will sometimes ensue within the confines of relationships, especially for Christians. Because their father is the ruler of this dark world, people not following Jesus Christ will make persecutory comments toward the believers of Jesus Christ. Unbelievers don't understand the things of God, and at times they will even vehemently oppose them. Christians are often ridiculed, stigmatized, rejected, and slandered by those who oppose the Christian faith, but God can and often does still bless them in hope that the blessing will bring them to Him.

My friends, just because we don't see the punishment given out to the unrighteous doesn't mean that they have gotten off totally free. Just as we will account for all of our deeds, the unjust will also. God is a righteous God. He is the judge, not us. Matthew 7:1-2 gives us a good warning, **"Judge not, that you be not judged. For with the judgment you pronounce you will be judged, and with the measure you use it will be measured to you."** What we need to concentrate on is our walk. Are we living a life that is pleasing to God? Are we offending others by our words, actions, attitudes? If we are, then we had better change our ways as time is running out.

We need to build each other up not tear each other down. If we do this we will not have to worry about offending anyone. Hebrews 10:24-25 **"And let us consider how to stir up one another to love and good works, not neglecting to meet together, as is the habit of some, but encouraging one another, and all the more as you see the Day drawing near."** This is what Christian living is all about.

Are you praying

January 19th

Matthew 6:13 –"And lead us not into temptation but deliver us from the evil one."-NIV

God's Word speaks about the tempter and the evil one, known as the father of lies, the Prince of Darkness, or Satan, and also of our need for deliverance from his seduction. We should strive in our daily walk for a connectedness with our Heavenly Father that surpasses the things that we can touch, taste, smell, hear and see in this world. We need to surrender our will to Christ and allow His power and authority to draw us into His presence. Philippians 1:21 says **"For to me to live is Christ, and to die is gain."** Paul's life is not a matter of seeking his own comfort or advancement and ours shouldn't be either. It is all about seeking the advancement of Christ's kingdom: to live is tantamount to serving Christ. In fact, to die should be seen as gain also, because it would mean that we would be freed from this trouble-filled life on earth to rejoice in Christ's presence in Heaven. In other words, we surrender our will and choose to follow Christ and His precepts and if we should die in the process we have the ultimate payoff.

God and His Word need to be everything in our lives Psalm 138:2 **"I bow down toward your holy temple and give thanks to your name for your steadfast love and your faithfulness, for you have exalted above all things your name and your word."** God needs to be our very sustenance. We need to thank Him for who He is and for what He has done in our lives. Ephesians 5:20 says **"give thanks always and for everything to God the Father in the name of our Lord Jesus Christ."** God needs to become more powerful and needed in our lives than the very air that we breathe and the water that we drink. He needs to be elevated to a place which is far above our relationships, our material possessions, our careers, our education, and our own selves. If God isn't first in our Christian walk and existence than anything we do in this life is worthless. If God isn't first in our life than our life will not be completely empowered by God to the degree that we need it to be in order for us to fight **The Waging War Within** successfully.

God needs to take precedence in our thought life, our work life, our prayer life, our church life, our physical life, and our daily devotions, our relationships with others, our family, and our finances. From the time we wake up to the time we retire at night we need to reflect on the things of God. In order to become more like Christ we need to think more about Him and who He is in our lives. If we don't allow God to mold us, refine us and subdue our will, the world culture will prevail and we will lose our focus. The world doesn't mold humans into the image of God, only God can do that. The world tries to pervert and distort who God is and what He has in store for our lives. It definitely doesn't refine a soul. Once we're subdued by the world, we're dead. The enemy is waiting to destroy your life, to devour and ultimately kill you as we are told in 1 Peter 5:8, **"Be sober-minded; be watchful. Your adversary the devil prowls around like a roaring lion, seeking someone to devour."** Don't ever let your guard down. Once you let your guard down, it's too late; you've let the enemy in. He's like the proverbial fox in the hen house. Remember, the sneaky serpent comes in all shapes and sizes just waiting to deceive and annihilate you. Be forever vigilant.

I believe we spend our whole life searching for deliverance from various things. In God's Word, He specifically states that He will deliver us from the enemy. If we call on Jesus in our time of need, He will deliver us from the enemy's hands, 1 John 5:14-15 **"And this is the confidence that we have toward him, that if we ask anything according to his will** he hears us. **And if we know that he hears us in whatever we ask, we know that we have the requests that we have asked of him."** Satan will no longer have a grip on us. Satan will no longer have any power over us because he doesn't have any power over God. Satan only has power, in many cases, when we allow him to sneak in and rob, kill and destroy. Otherwise, Satan is powerless, hopeless, detestable, and a loser in the eyes of God. Satan has lost the battle that has been already waged and won by God on the Cross of Calvary. Praise God!

We need to ask God every day for an awareness of the things that might tempt us away from Him. Ephesians 4: 22-23, **"Put off your old self, which belongs to your former manner of life and is corrupt through deceitful desires, and to be renewed in the spirit of your minds."** We need to thank God for all of the things that He has blessed us with, our health, our loved ones, our very existence, and mostly because He found something in us that we didn't necessarily see in ourselves, our worthiness of being called a son or daughter of the Most High. There can be no compromise, no looking back, and no looking to the left or the right but focus on God. Proverbs 4:25 says **"Do not swerve to the right or to the left; turn your foot away from evil."** This is telling us to avoid evil in speech and action. We should only look onward and upward with Jesus in our sight, for He alone will help us. 1 Timothy 6:12 says to **"Fight the good fight of the faith. Take hold of the eternal life to which you were called and about which you made the good confession in the presence of many witnesses."** We need to flee from sin and pursue virtue.

The Deliverer
vs.
The tempter

Matthew 6:15- **"But if you do not forgive men their sins, your Father will not forgive your sins."-NIV**

Forgiveness is about walking in the Spirit of Christ. The antithesis of living in the Spirit of Christ is living to please our carnal nature and our flesh. True, unwavering and authentic forgiveness can only be obtained through Jesus Christ. After all, it was Jesus Christ (God Himself) that died on the cross and offered mankind the passage to true forgiveness. He sacrificed His life that we might live life on a higher plain and experience life more abundantly. He died so we might live! Now we must take upon ourselves His nature. We must die to ourselves in order to live in Him and experience all that He has to offer us. 1 Corinthians 15:31 **"I protest, brothers, by my pride in you, which I have in Christ Jesus our Lord, I die every day!"** He desires to give all that surrender to Him, spiritual blessings. One of these blessings is the ability to forgive others when we have been treated wrongly by them. Matthew 7:1-5, **"Judge not, that you be not judged. For with the judgment you pronounce you will be judged, and with the measure you use it will be measured to you. Why do you see the speck that is in your brother's eye, but do not notice the log that is in your own eye? Or how can you say to your brother, 'Let me take the speck out of your eye,' when there is the log in your own eye? You hypocrite, first take the log out of your own eye, and then you will see clearly to take the speck out of your brother's eye."** Unless the forgiveness of Christ overflows in and out of our lives, a **Waging War Within** will exist within us and permeate our entire being.

My friends, did God ever go on leave and put you on the throne? I didn't think so because I never received that memo. We cannot afford to pass judgment on others because if we do we will be judged with the same measure we use on them. Can you imagine how harsh that would be? We can become very critical of others. We can also be very critical on ourselves. We need to go easier on everyone around us and ourselves if we are judgmental people. We need to put that dog to bed. Judging of others is a commodity we cannot afford.

Judge not lest ye be judged

Matthew 6:15- "But if you do not forgive men their sins, your Father will not forgive your sins."-NIV

The very essence of Christianity has to do with God's forgiveness of mankind. Jesus Christ displayed His love for us by dying on the cross; by doing this He declared His love and forgiveness for all. 1 Peter 3:17-18 says **"For Christ also suffered once for sins, the righteous for the unrighteous, that he might bring us to God, being put to death in the flesh but made alive in the spirit."** The crucifixion was all about forgiveness. Jesus Christ became the blood sacrifice offered up to God as an offering for the sin of the world. Salvation is all about our forgiveness from God.

Taking up our cross and following Jesus is all about acknowledging God's love and forgiveness through the sacrifice of Jesus Christ. In order to be restored, one must be forgiven. In order to be saved, one must be forgiven. Christ was the penalty that was paid on the Cross of Calvary. He was the propitiation for our sins. He died for all in order that we might live.

The great mystery of this is clearly revealed by the prophets of old from within the pages of the Holy Bible. See for yourself, go ahead and crack the covers. Open your Bible, blow off its dusty cover and reveal its hidden treasure. In order to protect yourself in a physical war you would want a gun and some body armor. To protect yourself in a spiritual war you need the armor of God. Ephesians 6:10-18 explains the Armor of God; **"Finally, be strong in the Lord and in the strength of his might. Put on the whole armor of God, that you may be able to stand against the schemes of the devil. For we do not wrestle against flesh and blood, but against the rulers, against the authorities, against the cosmic powers over this present darkness, against the spiritual forces of evil in the heavenly places. Therefore take up the whole armor of God, that you may be able to withstand in the evil day, and having done all, to stand firm. Stand therefore, having fastened on the belt of truth, and having put on the breastplate of righteousness, and, as shoes for your feet, having put on the readiness given by the gospel of peace. In all circumstances take up the shield of faith, with which you can extinguish all the flaming darts of the evil one; and take the helmet of salvation, and the sword of the Spirit, which is the word of God, praying at all times in the Spirit, with all prayer and supplication. To that end keep alert with all perseverance, making supplication for all the saints."** Your sword is your Bible and it only works if you open and read it. **The Waging War Within** is an internal war that is carrying itself out on the playing field of the real world with your life at stake. This isn't a dry run for a play! It's the real McCoy and it's happening whether you are aware of it or not. You my friend have to pay attention with what is happening in your thought life and your physical life as well.

God has given us one life on this side of heaven. Let's give it to Him to mold, to form, to lead, to guide, and to transform. Let's not live in the mundane. He wants us to live life. John 10:10 explains the mission of Jesus Christ; **"The thief comes only to steal and kill and destroy. I came that they may have life and have it abundantly."** He has given, not as the world gives, but as God gives! John 14:27; **"Peace I leave with you; my peace I give to you. Not as the world gives do I give to you. Let not your hearts be troubled, neither let them be afraid."** The peace of God surpasses every kind of peace you could ever begin to imagine. It is a peace of passion.

Have you ever gone out into the middle of nowhere and just sat there and admired God's creative wonder? Just try it, it is so awesome, so serene. I love to do that. I grew up on the shores of Lake Michigan and I would drive down to the shore and just lay out on the hood of my car and just veg out and enjoy a peace that was near perfect. That is kind of like God's peace, but His is even more than that. He's perfect and so is His peace.

God is peace! He's immortal! He's eternal! He's revolutionary! And most importantly, He's forgiven us of all of our sins. He doesn't hold anything against us. When we ask God for forgiveness and we are earnest about it, He grants us that forgiveness. Now when we ask it a second time for the same offense, He says "What are you talking about?" When God forgives us of a sin He remembers it no more. He forgives us completely.

Think about this next section long and hard. If God can forgive those who sinned against Him, and if He can forgive us of our sins, why is it that we have such a hard time forgiving others who have sinned against us? How can we deny someone forgiveness when Jesus Christ suffered far worse that we can ever imagine and He forgave those who sinned against Him? They beat and killed the Son of God and He forgave them. We are mere humans and we find it hard to forgive someone who called us a name or spoke behind our back or somehow did an injustice to us. How can this be? Some of us can't even find it within ourselves to forgive ourselves of an injustice we committed. Now you on the other hand may not have forgiven yourself. That is sometimes harder to do than asking God for His forgiveness. His life, death and resurrection have already paid the price for our sin, we don't have to crucify ourselves, the blood has already been shed for our sins. It's done! It's finished! It's over! Praise God!!

Forgiveness
vs.
Unforgiveness

January 22nd

Matthew 6:19, 21-24-"Do not store up for yourselves treasures on earth, where moth and rust destroy, and where thieves break in and steal. But store up for yourselves treasures in heaven, where moth and rust do not destroy, and where thieves do not break in and steal. For where your treasure is, there your heart will be also. The eye is the lamp of the body. If your eyes are good, your whole body will be full of light. But if your eyes are bad, your whole body will be full of darkness. If then the light within you is darkness, how great is that darkness! No one can serve two masters. Either he will hate the one and love the other, or he will be devoted to the one and despise the other. You cannot serve both God and Money."-NIV

Wow, talk about a powerful passage of scripture! Such a vivid portrait is painted here for us of what can happen if we let the worldliness of our society and culture permeate our spirit, mind, and our soul. God is warning us that our temporal existence shouldn't overshadow our life in Christ. Have you ever seen labels or signs that say, "Danger", "Warning", "Keep Out" or "Enter at your own risk?" God, throughout His Word, is clearly drawing a line in the sand for us. He's saying, "Do not value the things of this world more than me". God is asking the question, "Where is your heart?" Who or what are we serving? Are we serving God or money? Whatever it is our heart is after will have a certain level of control over us if we allow it to.

The awareness that we have that our lives within the physical realm are temporal and within the Heavenly realm are eternal is of the utmost importance when wrestling with these two opposing points of view. On the one hand, you have the world telling you that you need to consume everything in order to feel complete. You not only have to "Keep up with the Jones", but you have to surpass them. The expression, "In the end, whoever has the most toys wins," is a popular American saying. Unfortunately for many, it has become a way of life! A segment of American culture has built their philosophy of living around these two sayings. In other words, it's not the internal that we should be concerned about, but the outer existence and the things we can accumulate, possess, control, use, and buy, sell and manipulate! This is scary! Many of us are in denial as to how much this type of thought has permeated our culture and our individual lives. When individuals start loving money and feel that using other people for their own gain is acceptable, then something is way out of whack. Matthew 6:24 informs us of a fact of life; **"No one can serve two masters; for either he will hate the one and love the other, or he will stand by *and* be devoted to the one and despise and be against the other. You cannot serve God and mammon (deceitful riches, money, possessions, or whatever is trusted in)."**

We as Christians are the other side of the above saying. We are to live our life as one pleasing to God. The expression, "One hundred years from now none of this will matter", can only truly be grasped through the lens of Christ. Christ is our example, our Leader and His life should be our compass that allows us to avoid these pitfalls. How many of us have ever seen a mortgage, a house, a car, a boat, a bank account, stocks, mutual funds, an armored car, or a 401k plan attached to a hearse or in a funeral procession as it takes a person to the cemetery? Life is all about perspective isn't it?

Where are we finding our worth? Who are we modeling our lives after? Where is our heart pointed? Hopefully it is pointed in the right direction. Hopefully we all can sing "Christ is all I need, all other ground is sinking sand." Warning! Be careful where you build your house Matthew 7:26; **"And everyone who hears these words of Mine and does not do them will be like a stupid (foolish) man who built his house upon the sand."** Have you ever seen a new comer get all fired up and then when the going gets tough they fall apart and get bitter? How about the reverse, where a newcomer enters the fold when their life is falling apart and they have nowhere else to turn but to God and He gets their ship back on an even keel and once their ship is righted they feel they don't need Him anymore and they leave? Why is it that He settles our lives for us and then we feel we don't need Him anymore?

The depraved conceptions of our minds provoke us to transgress the law. In other words, the devil has twisted man's mind into going with temptations and the ways of the world instead of going the way of God. The devil has no direct ability to touch our mind directly but what he does is he places obstacles in our paths which allow the opportunity for us to fall short of the glory of God and His righteous ways. We need to be cautious what we allow to enter our minds. Romans 7:21 tells us; **"So I find it to be a law that when I want to do what is right *and* good, evil is ever present with me *and* I am subject to its insistent demands."** I can relate to this. Can you? How do we overcome this obstacle? We renew our minds. We seek to follow God with everything we have in us and we call on God for His help and guidance. Romans 12:2 gives the instruction on how to beat the devil at his game; **"Do not be conformed to this world, but be transformed by the renewal of your mind, that by testing you may discern what is the will of God, what is good and acceptable and perfect."** See that? And you thought I was making all of this stuff up. The answers to all of our questions are found in the mighty Word of God. Crack the covers and the answers pour out.

Seek the Word
and
you will find the answers

Hate is a powerful word. Hatred is the anti-thesis of forgiveness, just as light is the opposite of darkness. A **Waging War Within** exits between these opposing forces that operate in the world in which we live.

Light and darkness are constant prevailing forces being reconciled perpetually within every thought, feeling, action, reaction, and communication of our lives. Our life style and who we are can be defined either by light, or the darkness. Are we children of the light or are we children of the darkness? If we are children of God, then we are to be of the light and we should be allowing our light to shine before men. Matthew 5:16 informs us; **"Let your light shine before others, so that they may see your good works and give glory to your Father who is in heaven."** The world will see the **light** of the kingdom through the good works done by Jesus' disciples (you and I), with the result that the Father who is in heaven will also be glorified. How can you do this if you are living and walking around with hate and discontent in your heart? You can't. You need to clean house and empty yourself of anything not of God.

Make some changes in your lives to allow you more time to study God's Word. If you are earnestly seeking Him you will be willing to make the necessary alterations to your schedules. Ask God to show you how your watching TV, movies, reading things that are not bringing glory to Him, certain magazines, books, even listening to certain kinds of music or talk radio shows, all of these things have caused you to relax your moral standards which has compromised your walk and what Scripture clearly teaches about righteous Christian living. My brothers and sisters, let's make a promise to rid ourselves of anything that is not Godly, pure, anything that is not true or noble, right, or admirable, and let's ask God to give us the strength to rid ourselves of toxic things, anything that is not of God. He will help us think about that which is excellent and praiseworthy, but He won't force His will on us, we have to ask that His will be done in our lives. When you ask, it is an act of faith, and He will answer.

Hate is powerful

Matthew 6:31-34- "So do not worry, saying, 'What shall we eat?' or 'What shall we drink?' or 'What shall we wear?' For the pagans run after all these things, and your heavenly Father knows that you need them. But seek first his kingdom and his righteousness, and all these things will be given to you as well. Therefore do not worry about tomorrow, for tomorrow will worry about itself. Each day has enough trouble of its own."-NIV

Many of us would respond to the above scripture, "easier said than done." God's Word is explaining that there should be a clear separation between the values of all Christians and the world with respect to the way we live, where our focus is, and how we respond to the pressures placed upon us. Individuals and families today are immersed in an American culture that is consumer driven which is resulting in many having difficulty between distinguishing a want from a need.

Worry, worry and more worry! Many, even some Christian's, are plagued with worry. Both the churched and the un-churched worry about their bills, their finances, their health, their job & and their career. These are all temporal things. God's Word guides us to the eternal things and the realization that the way we, the created, perceive things to be isn't always the way they are. After all, we're the created and He is the Creator, aren't His ways above our ways? Isaiah 55:8-9 tells us; **"For my thoughts are not your thoughts, neither are your ways my ways, declares the LORD. For as the heavens are higher than the earth, so are my ways higher than your ways and my thoughts than your thoughts."** Didn't He create the Heavens and the Earth, or did we? Isaiah 45:18 **"For thus says the LORD, who created the heavens (he is God!), who formed the earth and made it (he established it; he did not create it empty, He formed it to be inhabited!): "I am the LORD, and there is no other."**

Has humanistic Darwinism crept into your thinking? These are all philosophies and ideologies that have permeated our culture and as a result they have influenced the Church of Jesus Christ. Faith in the absolute power of God is contrary to placing one's faith in man or oneself. They are polar opposites! This is the reason why there is **A Waging War Within** us.

Christianity
vs.
Worldly ways

January 25th

Matthew 7:1-2- "Do not judge, or you too will be judged. For in the same way you judge others, you will be judged, and with the measure you use, it will be measured to you."-NIV

Judgment over legal matters belong to earthly judges, however eternal judgment belongs to God! God alone judges the inner most thoughts, motives, intents of the heart and deliberations of mankind. His Word guides us also. The Word of God then acts as God himself, so that one's innermost thoughts and intentions are exposed. This happens constantly in Christians' lives.

How many times have you heard it said "that person or couple is so judgmental"? Or, "they're snobby and stuck-up"? Some are more judgmental than others. However, we all have the capacity to be critical of others. Sometimes our human nature kicks in and takes over and we run as the world runs. We go on auto pilot, operating in the flesh. Maybe someone has wronged us and we're wrestling with unforgiveness. There are many unrecognized, unresolved, and never relinquished issues within our lives that can cause us to be judgmental of others. We really need to remember that sometimes we're wrestling against our own flesh. We can and have to make a conscious effort to be non-judgmental toward others. After all it's a choice, a decision. We're not puppets controlled by our flesh, we have control. We should consciously be making every attempt upon earth to walk in the Holy Spirit and the One that saved our souls, Jesus Christ. 1 John 1:7, **"But if we walk in the light, as he is in the light, we have fellowship with one another, and the blood of Jesus his Son cleanses us from all sin."**

If we change our thinking and walk in the light then others we are close to would see a change in our lives, attitudes, words, and mannerisms and perhaps they would also want to make a change in their walk also. Can you imagine the impact on society if one person at a time would change their ways and that caused another to change also? Let's give it a try shall we?

God alone judges

January 26th

Matthew 7:3-5 **"Why do you look at the speck of sawdust in your brother's eye and pay no attention to the plank in your own eye? How can you say to your brother, 'Let me take the speck out of your eye,' when all the time there is a plank in your own eye? You hypocrite, first take the plank out of your own eye, and then you will see clearly to remove the speck from your brother's eye."-NIV**

What a metaphor! Specks of sawdust and planks within eyes! Powerful! What more of a fitting analogy could God use than this? It is descriptive and it goes right to the point. This is where the rubber meets the road. Humanity is quick to point out the faults, frailties, insecurities, wrongdoings and even the sin of others. People don't hesitate to verbally assassinate others with their loathing arsenal of verbal onslaughts. We all have a **Waging War Within** us. The question is, what are we going to do with it? Are we going to allow it to consume us and let the devil win, or are we going to let the Holy Spirit guide us and let the light shine? Are we going to let Jesus win? I pray that we do.

Can you imagine how much good we could do with all of the time we spend on negative thinking and actions? Think about all of the time we waste with all of the negativity. It's truly amazing all of the time and energy we spend on the negative. Break the curse my friends. Dare to be different. Time is too precious to spend on the darkness. Dare to be light.

I have heard people use the excuse that everyone else is so negative so they fall in the trap. That is a load of manure. They fall in the trap because they allow others negativity to impact them. Change your thinking people. If you are in a room that is totally dark, I mean it is so dark that you can't even see your hand when it is right in front of your face, and you have a tiny pinprick of light to enter the room is no longer dark. Think about it. Light has entered so it is no longer dark am I right? I know I am that's why I said it. Be that light. Don't let the devil win.

Specks
vs.
planks

Matthew 7:6,-"Do not give dogs what is sacred; do not throw your pearls to pigs. If you do, they may trample them under their feet, and then turn and tear you to pieces."-NIV

Is God warning us and attempting to prevent our premature demise to those that aren't following Jesus? God is attempting to guide us away from those that would love to stomp us like a bull would his rider. Many people are at odds with those that are believers in Jesus Christ, ultimately because of **the Waging War Within**. 1 Timothy 4:1-2 shares this truth; **"Now the Spirit expressly says that in later times some will depart from the faith by devoting themselves to deceitful spirits and teachings of demons, through the insincerity of liars whose consciences are seared."**

God desires all to know Him, but the reality is that not all want His will for their lives. Matthew 10:14 tell us how to react if someone denies the Lord; **"And if anyone will not receive you or listen to your words, shake off the dust from your feet when you leave that house or town."**

The war that exists within the spiritual realm is a reality which we need to grasp. Too many think that it is a fallacy, well it is very real. NBC has a comedy program, "Saturday Night Live", it had a character known as the "Church Lady" who attributed everything to "Satan!" People in the audience and all over America roared in laughter at the characterization of a Christian who attributed events to a being known as Satan". The sad thing is that people believe Satan is a joke. Satan according to the Bible is a very real being, who is opposed to God's work in every facet possible. According to Jesus, he (Satan) is the father of lies. John 8:44 explains; **"You are of your father the devil, and your will is to do your father's desires. He was a murderer from the beginning, and has nothing to do with the truth, because there is no truth in him. When he lies, he speaks out of his own character, for he is a liar and the father of lies."** There is no truth in him. Therefore, with millions of people watching, Saturday Night Live plays its role in causing many to doubt Satan exists, bringing doubt to the words of Jesus in the Bible. This is just one of many examples of the Spiritual War which is taking place all around us. He is very real. There is a waging war taking place for your very soul my dear brothers or sisters. Believe me, it is real and it is ugly.

Pigs and pearls

January 28th

Matthew 7:7-8 -"Ask and it will be given to you; seek and you will find; knock and the door will be opened to you. For everyone who asks receives; he who seeks finds; and to him who knocks, the door will be opened." (NIV)

My friends, how many of you have searched for a helpmate? You know how hard it can be to find that special someone who is compatible with you. You want that someone who takes your breath away when you see them and someone who brings a tear to your eye when you can't. It is so awesome to have someone to come home to and someone you can share your deepest thoughts with and someone you can laugh and even cry with. Someone who can complete your sentences for you because you are so in tuned with them. We all want that. We have to remember that when we are searching and praying for that partner in life we have to be equally yoked.

Light cannot associate with darkness, neither the ungodly with the Godly. The verse of 2 Corinthians 6:14 **"Do not be unequally yoked with unbelievers. For what partnership has righteousness with lawlessness? Or what fellowship has light with darkness?"**, 1 Corinthians 5:9, **"I wrote to you in my letter not to associate with sexually immoral people"**, Deuteronomy 22:10, **"You shall not plow with an ox and a donkey together"**, Ephesians 5:7, **"Therefore do not associate with them"**. Do you see all the references on the separation that is called throughout the Bible on being equally yoked with other believers? The reason is that it is impossible to stay spiritually strong if you are partnered with an unbeliever.

Imagine yourself in a battle with someone who is not committed to the mission and what it represents, can you trust your life into their hands, no way. My brothers and sisters, we are in a battle. We are on a mission. We need to wake up and realize this fact. There is a war waging all around you each and every day and every waking hour of the day. If you want to win this war, get yourself an accountability partner and get serious with your walk people.

Typically, unless the Holy Spirit is bringing one into the realm of salvation, a friction, a wedge, and even a dislike and hatred are characteristic trait's the unsaved have toward those that have received Christ. God is warning us to be shrewd in our dealings with unbelievers and not unaware that their father is the prince of this world.

Be careful of those you surround yourself with, whether they be extended family members, friends, business partners, acquaintances, colleagues, or even those within the Christian Church. Some are just not going to build you up in the most precious faith. I'm not saying don't associate with them. Help them in their faith. However, if you want to grow and mature in the Lord, you yourself have to associate with Christians that are on fire for the Lord Jesus Christ. Remember standing in a church doesn't make you a Christian any more than standing in a garage makes you a car. The devil arrives at church before anyone else. Be wise in your relationships and use the discernment which God entrusted to you.

Christians that are dedicating their life's blood and works to Jesus are people that can see Jesus for who He is and are walking with Him on a daily basis. You want to interact with Christians that can challenge you in the Christian Faith in a positive way and that can awaken you to new, exciting, and uncharted territory in your spiritual lives. 1 John 1:7; **"But if we walk in the light, as he is in the light, we have fellowship with one another, and the blood of Jesus his Son cleanses us from all sin."**

When you associate with garbage, garbage you'll become. When you associate with people that are living a humdrum Christian Life, than a humdrum life is what you'll get. When you hang with people that are mediocre, mediocre is what you'll become. We have to aspire to something greater, bigger, loftier, and most importantly, Godlier. We're created in the very image of God. Genesis 1:27; **"So God created man in his own image, in the image of God he created him; male and female he created them."**

God desires great things for us. He desires us to be successful, fulfilled, wonderful, beautiful, illuminating, brilliant, terrific, profound, talented, gifted, radiant, and also challenged. God wants the best for us, and the best is what He deserves. Dear brothers and sisters, think about this please, **He has called you to be a son or daughter of the Most High!** How can you even consider giving Him anything but your very best? He has called us to be His children. How awesome is that!!

He has called us to be His!

We are
sons and daughters
of the Most High God!

January 29th

Matthew 7:13,14- "Enter through the narrow gate. For wide is the gate and broad is the road that leads to destruction, and many enter through it. But small is the gate and narrow the road that leads to life, and only a few find it."-NIV

"There is only one name under Heaven whereby we must be saved and that name is the name of Jesus Christ", Acts 4:12. "Confess with your mouth and believe in your heart that Jesus Christ is Lord and you will be saved", Romans 10:9-10. This is the salvation message. We must cling to the cross of Calvary and the atonement made through Jesus Christ while He hung on it. Nothing we can do will ever earn us salvation. This is why accepting Jesus Christ is difficult for many, because they feel that this is just way too simplistic.

Many feel that they have to earn their way into Heaven or that good works will get them there. There is nothing we can do to earn or buy our way into Heaven, nothing. Jesus is all about simplicity. He specifically didn't make salvation complex. Is your intellect battling with God? Is the creature questioning the Creator? Bring this battle, **the Waging War Within,** to God. He wanted and presently still wants everyone to be saved. 2 Peter 3:9 says; **"He does not want that one should perish, but all to come to have everlasting life".** God doesn't require us to earn a PhD so that we will have worth in his eyes. All that matters to Jesus is the condition of our hearts. John 3:16 says; **"For God so loved the world, that he gave his only Son, that whoever believes in him should not perish but have eternal life."** There are no stipulations whereas your works will allow you entrance into Heaven are there? None!

"Works" is used by Paul and James, in a special sense, as indicating those legal performances by means of which men sought to be accepted of God, in opposing distinction to that faith in Christ through which the sinner is justified apart from all legal works (Romans 3:27; Romans 4:2, 6, etc.; Galatians 2:16; Galatians 3:2, 5, 10), "working through love" (Galatians 5:6 1 Thessalonians 1:3), and is fruitful in all truly "good works," in which Christian believers are expected to abound (2 Corinthians 9:8 Ephesians 2:10 Colossians 1:10 2 Thessalonians 2:17, etc.). When James speaks of being justified by "works" as well as by "faith" (2:14-26), he has in his view those works which show faith to be real and vital. "Dead works" avail nothing (Hebrews 9:14; Hebrews 10:24). We are known as Christians because we display God's love to the unloved and at times the unlovable. We are saved by a confession of Christ as our Savior and Lord, not by our deeds. There is nothing we can do aside from our confession that will gain us entry into Heaven. Nothing at all. Jesus Christ paid that price already.

January 30th

Men and women both love to take control of their own lives. Let go and let God, please! We humans can get so hung up on ourselves that we become the center of our own universe. Me myself and I seem to be the new trinity. Why do you think mirrors are so popular? The mirror is all about me, not you and or anyone else. Let's take our eyes off of ourselves, our own issues, our own feelings, our own thoughts, our own lives, and start living everyday thinking about God and others. We can give our thought life to God as a sacrificial offering and ask Him to dissect it and clean it out so that it pleases Him. We consciously have to give Him the scalpel and the issues of our life so that He can surgically heal, mend, and remove as He sees fit. Why not submit to the Creator who's calling His creation into a relationship with Him? Submit to **The Waging War Within.** Let Christ be at the center of your Life. He is the Master Surgeon. Dr. Jesus Christ, M.D. Absolutely! Pretend that He went to Yale Medical School! With Dr. Jesus in control we have need for no other.

Jesus is The Way, The Truth and The Life. John 14:6, **"Jesus said to him, "I am the way, and the truth, and the life. No one comes to the Father except through me",** John 1:4-5, **"In him was life, and the life was the light of men. The light shines in the darkness, and the darkness has not overcome it."** Salvation comes through Christ and no one else. There is only one way to Heaven. There is only one whereby we can be saved from the clutches of hell and translated to an eternal Heaven. Forever and ever our souls will live with Christ Jesus, far from the earthly difficulties and problems that we face in this life. This is a promise from Him. He has promised to save us if we accept Him as Lord and Savior and place our trust in Him. There is no other name under Heaven whereby we must be saved. Acts 4:12 states; **"And there is salvation in no one else, for there is no other name under heaven given among men by which we must be saved."** Jesus is the narrow road that leads to life. Matthew 7:14; **"For the gate is narrow and the way is hard that leads to life, and those who find it are few."**

Many religions promise this same path, however, only one God, Jesus Christ, has lived, died, and risen to the right hand of God. John 14:6 tells us; **"Jesus said to him, "I am the way, and the truth, and the life. No one comes to the Father except through me."** He is the only way. If you try something else it is not of Him and you will only be spinning your wheels.

Heaven
vs.
Hell

Matthew 7:15-20- "Watch out for false prophets. They come to you in sheep's clothing, but inwardly they are ferocious wolves. By their fruit you will recognize them. Do people pick grapes from thorn bushes, or figs from thistles? Likewise every good tree bears good fruit, but a bad tree bears bad fruit. A good tree cannot bear bad fruit, and a bad tree cannot bear good fruit. Every tree that does not bear good fruit is cut down and thrown into the fire. Thus, by their fruit you will recognize them."-NIV

How many well-known ministers have fallen? Many scandalous things have happened in the name of ministry. **A Waging War Within** exists within the realm of Satan and God's Kingdoms. These two opposing kingdoms are very real. The devil is the king of this world. He is the ruler of the kingdom of the air and he controls and manipulates the things of this world. His main goal is not only to distract Christians from Christ, but to steal, kill and destroy (John 10:10). Christ came to seek and save the lost (Luke 19:10). There is a huge difference. Now do you believe that we're fighting a war? We are engaged in warfare with an arch enemy and our very own flesh. God's Word speaks of ferocious wolves who are dressed as sheep which can look like one of us Christians and even be in church with us. However, they're practicing evil deeds like deceit, trickery, manipulation, and lies.

Beware, lest you be led astray and captivated by false pretenses. Beware, or else you'll be lead down the wrong path by leaders that have worldly gain as their motive and not Christ Jesus. You cannot serve two masters, either you will love the one and hate the other (Matthew 6:24). Some leaders twist the Word of God for their own financial benefit. Beware of this, it can devastate your spiritual life and thwart your relationship with God Almighty. God is warning us that deception even takes place within the realm of the church and among God's chosen people. We must not close our eyes and we must always test things in the light of scripture if we're going to be well grounded in the Truth.

Be careful of being hoodwinked by smooth talking preachers that promise you the world instead of the things of God. To be a Christian, you belong to the One above and are daily allowing yourself to be conformed to His image, not the image this world has to offer (Romans 12:2). This is why Bible study, prayer, fellowship, Sunday school classes, Biblical teachings, and becoming grounded in a solid Bible believing church is of utmost importance.

Beware of false prophets

FEBRUARY

February 1ˢᵗ

Matthew 7:21-"Not everyone who says to me, 'Lord, Lord,' will enter the kingdom of heaven, but only he who does the will of my Father who is in heaven."-NIV

Powerful, powerful, powerful are these words! How many of us Christians are striving to find, understand, and carry out the will of the Father in our own precious lives that He has blessed us with. God desires for us to carry out His will for lives right here on Earth, on this side of Heaven. Many of us are making attempts to humble ourselves and surrender our will and our life to our Creator, realizing that His Ways are above our own ways and that He knows what is best for us. Romans 12:1-3 shows; **"I appeal to you therefore, brothers, by the mercies of God, to present your bodies as a living sacrifice, holy and acceptable to God, which is your spiritual worship. Do not be conformed to this world, but be transformed by the renewal of your mind, that by testing you may discern what is the will of God, what is good and acceptable and perfect."** How wonderful it is to have God on our side! For God to lead us, to guide us, and direct us throughout our earthly existence is an awesome privilege.

God gives us a warning and attempts to open our spiritual eyes to **The Waging War Within.** God is speaking to the importance of us carrying out His Will for our lives, not our own, daily dying to ourselves, so that we might live for Him, allowing Him to operate through us on a daily basis. 1Corinthians 15:31; **"I protest, brothers, by my pride in you, which I have in Christ Jesus our Lord, I die every day!"**, Mark 8:34-35; "And he called to him the crowd with his disciples and said to them, **"If anyone would come after me, let him deny himself and take up his cross and follow me. For whoever would save his life will lose it, but whoever loses his life for my sake and the gospel's will save it."**, Luke 9:23-24; " And he said to all, **"If anyone would come after me, let him deny himself and take up his cross daily and follow me. For whoever would save his life will lose it, but whoever loses his life for my sake will save it."** Do you see how important it is to deny ourselves our own selfish wants?

Dying to oneself is a continuous theme throughout the New Testament. It is mentioned 26 times. I believe there is a reason for this. If you are not practicing dying to yourself daily, please pray that you will eventually get it. Your walk will change dramatically once you make this a daily practice. Let's pray right now! "Dear Father in Heaven, I pray Lord that you take my selfish ways about me and allow me to die to myself and take up my cross for you. Lord, I know I am not worthy to be called a son or daughter of the Most High Lord, but I thank you immeasurably for finding something in me that has appealed to you. Lord, please work with me as I endeavor to please you and mimic the walk of Your Son, Jesus Christ, my Lord, and my Savior. And Lord, when I do err in my walk, I pray that you will forgive me once again. I ask these things Father in the name of your son, Jesus Christ, my Lord. Amen and Amen."

How glorious it is that we have the capacity in allowing the Creator of the Universe to live in us and to work through us with His mighty power. The insurmountable importance is revealed within the scripture above. Our spiritual existence may be in question. It's obviously important to God that we do His Will and not our own. Our prayer should be that His will be done and not our own. The Lord's Prayer is a great example of how we need to pray, **"Father, Thy will be done and not mine"**. The 23rd Psalm is a great example of a statement of confidence in our Lord. **"The Lord is my shepherd; I shall not want. He makes me lie down in green pastures. He leads me beside still waters. He restores my soul. He leads me in paths of righteousness for his name's sake. Even though I walk through the valley of the shadow of death, I will fear no evil, for you are with me; your rod and your staff, they comfort me. You prepare a table before me in the presence of my enemies; you anoint my head with oil; my cup overflows. Surely goodness and mercy shall follow me all the days of my life, and I shall dwell in the house of the Lord forever."** How easy it is to say it and how altogether different it is to live it out in our life. Our wrestling match is with **The Waging War Within** ourselves. We wrestle with our will, our pride, ego, self-centeredness, conceit, vanity, arrogance, lust, weaknesses, and our flesh. They all lead us down the wrong road. How far will we allow the spirit of the flesh to take us? Will it lead us to destruction? To ruin and collapse? To insanity or an inability to even see the things of God? Will it lead to incapacity to escape the idea that we're not the center of the universe? Will it lead to the lack of understanding that the finite cannot possibly fathom the infinite?

Our will must decrease and He must increase. God, please do what you will with me. God, I pray that you make what you must out of me. Dear Lord, please take me, mold me and have your own way, please God, in my life. God, I need you now. Rescue me from my plight, my vain existence, and make more of me than I can ever make of myself or that I can even imagine. May I not live for myself, but may I live for you and you alone. God, please lay a path for me that I cannot even fathom, for I know that your path is one I can trust and that it will lead me to everlasting life. Thank you Lord. I love you.

Is the Creator
living through you?

February 2nd

Matthew 7:22-23-**"Many will say to me on that day, 'Lord, Lord, did we not prophesy in your name, and in your name drive out demons and perform many miracles?' Then I will tell them plainly, 'I never knew you. Away from me, you evildoers!"-NIV**

False disciples do have the ability to exercise power in Jesus' name but their ministrations are meaningless because they deceive themselves and other believers, they only want attention for their own spectacular displays. Mighty works are not proof of the Father's will since they can come from sources other than God, including demons and human manipulations. Acts 19:13–16; **"Then some of the itinerant Jewish exorcists undertook to invoke the name of the Lord Jesus over those who had evil spirits, saying, "I adjure you by the Jesus, whom Paul proclaims." Seven sons of a Jewish high priest named Sceva were doing this. But the evil spirit answered them, "Jesus I know, and Paul I recognize, but who are you?"** 2 Thess. 2:9–12; **"The coming of the lawless one is by the activity of Satan with all power and false signs and wonders, and with all wicked deception for those who are perishing, because they refused to love the truth and so be saved. Therefore God sends them a strong delusion, so that they may believe what is false, in order that all may be condemned who did not believe the truth but had pleasure in unrighteousness."** Rev. 13:13–14; **"It performs great signs, even making fire come down from heaven to earth in front of people, and by the signs that it is allowed to work in the presence of the beast it deceives those who dwell on earth, telling them to make an image for the beast that was wounded by the sword and yet lived."**

Jesus says that he will one day exercise the prerogative of condemning people to hell, something that only God can do. John 5:22; **"The Father judges no one, but has given all judgment to the Son."** Though these condemned prophets appeared to belong to Jesus, they were never truly saved, for Jesus because Jesus said He never knew them.

Oh, some will preach Jesus from false motives, not sincerely, some seeking for financial gain, some wanting to exalt self, looking for fame and fortune. Jesus is looking at the heart of His believers, not what they're doing externally. God is in the business of performing spiritual surgery, which is on the inside of a man. What is the condition of a man's heart? Since Jesus created our heart, He's aware of its functioning. Do you exist with a heart that seeks after God, and is turning from the things of the world? Where do you stand? How is the condition of your heart? Whatever has our heart has us entirely.

God is making it clear that He's not as concerned with what one is outwardly as much as He is our inward existence. Seek ye first the Kingdom of God and all these things will be provided to you (Matthew 6:33).

February 3rd

Matthew 7:23-" Then I will tell them plainly, 'I never knew you. Away from me, you evildoers!"-NIV

Apart from God, the heart is full of wickedness and deceit. Ecclesiastes 9:3; **"This is an evil in all that is done under the sun, that the same event happens to all. Also, the hearts of the children of man are full of evil, and madness is in their hearts while they live, and after that they go to the dead."** Romans 8:7; **"For the mind that is set on the flesh is hostile to God, for it does not submit to God's law; indeed, it cannot."** Psalm 53:1; "The fool says in his heart, **"There is no God." They are corrupt, doing abominable iniquity; there is none who does good."** Strive and pursue the heart of God and seek His will for your life. Worship, praise, and prayer, all three must spring from the heart in order to be authentic. Sometimes our flesh doesn't feel like drawing closer to God, but we must combat **The Waging War Within.**

How many are doing things in the name of God to be seen, recognized, revered and given accolades by men? Matthew 6:2; **"Thus, when you give to the needy, sound no trumpet before you, as the hypocrites do in the synagogues and in the streets, that they may be praised by others. Truly, I say to you, they have received their reward."** Many, God says it therefore I believe it. Today, and in times past, there have always been those that seem to do the miraculous in the name of Jesus. God is clearly pointing out that there are counterfeits in the faith. Things are amiss and evil in the sight of the Lord. I didn't say this hard word, God did. Read it for yourself. Matthew 7:15; **"Beware of false prophets, who come to you in sheep's clothing but inwardly are ravenous wolves."** God is saying in a straightforward manner not to believe everything that you see and hear. He wants us as Christians to be discerning.

You have to ask yourself the question, are the many ministries that are bringing in millions and millions of dollars per year really of God or are they just lining someone's proverbial pocket? Where is the money going? Is it going to others selfish and materialistic pursuits? Is it going to spreading God's Word, or is it going to self-aggrandizement? This is the litmus test we need to apply.

The saved
vs.
Evil doers

February 4th

Matthew 7:24-27- "Therefore everyone who hears these words of mine and puts them into practice is like a wise man who built his house on the rock. The rain came down, the streams rose, and the winds blew and beat against that house; yet it did not fall, because it had its foundation on the rock. But everyone who hears these words of mine and does not put them into practice is like a foolish man who built his house on sand. The rain came down, the streams rose, and the winds blew and beat against that house, and it fell with a great crash."-NIV

Practice, practice, practice. God doesn't want us to just listen to the preaching of His Word, nor does He want for us to just read it. He wants us to apply it to our lives. God equates this with building yourself on the Rock. A man's life built on the rock cannot be moved, swayed, or destroyed. Actually, living out His Word in our lives is what He desires from us. This is His true passion. Remember, the Word is alive. Hebrews 4:12; **"For the word of God is living and active, sharper than any two-edged sword, piercing to the division of soul and of spirit, of joints and of marrow, and discerning the thoughts and intentions of the heart."** The Word is the Sword of the Spirit spoken of in Ephesians. Ephesians 6:10-18 is the Armor of God chapter; **"Finally, be strong in the Lord and in the strength of his might. Put on the whole armor of God, that you may be able to stand against the schemes of the devil. For we do not wrestle against flesh and blood, but against the rulers, against the authorities, against the cosmic powers over this present darkness, against the spiritual forces of evil in the heavenly places. Therefore take up the whole armor of God, that you may be able to withstand in the evil day, and having done all, to stand firm. Stand therefore, having fastened on the belt of truth, and having put on the breastplate of righteousness, and, as shoes for your feet, having put on the readiness given by the gospel of peace. In all circumstances take up the shield of faith, with which you can extinguish all the flaming darts of the evil one; and take the helmet of salvation, and the sword of the Spirit, which is the word of God, praying at all times in the Spirit, with all prayer and supplication. To that end keep alert with all perseverance, making supplication for all the saints."** You can never hear too much about the Armor of God. The Armor of God can and will save your soul if you take it and claim it and place it in your heart.

Things will come against us in our lives, however, by trusting and placing our faith in the inerrant, infallible, and God inspired Bible, we will be able to withstand the fiery dart of the enemy. We will be able to stand when all others fall. We aren't supposed to be wavering and having our faith and confidence in our own strength. We have been bought with a price. You believe that don't you? If you don't, change your thinking. Jesus Christ wasn't hanging on that cross because He had nothing better to do with His time. He died for you and me so that we can enjoy eternal life with Him. 1 Corinthians 6:20; **"For you were bought with a price. So glorify God in your body."**

We are no longer our own, but we are God's chosen people. We're God's workmanship which has been created for His purpose. Ephesians 2:10; **"For we are his workmanship, created in Christ Jesus for good works, which God prepared beforehand, that we should walk in them."** Are you walking in His ways? Are you walking in your own way? Do yourself a favor and take a serious self-examination and think about what it is you are living for. Are you living for self-aggrandizement? Are you living to get big money so you can have a better Harley or a big house on a hill for the whole world to see? Are you living to better your influence with big shots at the company you work for? What is your purpose in life? Think about it.

The Word tells us that we are to live for God. Colossians 1:10; **"walk in a manner worthy of the Lord, fully pleasing to him, bearing fruit in every good work and increasing in the knowledge of God."** Are you walking in a manner which is pleasing to God? I pray you are. If your answer was no, it is not too late to amend your walk. There is still time to make the necessary changes if your walk is contrary to the Word of God.

One thing we can all benefit from in our walks is accountability partners. Find a man or a woman, men with men and women with women, someone who has a proven walk and a strong background in the Word who is someone you would like to become in your walk. I am not talking of worshipping that person or putting them on a pedestal, that wouldn't be fair to them, just someone whom you can talk to on a regular basis and glean wisdom from. There are people out there who have been through so much and they stood strong when the storms raged around them. Find that someone and get to know them and ask them to work with you. The church is full of sage individuals. Tap into the resources around you. Sharing with someone who has been around the block a few times is a double blessing. These people you share with can also learn from you. I have dared to do this and I have been so abundantly blessed by it. Share your thoughts with them. Share your fears with them. You are sure to come out the victor in your relationship with them. What have you got to lose?

The Rock
vs.
The sand

February 5th

Matthew 7:27- "The rain came down, the streams rose, and the winds blew and beat against that house, and it fell with a great crash."-NIV

God often uses things from His creation to teach us and draw us closer to Himself. Rain, streams, and winds are all things we see in nature. Here, we understand them to be related to trials, tribulations, and even hardships that we have and will face within the realm of our earthly existence. There is a **Waging War Within** battling for domination of our personhood trying to get us to fall prey to the ruler of this present darkness. We need to stand on the side of righteousness and trust in God. If we do this, we will win in the end.

Even with all the pounding our lives take as Christians, we can stand without being overcome. By faith, trust, and hope in God we will be able to withstand the pressures that will thrust themselves upon us. Nothing in all of creation will be able to separate us from the love of God if we follow the roadmap given to us in the Bible. What is the Bible after all? The Bible is **B**asic **I**nstruction **B**efore **L**eaving **E**arth! No one can fathom the depth of God's undying, unwavering and infinite love that He has for His children. He cradles us within His loving arms. Hebrews 13:5; **"I will never leave you nor forsake you."** Deuteronomy 4:31; **"For the LORD your God is a merciful God. He will not leave you or destroy you or forget the covenant with your fathers that he swore to them."** 2 Corinthians 4:8-10; **"We are afflicted in every way, but not crushed; perplexed, but not driven to despair; persecuted, but not forsaken; struck down, but not destroyed; always carrying in the body the death of Jesus, so that the life of Jesus may also be manifested in our bodies."** We need to take these verses and claim them and make them our own. God only wishes for us to have the very best He has to offer. The decision is ours whether we wish to accept Him or not.

Establishing a foundation is of priority in maintaining a healthy Christian life and a well-balanced household. We need to realize the foundational truths of the Bible are of tremendous importance to the believer in Christ. As a construction worker buttresses foundations with cement, rod iron, and steel for reinforcement, so must we strengthen ourselves with the divine Word of God. Our foundation in God's Word is a key factor in all that we do, all that we become, and all that we are in Him. We need to take the Word and read it, study it, and imprint it on our hearts. We need to tattoo the Word in our hearts and in our minds. Never mind the body art, tattoo the Word on the core of your being.

A **Waging War Within** exists when we're making our own way in life. It's easy for us to forget the things of God if we don't read and heed His Word and practice the walk. Professional athletes practice for hours and hours a day in order to be at their peak performance. How long do you read your Word a day? Have you read it at all? Make it a habit. We can become complacent in our walk with God and take His blessings for granted, but woe to you if you do. You can and will eventually receive the Holy smack down. My dear brothers and sisters, when God takes you to the woodshed, it hurts. If you want to avoid the sting of His punishment obey His Word. The only way you can obey the Word is if you read it. So read it and heed it!

Complacency is probably one of a Christian's worst enemies. A complacent Christian no longer possesses a passion for Christ. They will lose their zeal, tenacity, and grit in pursuit of the things of God. They lose perspective completely. Some backslide into the things of this world because they never established themselves on the truth of God's Word.

51~ The Waging War Within

If we want to stand we must be grounded with a firm foundation. Head knowledge is great, but without heart knowledge it will do you no good what so ever. If you want to win the **Waging War Within**, you will need to combine both the head knowledge with the heart knowledge. All other ground, beside the fertile Word of God, is sinking sand. Matthew 7:24-27; **"Everyone then who hears these words of mine and does them will be like a wise man who built his house on the rock. And the rain fell, and the floods came, and the winds blew and beat on that house, but it did not fall, because it had been founded on the rock. And everyone who hears these words of mine and does not do them will be like a foolish man who built his house on the sand. And the rain fell, and the floods came, and the winds blew and beat against that house, and it fell, and great was the fall of it."** On Christ the solid rock I stand, all other ground is sinking sand. Amen!

Wisdom is needed when we make decisions my friends. The ways of the world is death. Proverbs 7:27 speaks of the ways of the world; **"Her house is the way to Sheol, going down to the chambers of death."** Proverbs 8:32-36; **"Blessed are those who keep my ways. Hear instruction and be wise, and do not neglect it. Blessed is the one who listens to me, watching daily at my gates, waiting beside my doors. For whoever finds me finds life and obtains favor from the LORD, but he who fails to find me injures himself; all who hate me love death."** We need to use wisdom in all that we do. Proverbs 1:7; **"The fear of the LORD is the beginning of knowledge; fools despise wisdom and instruction."** We need to use the wisdom God gave us.

A firm foundation
vs.
A leaky, cracked laden foundation

February 6th

Matthew 7:29- "…because he taught as one who had authority, and not as their teachers of the law."-NIV

Authority! Today, so many children, as well as adults are rebelling against the very thing that God has put in strategic places, authority. Parents, grandparents, teachers, police officers, pastors, ministers and others that hold positions of power and authority are vehemently being rebelled against. There is absolute, unadulterated, and unconscionable rebellion taking place everywhere, even in some churches.

We have become inundated with news. We are living in a time when news programs, either via the T.V. or the radio, are becoming the source of information that's relied upon by people everywhere. People aren't opening books nearly as often as previous generations. Sadly enough, books are collecting dust in our local libraries. People want their information quick, concise and with some spin. So many TV and radio programs are propagated by hype in-order to increase the ratings. The authorities today consist of nationally syndicated propagandizing machines on major television networks. There are so many multi-millionaires that just love to hook you into their media station by sensationalizing the atrocities of the world. It reminds me of the 1982 Don Henley song "Dirty Laundry". The song says it all. People love dirty laundry.

Do people look for the truth anymore? Open your Bible people! Do you want to know the forecast for today and tomorrow on the political and economic fronts? Open God's Word. A great verse is in the book of Ecclesiastes, chapter 7, verse 12, **"For protection of wisdom is like the protection of money, and the advantage of knowledge is that wisdom preserves the life of him who has it."** Wisdom is similar to money in that both offer the possessor some real protection against the misfortunes of life. A point in favor of wisdom, however, is that it preserves the life of him who has it. As a general rule, living wisely receives God's blessing, including long life, even if it cannot provide eternal life.

Are you rebelling?

February 7th

Matthew 7:29- "...because he taught as one who had authority, and not as their teachers of the law."-NIV

God is the ultimate authority that people are running away from. There has been such a shift in society in the last 50 plus years. It wasn't all that long ago where a class would stand with their hands over their hearts and say the Pledge of Allegiance and this is pathetically a thing of the past. Prayer was another common occurrence in school. This is now ruled unconstitutional, and we sit and wonder why our country turned out the way that it has. Our government has been threatened to legislate God out of the money, God out of marriage, God out of schools in both prayer and the pledge of allegiance. Some no longer want one nation under God recited in the Pledge in order that no one is offended. We live in a day when millions and millions of abortions have been allowed to happen throughout the United States of America and the rest of the world and hardly an eye is being batted at the rate of occurrence. How can millions of babies be murdered every year with no one seeming to care? I now know that it was by the grace of God that I was even given a chance to live on God's green earth. I could have been politically funneled to death before I even came down the birth canal to take my first breath apart from my mother.

America needs to return to God. We need to humble ourselves and cry out to God for forgiveness and for His grace in this time of need. Remember, the God of old is the same today, and He is waiting for us to return to Him. Do you want to follow the religious leaders of today and believe that we are ok, or do you want to seek God? The battlefield for your heart, soul, and mind is taking place this very minute. It's **The Waging War Within.** It doesn't take a rocket scientist to figure out that people have fallen away from a true relationship with God. God is the authority! There is only one name under Heaven whereby a man must be saved and it's Jesus Christ (2 Corinthians 5:17, Acts 4:12). There is only one God, one way to salvation, and one authority. Who's the authority in your life? Is it you, a loved one, a mentor, a friend, or a famous person? Or is it God and God alone? We are running out of time and you need to truly decide now. I pray you make the wise choice.

Pray for wisdom

Matthew 8:3- "Jesus reached out his hand and touched the man. "I am willing," He said. "Be clean!" Immediately he was cured of his leprosy."-NIV

Isn't faith wonderful? By faith God heals! By faith God restores! By faith God sets free! By faith we as Christians can live, breath, and have our being. It comes by faith in the Son of God. As you know, faith is being sure of what we hope for and certain of what we do not see (Hebrews 11:1). A mysterious thing is this word, faith.

The atheists don't like the word. In order to have faith you have to believe in something. When you don't believe in anything, it's really difficult to find comfort in such a word.

Humanists don't like the word faith because it can't be scrutinized by the scientific method. In other words, this thing called faith is too abstract and can't be observed, analyzed, and dissected under the microscope. Will you put your hope in the faith you have in Christ, or what the world has to offer in its ideologies, philosophies, and half-truths? **A Waging War Within** exists in your mind, your heart, your soul, and your very life.

The word faith isn't intellectually captivating enough for the humanist. Did Darwin have faith when he came up with the theory of evolution? Who did he place his faith in? Was it the Creator? I don't think so, but right now I can guarantee you that he wishes he did.

The Bible specifically states in Genesis how the earth was created (Genesis 1:1-2:3). But creation takes faith to believe in, doesn't it? My prayer is that God would bring all Christians, all over the world, in such a time as this, closer to Him than ever before. By faith, our relationship with God can be restored and/or rejuvenated. By faith, our marriages and our relationships with our children can be strengthened and renewed. By faith, our lives will be living testimonies to the wonderful grace and power of God to those all around us.

Faith.
Isn't it wonderful?

February 9th

Matthew 8:8- "The centurion replied, "Lord, I do not deserve to have you come under my roof."-NIV

How applicable for so many of us. We don't feel like we deserve all that God has to offer us because of prior life experiences or whatever hang-ups we might have or things we have done. We think that we are unworthy to be called His son or daughter. God has come to forgive sinners and to set them free (Isaiah 61:1). He has set us free from whatever has held us captive. He has come to all those in need, whether rich or poor, black or white, American Indian, Asian, European, Russian, Indian, Latino, whatever culture, nationality or faith they practice. God has come for all. Jesus Christ has died so that all might live, and live more abundantly through Him. The devil has come to steal, kill, and destroy. (John 10:10).

This is a difficult concept to grasp. I suffered with the thought of unworthiness. I was told many times throughout my life that I was worthless and unwanted. I was part of a certain denomination that had me convinced I was going to hell from a very early age. After a while you really start to believe it. I did. This thought of unworthiness is a lie from the pits of hell. You are created in God's own image. Genesis 1:26-27, **"Then God said, "Let us make man in our image, after our likeness. And let them have dominion over the fish of the sea and over the birds of the heavens and over the livestock and over all the earth and over every creeping thing that creeps on the earth." So God created man in his own image, in the image of God he created him; male and female he created them."** Do you honestly believe that He created something in His own image and that that creation is unworthy to be called His? You are a son or daughter of the Most High! Believe it! You hold your head High! You belong to the one true and most high God. Be proud of that. And in case you haven't heard it in a while, you are loved. I love you. If I didn't, I wouldn't have spent so much time and sweat on this book. Believe that you are worth it.

Are you worthy?

February 10th

Matthew 8:10- "When Jesus heard this, he was astonished and said to those following him, "I tell you the truth, I have not found anyone in Israel with such great faith.""-NIV

I believe that Jesus was sensing the Centurion's feelings of being unworthy. The Centurion was conveying his humility at the sight of Jesus. Remember that a Centurion was of equivalent public official ranking as that of a mayor. He wielded a lot of power. To find a high ranking Roman official who was also a Christian was almost unheard of. Obviously, the Centurion was captivated by the presence of Jesus. Jesus sensed the humble spirit the Centurion demonstrated toward Him. He demonstrated not only his humility he also demonstrated great faith in Jesus Christ, his Lord. How relevant for today's believer.

In a day and age when so many people have great pride, extreme arrogance, and haughty attitudes to beat the band, God is looking for His people to humble themselves in order that He can exalt Himself through His believers. He can't work through us if we don't humble ourselves in and through Him. Remember that ego is **E**dging **G**od **O**ut. Do you have an ego problem? Do you need to ask Him to alleviate you of your ego or any other problem?

We need to drop to our knees and remember all that God has done for us. We need to swallow our pride and get right with Him. We also need to start cleaning our carpets, and a great way to do it is with our knees. We need knees like that of a camel, rough and callused.

Are we on our knees? Are we really and truly humbled in our attitudes towards God? Do we astonish Jesus today with our great faith? If not, it's time to get started and there is no better time to start than the present.

Great faith vs. Luke warm faith

February 11th

Matthew 8:12-"But the subjects of the kingdom will be thrown outside, into the darkness, where there will be weeping and gnashing of teeth."-NIV

People have been led astray by false doctrines and by the deceitfulness of men in their scheming. This is a horrific picture of what it will be like for those that don't accept Jesus on the terms that God has set for us within the Bible.

This reveals the paramount importance of sound doctrine, teaching, and instruction in the Word of God. How critical it is to understand and comprehend Scripture. How important it is to get connected to a strong Bible believing church where a believer can grow in the grace, the mercy, and the love of God with fellow believers in Jesus Christ! A believer must understand that salvation comes from accepting and believing in one's own heart that Jesus Christ is Lord (Acts 16:30-31). One must confess with one's mouth and believe in one's heart that Jesus Christ is Lord (Romans 10:9-10). Once someone confesses and believes in their heart that Jesus Christ is God, they're saved by the blood that Jesus already paid on the Cross of Calvary. We're saved through God's grace that is freely given to all of humanity. This is not of works, so that no one can boast in who he or she is or in what they've accomplished.

Being thrown into outer darkness where there is weeping and gnashing of teeth is not something that neither I nor anyone else should knowingly want for themselves or their loved ones. God warns us specifically in the Word of God that many will be led astray for various reasons. It is our responsibility to arm ourselves through prayer, the Word of God, Godly instruction, Godly teaching, and being connected to a Godly church, one where we can grow spiritually in the things of God. What more do we need as Christians other than this above scripture, to grasp the urgency and need, to allow God's Word to penetrate our hearts and the hearts of others. Life is but a breath! It's over before we can even fathom it. Time is of the essence! Let's go into all the world and preach the Gospel as we were told to do (Matthew 28:19-20, The Great Commission). Let's go into our schools, our communities, our homes, our families, our cities, and even to distant lands.

Dear brothers and sisters, isn't it a shame that the United States used to be the biggest exporter of Missionaries throughout the world and today we are the biggest importer of them? We have third world countries seeing the sorry state of affairs that our once great nation has become and they want to save us. How ironic. What has happened to us as a country? I think we have become too complacent in our walks. We need to shine our light before men and not be ashamed of it (Matthew 5:16). We have our hope and faith in God the Father, Jesus Christ His Son, and our helper the Holy Spirit. With them on our side what else can we possibly need?

February 12th

Matthew 8:13- "Then Jesus said to the centurion, "Go! It will be done just as you believed it would." And his servant was healed at that very hour."-NIV

God reveals the importance of belief and faith in Him. We need to have trust and vision in the God of the universe. God is the Creator of Heaven and Earth! Should we place our trust in any other? Absolutely not! We can if we want to be led astray and destroyed by the world and its rulers. We need to turn from our earthly ways and take a stand that is emphatically and unequivocally Christ centered. We need devotion to God! Devotion to the Truth! Devotion to our destiny, our calling, and our purpose in God! Let us have faith in the power that rests in Christ alone. Faith is powerful! Faith in God has the power to move mountains, transform lives, restore broken homes, and heal the broken hearted (Matthew 17:20).

We can believe in our victory through Christ Jesus because He has already paid the price for our salvation and that of our souls. Those that accept Christ and trust in Him as their personal Savior have the eternal assurance that they're heaven bound. Isn't that a great insurance policy? It is an assurance policy. You can't get that from State Farm or anywhere else.

Let's keep pressing in to God and allowing Him to transform us from the inside out. When in the valley, God is there. When in the storm, God is there. When you are in the most trying times of your lives, God is there. He will never leave us nor forsake us (Genesis 28:15, Hebrews 13:5). We have this assurance. Ask, seek, knock, and the door will be opened (Matthew 7:7-8). Let us draw closer to God, realizing that He has our best interest in mind. He will give us nothing less than the very, very best.

Belief
vs.
Unbelief

February 13th

Matthew 8:16,17-" When evening came, many who were demon-possessed were brought to him, and he drove out the spirits with a word and healed all the sick. This was to fulfill what was spoken through the prophet Isaiah: "He took up our infirmities and carried our diseases."-NIV

God sacrificed Himself that we might live and have life more abundantly (John 10:10). He has warned us of the demon-possessed spiritual world of darkness that is permeating our planet with its horrors, atrocities, wars, crimes, violence, and decaying refuse. Ephesians 6:12; **"For we do not wrestle against flesh and blood, but against the rulers, against the authorities, against the cosmic powers over this present darkness, against the spiritual forces of evil in the heavenly places."** Christ desires to set His children on a higher plane, far above the things of this world. He will protect us, guide us, and lead us in the right direction. He will heal those that need healing. Our churches were never meant to be spiritual country clubs. The church is a spiritual hospital for those that are in need of spiritual care for mental, emotional, psychological, and in some cases, physical healings.

Our individual lives, our families, and everyone within the realm of our planet, are in need of Him. Have you ever seen so much pain, hate, unhappiness, and such a state of both inner and outer turmoil? There is such a need for the peace of God in our world today. We can help spread the love of God one soul at a time if we just get over our insecurities and selfish hearts. Do you remember the day you were saved? Do you remember how good you felt? Who are you to deny someone else that very same sense of elation? Come on people, time is running out.

God is love, and our prayer should be that this love will be shared, revealed, and conveyed to others within our lives. Let us humble ourselves so that He might lift us up, so that we might be a light to others in this dark world. Light shines in the darkness, uncovering deceitfulness, untruths, hidden secrets, and ultimately, peoples destructive paths. Let us cling to God so that He might equip us with the spiritual power that's inherent in the Holy Spirit, to conquer Satan and his demonic forces. Our daily prayer should be; "Dear God, cover us, our families, our loved ones, and our church with your blood covering and your finished work on Calvary."

The Kingdom of God
is near

February 14th

Matthew 8:22- "But Jesus told him, "Follow me, and let the dead bury their own dead.""-NIV

Sounds drastic! It is drastic, to follow Jesus with all your heart, with all your soul, with your entire mind, and with all your strength, is totally radical. Think about it. Shouldn't the created follow the Creator? Makes sense to me, does it to you? Should anything or anyone ever come between you and God? I think not. God is giving us an example of the perspective that He expects from His followers. He says, "Follow me." Then He says, "Let the dead bury their own dead." God is explaining to us here the importance of giving of our total self to Him. Everything! He deserves nothing less. Giving totally of ourselves to His plan, purpose, and calling within our lives is what is pleasing to Him. Should we not give completely to the one that died for us, so that we might live a life carrying out His divine destiny here on earth? This is a call to total commitment. The call to follow Him rises above all other allegiances. Anything that hinders unqualified commitment to Him and the new covenant family of faith must be set aside.

Could you imagine Jesus saying to God when He was called to suffer and die on the cross, "Hey dad, I'm sorry, but I'm going to go shoot pool tonight, so Gregg and Jason are just going to have to wait till tomorrow to get a chance to go to Heaven"? That would really stink, don't you think so? I do. When the call is given, we expect Him to jump. Why should He jump for us if all we do is put Him on hold when He calls? Doesn't that make you think? We really need to get our priorities in order. Don't think that you're the lone man in the boat because I am there with you. I have blown plenty of opportunities in the past. I felt like a real heel after but I also learned from those experiences. It's not a good feeling and I try not to do it anymore.

While writing this book opportunities have presented themselves where people have come up to me and they asked what I was doing. They would say, "Gregg, what are you doing writing a book?" kind of smart-allecky like and I would say, "Yes I am actually". This would stop them in their tracks and I would ask them if they would like to read a page or two before telling them what it is I am working on. This was a great opportunity to witness to them about our Lord and Savior and I would take it. I would ask if they read their Bible or if they even have one.

I drive around with a case of paperback Bibles in my truck and a case of New Testaments also. I am always ready to give one away to someone who is seriously willing to read it. I won't accept money for it if offered either. I tell them to pass on the gift to someone they share the opportunity with. This salvation we have is a gift worth passing on don't you think? It is the gift that keeps on giving. Share it please.

February 15th

Matthew 8:24-25-**"Without warning, a furious storm came up on the lake, so that the waves swept over the boat. But Jesus was sleeping. The disciples went and woke him, saying, "Lord, save us! We're going to drown!"-NIV**

Are you going through a turbulent time? "Relax, relax, relax," Jesus would say. "Quiet down, don't you know I'm God?" "Don't you know that I am omnipresent, omniscient and omnipotent?" "Don't you know that if it weren't for me you would not even exist?" "Are you rotating the earth or am I?" "Did you create the universe or did I?" "I've created the sea and every living creature in it, and I've created everything on land as well." "Do you not think that I can manage a storm that comes on you suddenly and unexpectedly?" "Don't carry your fear, your hurt, and your pain; I'll carry it for you." "Let go and let me carry you, I will never lead you astray." "Trust and place your faith in me and in me alone."

Easier said than done right? Not really. If you have lived any time at all you have had to trust in something. You trusted your parents at some point in your life. They may have let you down, that I don't know. You may have trusted brothers and sisters and been burned by them, again I don't know. I will tell you what I do know, that is that Jesus will never let you down. That is a promise you can take to the bank. He says, **"I will never leave you nor forsake you"** (Hebrews 13:5). One thing for sure, God doesn't lie. He can't. People will let you down, God won't. If He says He'll do it, rest assured, He will.

You who are parents want nothing but the best for your kid's right? God wants nothing but the best for us His children. Luke 11:11; **"What father among you, if his son asks for a fish, will instead of a fish give him a serpent; or if he asks for an egg, will give him a scorpion? If you then, who are evil, know how to give good gifts to your children, how much more will the heavenly Father give the Holy Spirit to those who ask Him!"**

Are you playing God?

February 16th

Matthew 8:26-"He replied, "You of little faith, why are you so afraid?" Then He got up and rebuked the winds and the waves, and it was completely calm."-NIV

God used His creation to explain His power. He realized that these men needed to see His miracles and His miraculous power. God did this to strengthen their faith. How much more can He calm the storms of our lives even in the most horrendous of situations and circumstances? Philippians 4:7; **"And the peace of God, which surpasses all understanding, will guard your hearts and your minds in Christ Jesus."** This true peace can only come from the One and only true God. Proverbs 3:5 says that we as Christians are to lean not on our own understanding, but in all of our ways we are to acknowledge God and He will make our paths straight. Sometimes God will use the storms, the valleys, and the perils of life to test, refine, and mold our faith. Being a Christian isn't easy. If it were, don't you think that everybody would be one? It's comforting to know that God's in charge isn't it?

My brothers and sisters, we must remember that precious gold must go through the smelting fires in order to be made pure. The clay at the potter's house must be rolled and shaped into a ball and then thrown against the wire and halved in order to have the impurities exposed and plucked out. This life we live is just that for us, it is where our impurities are exposed in order for us to be made acceptable to our Lord and Savior, Jesus Christ. Don't fight the refining power of God, accept it. It only hurts for a little while and then we reap our rewards in Heaven.

I remember the frustrations that I had when things always seemed to foul up and everything I did seemed to be wrong. One day I realized that God was refining me. It was a relief after a while when I started hearing people saying, "Hey brother, you're really shaping up." I even remember a young lady telling me that I was the most secular person she knew. I thought that was a compliment at the time, but now I know the definition of secular and I am not so proud of that comment. I didn't think that I was really all that bad, but then again, we are usually the last to know aren't we? We are all a work in progress, so don't give up. God's not finished with you yet.

Peace
vs.
Chaos

February 17th

Matthew 8:28- **"When he arrived at the other side in the region of the Gadarenes, two demon-possessed men coming from the tombs met him. They were so violent that no one could pass that way."-NIV**

The prince of the power of the air is waging, and has from the beginning of time, a war against the souls and the eternal destiny of mankind. We cannot fathom the occult occurrences that are taking place within the spiritual realm of our existence. God clearly shows us examples throughout His Word of this demonic realm.

Have you ever met a person who no matter what you did or said they would want to bite your head off? Perhaps you were one of those people, or possibly you still are. Sad isn't it? They just seem to be eternally miserable. If you stood on your head and spit dimes for them they would be upset that they weren't quarters. It's a no win situation. We need prayer at your churches for people like that. Pray that God will touch them and that He will develop a relationship with them. They need to feel the loving arms of God wrapped around them giving them a hug. Hugs and a kind word can have dynamic results.

People who seem miserable all the time are usually just lonely. Somewhere in their life they were hurt and they don't know how to act any better than they do. If you just pray and ask Jesus to change their heart, He can. Are they worth the effort? Were you worth the prayers someone lifted on your behalf before you were saved? That was a rhetorical question. Of course you were worth the prayers and the effort people invested in you. Often time's people don't care how much you know until they know how much you care. Let them know that you care and that they are valued. Take time out of your busy schedule and shed a little light into their lives. Be a friend to the friendless.

Filled with the Holy Spirit
vs.
Demonic possession

February 18th

Matthew 8:28- "When he arrived at the other side in the region of the Gadarenes, two demon-possessed men coming from the tombs met him. They were so violent that no one could pass that way."-NIV

As a Christian Counselor I have often wondered and questioned myself of the mysteries inherent within the realm of demonic possession and deliverance of these satanic forces. The Bible speaks clearly, as in the above scripture, of demonic possession. What we take in as human beings opens us up to various spiritual forces. As the old adage says, "The eyes are the windows to our souls". What we take in through our eyes has the capacity to influence our thoughts, our actions, our beliefs, our values, and ultimately, our divine destiny. This truth becomes even more powerful when you stop and think of our eternal destiny, and not just our temporal existence.

Working within the mental health field for the past twenty years, I have witnessed first-hand, individuals that exhibit various forms of psychosis and mental health issues. Spiritually speaking, I have questioned whether or not some of these extreme cases have been either possession or oppression of demonic forces.

Many individuals that are diagnosed with psychotic disorders can become so violent towards themselves and others, that as a Christian Counselor, I naturally question the influence of demonic activity within the realm of their individual lives. When we look at the things our kids watch on television or at the movies it is really scary. There is so much interest in the occult. We see shows popularizing witchcraft, vampires, demons, all sorts of evil. People, we are in charge of our children and if you want them to be healthy and functional spiritually, as well as physically and psychologically, you need to monitor what they are taking in. The electronic babysitter sitting in your living room or den is not fit to watch a child; it is our responsibility to our kids, and to God, to better watch them. When I think of how far our entertainment industry has slipped into that abyss of filth from when I was growing up I want to cry. Let's pray for the advancement and influence of morals all across this country and the whole world ok? Please.

Let's live our morals
for all the world to see

February 19th

Matthew 8:32- "He said to them, "Go!" So they came out and went into the pigs, and the whole herd rushed down the steep bank into the lake and died in the water."-NIV

In His Word He has the power to cast out these demonic forces and to deliver people of possession. According to the Word of God, there is no other name under Heaven, other than Jesus, that one can access this pervasive power to deliver people (Acts 4:12).

One of the prayers that I pray daily for myself and my family is that we would be covered by the blood of the Lamb. I believe that there is power in pleading the blood of Jesus over our lives and the lives of others since He was the divine and ultimate sacrifice for our sins and the sins of the entire human race. There is tremendous power in prayer.

If we practice strengthening our prayer life, just imagine the power that we would possess. We practice our golf and bowling, perhaps football or softball, running distances and biking, why not prayer? If you want to be good at something it takes practice. Try praying for 15 minutes at a time each day for a week and then extend it to ½ hour the next week. Do this for a month and you will be praying for an hour at a time a day. Imagine what you will be able to accomplish. You will be a mighty warrior in God's army. Now try to convey this idea to your church leaders and have a night of pray at your churches. We have it at our church on Saturday night. There is power there. We also pray with our pastors before they ascend the pulpit. We get a group of men together in the "Holy Hallway" and we pray with everything we have for our pastor and that God's message will be brought forth, and that the forces of hell will be staid and that the Holy Spirit will flow forth and touch everyone present. We pray that God will have His way during our service and that if there are any who are sick and infirmed that they will be blessed with good health by our Lord Jesus Christ. My friends this is done before every service. Try this at your churches and you will be blessed.

God has the power

February 20th

Matthew 9:2- **"Some men brought to him a paralytic, lying on a mat. When Jesus saw their faith, he said to the paralytic, "Take heart, son; your sins are forgiven."-** NIV

Faith is the realization that all power exists within Jesus and that outside of Jesus there is no sure foundational truths. Hebrews 11:1 says; **"Now faith is the assurance of things hoped for, the conviction of things not seen."** In faith we believe that God will answer our prayers, heal us of our infirmities, and ultimately forgive us of our sins. Any barrier that gets in the way of this reality for us must consciously be set aside and put to rest. We must train our minds and our hearts to take action in the present, not relying on our own goodness, but relying on the goodness of God and His ability to transcend our humanity. God is Omni-benevolent in that all goodness is in Him. God only wants what is best for us.

I have heard people say that God never answers their prayers for them. Have you ever heard this? I tell you the truth, it drives me nuts. God answers all prayers, people. If you think otherwise, you need to change your thinking. Those of you who are parents, do you give your kids everything they ask for? Of course you don't. Why not? You don't give them everything they ask for because they would probably hurt themselves, or they might get sick, or perhaps they would turn out to be spoiled brats, right? God is no different. He is our Father right? He's a good parent. Perhaps we don't necessarily need whatever it is that we prayed for. Perhaps whatever it is we prayed for would hurt us. Perhaps it would pull us away from God. He doesn't want us to be spoiled, sick, or hurt.

Prayer is our hotline to God. It is our lifeline. When we pray we are praying to God and asking it through our intercessor, Jesus Christ. When you finish your prayers don't you say "I ask this in the name of your Son, Jesus Christ, my Lord." When we pray, our prayers are heard by God and answered by Jesus. Jesus is asked by God, and if we are known to Him, Jesus, He says, "Go ahead Dad, He's one of mine." So, all prayer is answered, it may be that the answer is no, or perhaps not right now. God hears all of our prayers my friends; not some, but all of them.

Faith & forgiveness
vs.
Unbelief/unforgiveness

Matthew 9:10-11- **"While Jesus was having dinner at Matthew's house, many tax collectors and "sinners" came and ate with him and his disciples. When the Pharisees saw this, they asked his disciples, "Why does your teacher eat with tax collectors and sinners'?"-NIV**

We must move away from the rigidity of religiosity and toward the free work that can be found in Christ. Christ did not come to make us a more religious people, He came to save sinners and to set the captive free (John 8:36). He came to deliver us from the various bondages that can be all consuming within our lives. No matter what your walk of life, no matter what your profession, no matter what your past and no matter what your family history, God can set you free. Jesus is all about the soul, not about the external things of this world.

He's not about how we compartmentalize people into various groups, nor is He about boundaries and walls. He's about breaking down these various aspects of our lives and giving us spiritual lenses to see others how He sees them. God is in the business of removing our blinders. We must allow God to remove these preconceived notions, these images and prejudices that we have toward others in Christ. Do you know the heart of a man, like God? I didn't think so. We need to be careful of what comes out of our mouths and our hearts.

How would you feel if someone judged you the very same way that you judge others? Chances are, you would feel pretty crummy. Am I right? Admit it, you know I am. Let's, starting today, ask God to remove from us our judgmental hearts and our preconceived notions of other people and let's ask Him to cleanse us from the inside out. Sound good? Let's do it! We can't afford to walk around life feeling ill will towards a certain ethnic group or denomination other than the one we practice. Life is too precious to spend it on things so insignificant.

Have you ever thought of what Heaven will look like? I can guarantee you one thing; it won't be broken up into different barrios. Could you imagine Jesus walking down the street with you in heaven and saying to you, "Hey buddy, look over there! And then you would say, "What is it Jesus?" And He would reply, "They have a new kid over there in the Baptist barrio." This sounds pretty ignorant doesn't it? Yeah, I thought so. It does to Him too, but isn't that what we are doing when we talk about other religions in a negative way? We need to practice love.

Jesus came to save!

Matthew 9:12-13-"On hearing this, Jesus said, "It is not the healthy who need a doctor, but the sick. But go and learn what this means: 'I desire mercy, not sacrifice.' For I have not come to call the righteous, but sinners.""-NIV

God is in the business of restoration of a fallen mankind. He longs to make us whole and to heal our wounds, whatever they may be. Apart from God we're incomplete. Even with God, we should be in a constant state of change, growth, and spiritual renewal. All this takes place within the inner man. God works from the inside out. He's able to penetrate the many layers and complexities of our human nature, changing, molding, and creating a spiritual inner man, where their once was none. Us knowing God changes oh so many things. We're new creations in Christ Jesus (2 Corinthians 5:17). We're born again, not of our mother's womb, but of God (John 3:3). We're born of the God of all creation, the God of both Heaven and Earth.

God has had mercy on us, so shouldn't we have mercy on others? We're called to look to the needs of others above and beyond our own needs. This is the example that Jesus Christ has given us to live by. God, with all His power, looked down from Heaven, and He sent Jesus Christ in human form to die and sacrifice His life for us. I can't even begin to fathom that.

How many of us would be willing to truly die for a loved one? Not too many I would bet. Imagine this, God died for you and for me! Can you imagine that? This totally blows my mind. God found me worthy enough that He gave up his life for me. He did the same for you too. Imagine that!! We need to see ourselves as God sees us. When He stretched out His arms on that cross He showed us how much He loves us.

Picture a little one when you ask them how much they love you and they throw out their little arms and they say, "This much." They can't reach anymore they are stretched so far. My dear brothers and sisters, that is how much God loves us. Believe it! It's true. I wouldn't lie to you. Oh, please God; let us grasp what we have in you and how much you love us. In you we have everything. Have us believe it please.

Mercy vs. Sacrifice

Righteousness vs. Sin

February 23rd

Matthew 9:22-"Jesus turned and saw her. "Take heart, daughter," he said, "your faith has healed you." And the woman was healed from that moment."-NIV

In the Holy Scriptures, Jesus talks about the importance and significance of our faith. Our faith in Him is of paramount importance, according to Scripture. According to the Bible, there are many positive outcomes that take place in individual lives when one has faith. Faith in God isn't just wishful thinking, or positive thoughts, it's trusting in our Creator with every aspect of our being. How much are we really relying on Jesus? Do we trust in ourselves and in our own strength more than we trust in Him? I sure hope not people. We really have to throw away the old saying, "Lift yourself up by your own bootstraps and do something with your life!" My friend, where is God in that statement? If we take the perspective of relying on me, myself and I, you know them, the new age trinity, then life will quickly become a very self-centered existence. Healing is a pervasive term. It signifies the absolute and complete change of a condition, situation, or circumstance within our lives. God longs to intervene and make things right for us. The question is, how much of our existence, of our lives, are we allowing Him to have? Are we going to Him with everything, or are we holding back something due to lack of trust? Imagine the healing that could take place in our lives if we brought everything in our life to the foot of the Cross of Christ? Let's lay it all and leave it at the foot of the cross. What is so important that you can't trust it to God? Don't you want to be free of it? Give it all to Him.

Can you imagine how awesome life would be if you were worry free? Think of all the time you would have on your hands without all of the negativities of life bogging you down. Think of all the great things God would have you do. You are cheating not only God but yourself also by holding onto them. Give them to Him. He's begging you for them. Do it and move into the next stage of your new life in Him. He's waiting.

Faith!

Matthew 9:28-30**"Do you believe that I am able to do this?" "Yes, Lord," they replied. Then he touched their eyes and said, "According to your faith will it be done to you"; and their sight was restored."-NIV**

Let's not question God. Let's not transfer our tainted and limited human understanding onto the Almighty God. God longs for us to come to Him as little children, in faith, believing that all things are possible through Him. Look at how children come running for their loved ones with outstretched arms and huge smiles on their little faces just wanting love. They trust completely. How beautiful! That's how our Father wants us to come to Him.

Have you ever watched children when they are coming out of elementary school after their first day of school and they see their mom or dad at the fence to pick them up? They are beaming from ear to ear with excitement at the sight of their parent. That is God when He sees us living for Him. He is smiling big time when we finally make the decision to follow Him completely. That is all He asks for.

In an age where we are measured according to grade point averages and initials after ones name, we must not lose sight of what our loving Savior longs to do in our lives. So much of our lives are built upon conditions, ultimatums, both institutional and societal, and cultural pressures. God loves us unconditionally. He says in Mark 8:34; **"And he called to him the crowd with his disciples and said to them, "If anyone would come after me, let him deny himself and take up his cross and follow me."** We are to place our lives in Him. Place your faith in Him and He will guide, heal, transform, and totally revolutionize your life. God has a divine destiny for our lives. He's able to see the big picture which we can't. We need to have faith and never lose hope in the truth that's in Christ Jesus our Lord.

Restoration vs. Deterioration

February 25th

Matthew 9:34-"But the Pharisees said, "It is by the prince of demons that he drives out demons.".-NIV

How far off was the discernment of the religious leaders of that day? They thought that Jesus was driving out demons with another power besides that of God? Those that don't have the Holy Spirit operating within their lives are spiritually blinded to the things of God. Unbelievers cannot understand nor comprehend the things of God, only those exposed and walking in the light can (1 Corinthians 2:9-16). We need the power of the Holy Spirit to illuminate our minds and our hearts to even have an inkling of what God says in His Word. If we don't allow the Holy Spirit to reveal His Word to us, then we are kidding ourselves with the reliance of self to interpret the Word of God.

How deceived the Pharisees were to think that demonic forces drive out demonic forces. Darkness does not drive out darkness, only light can drive out darkness. Only God can drive out the things of Satan. Man alone cannot, apart from God, fight against the spiritual forces of darkness. The Pharisees were confusing the light of Christ with the darkness of the evil one. They were spiritually in the dark, unaware of the need of the Holy Spirit to open their eyes to the things of Jesus Christ.

Have you ever been in a room with absolutely no light at all? Scary isn't it? If you are in a room like that and all of a sudden there is a little pin prick of light it shines like a beacon and the room is no longer totally dark. That is our life. We have the light in us and shining through us. The more we dig into the Word the brighter the light. The brighter the light, the more people will be drawn to us. Remember the summer nights when you had your porch light on and all the bugs were swarming around it, they wanted the light, and they needed the light. We are the same way the bugs on a summer night do. We need it to survive in this our present darkness.

What's your discernment say?

February 26th

Matthew 9:37-"The harvest is plentiful but the workers are few. Ask the Lord of the harvest, therefore, to send out workers into his harvest field."-NIV

Billions of people throughout the world are in need of a Savior. The problem is that many within the realm of the church are not reaching the lost for Jesus Christ. So much of the world continues to be in need of hearing of the love of our Lord. People all over the world are waiting for the Good News; however, there is no one to share His love with them. The church is in need of visionary leaders that can obtain, and maintain, a vision of the great commission to reach the lost for Him. In many instances, the great commission has been the great omission. This is a shame.

God says specifically in His Word how we're to allow the Lord to move, I believe that this comes about by prayer. Prayer will be the releasing power that allows the Holy Spirit to move in the hearts and minds of people throughout the world to get involved with the Great Commission and the realization that we're called to preach the gospel to all nations, all tongues, and to all tribes. Matthew 28:19-20; **"Go therefore and make disciples of all nations, baptizing them in the name of the Father and of the Son and of the Holy Spirit, teaching them to observe all that I have commanded you. And behold, I am with you always, to the end of the age."**

Do you remember what your life was like before you heard the Good News? Mine was very bleak. I am so grateful that someone took the time to share it with me. I can remember the first time I went witnessing how scared I was at being spurned by someone or having someone embarrass me by asking a question I couldn't answer. Does this sound familiar? All we have to do is to make the effort to witness and God will do the rest. He will work both in and through us if we allow Him to. We have to be willing to do our part, and if we do, He will be faithful to follow it through to completion. We just have to be willing.

Do you know your Savior?

February 27th

Matthew 10:7-8-"The Kingdom of Heaven is near. Heal the sick, raise the dead, cleanse those who have leprosy, drive out demons. Freely you have received, freely give."-NIV

Life is but a breath. How quickly life passes. We plan our short-term and long-term goals, and we spend much of our lives accomplishing and accumulating things. How many of us are involved in the divine destiny that God has for our life? Are we allowing God to be part of our destiny?

Let's dedicate our lives in the service to others, delivering them and setting them free with the power that's inherent within Jesus. God's gift of salvation was free, even though He paid the ultimate price, which was the sacrificial offering of His life on the Cross of Calvary. One died for all so that all might live. Let's offer up ourselves as a fragrant offering to the Lord, so that we can carry out His Will while we are here on earth.

What can be a larger step of faith than healing in the name of Jesus? We all know people within the church who are seeking physical, financial, emotional, psychological, and spiritual healings. God is in the business of healing. How comforting it is to know that we can come before the throne of God in prayer, with requests and petitions, calling out to our Heavenly Father to intercede for us and to heal us of all our infirmities. What a blessing. How powerful! Awesome! What would any of us do without the life we presently have in Christ?

I have heard testimony after testimony of what God is doing all over the world, and not just from missionary's that have come to the church I attend. I have heard it by meeting with Christians from other countries that have told me what God is doing in their countries. A friend from Africa has shared with me on several occasions the wonderful healings and miraculous things that God is doing in Africa. Africans walk for miles to attend church. Sometimes their praises and their worship, their prayers and preaching's, can go on and on for days. They cry out to God! They're spiritually focused and also they are spiritually minded, open to what God would have them do in their lives. What a great example for us to follow.

Freely you have received,
freely give

February 28th

Matthew 10:16-"I am sending you out like sheep among wolves. Therefore be as shrewd as snakes and as innocent as doves."-NIV

Jesus warns the disciples about the persecution that missionary disciples will endure. We are to be wise as serpents and innocent as doves. The serpent was the symbol of shrewdness and intellectual cunning. Gen. 3:1; **"Now the serpent was more subtle and crafty than any living creature of the field which the Lord God had made. And he [Satan] said to the woman, can it really be that God has said, you shall not eat from every tree of the garden?"** Ps. 58:4–5; **"Their poison is like the venom of a serpent; they are like the deaf adder or asp that stops its ear, which listens not to the voice of charmers or of the enchanter never casting spells so cunningly."** The dove was emblematic of simple innocence. Hos. 7:11; **"Ephraim also is like a silly dove without heart or understanding."**

God is clearly and definitively warning us that we must be alert and on guard at all times. We will be surrounded by wolves in sheep's clothing. John 10:10 tells us that **"The thief comes only in order to steal and kill and destroy. I came that they may have and enjoy life, and have it in abundance (to the full, till it overflows)."** We must be vigilant and aware that the enemy is lurking in the shadows waiting to pounce on us like a wild beast. We need to be prayed up like a fortified city that is expecting an attack from the enemy, while at the same time maintaining our composure and calmness in the face of the storm. God uses the metaphorical terms of "sheep among wolves" and "being shrewd as snakes and innocent as doves" to grab our attention. How much clearer does He have to be for us to get the picture and wake-up?

I remember times in the military where we would set up camp. The most important thing we had to consider when setting up camp was a route for egress if a situation were to occur. Once in camp we needed to secure and maintain an outer perimeter. We had guards posted 24/7. If anyone was to try to sneak up on us they were challenged. If when challenged they didn't know the password they were dealt with accordingly. We need to have the same perimeters in place. What perimeters have you got in place? Do you have any? Are you maintaining a vigilant watch over your family? They were entrusted to you by our Lord. We need to keep the same vigilant watch on our hearts, souls, and salvation that a soldier keeps on his camp. Our hearts, souls, and salvation were bought with a price. They are precious to us as well as to the Lord and they are well worth the protection needed to maintain them.

Be wise

February 29th

Matthew 10:21-23-"Brother will betray brother to death, and a father his child; children will rebel against their parents and have them put to death. All men will hate you because of me, but he who stands firm to the end will be saved. When you are persecuted in one place, flee to another. I tell you the truth, you will not finish going through the cities of Israel before the Son of Man comes."-NIV

Things are going to seem out of control, chaotic, and utterly detestable in the last days in the eyes of God. People will be killing each other unmercifully. Hatred and discord will run rampant throughout the world. It's difficult to imagine all of this happening with a greater degree than is presently taking place, but it will. We are seeing hate and discontent played out before us daily when we turn on our TV's and see the news from around the world. We are seeing people killing each other for no reason at all. We are seeing children killing children just to see what killing someone feels like. We are seeing kids raping other kids for something to do. Young people are running in packs like wild dogs and attacking innocent people and destroying their lives for no other reason than because they had nothing else to do. The value of human life has been degraded to an all-time low. I sometimes cry when I see what is taking place in our world, sometimes even in our own neighborhoods. It is going to get worse however.

God is calling us to stand firm my friends. God is calling us to stand firm to the very end. Ephesians 6:10-11 says to **"Be strong in the Lord and in the power of His might. Put on the whole Armor of God that you may be able to stand against the wiles of the devil."** We must be strong. We must not waver or swagger in our walk or in our Faith in Christ Jesus. We must do everything within our power to stand steadfast in our most precious Christian Faith, and when we feel that we can't stand anymore, we must trust in our Most High God. When we are at the end of our rope, we are at the beginning of His. When everything starts coming at us from all directions, urging, prodding, and coaxing us to go with the flow of our culture, just remember this, you are not alone, He is with you. These calamities are just a sign of the times. His coming is nearer than we may think. Let's not lose heart, but stand steadfast in the face of the enemy. We don't know when He is going to reappear, but we do know that He will.

Stand Firm!

MARCH

March 1st

Matthew 10:25-"If the head of the house has been called Beelzebub, how much more the members of his household!"-NIV

Think about this verse my friends. If they were accusing Jesus of being the devil, how do we think we are going to get by without accusations being thrown at us? The truth is we won't. We just need to make sure we are toeing the line with God in all aspects of our life.

A Godly home is nothing to take lightly, especially in this day and age. We need to maintain a Godly home. Our Lord has entrusted us with morals and values and we are seeing what can happen if we lose those. If there is any doubt, turn on the nightly news or pick up a newspaper. It is all through whatever form of media you chose to gather for your news source. We need to pray over our loved ones and/or husbands or wives? What about praying over your children? You do pray over your children don't you? You really need to pray a hedge of protection over your family members. Do you pray over your properties? They are all gifts from on high. We can lose them just as fast as we received them. This is a great practice to get into. Pray over your loved ones before they leave the house, or you leave the house, whichever the case may be, just do it. This may seem foreign at first if you are not used to it, but what a great practice to get into. What about praying over your food? Do you do it? If not, start. Pray over it not only at home but at restaurants also. Don't be ashamed of the fact that you are Christian, be proud of it.

The prince of the power of the air, otherwise known as Satan, is ruling the homes of unbelievers. Don't let him get control of yours. Unbelievers are prone to the influence of the anti-Christ spirit that now is at work in the world with a great intensity and zeal for destruction. Satan and his demonic cohorts are subtly, discreetly, and sometimes even blatantly, annihilating and obliterating the homes and families within the United States of America and throughout the world. Don't fall victim to his path of destruction. He would love nothing more than to get a hold of another Christian who let his or her guard down. Pray for strength in the battle and He will give it to you.

Be strong in the Lord

March 2nd

Matthew 10:28-"Do not be afraid of those who kill the body but cannot kill the soul. Rather, be afraid of the One who can destroy both soul and body in hell."-NIV

Let's not fear men and their ungodly devices. Christians need to develop a healthy fear of the Lord in order to capture the divine destiny of their souls. The soul is an eternal entity, whereas the physical body is only a temporal manifestation of who we are. Our souls will last eternally either in Heaven or hell. The decision is ours, and only ours, to make. Decisions determine our destiny and where we will spend eternity.

When man is great and God is insignificant, human beings have a tendency of giving men more power than they deserve. We should never allow men to become greater in our minds eye than our reverence for God. Within God, there is all power; unequaled, and unparalleled authority. Remember that all wisdom begins with the fear of the Lord (Psalms 111:10). This fear is tremendous respect, not boot quaking scared to death fear, but deep honor and respect fear.

There is a difference between fear and being afraid. With a healthy fear, there can be reverence and respect toward God. Being afraid is being fearful and distrustful of what one might do on his or her own. Humans are typically afraid of those that don't have their best interests in mind. Our enemies can cause us to be afraid. For those of us that have been mugged or taken advantage of in some way, we know what it is to be afraid. Having a fear of the Lord is the beginning of knowledge and wisdom. This wisdom is not as the world gives, but it is a wisdom that God gives.

Man can kill the body. We're witnessing this presently in the wars within Iraq and Afghanistan. Men, women, and children are dying daily. Human beings have always died in war. Their physical bodies are being destroyed, with only memories left for their families. Man can kill the human body; however, God has the power of bringing our eternal soul to remain in Heaven with Him. Man has a distinct choice between good or evil, right versus wrong, believing in God or rejecting God. Heaven and hell hang in the balance of these decisions. Life is full of difficult choices. Real choices have real consequences. Life isn't a joke. We have the God given gift of being born, living life, and eventually dying. Let's not reject God and our Creator in the process.

Fear and
revere God!

March 3rd

Matthew 10:34-37"Do not suppose that I have come to bring peace to the earth. I did not come to bring peace, but a sword. For I have come to turn "a man against his father, a daughter against her mother, a daughter-in-law against her mother-in-law- a man's enemies will be the members of his own household.".-NIV

Many will turn away from you once you become a true believer in our Lord Jesus Christ. Christians should not be amazed or perplexed when this happens. According to God, this is an expected phenomenon. We may not understand it but He does.

When a person becomes born again of the Spirit, God is within them and they are His. Christ calls us as Christians to take up our cross and to follow Him (Mark 8:34-35); everything else becomes peripheral and secondary to Jesus. Rightfully so! The Christian has found God and he no longer is holding dear the things of this world. We're looking to a builder and a maker of a Kingdom that is not of this world. We become mindful of Heavenly things and we are no longer consumed and conformed to the things of this world (Romans 12:2).

When someone accepts Jesus Christ as their Personal Lord and Savior, others that are unbelievers, or people of other faiths, they may not understand what has happened to the individual who has accepted Jesus. They won't understand the transformation. People of the world find Christians to be a perplexing phenomenon.

Christians that are radically sold out for Christ will become ridiculed and rejected in some cases. What binds the people of this world should no longer bind the Christian. Our minds, hearts, souls, and spirits, have all been renewed with the power of the Holy Spirit. The saving work of God now lives in us. The spirit of the anti-Christ has no power over us. Don't be surprised when a **Waging War Within** takes place all around you. This is a sign that the chains, the bondages, and the vices of this world, are being relinquished and no longer have a grip on you. Praise God!

Are you turning away?

March 4th

Matthew 10:37-39-"Anyone who loves his father or mother more than me is not worthy of me; anyone who loves his son or daughter more than me is not worthy of me; and anyone who does not take his cross and follow me is not worthy of me. Whoever finds his life will lose it, and whoever loses his life for my sake will find it."- NIV

When we abandon ourselves to the Lord Jesus Christ we must count the cost. We would be in utter denial in thinking that following Jesus doesn't come with a cost. God specifically warns us of the cost in following Him. Luke 14:28; **"Any one of you who does not renounce all that he has cannot be my disciple."** He explains how it might cost us in changing our present and future existence. Nothing and no one can ever come before Jesus Christ. He's our all and all. He's numero-uno. He's number one. He is the Macaroni and we are merely the cheese.

God explains that by following Him, we'll actually gain our life once we have crucified the flesh and get off our sinful beaten track. Galatians 2:20; **"It is no longer I who live, but Christ who lives in me. And the life I now live in the flesh I live by faith in the Son of God, who loved me and gave himself for me."** God transcends our earthly relationships and the things that bind us here to earth. In following God, we begin to realize that our lives are fleeting and that at any moment God could call us Heavenward, to be with Him and Christ Jesus. Our entire reason for being is totally transformed once we know God and His love for us.

The cross is the representation of God's love for us. He not only died on the Cross for our sins, but He was raised from the Cross for our justification and salvation. We have been reconciled to the Cross of Christ by Jesus Christ's resurrection from the dead. Upon acceptance of our Lord and Savior, we now have the same power that raised Jesus from the dead, working within our earthly and mortal bodies. This means that we can do things that are otherworldly impossible. We have the power within us through Him to heal the sick, intercede for others in times of prayer, and so much more. John 14:12; **"Truly, truly, I say to you, whoever believes in me will also do the works that I do; and greater works than these will he do, because I am going to the Father."** How awesome is that? It's well worth the tradeoff isn't it? Our life for His? It's really a no brainer.

Take up the cross of Christ

March 5th

Matthew 10:39-"Whoever finds his life will lose it, and whoever loses his life for my sake will find it."-NIV

There is no guarantee that you will not face opposition when you become a Christian. There is a long history of persecution and martyrdom that are in the annals of Christianity. Look at the original disciple's, all but John died a martyr's death. The term martyr means witness in the Greek language. Revelation 6:9 speaks of martyrdom; **"When he opened the fifth seal, I saw under the altar the souls of those who had been slain for the word of God and for the witness they had borne."** Revelation 20:4 is another; **"Then I saw thrones, and seated on them were those to whom the authority to judge was committed. Also I saw the souls of those who had been beheaded for the testimony of Jesus and for the word of God, and who had not worshiped the beast or its image and had not received its mark on their foreheads or their hands. They came to life and reigned with Christ for a thousand years."** God wants our all whatever that may be.

God wants our entire beings to be united with Him. He desires us to follow Him with all of our heart, our soul, and our strength. He desires for us to give our entire self to Him, to follow Him, and to live for Him, and when necessary to die for Him also. God wants us to have a relationship with Him knowing that He is always with us, for us, and not against us. God longs to bless our lives, our family's lives, and our future. He wants us to walk daily with the realization that our lives are not our own, they are His. The very One that created us wants us to rely on Him more than the air that we breathe, the water that we drink, and the food that we eat.

God wants us to run to Him, not recklessly, but without regret, to abandon our lives and our wills to Him, with all that we do. We must not compromise the divine destiny that God has for our lives. He wants to work in us and through us. He wants this so that we can win the world to Him. Our lives must become living sacrifices to Him daily. Romans 12:1-5; **"I appeal to you therefore, brothers, by the mercies of God, to present your bodies as a living sacrifice, holy and acceptable to God, which is your spiritual worship. Do not be conformed to this world, but be transformed by the renewal of your mind, that by testing you may discern what is the will of God, what is good and acceptable and perfect. For by the grace given to me I say to everyone among you not to think of himself more highly than he ought to think, but to think with sober judgment, each according to the measure of faith that God has assigned. For as in one body we have many members, and the members do not all have the same function, so we, though many, are one body in Christ, and individually members one of another."**

March 6th

Matthew 11:12-15- "From the days of John the Baptist until now, the kingdom of heaven has been forcefully advancing, and forceful men lay hold of it. For all the Prophets and the Law prophesied until John. And if you are willing to accept it, he is the Elijah who was to come. He who has ears, let him hear."-NIV

Just think, God's people have been growing in number for a couple of thousand years. People of all walks of life, every nationality, every tribe and every nation, have chosen to follow Jesus and accept Him as their Lord and Savior. This is incredible! Human beings from every country in the world have accepted Jesus as Savior and are Heaven bound for eternity. Why is this? It is because someone took the time to speak as we were told to do in the Great Commission of Matthew 28:19-20. They spoke of the saving power of one Jesus Christ. Not only that, the people had ears to hear (Matthew 11:5).

In a day and age when Christians are being attacked on the political front for being rigid, close minded, backward, and not progressive, the multi-ethnic, multi-pluralistic, and multi-cultural dynamic of Christianity worldwide is growing. How ironic. Faith in Jesus Christ is being portrayed by some segments of society as being behind the times. I guess many should rub shoulders with the Christians of other parts of the world, prior to making a judgment call.

We look upon the United States of America as a melting pot of humanity, imagine Heaven! Every tongue, every culture, and every people will be represented in Heaven. With God, there is no border control. God is in the eternal security business! Instead of keeping people out, He's attempting to bring them in. God says that all, no matter what background or demographic, can accept Jesus Christ as Savior and receive salvation for their souls. I myself was led to Christ by an African Missionary who was visiting the United States at a mission's convention. God crosses all borders, all boundaries, all people groups, and all classes around the world with His message of salvation.

We must have passion as Christians. It is this passion for the things of God that will allow the message of Jesus Christ to forcefully advance on every front throughout the world. God knows that His creation desires salvation. We as Christians must find ways of spreading the Gospel throughout the world until Jesus comes again. We must never lose our vision for reaching the entire world with the message of the Word of God.

Give God your all

March 7th

Matthew 11:19-"The Son of Man came eating and drinking, and they say, 'Here is a glutton and a drunkard, a friend of tax collectors and "sinners."' But wisdom is proved right by her actions."-NIV

Misconceptions, false interpretations, and sheer misrepresentations by the religious leaders of the time judged Jesus Christ. Thank God the Father, He sent Jesus to save sinners. What would a big ship do without a Captain? How about a plane without a pilot? You can imagine the difficulties that would be obvious consequences to these questions. I am sure you can bring to your imagination the devastating consequences that would prevail if both the ship and the plane are left without a competent authority to take charge. There would be utter chaos and confusion. People wouldn't know what to do. People would be left to their own devices.

What do sinners do when left to their own devices? They sin and continue to go on a wayward course that ultimately will lead to their destruction. Thank God that He came to save sinners from their own incapacity to save themselves. Man cannot save himself, only God can do that. God acted on our behalf because He knew that we couldn't.

By God meeting with the downtrodden and common place people He demonstrated His capacity to love and gave us an example to live by. Jesus didn't consider Himself better than these people, despite the fact that He was God. He humbled Himself even to death on a cross, so that we might live (Philippians 2:8). Let's be careful that we don't develop a false sense of who we are in Christ Jesus. Let's never think of ourselves more highly than we should. Our prayer should be that God would make us to be the extended eyes, ears, arms, hands, legs, feet, and voice of Jesus to a dying, decaying, and lost world.

Jesus' life displayed the divine. He was complete divinity, God Himself in human form. God designed and engineered a perfect way to let man know who He was and what He came to do. How could man ever relate to God if God wasn't sent here to live on earth in human form? How could God possibly bridge the separation between Himself and humankind if He didn't send His son Jesus Christ? What perfect sacrifice could God have made in place of Jesus Christ? I don't even want to think about it.

Actions speak volumes

March 8th

Matthew 11:20-"Then Jesus began to denounce the cities in which most of his miracles had been performed, because they did not repent." -NIV

Repentance is key to both Christianity and also to having and maintaining a relationship with our Lord Jesus Christ. When we repent, we're humbling ourselves before God. God places a high priority on repentance. The very act of repentance allows all sinners to get right, and stay right, before both God and our fellow man. Repentance transcends our temporal existence and allows us to gain a perspective and also to access our eternal reality in Christ Jesus.

Our hearts are in a right place when we repent of our sins. All pride, jealousy, anger, hatred, animosity, fear, distrust, or anything else within us that isn't from God, is able to be cleansed and washed away forever. Through heartfelt repentance, we're able to be in right relationship to God our Father. Our prayer should be that God would send His Holy Spirit to reveal anything within ourselves that He wishes to change, heal, or deliver us from. Through true repentance, we can be honest with God as He searches our souls. We should ask God for His Holy Spirit to give us discernment and wisdom in our prayer of repentance.

The very act of repenting allows God to intervene in beautiful ways in our lives. While He is transforming us more into His image, we will notice changes taking place. He longs to create in us a clean heart and to renew a right spirit within us. The very nature of our flesh and carnal nature requires us, as Christians, to daily repentance and spiritual renewal. We should be praying for God to renew ourselves daily in order to live and carry out our Christian Faith. It's exciting to see how God can work through us when we're walking with a repentant spirit. Repentance allows God to transform and revolutionize our spiritual journey and our relationship with Him.

There is nothing more powerful that happens in my life than when I bow down and lower myself to my knees and cry out to God to forgive me of my sins. God descends to me, forgiving me, and He restores me in this process. Prayer and repentance are so very powerful. The way to triumph as a Christian is to bow down to the Master of Heaven and Earth. God hears our cry and will answer our prayer. He has already won **The Waging War Within** for us.

Repent before God

March 9th

Matthew 11:22-"But I tell you, it will be more bearable for Tyre and Sidon on the Day of Judgment than for you."-NIV

God clearly is warning us throughout His world that without a repentant heart, our lives will carry judgment upon them. God required the people in the past to repent. He also requires us to heed this same advice and counsel. Let's listen to and submit to God's authority, allowing all of His spiritual blessings to flow through our lives.

Look at what we have as the church of the 21st century. We have wonderful Christian Churches throughout the world, packed with Bibles, allowing the whole Word of God being preached and us the opportunity to follow along. God has revealed to us, and has given us, so much. We're blessed through and through. God's church is growing by leaps and bounds all around the world. God is using all types of venues to spread His Word. He's using the press, books, the movie industry, radio, and television, to spread His Word. God is using technology to spread His Word like never before. His Word and the Gospel message are spreading to the outer most parts of the earth.

When much is given, much is expected. Luke 12:48; **"But the one who did not know, and did what deserved a beating, will receive a light beating. Everyone to whom much was given, of him much will be required, and from him to whom they entrusted much, they will demand the more."** God has blessed us with the means of taking the entire country and the world for Him. With the advent of technology the spreading of the Good News is easier to do today than any time in the history of the world. God asks us the following: "What are you doing with all that you've been given?" Are you giving the Gospel Message all that you have? Are you sold out for Christ? Are you doing everything within your power to reach the people that haven't been reached with the Gospel? If not, why? If not, when? If you're not, who will go? Will you?

Repent of your wrongs.

Matthew 11:24-"But I tell you that it will be more bearable for Sodom on the Day of Judgment than for you."-NIV

God warns, using historical examples of Sodom and Gomorrah and of how devastating it can be if repentance and unbelief aren't operating within our lives. Let's read that account. Genesis 19:1-29; **"The two angels came to Sodom in the evening, and Lot was sitting in the gate of Sodom. When Lot saw them, he rose to meet them and bowed himself with his face to the earth and said, "My lords, please turn aside to your servant's house and spend the night and wash your feet. Then you may rise up early and go on your way." They said, "No; we will spend the night in the town square." But he pressed them strongly; so they turned aside to him and entered his house. And he made them a feast and baked unleavened bread, and they ate. But before they lay down, the men of the city, the men of Sodom, both young and old, all the people to the last man, surrounded the house. And they called to Lot, "Where are the men who came to you tonight? Bring them out to us, that we may know them." Lot went out to the men at the entrance, shut the door after him, and said, "I beg you, my brothers, do not act so wickedly. Behold, I have two daughters who have not known any man. Let me bring them out to you, and do to them as you please. Only do nothing to these men, for they have come under the shelter of my roof." But they said, "Stand back!" And they said, "This fellow came to sojourn, and he has become the judge! Now we will deal worse with you than with them." Then they pressed hard against the man Lot, and drew near to break the door down. But the men reached out their hands and brought Lot into the house with them and shut the door. And they struck with blindness the men who were at the entrance of the house, both small and great, so that they wore themselves out groping for the door. Then the men said to Lot, "Have you anyone else here? Sons-in-law, sons, daughters, or anyone you have in the city, bring them out of the place. For we are about to destroy this place, because the outcry against its people has become great before the LORD, and the LORD has sent us to destroy it." So Lot went out and said to his sons-in-law, who were to marry his daughters, "Up! Get out of this place, for the LORD is about to destroy the city." But he seemed to his sons-in-law to be jesting. As morning dawned, the angels urged Lot, saying, "Up! Take your wife and your two daughters who are here, lest you be swept away in the punishment of the city." But he lingered. So the men seized him and his wife and his two daughters by the hand, the LORD being merciful to him, and they brought him out and set him outside the city. And as they brought them out, one said, "Escape for your life. Do not look back or stop anywhere in the valley. Escape to the hills, lest you be swept away." And Lot said to them, "Oh, no, my lords. Behold, your servant has found favor in your sight, and you have shown me great kindness in saving my life. But I cannot escape to the hills, lest the disaster overtakes me and I die. Behold, this city is near enough to flee to, and it is a little one. Let me escape there— is it not a little one?—and my life will be saved!" He said to him, "Behold, I grant you this favor also, that I will not overthrow the city of which you have spoken. Escape there quickly, for I can do nothing till you arrive there." Therefore the name of the city was called Zoar. The sun had risen on the earth when Lot came to Zoar. Then the LORD rained on Sodom and Gomorrah sulfur and fire from the LORD out of heaven.**

And he overthrew those cities, and all the valley, and all the inhabitants of the cities, and what grew on the ground. But Lot's wife, behind him, looked back, and she became a pillar of salt. And Abraham went early in the morning to the place where he had stood before the LORD. And he looked down toward Sodom and Gomorrah and toward all the land of the valley, and he looked and, behold, the smoke of the land went up like the smoke of a furnace. So it was that, when God destroyed the cities of the valley, God remembered Abraham and sent Lot out of the midst of the overthrow when he overthrew the cities in which Lot had lived."

We want God's blessing not His wrath to be poured out upon us and our lives. Our society may be steadily heading toward judgment from God due to the millions and millions of abortions, the abuse and neglect of its children, the increased focus on self and materialism, locking God out of our schools and our families, the redefinition of the American family, the lack of discretion in our lives and the increase in crime within its borders. If America continues to blatantly turn her back on the Living God, Jesus Christ, and the precepts given to us by God, then the people within its borders will suffer the consequences of its own sin just as Sodom and Gomorrah did. History can and often does repeat itself.

The day and the hour
is fast
approaching!

Are you ready
for it?

March 11th

Matthew 11:25-26-"At that time Jesus said, "I praise you, Father, Lord of heaven and earth, because you have hidden these things from the wise and learned, and revealed them to little children. Yes, Father, for this was your good pleasure."-NIV

Sometimes our intellectual minds can interfere with our childlike faith and trust in Jesus. Not that we should be ignorant, impulsive or childish. God uses children as examples for us to emulate. Children have innocence about them. Children haven't yet been tainted by the world system like adults.

The great minds of our time, even those that have attempted to speculate the origins of our world have found it difficult to accept and understand the things of God. God requires our faith to metaphorically speaking be that of a little child (Matthew 18:3-5). As an earthly child can trust his or her earthly father and mother to guide and lead them across a busy intersection, we as Christians should be trusting God to guide us through our temporal existence here on earth and then into the eternal beyond.

Jesus Himself appeared to us a baby in a manger (Matthew 1:18-2:23). To think that God Himself sent us His image in the form of a little infant lying in a manger is prolific and allows us to fathom the heart of God. God loves children. God could have chosen to come to humanity in many forms; however He chose the likeness of a child. God transcended to all of humanity by coming into the world as a new born baby. Not one of us, no matter what walk of life, came into the world in any other fashion than that of a newborn baby.

God desires us to place our lives in His merciful hands, because He knows what is best for us. Our loving Heavenly Father wants us to prosper, to mature in Him and to grow spiritually. He wants the foundation of our lives to be poured out with the finest spiritual substance so that our lives will be a reflection of who He is. We need to have a simple faith, a simple trust in Him. He longs to guide us onward and upward in our Christian life and faith. He would not wish for us to stumble off of the path He has for us which leads to everlasting life. He desires for us to build a rock solid foundation that can withstand even the toughest warfare. He knows that a **Waging War Within** exists. He longs to be that rock solid foundation in our lives so we won't be moved. Let's trust in Him.

Seek the hidden things of God

March 12th

Matthew 11:27-"All things have been committed to me by my Father. No one knows the Son except the Father, and no one knows the Father except the Son and those to whom the Son chooses to reveal him."-NIV

God has chosen His people. His people are the people that have chosen Him. That's why we're called a chosen people, not of this world, but chosen of God. God has desired that within the fullness of time we be saved and committed to Him. How comforting it is for us to know that God the Father knows us, because He has revealed His Son Jesus Christ to us. God has chosen to reveal Himself to us so that we in turn can be changed into His image and transformed into His likeness.

Knowing someone implies that you have a relationship with them and that you have established communication and interaction with each other. How are we allowing God to come into our lives to work within us and change us? We should be experiencing change, growth and attempting to move toward spiritual maturity as a believer. This change into Christ likeness can be evidenced in our outward behaviors, our words, our relationships and the way we carry ourselves. Inwardly, knowing Jesus Christ, we should be experiencing and striving to have pure thoughts, a pure heart, pure intentions, pure motives and ultimately a wholesome thought life (Matthew 5:8).

Walking in a revelation of Jesus Christ is our aim. God's divine destiny in revealing His Son to us is to access salvation; however it's also to radically change every aspect of our lives. Knowing and being in Jesus should be providing us with His life giving Holy Spirit on a daily basis. Just as sure as we breathe air to keep our physical bodies alive, we should be allowing Jesus every second to keep our spiritual life intact.

It is impossible to know God without knowing Jesus Christ (John 14:6). Both God, and Jesus Christ are one is the same (John 1:1-3). God knew before He created the foundation of the earth that He was sending His son to earth in human likeness. This was His way of bridging the chasm between Earth and Heaven and providing the ultimate bridge of salvation so that people could enter His gate. There is no other name under Heaven whereby one must be saved and that name is Jesus Christ (Acts 4:12).

Let's know Christ as our Savior

Matthew 11:28-"Come to me, all you who are weary and burdened, and I will give you rest."-NIV

We live in a fast paced society and culture where we all are on the go twenty-four seven. We're on the move, going here and there and everywhere. If your life is like mine, you never have any down time unless you take the time to step back and relax. It's comforting to know that Jesus knew that we were going to be weary, burdened, and in need of some rest. What would we ever do without Jesus? We would be stressed, anxious and running ragged without Jesus giving us perspective. Let us continue to tap into His strength, His power, His majesty and His love. When we draw unto God, God will draw unto us (James 4:8).

More than ever we see an increase in depression, anxiety and stress for both adults and children. Never before in history have more people been on psychotropic medications for mental health issues. The prevalence of suicides due to mental health issues is increasing at a staggering rate. The increased abuse of alcohol and drugs has permeated our culture. People in many cases have allowed **The Waging War Within** to penetrate, infiltrate and annihilate their lives. Our lives spiritually can be equated to a military person in combat, experiencing heavy artillery. As a soldier needing the proper gear to carry out his or her mission, we as Christians are in need of the proper armor. One set of gear is provided by the United States Government, another by God (Ephesians 6:10-18).

Christians have to put on the full armor of our salvation and to gird up ourselves with the Word of Truth so that we can withstand the attacks of the enemy. Satan will attack us from every angle. He will find a way to destroy us if we're not vigilant both offensively and defensively. Our strategy must be from God. He specifically tells us that we have to be in God's Word and prayer on a daily basis. We also have to be committed to a local body of believers. We can't do it alone. God stresses the importance of fellowship with others of like precious faith (Hebrews 10:24-25). This will allow us to be built up in the faith so that we can withstand the fiery darts and sometimes the missiles that Satan will throw at us.

We have to do our part in living a disciplined Christian Life if we're going to experience God's favor. God does require us to take active participation in living a Christian Life. A Christian Life isn't something that is just given, it has to be lived consistently, steadfastly and with perseverance. It's a marathon, not a sprint.

Rest in Jesus

March 14th

Matthew 11:29-30-"Take my yoke upon you and learn from me, for I am gentle and humble in heart, and you will find rest for your souls. For my yoke is easy and my burden is light."-NIV

Alone time with God is a must. Let us never forsake spending time with God individually. God longs for us to spend quality time with Him. Our earthly relationships require time to nurture, so does our relationship with God. All relationships benefit from frequent communication. God hears from us in our prayer time. How is your prayer life? Prayer is a matter of practice and conditioning. You do not just start off with a perfect prayer life, it takes time to build it up and it takes practice and discipline. You have to discipline yourself if you want a healthy and productive prayer life.

How many of us are burdened with the cares and responsibilities of life? God knows how to mend our wounds, carry our problems, guide and counsel us through life. He wishes for us to have life more abundantly. John 10:10; **"The thief comes only in order to steal and kill and destroy. I came that they may have and enjoy life, and have it in abundance."** Being fulfilled and content within our inner man is a priority that God desires to fill.

Open up your Bible and read the Word of God. Pray, fast, sing songs of praise from your heart to God, fellowship with other believers, create a prayer group, attend some worship rallies and most importantly be actively involved in your local assembly of believers. What you cannot do alone, you can do collectively. God uses people to refine one another, to befriend each other and to encourage each other. Proverbs 27:17; **"As iron sharpens iron, so one man sharpens another."** Don't ever forsake yourself gathering with others of like precious faith. If you do forsake this gathering it will be your downfall. You need to be active and associating with other like-minded people if you plan on having a fruitful life. You need to be equally yoked with other people of the same mindset if you plan on remaining strong.

Remember, God's burden is light and He desires to take all, not just some, of your burden. We at times find it hard to relinquish our will to Him, because we think we can make it alone. Let's not fool ourselves. Living without God is like a passenger of a plane which is flying without a pilot.

Be gentle and humble of heart

March 15th

Matthew 12:2- "Look! Your disciples are doing what is unlawful on the Sabbath."-NIV

Here we have the Pharisees accusing Jesus and His followers of being in league with Satan. There was a constant flowing of condemnation from the religious readers of the day. Today we have a similar trend where we are being persecuted by other denominational leaders and the leaders of society. We need to stand on the Word and follow its precepts no matter what comes against us. In order to do this we have to first know the Word. How do you do this you might ask? You crack the covers and get down to business. You study. 2 Timothy 2:15; **"Do your best to present yourself to God as one approved, a worker who has no need to be ashamed, rightly handling the word of truth."**

Constant and frequent persecution was heaped upon Christian believers in the days of Christ's ministry as well as today. We are harangued by societal rules, whims, traditions and ultimately the leaders of society. Following Jesus comes at a price. As it was then, so it is today, we're free in Christ Jesus. We are not free to live any way we wish, but we do have freedom to worship and follow our God. We have to obey man's laws as well as God's laws. Matthew 22:21 tells us Christ's answer when asked by the Pharisees disciples what they should do with their taxes; **"Therefore render to Caesar the things that are Caesar's, and to God the things that are God's."** The Word says that we're free in Christ but that we are also to obey the laws of the land.

John 8:36; **"So if the Son liberates you (makes you free men), then you are really and unquestionably free."** When Christ sets you free from both the guilt and the life-controlling power of sin and from the influence of demonic activity, you are free. When we were still of the world we were doing the devils bidding for him. We were living lives that were undoubtedly sinful in nature and displeasing to God. We are on the other side of grace and our pasts are forgiven. We are free from our past if we are walking in Christ.

Stand on God's Word!

March 16th

Matthew 12:6-8-"I tell you that one greater than the temple is here. If you had known what these words mean, 'I desire mercy, not sacrifice,' you would not have condemned the innocent. For the Son of Man is Lord of the Sabbath."-NIV

Jesus challenged not only the Law but the Pharisees way of life. They were making themselves rich by forcing people who couldn't afford a sacrifice into going into greater debt by having to pay for a sacrificial animal or bird with what very little they had left. He came to show mercy to the poor and downtrodden. This went against the rules emplaced by the Pharisees. Jesus authoritatively interpreted every aspect of the law and here He points out to the Pharisees' their blindness to the actual intent of the Sabbath, which was to bring rest and well-being. He was showing that it was not works but rest that was needed. He both told and showed that it was not works that get you saved and into Heaven that it was faith and belief in Him. Christ showed mercy.

God sent His Son Jesus Christ so that He might have mercy on us. Mercy means that God outstretched His arm to reach out to us in our humanity. Salvation is an act of mercy on the part of God. God was merciful even to the merciless. While we were still in our sins, God came to set us apart from our sin and bring us into a right relationship with Him. Should we that have been shown mercy not be merciful to those in need of mercy? Mercy triumphs over judgment.

When is the last time you displayed mercy within your life? Mercy is a powerful entity. With mercy we're extending ourselves, giving our self and allowing the love of God to flow through our lives. Mercy is the key ingredient when we are restoring broken relationships and repairing relational wounds. We need to reach out to others despite the brokenness and waywardness of their lives. We need to be a people involved in Kingdom business. Let's restore the brokenhearted to a relationship with Jesus Christ.

Life is but a breath. I myself am incapable without the love of the Lord operating within my life. I am helpless, hopeless, and utterly inept without the power and transforming grace of our Lord Jesus Christ. **"Humble thyself in the sight of the Lord and He will lift you up"** (James 4:10). When we're weak we will become strong through the power and the working of the Holy Spirit.

I hope and pray that people will be merciful to me in my time of need. More importantly I pray that God's mercies would be new every morning in my life. I pray that His mercies would overflow in abundance to my wife and my three children. God showed unlimited favor and mercy by His sacrificial work on the Cross. His life, death and resurrection were the most merciful things He could have ever done for mankind. No greater act in the history of the world has ever been carried out like the crucifixion and resurrection of our and Savior Jesus Christ.

March 17th

Matthew 12:10-12-"Looking for a reason to accuse Jesus, they asked him, "Is it lawful to heal on the Sabbath?" He said to them, "If any of you has a sheep and it falls into a pit on the Sabbath, will you not take hold of it and lift it out? How much more valuable is a man than a sheep! Therefore it is lawful to do good on the Sabbath."-NIV

Accusations were flying everywhere. It's powerful to see how Jesus responds metaphorically and with a question. Jesus certainly makes people think. Jesus constantly attempted to make the religious leaders think logically, rationally and accurately. He could have said, "Of course I can heal, I can heal anyone any time I want, after all I'm God!"

The irony that's apparent with the religious leaders is that they're more concerned with the dos and don'ts of the Sabbath than about the suffering of humanity. It seems as though their priorities weren't in proper order.

Jesus explains the importance of human beings in this powerful passage. Human beings hold value. He gives credence here to every man, woman and child being worthwhile in His sight. Jesus is all about people. He has both an undying and unquenchable love for all the people of the world. It is people that He came to save. Jesus longs to deliver us from the difficulties we face in this life. He will help us to overcome even if He has to lift us out of a pit.

The leaders of His time had nothing better to do than to accuse Jesus. Religiosity will never prevail over the freedom that is experienced in Christ. As Jesus exemplified, we are to live free in God, without the bondages of the religious leaders of today. In Jesus there is freedom from all the things that might shackle us in this world.

God has shown that He will heal anyone, anywhere, and at any time that He wants. God doesn't have to submit to the worlds authorities. There is no authority over Him. God, and God alone, rules the world. He rules all of creation and the entire universe. God is over all. He owns everything. Nothing exists without God. Nothing belongs to man, it's all God's. Without God there would be nothing, everything would be void. I certainly wouldn't have the capacity to write this book without God.

Seek the lost

March 18th

Matthew 12:13-14-"Then he said to the man, "Stretch out your hand." So he stretched it out and it was completely restored, just as sound as the other. But the Pharisees went out and plotted how they might kill Jesus."-NIV

The miraculous healings that Jesus performed perplexed and angered the religious leaders of that day. The Pharisees couldn't stand that Jesus was healing people and claiming to be God. Upon repeatedly hearing these claims of Him being God, they began plotting to destroy Jesus. The supernatural force of the enemy was clearly at work within them. A definite **Waging War Within** existed.

The spirit of the anti-Christ was alive and well and working within the Pharisees. Man has always been unable to even grasp the things of God without the Spirit of God working from within. 1Corinthians 2:12-14; **"Now we have received not the spirit of the world, but the Spirit who is from God, that we might understand the things freely given us by God. And we impart this in words not taught by human wisdom but taught by the Spirit, interpreting spiritual truths to those who are spiritual. The natural person does not accept the things of the Spirit of God, for they are folly to him, and he is not able to understand them because they are spiritually discerned."** It is the Spirit of the Living God that will reveal Himself to people. He will open spiritually blind eyes and allow people a glimmer of the things of God.

Jesus healed on the spot. He saw the need and restored things as they once were, or as to how they should be. Jesus worked miracles and performed many healings while He walked the earth. Everything that Jesus was doing was for the good of mankind.

Jesus was healing many people of many afflictions. We are able to do the same today. John 14:12; **"Truly, truly, I say to you, whoever believes in me will also do the works that I do; and greater works than these will he do, because I am going to the Father."**

Healing rooms are opening around the globe staffed by people of faith. There are healings taking place at an astronomical rate due to people living the Word and having that mustard seed of faith. We should be Spirit filled Christians. We can live the same type of ministry that Jesus lived if we would only believe.

God is a God of restoration

March 19th

Matthew 12:18-21"Here is my servant whom I have chosen, the one I love, in whom I delight; I will put my Spirit on him, and he will proclaim justice to the nations. He will not quarrel or cry out; no one will hear his voice in the streets. A bruised reed he will not break, and a smoldering wick he will not snuff out, till he leads justice to victory. In his name the nations will put their hope."-NIV

God is again showing how pleased He is with His Son. He has given His Son tremendous authority, the authority to bring justice to the nations, to judge the world. Jesus brought the Good News to the world but the world rejected it. How sad is that? It is still going on today.

Jesus came as a herald to carry the news that He was the Promised Savior, the Messiah, only the people and the rulers of His time refused to listen to Him. He didn't come as the conquering warrior but as The Servant to mankind. Jesus as the servant showed tremendous compassion to those who needed mercy shown to them and He cared for the sick and infirmed. Are we following His example today? If not, why not?

God can put His Spirit on us today! The Lord Jesus has the desire to have His Holy Spirit poured out on all nations. 1 Timothy 2:3-4; **"This is good, and it is pleasing in the sight of God our Savior, who desires all people to be saved and to come to the knowledge of the truth."** God desires to save all people, people from all walks of life. Romans 8:28; **"And we know that for those who love God all things work together for good, for those who are called according to his purpose."**

His tears are falling from Heaven with the desire that all people from around the world will come into a relationship with Him and gain salvation over death, hell and the grave. The Holy Spirit is using people, situations, circumstances and many other means to reach the lost for Jesus Christ. What are needed are workers for the harvest fields.

My friends, how much are you doing to bring people to knowledge of Christ? Are you actively winning souls for the Kingdom? What would your life be like if someone never shared the Gospel with you? Do you think that you would be one of His if whoever that person was who brought you to knowledge of Christ hadn't bothered answering the call of the Great Commission? I know I wouldn't be here right now if it wasn't for that person. People, we are running out of time to win souls to Christ. We need to get busy. Matthew 28: 19-20; **"Go therefore and make disciples of all nations, baptizing them in the name of the Father and of the Son and of the Holy Spirit, teaching them to observe all that I have commanded you."**

In God we trust

March 20th

Matthew 12:23-All the people were astonished and said, "Could this be the Son of David?"-NIV

The people of Christ's time had a picture in their minds eye of what the Messiah would look and act like. They thought of David as a warrior and king and believed the Son of David would be a liberator. It was difficult for the people to comprehend that this gentle healer could indeed be David's promised Son. Bewildered, perplexed, dumbfounded and amazed! What, the Son of David! Could this be? Oh, how the human mind gets in the way. It did then and it does now.

Don't get me wrong, the mind and the intellect are two very important components of our God given genetic attributes. When the mind starts interfering with our faith, we need to be careful. **"Faith being the substance of things hoped for and the evidence of things not seen"** (Hebrews 11:1). Do we want to place our hope in our limited, finite capacities and capabilities, or do we want to trust in God, our Creator, our Redeemer and our everlasting Father? This would seem to be the wiser choice of the two.

The people being who they were had their preconceived notions of who the coming Messiah would look like and be. Don't we do this still today? God grants the desires of our hearts. Remember the Book of Samuel where the people wanted a king just like all of their neighboring kingdoms had? God granted their wishes and gave them Saul. Read it in 1 Samuel and follow through until you finish at 1 Kings 2. We are still doing the same thing today. God was the King of Israel and that wasn't good enough for the people, they had to have an earthly king like the Jones'. He gave them what they desired. He knows better what we need than we do. Why is it that we think we know better than Him? He is God. He created the heavens and the earth.

The next time you look into the heavens and see with your own eyes; the stars, the constellations, the sun, the moon, shooting stars, or a solar eclipse, or a rainbow ask yourself this question: Should I trust in the Creator of it all, or myself His creation? Just remember the greatness of God dwarfs anything in all creation, no matter how spectacular.

Remember, Father knows best!

March 21st

Matthew 12:24-"But when the Pharisees heard this, they said, "It is only by Beelzebub, the prince of demons, that this fellow drives out demons."-NIV

Remember that Beelzebub means "master of the house" and refers specifically to Satan. The accusation that Jesus was really Satan is totally twisted. The Pharisees were accusing Jesus of practicing magic. Practicing magic by Satan's power was a capital offense which was punishable by stoning. This view of Jesus as a sorcerer was common among the Jewish population even well into the early centuries of Christianity.

Disbelief has always been an ongoing problem with people, especially with those in a position of power, prestige and privilege. What, trust or even belief in a God? Many in positions of power believe that they are God. Some have trusted to such a degree in their own merits, their own ingenuity, cleverness and scheming that they can no longer even perceive who God might be. What God? Where's God? Who's God? The Bible clearly says that if a person is not following God, their God is the prince of the power of the air, the prince of this dark world. John 3:19; **"And this is the judgment: the light has come into the world, and people loved the darkness rather than the light because their deeds were evil."** Let's pray that our very own eyes would be enlightened by the Holy Spirit so that we ourselves can always differentiate between the true work of the Lord and the work that comes by the hands of man.

The Pharisees were not only attempting to minimize what Jesus was doing in His earthly ministry, but they were a downright nasty and destructive force to be reckoned with. They were attempting to discredit and classify Jesus' healings as coming from demonic forces. When people are blind to spiritual things they cannot see the things of God at work. Romans 1:18-20; **"For the wrath of God is revealed from heaven against all ungodliness and unrighteousness of men, who by their unrighteousness suppress the truth. For what can be known about God is plain to them, because God has shown it to them. For His invisible attributes, namely, His eternal power and divine nature, have been clearly perceived, ever since the creation of the world, in the things that have been made. So they are without excuse."** They think that it's trickery and slide of hand. There is no evil in God, only good.

God is good

March 22nd

Matthew 12:25-28-"Jesus knew their thoughts and said to them, "Every kingdom divided against itself will be ruined, and every city or household divided against itself will not stand. If Satan drives out Satan, he is divided against himself. How then can his kingdom stand? And if I drive out demons by Beelzebub, by whom do your people drive them out? So then, they will be your judges. But if I drive out demons by the Spirit of God, then the kingdom of God has come upon you."-NIV

How profound is this passage? God Himself is able to read the thoughts of men in their deceitful scheming. The demonic world is once again uncovered and lay bare by God. God exposes the things of darkness and brings them to light. 1 Corinthians 4:5; **"Therefore do not pronounce judgment before the time, before the Lord comes, who will bring to light the things now hidden in darkness and will disclose the purposes of the heart. Then each one will receive his commendation from God."** Only God can do this. He's the ultimate detective when it comes to sin.

Division and sin go hand and hand. Sin divides and conquers relationships of all sorts. Marriage is a relationship that has been marred by the ramifications of sinful acts. God doesn't just mention division as it relates to households, but He goes on to attest to the division of entire cities, states, and kingdoms.

How many churches, businesses, schools, colleges, universities, homes or marriages have been ransacked by Satan and his demonic cohorts? All we have to do is listen to the news, pick up a paper or magazine, or talk with family, friends, or acquaintances to discover that this is happening in our own world. Any organization that is run by human beings, Christian or non-Christian, will experience its share of conflict, discord and disagreement. Unfortunately, we hear of many church splits that have taken place. Conflict is a natural part of our human existence. It's not a matter of if we're going to experience conflict; it's a matter of when. Conflict is inevitable.

Division can be managed, solved, worked through and mediated. There are some conflicts whereby the two parties cannot come to mutual agreement and the relationship is relinquished, annulled, and ultimately terminated. These are cases of irreconcilable differences. These divisions are part of **The Waging War Within.**

Human beings like to have their own way. People can be selfish, bitter, backbiting, arrogant, jealous, angry and downright narcissistic. Many of these destructive tendencies are sinful acts and result from people acting out of the flesh rather than the Spirit of God. It is God that teaches us how we are to live and how we are to respond to specific situations and circumstances. He has given us commandments, teachings, and most importantly He has given us His Holy Spirit.

March 23rd

Matthew 12:29-30-"Or again, how can anyone enter a strong man's house and carry off his possessions unless he first ties up the strong man? Then he can rob his house. "He who is not with me is against me, and he who does not gather with me is against me, and he who does not gather with me scatters."-NIV

What has us bound in shackles? What of our flesh is preventing us from finding our fulfillment in Christ Jesus? We must determine what, if anything is in our way from allowing the Holy Spirit and God from having His complete way with us? We must move from denial and allow God to dissect our very internal being. Our prayer should be, "God show me if there be any wicked way within me and reveal to me what I need to change, surrender, renounce and work towards to find myself more complete in you, oh God, my Redeemer and my Friend."

God desires for us to work together, to have unity, and to be a witness to the world we live in. Matthew 28:19-20; **"Go therefore and make disciples of all nations, baptizing them in the name of the Father and of the Son and of the Holy Spirit, teaching them to observe all that I have commanded you. And behold, I am with you always, to the end of the age."** You can never hear or read this passage enough. This needs to be placed deep within your heart! Our heart must be given to Jesus, focused on Jesus, and surrendered to Jesus. A change of heart is monumental in grasping the depth of a relationship with Jesus Christ! God can allow us to have His supernatural presence and power in order to have a change of heart. The Creator who knit our very heart together has the power to mend, fix and clean out our heart from the impurities that would prevent us from fulfilling our divine destiny.

We will continue to gather together and have a unity like no other group because we're bound together in Christ Jesus. Are we letting God have His way in our lives? Our heart is a good place to start, remain, and continue to focus on/in our individual walk with Jesus. God Himself can hold our relationships, our families and our very churches in right relationship with Him. This takes prayer and it also requires our allowing of the power of God to minister to us. Without complete and undeniable surrender into the hands of Jesus Christ, unity will never happen. The acknowledgement of God in every aspect of our individual and collective lives must be priority!

Be with
And gather with Christ

March 24th

Matthew 12:33-"Make a tree good and its fruit will be good, or make a tree bad and its fruit will be bad, for a tree is recognized by its fruit."-NIV

Life empowered by the Holy Spirit; what a difference! The overflow from one Spirit filled Christian to another and ultimately unto the world, is a tremendous life altering experience. Bearing fruit and fulfilling God's desire to spread His Gospel to the outer most parts of the world is what we are called to do with the Great Commission found in Matthew 28:19-20, it says **"Therefore go and make disciples of all nations, baptizing them in the name of the Father and of the Son and of the Holy Spirit, and teaching them to obey everything I have commanded you. And surely I am with you always, to the very end of the age."** True Christians are recognized by their fruit. If we're allowing God to operate in us and through us then our life is a reflection of Him. Jesus draws all people to Himself. If we're living a life in which the God of all creation can flow through us then there is no other alternative other than to bear fruit. Fruit bearing can range from the seemingly insignificant to the most high mountain top experience. Fruit bearing is always powerful in some way, shape or form. Fruit bearing is God's providential plan.

Someone that is seriously following Jesus Christ is bearing fruit. Christians that are sold out for the Lord are touching the lives of others in a powerful way. Christians that are sharing Jesus with others, inviting people to church, living for the Lord, involved in various ministries, and living for God within their families are the ones that are bearing fruit. God didn't want us just to sit in a pew and be thankful to be Christians. He wanted us to live transforming lives. God wanted us to go into all the world and preach and teach the Gospel, this is why the Great Commission exists, so that we won't be selfish with the gift we were given. This may mean going down the street for some and off to a distant country for others. God wants us to spread the hope of the Gospel and the message of the Good News. It doesn't matter if we're not Missionaries, Pastors, Evangelists, Christian Authors or a Christian Counselor. It matters if we have a heart that's willing to take the world for the Cross of Christ. We're not something extra special if we're in full time ministry. God desires to have a heartfelt relationship and someone that walks the walk and doesn't just talk the talk. When someone is radically following Jesus Christ no matter whom he or she is they will influence the lives of others.

A life that bears fruit is a life that brings others to the Cross of Christ and leads others to salvation. The salvation of a soul is the most important thing in God's eyes. All of Heaven rejoices when one soul is saved by the Blood of the Lamb. When a man, woman, adolescent or child accepts Jesus as their Personal Lord and Savior the angels rejoice.

March 25th

Matthew 12:34-35-"You brood of vipers, how can you who are evil say anything good? For out of the overflow of the heart the mouth speaks. The good man brings good things out of the good stored up in him, and the evil man brings evil things out of the evil stored up in him."-NIV

The Pharisees own words revealed their hearts time and again. They were bad trees that needed to be put to the fire. Luke 6:45; **"The good person out of the good treasure of his heart produces good, and the evil person out of his evil treasure produces evil, for out of the abundance of the heart his mouth speaks."** We continuously need God to fill us with the Holy Spirit so we can walk in the Spirit and not be controlled and influenced by the spirit of this world. Being edifying to others and saying a kind word to uplift the spirit of another isn't easy all of the time, especially if we're down in the dumps and having our own difficulties. Words are influencing and all powerful. God Himself speaks to us through His Word. God chose to speak to us through His Bible, the Word of God. Words have the power to build up or tear down. A kind word has healing power in and of itself. A biting word can be cancerous and destructive to the point of wrecking marriages, sinking businesses, ruining careers, destroying friendships and ultimately being good to no one.

I am sure all who are reading this can remember a time when you were young and someone said something hate filled and it has still stuck with you till this very day. Am I right? Words are powerful. Proverbs 18:21; **"Death and life are in the power of the tongue, and those who love it will eat its fruits."** James 3:-12 speaks of the tongue. **"The tongue is a small member, yet it boasts of great things. How great a forest is set ablaze by such a small fire! And the tongue is a fire, a world of unrighteousness. The tongue is set among our members, staining the whole body, setting on fire the entire course of life, and set on fire by hell. For every kind of beast and bird, of reptile and sea creature, can be tamed and has been tamed by mankind, but no human being can tame the tongue. It is a restless evil, full of deadly poison. With it we bless our Lord and Father, and with it we curse people who are made in the likeness of God. From the same mouth come blessing and cursing, my brothers this ought not to be so."** We need to watch our words my friends.

The bottom line is that if we're not drawing close to God the evil manifestations of this world will eventually rip us apart. We need to be grounded in the Word of God. God continuously warns us of this. He doesn't want **The Waging War Within** to destroy us and tear us apart. He wants us to have more than a fighting chance to win the race of life.

March 26th

Matthew 12:36-37-"But I tell you that men will have to give account on the Day of Judgment for every careless word they have spoken. For by your words you will be acquitted, and by your words you will also be condemned."-NIV

Eternal judgment will await all of those who attempt to turn the people against Jesus by slandering accusations of blasphemy. By your words you will be justified means a person's words will be an outward evidence of their inward character. Evil people's evil words will be evidence by which they will be condemned. We need to guard our words.

No doubt, words are of paramount importance in our lives. Much of the entire book of James explains to us the importance of watching our words. What we speak, the words we say and how we communicate to one another conveys what kind of character we have and ultimately where we stand with God in our personal relationship with Him.

Carelessness can come into play when we don't give thought and attention to the words we speak within our home, within our churches, our places of business and our surrounding communities. It's impossible to take back a word you wish you didn't speak but actually did. If we put as much time into listening as we did speaking imagine how much nicer the world would be. Have you ever been with someone who wouldn't shut up for a second so that someone else could have a chance to speak? It is so very frustrating. It drives me nuts.

We all have habits we need to gain control of whether they are drugs, alcohol abuse, slothfulness, envy of others, gossip, whatever the case may be. We need to gain control of them before we are judged by them. An untamed tongue is probably one of the most harmful tools in the devils arsenal. With an untamed tongue you can bring down entire nations. It has the power of life and death. Proverbs 18:21; **"Death and life are in the power of the tongue, and those who love it will eat its fruits."** My brothers and sisters, there is a very powerful warning here. We are going to be judged by our own words which we speak. We need to watch what we say.

Putting our foot in our mouths happens to the best of us and it typically occurs when we least expect it. Our humanity will be forever plagued with misguided words unless we continue on a daily basis to be empowered by the Holy Spirit. Asking and praying for the Holy Spirit's guidance is of critical importance in preventing us from living a life full of careless words.

The words we speak
are powerful

March 27th

Matthew 12:38-40-"Teacher, we want to see a miraculous sign from you." A wicked and adulterous generation asks for a miraculous sign!"-NIV

We are ruled by our senses. Sometimes we have to see with our own eyes in-order to truly believe something (The story of Doubting Thomas, John 20:24-31). God is in the business of doing the miraculous; however our focus should not be in having to see the incredible prior to placing our faith in the Lord. We are saved by placing our faith in Him. Faith is trust in the unseen, the invisible and untouchable person and working of God and His Holy Spirit. God makes it very clear that some need a sign in-order to believe. Truth isn't enough for them to believe, because they cannot see or understand the truth. You can only truly comprehend God's Truth as the Holy Spirit reveals it. 1 Corinthians 2:14; **"The natural person does not accept the things of the Spirit of God, for they are folly to him, and he is not able to understand them because they are spiritually discerned."** The natural mind cannot see the things of God, because they're supernatural in origin. The natural mind needs to become illuminated by the Holy Spirit and this can only happen when someone is born from above.

Don't you feel special when someone you respect and love places their faith and trust in you? You feel special. It's a great feeling to be trusted and to have someone's faith being placed in you to make the right choice, the right decision and do the right thing.

Can you imagine how God must feel when we place our faith and trust in Him? He must get excited about this. He must be like, "Wow, there's my child placing their trust and faith in me." Jesus encourages us to place our trust, faith and hope in Him. He wouldn't have it any other way, would He? Of course He wouldn't. God sees all, hears all and knows all. He knows when we're placing our faith in Him. He probably is in Heaven rooting us on, encouraging us to run the race and finish with victory. I know that Jesus prays for us and intercedes for us at the right hand of God the Father.

You don't need to
See in order to believe.

Believe it in
Your heart.

March 28th

Matthew 12:43-"When an evil spirit comes out of a man, it goes through arid places seeking rest and does not find it."-NIV

Demons were often associated with waterless places, apparently because deserts were thought of as being devoid of the blessing of God that came with rainfall and abundant crops. That is the perfect description of a person before they come to Christ. We were all devoid and barren of God and His blessings. We were lost and forgotten by the world but wanted by God.

God warns the believer of evil spirits that inhabit people. The Bible makes it clear that evil spirits exist and they will make themselves manifest in the world in which we live. If we believe the Bible to be God's inspired infallible Word, then we must be aware that God wants us to know that evil spirits exist. The natural mind can recognize the fact that evil exists in the world, however the natural mind will not understand or be able to fathom how evil spirits influence the evil circumstances and situations in people's lives. One could ask the question, "Does the evil that is visible or made manifest in people's lives exist due to the evil spirits that have infiltrated them on a spiritual level?"

An awareness of evil spirits is of importance, but our focus needs to be on God. God wants us to be aware that warfare takes place in the supernatural and reveals itself in the physical world. God has given us a way to survive on the battle field, He has given us His armor. Ephesians 6:10-18; **"Finally, be strong in the Lord and in the strength of his might. Put on the whole armor of God, that you may be able to stand against the schemes of the devil. For we do not wrestle against flesh and blood, but against the rulers, against the authorities, against the cosmic powers over this present darkness, against the spiritual forces of evil in the heavenly places. Therefore take up the whole armor of God, that you may be able to withstand in the evil day, and having done all, to stand firm. Stand therefore, having fastened on the belt of truth, and having put on the breastplate of righteousness, and, as shoes for your feet, having put on the readiness given by the gospel of peace. In all circumstances take up the shield of faith, with which you can extinguish all the flaming darts of the evil one; and take the helmet of salvation, and the sword of the Spirit, which is the word of God, praying at all times in the Spirit, with all prayer and supplication."** We need to read this daily and take it to heart.

People's lives can be a reflection outwardly of what is happening to them spiritually. Our entire goal is to have the Holy Spirit fill us, lead us and guide us throughout our lives. Let's pray daily that we be filled with the Holy Spirit's power!

March 29th

Matthew 12:45-"Then it goes and takes with it seven other spirits more wicked than itself, and they go in and live there. And the final condition of that man is worse than the first. That is how it will be with this wicked generation."-NIV

The number seven is associated in Scripture with completion or perfection. In this verse it is perhaps signifying the completeness of demonic possession once the demon has returned. If this evil generation continues to reject Jesus as did the earlier generations, even after witnessing his divine authority over demons, their condition will be worse than if they had never seen him. We need to get the Word out my friends.

God is showing us how evil increases both within men and in our society by the multiplication of evil spirits. Generations of people have renounced God in their lives and have given themselves over to a licentious life-style that is contrary to God's Commandments and His Holy Word. Evil can be pervasive when God is removed from individual lives. This results in the removal of God's Holy Spirit from churches, homes, businesses, schools, institutions, and marriages and other significant relationships and entities. When humankind no longer sees the importance of allowing God in, then evil will be prevalent in the minds and hearts of people.

Are we still wondering why there is so much depravity in our society? We cannot begin to understand the things of God unless we have the mind of Christ. 1 Corinthians 2:12; **"Now we have received not the spirit of the world, but the Spirit who is from God, that we might understand the things freely given us by God."** Without God revealing this present age to us, we're walking around with blinders on.

We are running out of time. The longer we wait to get the Word to people we know and love, the more time we are giving the evil one to sow his evil and perverse seed into society. We need to act now while the fields are ripe for the harvest of souls.

Demonic possession
is very real

March 30th

Matthew 12:48-50-**"Who is my mother, and who are my brothers?" Pointing to his disciples, he said, "Here are my mother and my brothers. For whoever does the will of my Father in heaven is my brother and sister and mother."-NIV**

Jesus is not neglecting His family here; He is showing us that our loyalty to Him is of upmost importance. Jesus' messianic mission takes priority even over our familial loyalties. Rather than negating the importance of one's biological family, Jesus is demonstrating the preeminence of a person's commitment to Him and the Kingdom of Heaven. Jesus said to "Honor your father and mother." He still wants for us to do this. He is stressing the importance of our commitment to Him.

God is also revealing the importance of maintaining relationships within the family of God and among those that believe in Him. God, within His Word, is pointing to the profound necessity of inculcating, building, and maintaining strong Christian relationships. Those that we hold most dear to us should be those in the Kingdom of God.

We have an obligation to seek after and take care of those within the fold. People who are earnestly seeking after God and surrendering their will and their life for His will in their lives are the people we should be surrounding ourselves with. This doesn't mean that we are to abandon all of our relationships with our unsaved friends, workmates, neighbors, and family members. If we did that we would have no way of witnessing and bringing anyone into the fold. God says that we should never forsake the gathering together of the brethren. Hebrews 10:24-25; **"And let us consider how to stir up one another to love and good works, not neglecting to meet together, as is the habit of some, but encouraging one another, and all the more as you see the Day drawing near."**

We're going to be in Heaven for eternity with our fellow Christian brothers and sisters. God shares the importance of getting to know them on this side of Heaven as well. Fellow Christians that are seeking God's will for their lives should be the ones that we're relationally connected with to the highest degree. These are the people that can refine us in our faith. Proverbs 27:17; **"As iron sharpens iron so one man sharpens another."**

Do the will of
our Father in Heaven

March 31st

Matthew 13:4-9- "A farmer went out to sow his seed. As he was scattering the seed, some fell along the path, and the birds came and ate it up. Some fell on rocky places, where it did not have much soil. It sprang up quickly, because the soil was shallow. But when the sun came up, the plants were scorched, and they withered because they had no root. Other seed fell among thorns, which grew up and choked the plants. Still other seed fell on good soil, where it produced a crop-a hundred, sixty or thirty times what was sown. He who has ears, let him hear."-NIV

As the seeds were scattered by the farmers in all directions while the farmer walked up and down the field, (remember there were no tractors, in those days the sowing was done by hand) some would fall accidentally on the hard paths that surrounded the field, this was the rocky ground mentioned in the verse. The terrain in Jesus' area was very uneven and rocky, covered by a thin layer of soil, which were the thorny areas that He mentioned. Competing for nutrients from the soil, weeds choke out the good plants, which are then unable to reach maturity and bear fruit. A typical harvest would bring in a yield of roughly fivefold to fifteen fold, with a tenfold being a good harvest. Genesis 26:12; **"Isaac sowed in that land and reaped in the same year a hundredfold."** Now that is a yield a farmer would love to have.

The environment seems an area of the utmost importance in not only our survival, but the survival of a mere crop of seed. In the case of the seed, the soil is the environmental condition that needs to be good in-order for vegetation to grow. Human beings are in need of a healthy environment to be fruitful. The environment must be nurturing, loving and caring.

God makes the comparison of His creation and conditions related to our spirituality. Just as fruits and vegetables need proper soil, the human spirit, soul, mind and body need a healthy environment that fosters intellectual, physical and spiritual vitality. Without these important facets of our existence, our spirituality won't be nourished.

A **Waging War Within** happens even on the most seemingly insignificant level. God demonstrates important aspects of living and spiritual sustenance through plants, soil and ultimately survival. Our survival in society and the world as Christians can be thwarted and hindered by external factors within our culture that try to choke our belief. These forces can either make or break us in our spiritual walk with the Lord Jesus.

We have a choice. Are we going to be tossed back and forth or are we going to hold our ground and persevere under trial? Even when the conditions for growth are against us, we must display our solid root in Jesus and remain attached to the true vine of life.

APRIL

April 1ST

Matthew 13:11-13- He replied, "The knowledge of the secrets of the kingdom of heaven has been given to you, but not to them. Whoever has will be given more, and he will have an abundance. Whoever does not have, even what he has will be taken from him. This is why I speak to them in parables:-NIV

A secret is typically something that is shared with a select few. Secrets are communicated to those that are usually close to us and to those that we can trust. Secrets are intended to be kept in confidence and not shared with those on the outside of the confines of the one bearing the secret. For those wishing to know the secrets of the Kingdom of Heaven, they must search intently to find out what the secret is all about. Luke 8:10; **"To you it has been given to know the secrets of the kingdom of God, but for others they are in parables, so that seeing they may not see, and hearing they may not understand."** Secrets draw people's attention because they aren't shared openly with others. People become curious about secrets, it's just human nature. Have you ever been around someone who whispers a secret in the ear of another? Didn't you get curious and wonder what was said? Of course you do. If you didn't, you wouldn't be human.

God wants us to seek the things of Him with all our strength, power, and might. It is something we should want to know. Matthew 7:7; **"Ask, and it will be given to you; seek, and you will find; knock, and it will be opened to you."** God wants us to cling to Jesus, search the Scriptures, and pray with tenacity. He wants us to be the most dynamic Christians that the world has ever seen. He desires that our minds, our hearts, lives, families, churches, schools and communities, that they be radically changed with the Light of the Gospel. He wants for us to yield to His will for our lives. He wants for us to be completely absorbed and caught up in Kingdom business. God has a great destiny for us, to prosper us, and, to make our future bright and beautiful. Now when I say to prosper, that doesn't necessarily mean in the financial realm. Prospering could be physical, emotional, psychological, spiritual, etc... We receive our rewards ultimately in Heaven, not here on earth.

Have you searched the secrets of the Kingdom of God? The Bible is God's Word that literally could be studied and studied and studied forever. Every time I read the Bible I realize again and again just how much I don't know. Just as every time I read the scriptures I can read the same chapter and verse every day for a month and get something revealed to me that I never realized before. The Word of God is illuminating to the various aspects of God. Theologians and Bible Scholars continue to search the scriptures, uncovering truths that have been hidden in the secret place of God since the foundations of the Earth. We need to be scholars in our own rite as the Bereans were. 2 Timothy 2:15; **"Do your best to present yourself to God as one approved, a worker who has no need to be ashamed, rightly handling the word of truth."** We need to be studious in our approach to the Word. We need to be prayed up when we open the Word. We need to pray that God would illume a certain Scripture or passage to us. Always pray before you read the Word that God would give you discernment in regards to it. We need to pray that we get out of the Word exactly what God desires for us to get out of it.

God desires to challenge us, to draw us in with the intention of having us to critically think, to use our minds, and to seek Him with passion. He also realized that some of us wouldn't get it if He didn't use comparisons and talk of things of everyday life. Some of the best authors of our day have used metaphors to emphasize and expand upon a point. Jesus was a creative genius in using parables to bring His point home. Praise God!

There are secrets in the parables spoken by Jesus

April 2nd

Matthew 13:13-17-"Though seeing, they do not see; though hearing, they do not hear or understand. In them is fulfilled the prophecy of Isaiah: "You will be ever hearing but never understanding; you will be ever seeing but never perceiving. For this people's heart has become calloused; they hardly hear with their ears, and they have closed their eyes. Otherwise they might see with their eyes, hear with their ears, understand with their hearts and turn, and I would heal them.' But blessed are your eyes because they see, and your ears because they hear. For I tell you the truth, many prophets and righteous men longed to see what you see but did not see it, and to hear what you hear but did not hear it.-NIV

Many eyes and ears aren't spiritually tuned in to the things of God. One cannot even fathom the things of God without the Holy Spirit illuminating their mind. John 14:26; **"But the Helper, the Holy Spirit, whom the Father will send in my name, he will teach you all things and bring to your remembrance all that I have said to you."** Having Godly visions comes with a price. One must not only deny themselves the pursuits of the flesh and the things of this world, but must cling to the things from above. Luke 9:23; **"If anyone would come after me, let him deny himself and take up his cross daily and follow me."** Our focus becomes key to our beginning to understand and comprehend the awesome things of God.

The eyes and the ears are the vehicles that God uses to transmit the deep and hidden things of Him to our hearts, our souls, and our spirit. Spiritually minded things come from God and have the power to radically transform our lives from the inside out. We must pray to God to send the Holy Spirit in our times of prayer, our times of reading the Holy Bible, our times of attending church, and our times of fellowship with other like-minded individuals. We must ask God to give us a discerning spirit that is able to properly divide the Word of God and distinguish the things of God from the things of the world. Hebrews 4:12; **"For the word of God is living and active, sharper than any two-edged sword, piercing to the division of soul and of spirit, of joints and of marrow, and discerning the thoughts and intentions of the heart."**

God wants us to be able to reach a spiritual maturity in-order to advance His Kingdom. We must be a transformed people. Romans 12:2; **"Do not be conformed to this world, but be transformed by the renewal of your mind, that by testing you may discern what is the will of God, what is good and acceptable and perfect."** We must be a people willing to follow Jesus no matter what the cost. Anything worthwhile attaining comes with a price, not necessarily a monetary price, but in the form of time, commitment, dedication, discipline, training, and endurance. The things that take blood sweat and tears on our part are usually the things within our lives that are the most worthwhile.

God is making a clear delineation in this passage between those that can and those that cannot understand what He is all about. Some clearly will never understand because they're not even attempting to strive to understand the things from above. Some people are focused on their temporal existence and never give the eternal things of God a second thought. They are so consumed with what they want to accomplish in this world that they never consider the great things that God has to offer them or the eternal. The eye and the ear by nature naturally work to allow us to live in the physical world. In order to get a glimpse into the things that are spiritually discerned, we must train ourselves to discern our own existence through the lens and the standpoint of God.

My friends, how are we ever going to attain the things of God if we can't even get the focus off of ourselves? If we can remove the focus off of ourselves and put it on Kingdom things, what a beautiful existence we can have. Granted it won't be totally rosy, but it will be better for us as we are better focused on God. We need to keep the proper trinity in mind; it is God, Jesus Christ, and the Holy Spirit, not me, myself and I. God can and will use us if we avail ourselves to His service.

Have you ever had someone tell you that they want to get involved in church happenings only to have them turn you down each time you call them for assistance? It's frustrating isn't it? It drives me nuts. Why is it that they can make time for anything else but things of the Kingdom? Their focus is off. They need to change their thinking. They are consumed by the things of this world. They need to transform and renew their minds.

Holy Spirit,
open our eyes and ears

April 3rd

Matthew 13:18-26- "Listen then to what the parables of the sower means: When anyone hears the message about the kingdom and does not understand it, the evil one comes and snatches away what was sown along the path. The one who received the seed that fell on rocky places is the man who hears the word and at once receives it with joy. But since he has no root, he lasts only a short time. When trouble or persecution comes because of the word, he quickly falls away. The one who received the seed that fell among the thorns is the man who hears the word, but the worries of this life and the deceitfulness of wealth choke it, making it unfruitful. But the one who received the seed that fell on good soil is the man who hears the word and understands it. He produces a crop, yielding a hundred, sixty or thirty times what was sown." "The kingdom of heaven is like a man who sowed good seed in his field. But while everyone was sleeping, his enemy came and sowed weeds among the wheat, and went away. When the wheat sprouted and formed heads, then the weeds also appeared."-NIV

The seed in the parable is the Word of God. Jesus explains that the Word is sown and if the people are not willing to listen to the Word, they will be like the seed that does not benefit from the fertile soil and the seed withers and dies. We need to not only plant the seed, we need to try to nourish it and groom it also. That is our responsibility as Christians, to plant the Word into people's hearts and assist them in their walk. Not everyone will be receptive to the Word sadly enough. If they are not, we need to move on and speak to those who are. We must remember that we are living in the devils realm.

A battle is taking place between good and evil, between the things of this world and the things of God. The things that are earthly and temporal and things that are Godly and eternal are two diametrically different focuses. We cannot be so wrapped up in ourselves that we miss out on what God has planned for our lives. God has to be our centrifuge, our source of life, our watering well, our place of spiritual nourishment, and our dwelling place. If God is going to be this for His people, we as Christians need to develop an acute spiritual awareness for every waking moment of our lives. This is not to be a political posture or a theoretical construct. We need to establish a personal and a very real relationship with our Creator and the source of our existence here on earth.

If we plan on finishing the race as Paul spoke of in 2 Timothy 4:7; **"I have fought the good (worthy, honorable, and noble) fight, I have finished the race, I have kept (firmly held) the faith"**, we really need to pull in close with God. We can never win the war on our own; the power of the Holy Spirit accomplishes this with and through us.

April 4th

Matthew 13:27-"The owner's servants came to him and said, 'Sir, didn't you sow good seed in your field? Where then did the weeds come from?" -NIV

God sows and bears good fruit, the enemy (Satan) sows and bears bad fruit. God pleases the Holy Spirit and Satan pleases the flesh. Both the Spirit and the flesh are at war with each other. The wheat represents the fruit of the spiritual truth and fervor of God working through man. The weeds represent everything that is not from God, everything that can potentially strangle the wheat from growing and becoming a valuable natural resource. God uses His creation to articulate, elaborate, and teach specific truths. The entire world is God's canvas. God's handy work emanates throughout all that He created since the beginning of time. Let's have vigilance in not letting the ungodly things of this worldly system to filter in to our lives. We can do this by being prepared for the battle for our souls which began with the beginning of man's existence.

Our own personal battle begins as soon as we open our eyes and we realize that God has given us another chance to get it right. We need to don our spiritual armor as in Ephesians 6:11-18; **"Put on God's whole armor..."** Once we have our physical eyes open, then we need to open our spiritual eyes as well and get down on our knees and thank God for allowing us another opportunity to live and spread His gospel to those we come in contact with. Matthew 28:19-20; **"Go then and make disciples of all the nations, baptizing them into the name of the Father and of the Son and of the Holy Spirit, teaching them to observe everything that I have commanded you."** We're created in the image of God, not in the image of the prince of this dark world. Our prayer should be to ask God to deliver us from anything that He finds within us, around us, and coming forth from us that is unpleasing to Him. God is the ultimate power that is able to prune us and make us more into the image of His Son.

Are there weeds in your garden?

April 5th

Matthew 13:28-"An enemy did this, he replied. "The servants asked him, "Do you want us to go and pull them up?"-NIV

An enemy is someone that stands against us and our way of life. This someone isn't looking out for our best interest, in fact, an enemy would like to see us destroyed, annihilated, and ultimately wiped off of the face of the earth. Evil is represented within and encompassed around our enemies. We believe in the truth of God's Word, and anything that is contradictory to our Faith in God is antagonistic to the foundational truths of which we believe. We need to stand firm on the Word of God. 2 Thessalonians 2:3; **"Let no one deceive or beguile you in any way."** We need to know the Word in order to stand on it and we need to be able to discern the truth from lies.

Enemies can take many forms and come in a diverse array of packaging. We must guard ourselves from the things that war against us. We must be vigilant in combat and battle the enemies of our Lord and Savior Jesus Christ. Our enemies can be individuals that are practicing Satanists, atheists, and humanists that represent philosophies and ideologies that are contradictory to God's Word. Enemies to the Cross of Christ could be human beings that have the spirit of the anti-Christ within them due to their belief in false religions, the worship of idols and graven images, created not by God, but by the very hand of man. There are a plethora of different spirits and sins associated with them. There are also wolves disguised as lambs that we need to be able to discern from those who really are of the flock.

The very spirit associated with materialism is contrary to God's Word. God warns us over and over within the Word to beware of things that are contrary to His teachings. The things of God have eternal rewards, but the things of this world are temporal in nature and can lead to eternal consequences. Eternity in Hell is the ultimate in consequences. The things of God are bound in Heaven and can also be bound on earth. Matthew 18:18; **"Truly I tell you, whatever you forbid and declare to be improper and unlawful on earth must be what is already forbidden in heaven, and whatever you permit and declare proper and lawful on earth must be what is already permitted in heaven."** An eternal blessing in Heaven is our life's goal.

God knows how to weed out the crops

Matthew 13:29-30-"No, he answered, because while you are pulling the weeds, you may root up the wheat with them. **Let both grow together until the harvest. At that time I will tell the harvesters: First collect the weeds and tie them in bundles to be burned; then gather the wheat and bring it into my barn."-NIV**

Any attempt to gather the weeds would only endanger the wheat, because the roots of the weeds would be intermingled with those of the wheat. Let both the wheat and the weeds grow together. God allows both believers and unbelievers to reside in the world together until the day He comes in judgment.

Remember that God is the ultimate harvester! He knows who belongs to Him and who doesn't. God knows the heart that is beating with the things of Him and the heart that is beating with the things of this world. We can be tempted as human beings to do our own thing, without the discernment, without the help, and without the ultimate work that only God can do in His infinite wisdom. God alone is able to save and to destroy. James 4:12; **"One only is the Lawgiver and Judge who is able to save and to destroy, He is the One Who has the absolute power of life and death. But you who are you that you presume to pass judgment on your neighbor?"**

We need to remember that we are not to judge others. Judging and paybacks are to be left to God. Romans 2:12-16; **"For all who have sinned without the law will also perish without the law, and all who have sinned under the law will be judged by the law. For it is not the hearers of the law who are righteous before God, but the doers of the law who will be justified. For when Gentiles, who do not have the law, by nature do what the law requires, they are a law to themselves, even though they do not have the law. They show that the work of the law is written on their hearts, while their conscience also bears witness, and their conflicting thoughts accuse or even excuse them on that day when, according to my gospel, God judges the secrets of men by Christ Jesus."** God knows and He has implanted the Word on the hearts of all. We all know right from wrong. Also paybacks are God's and His alone. Romans 12:19; **"Beloved, never avenge yourselves, but leave it to the wrath of God, for it is written, "Vengeance is mine, I will repay, says the Lord.""** And again in Hebrews 10:30; **"For we know him who said, "Vengeance is mine; I will repay." And again, "The Lord will judge his people.""** So don't worry about paybacks as God is in charge of that department. He has our backs. God knows what He's doing!

Trust in the Lord!

April 7th

Matthew 13:37-39-"The one who sowed the good seed is the Son of Man. The field is the world, and the good seed stands for the sons of the kingdom. The weeds are the sons of the evil one, and the enemy who sows them is the devil. The harvest is the end of the age, and the harvesters are angels."-NIV

As you can see, the parable is a representation of our earthly battle of good versus evil. We are the good seed and the worldly man is the bad seed. We are given the Word to guide and teach us. We are represented as a few different examples throughout the parables, sheep, seed, fish, etc... The point is always the same; we need to be fed the Word when it is presented to us. We need to feast on the Word.

Have you ever planted a garden? If you have, you will know how frustrating the war with weeds can be. You can work in your garden day and night to keep it nice and weed free and be proud as a peacock of your endeavor and then go on vacation for a few days and you're right back at square one in the battle of the weeds. You know once you have faced this battle how you have to be on guard constantly against the weeds at all times, the same attention to detail needs to be paid for the security of your soul, your eternal salvation.

This above mentioned battle is a simile for the battle of **The Waging War Within**. This war is one that is raging day and night my friends. This battle for our souls is a serious battle that must be won. We have to prevail as soldiers of Jesus Christ and the children of God in this battle for our soul. We must come out victorious, on the side of good versus the side of evil, light versus darkness, right versus wrong, angels versus demons, Heaven versus hell, blessing versus cursing, righteousness versus blasphemy, and God versus the devil. How are we going to win this battle? We win it by planning ahead. We win it on our knees. We have to remember that we are a chosen people. Matthew 7:21; **"Not everyone who says to Me, Lord, Lord, will enter the kingdom of heaven, but he who does the will of My Father Who is in heaven."** We are a holy race created in the image of the one true God. Genesis 1:26-28; **"God said, Let Us, Father, Son, and Holy Spirit, make mankind in Our image, after Our likeness, and let them have complete authority over the fish of the sea, the birds of the air, the tame beasts, and over all of the earth, and over everything that creeps upon the earth. So God created man in His own image, in the image and likeness of God He created him; male and female He created them."**

Get ready! God is coming soon!

April 8th

Matthew 13:40-43-"As the weeds are pulled up and burned in the fire, so it will be at the end of the age. The Son of Man will send out his angels, and they will weed out of his kingdom everything that causes sin and all who do evil. They will throw them into the fiery furnace, where there will be weeping and gnashing of teeth. Then the righteous will shine like the sun in the kingdom of their Father. He who has ears, let him hear."-NIV

This is a wakeup call to the Church of Jesus Christ! Let us turn our eyes upon Jesus, the Author of our faith. God is warning us to turn completely, with every ounce of our being, to follow Him. We have to complete and unequivocally surrender to God and He will heal our; broken lives, our churches, our families, our communities, and most importantly, our relationship with Him. God is attempting to guide, to lead, to prosper, to protect, to bless, to sanctify, and to save, His created human race. Every ounce of God, every moment of every twenty-four hour day of our whole entire life, God desires us to draw closer to Him.

God desires us to be righteous just as He is righteous. He desires us to inherit the Kingdom that He has created for us, not of this world, but of the world to come. Let's not be like the weeds. Let's be like the wheat! Let's partake of the harvest that's going to happen at the end of the age. Let's be the wheat that is translated heavenward to be with God for eternity, not the weeds that are going into the lake of fire.

Who would desire to experience the pain of hell for eternity? Who would want to go where there is weeping and gnashing of teeth? Don't think that hell is just a make believe place. It does exist. Some people make their hell right here on earth and live it for eternity after they die. It's a choice, a decision. You can either accept God or reject God and His message of salvation. People choose Heaven and Hell on a daily basis. Matthew 7:14; **"But the gate is narrow and the way is straitened and compressed that leads away to life, and few are those who find it."**

Choose this day whom you will serve. Will it be God or Satan? This is **The Waging War Within**, the very battle for our souls. Complete surrender to God is what is needed. Yes, complete surrender. Nothing else will do, nothing and nobody but Jesus, the answer to all of our problems.

The righteous will shine like the sun

April 9th

Matthew 13:44-"The kingdom of heaven is like treasure hidden in a field. When a man found it, he hid it again, and then in his joy went and sold all he had and bought that field."-NIV

Treasure in the day of Christ walking the earth was often hidden in fields, since formal banks didn't exist. When the verse speaks of the man buying the field it doesn't necessarily mean that the man earned his salvation; instead, the parable emphasizes the great value of the hidden treasure which is the kingdom of Heaven, which is worth far more than any sacrifice one could make to acquire it. We cannot buy our way into Heaven; we earn our way there through our belief in Jesus Christ and what He gave for us. He made the ultimate sacrifice for our salvation.

Let us give of every aspect of our lives for the things of God. First we have to be illuminated by the power of the Holy Spirit to even comprehend the reality of who God is and what He has done for us. John 14:26; **"But the Helper, the Holy Spirit, whom the Father will send in my name, he will teach you all things and bring to your remembrance all that I have said to you."** We cannot completely and freely give of ourselves to the building and working of God's Kingdom until this understanding has been breathed into our individual existence.

The internal treasures that belong to us in Jesus Christ are more powerful than the wealthiest material treasures we have here on Earth. The treasure inherent within the confines of Jesus Christ is eternal and everlasting. The chains of death, hell, and the grave, no longer have a hold on us. No matter what walk of life we come from, God has made us a new creation in Christ Jesus. The old has gone and we have been born again. 2 Corinthians 5:17; **"Therefore, if anyone is in Christ, he is a new creation. The old has passed away; behold, the new has come."** We are born a physical birth into the physical world. We can see, touch, taste, smell, and hear the things within this physical world. The hidden treasure is in the spiritual world that we're now destined for once we're born from above. The hidden treasures are the things of God; His Word, His salvation, His Kingdom, and His Heaven.

Heavenly treasures are far greater than earthly ones

Matthew 13:45-46-"Again, the kingdom of heaven is like a merchant looking for a fine pearl. When he found one of great value, he went away and sold everything he had and bought it."-NIV

Unlike the man who stumbled upon the hidden treasure, this merchant searched diligently for the fine pearls. But when he found the one pearl of great value which is the kingdom of Heaven, his reaction was the same: he sacrificed all that he had and bought it. What sacrifice are you willing to make for the great pearl? Are you willing to give up your way of life to follow Jesus? The things of God are worth far more than you could ever imagine. Think about it.

Who can even begin to fathom the things of God? Who can fathom the greatness of the Great I Am, The Alpha and the Omega, The Beginning and the End, The Prince of Peace, The Lion of the Tribe of Judah, The Shepherd and Bishop of Souls, The Head of The Church, The Bright Morning Star, The Son of Righteousness, The Root of David, The Word of Life, The Advocate, The Way, The Day Spring, Our Everlasting Father, The Lamb of God, The Holy One, and The King of Kings and the Lord of Lords? The truth is that no one can. Our minds cannot even come close to grasping anything remotely close to the glory of God and the things He knows.

Who can even compare to our King? Where can we even begin to find anything or anyone that compares to Jesus Christ, The Son of God? We can't find anyone or anything that compares. He found us. He has the perfect divine destiny for our lives.

What can compare to the riches that are ours in Christ Jesus. Romans 10:12-13; **"For there is no distinction between Jew and Greek; the same Lord is Lord of all, bestowing his riches on all who call on him. For everyone who calls on the name of the Lord will be saved."** Jesus Christ has many riches stored up in Heaven for those who are faithful to Him. Christ has already paid the ultimate price for us so that we can have all the riches of Heaven. If we follow the plan presented to us and if we remain faithful to Christ Jesus, He will open the storehouses of Heaven and pour out the bounty on us. Who could possibly want anything else?

This pearl is free to all,
but it came with a great price!

April 11th

Matthew 13:47-50-"Once again, the kingdom of heaven is like a net that was let down into the lake and caught all kinds of fish. When it was full, the fishermen pulled it up on the shore. Then they sat down and collected the good fish in baskets, but threw the bad away. This is how it will be at the end of the age. The angels will come and separate the wicked from the righteous and throw them into the fiery furnace, where there will be weeping and gnashing of teeth."-NIV

The net that gathered the fish is representing judgment day when Jesus meets with His Father and they judge all man. The fish were separated the good from bad. The bad and unclean were the ones which had no scales or fins. The same will be done on judgment day where the believers and the unbelievers will be separated one from the other. One will go to Heaven and the other will be going to Hell.

Heaven my friends is a real place, not a fictional place. God, Heaven, angels, demons, the devil, hell and good versus evil are real and live working entities within the world in which we dwell. Heaven is gained at the acceptance of Jesus Christ as your Personal Savior. When we confess with our lips and believe within our hearts that Jesus Christ is God and that He has the capacity to save us, redeem our lives by breaking the curse of sin within our earthly carnal corpses, we're born into His Heavenly Kingdom. 1 John 4:15; **"Whoever confesses that Jesus is the Son of God, God abides in him, and he in God."** Romans 10: 9-10; **"If you confess with your mouth that Jesus is Lord and believe in your heart that God raised him from the dead, you will be saved. For with the heart one believes and is justified, and with the mouth one confesses and is saved."**

God's Word paints a vivid and clear picture of what it will be like when Jesus arrives on the scene. Some will be talking and one will go, some will be working and one will go, some will be marrying and one will go, some will be divorcing and one will go, some will be giving birth and one will go, and some will be sleeping and one will go. The righteous will be taken with God into the air, the ones that have rejected Jesus Christ and the message of Salvation will go into eternal hell, where there will be no end to pain and misery. This is all due to their choice to reject God and the salvation that comes through Him. This is not God's plan for our lives, but it is the residual effect due to rejection of Him. God would like everyone on earth to come to the knowledge of the saving grace. Jesus Christ has purchased our salvation through the blood which He shed on the cross and His resurrection from the grave.

You can discern people walking in darkness. There is a clear and a very distinct difference between those living in darkness and those living in His light. There is a difference in the way they act, the way they think, the way they talk and the way they live. There is a difference in the way they spend their money, the way they spend their time, and very much so in the way they use their talents, gifts and abilities.

It's ironic that God makes such a distinction between the good and bad and the world has not only blurred the distinction between right and wrong, but the world has made wrong right and right wrong. Heaven forbid that someone believe in the Bible, God, right and wrong, Heaven and hell, angels and demons, and eternity. We can believe that the universe goes on forever, but not that there is such a place as an eternal Heaven. One you can scientifically explore and the other you have to believe by faith. Natural man is inclined to want to follow his carnal mind. Romans 8:7; **"For the mind that is set on the flesh is hostile to God, for it does not submit to God's law; indeed, it cannot."** Ecclesiastes 9:3;

"The hearts of the children of man are full of evil, and madness is in their hearts while they live, and after that they go to the dead." Psalms 53:1; "The fool says in his heart, "There is no God." They are corrupt, doing abominable iniquity; there is none who does good."

Faith is a major factor in how we as Christians conduct our affairs and ultimately our lives. Wouldn't you rather live by a set of beliefs and not have to worry about wronging someone, or would you rather live a life where you wrong someone and then live looking over your shoulder constantly worried that that someone you have wronged has tracked you down and is about to exact their revenge on you? A Christian's life is not an easy life. We all face challenges in life, the difference is how we deal with the challenge when it comes. God never said we wouldn't face challenges, He said He would deliver us through the challenge. After all, it is not the mountain top experiences where we grow; it is when we are in the valley that we learn the most about not only ourselves, but we learn about God also. It is while we are in the fire that we are being refined. Character is not built when we are challenged, it is revealed. What does your character say about you?

You need to plan for your future; will you be spending it in Heaven or in Hell?

April 12th

Matthew 13:57-58-"And they took offense at him. But Jesus said to them, "Only in his hometown and in his own house is a prophet without honor." And he did not do many miracles there because of their lack of faith."-NIV

Hard-heartedness and rejection of Jesus as the Son of God prevent the Holy Spirit's healing ministry, just as they prevent forgiveness of sin. The Holy Spirit does not force his miracles on a hostile, skeptical audience and neither does God the Father or His Son Jesus Christ. People have to have a believing heart in order to receive any of the gifts of God. Faith in Jesus is a great place to start.

Faith is something that has the capacity to put things into action, to make things happen, to bring something to fruition, to take something that wasn't and make it a reality. Hebrews 11:1; **"Now faith is the assurance of things hoped for, the conviction of things not seen."** Faith is powerful. With faith we have the capacity to move mountains and to rise above circumstances with our trust in God. Matthew 17:20; **"For truly, I say to you, if you have faith like a grain of mustard seed, you will say to this mountain, 'Move from here to there,' and it will move, and nothing will be impossible for you."** With God, there is no wondering if we are capable of doing something, He tells us that our faith makes it possible if we would only believe it can be done.

God calls us to have an insurmountable faith in Him, the Creator of Heaven and Earth. We have to trust in God. It is imperative that we trust in Him. He is our Father. God is pleased when His chosen people demonstrate faith within their everyday lives and they put their complete trust in Him. Faith is a powerful substance and entity. God can heal marriages that are ransacked by the attacks of the enemy; He can heal people in multiple ways; physically, spiritually, mentally and emotionally. Faith is the key element in which God operates.

People have the capacity to work in their own power, in their own volition, in their own way, and on their own terms, but God has instructed us in Proverbs 3:5-6 that we are not to rely upon ourselves, we are to trust in Him and in Him alone. Proverbs 3:5-6; **"Trust in the LORD with all your heart, and do not lean on your own understanding. In all your ways acknowledge him, and he will make straight your paths."** We cannot rely on ourselves or another person because we cannot be fully trusted to follow through. Man will fail, it is inevitable. God will show Himself to be faithful to those that have faith and confidence in Him.

Wait for God to reveal Himself!

April 13th

Matthew 14:9-12 -"The king was distressed, but because of his oaths and his dinner guests, he ordered that her request be granted and had John beheaded in the prison. His head was brought in on a platter and given to the girl, who carried it to her mother. John's disciples came and took his body and buried it. Then they went and told Jesus."-NIV

The decapitation of John the Baptist represents evil personified. Here we have a king that was capable of murdering another due to peer pressure by a young girl. A king was fearful of what might happen if he didn't commit such a gruesome murder. Even a king, with all of his mighty power, is susceptible to coercion.

Should we as Christians become baffled and hoodwinked when atrocities occur within the political sphere? I should think not! What we as Christians need to do is stand on the side of what is right, not sway with every wind that blows. If we don't stand for something, be it unpopular even though it is right, we will fall for everything that comes our way.

We have to start cracking the covers of our Bibles and really get into the Word of God. We need to see for ourselves what God has for us to do. We cannot do the popular thing because it is popular. We need to do what is right, even if it is unpopular and others may not like us for it. We need to part with the popularity bug, to put it to bed and take a stand on the Gospel of Christ. Philippians 1:27-28; **"Only let your manner of life be worthy of the gospel of Christ, so that whether I come and see you or am absent, I may hear of you that you are standing firm in one spirit, with one mind striving side by side for the faith of the gospel, and not frightened in anything by your opponents."** Being a Christian may not be popular, but it will sure pay off in the end.

We need to carry out the will of God in our lives and we will be rewarded for doing so. God's sovereign will is summed up in Matthew 22:36-39; **"Teacher, which is the great commandment in the Law?" And he said to him, "You shall love the Lord your God with all your heart and with all your soul and with all your mind. This is the great and first commandment. And a second is like it: You shall love your neighbor as yourself."** We need to persevere in our walk just as Christ did in His. Hebrews 10:36; **"For you have need of endurance, so that when you have done the will of God you may receive what is promised."** Jesus spoke of His desire to fulfill His Fathers will for His life in the Book of John 6:38; **"For I have come down from heaven, not to do my own will but the will of him who sent me."** Is that your will also?

What is the Father's will for your life?

April 14th

Matthew 14:13-"When Jesus heard what had happened, he withdrew by boat privately to a solitary place."-NIV

Jesus didn't withdraw from Galilee because He was afraid; He did it to prevent the escalation of violence that was brewing around Him and His mission. Jesus was sad indeed with the death of not only His friend but also His herald. John was the one who was heralding in Jesus as the Messiah. He was the one telling the people that the Messiah was there walking with them.

Jesus withdrew to draw close to His Father through prayer. Jesus realized that He needed to connect with God the Father privately, without any distractions or intrusions. He realized the extent of **The Waging War Within** the realm of humanity. Jesus was able to prioritize His relationship with His Heavenly Father. This example has been conveyed for us to emulate and to put into practice. Spending time with our Heavenly Father is of crucial importance in the life of Jesus Christ. It also needs to be priority one with us also. We need to pray and have that one on one time with God our Father. My friends strengthen your prayer life.

I can visualize Jesus going to a distant place to focus and pray to God for guidance, encouragement, strength, wisdom, and for God's ultimate will to be done in His life. How appropriate for us to model this prayerful strategy as we confront our own struggles and conflicts. Out of necessity, our focal point always needs to be the example of Jesus Christ. We need to pray always. Luke 21:36; **"But stay awake at all times, praying that you may have strength to escape all these things that are going to take place, and to stand before the Son of Man."**

Take notice in how Jesus practiced His prayer life. Jesus separated Himself from others and their possibility of distraction. Jesus always separated Himself when He prayed, but if you notice, He almost always had His disciples close at hand praying for Him. He had a forward guard so to speak, a couple of chosen men who were like an elite guard whom He could trust to pray through on whatever the need may have been. We need to copy this example and put it into practice. We all know of a few prayer warriors, the ones whom exemplify the warrior's heart when it comes to prayer. We can't rely on our own power to get us through situations but we can rely on the power of God to deliver us. There is power in numbers. Matthew 18:20 tells us **"When two or three come together in my name, there am I with them."**

What have you captivated, conquered, and controlled? Is it a substance, maybe a drug, or some sort of other addiction? Is it sexual bondage? Is it alcoholism? Is it pre-marital sex? Do you have a sexual addiction? Are you physically, emotionally, or verbally abusive to others? Are you in debt? Are you addicted to materialism? Are you struggling with your sexual orientation or your sexual preferences? Are you experiencing suicidal or homicidal ideation? Are you struggling with some form of mental illness? Do you have a strained family relationship that seems impossible to repair? We all face certain hardships in life, but we have a way to overcome them, prayer. Prayer is the answer to all that we face. Prayer is our lifeline to God.

What we need to do is to withdraw and pray. Seek God with everything that you have within you. Deuteronomy 4:29; **"Seek the LORD your God and you will find him, if you search after him with all your heart and with all your soul."** Ask God specifically to restore you in Him. God likes specifics. Do you like it when someone speaks in generalities all the time? Of course you don't. God wants for us to get specific with Him. Ask Him to restore your soul, your spirit, and your mind. He will. His promises are true. With God you will gain the victory. Your healing and full restoration could be instantaneous or it could take some time with prayer. Ultimately, if you seek Him, He will answer your prayers and heal your life. He may choose to use others or He may just choose to heal you Himself. He may choose to use a combination of things or other Christians with Himself in your restoration process.

I truly believe that Jesus is showing us how important it is to pray and to learn how to hear God speak quietly to our souls. He was emphasizing the importance of a solitary place. There are people building homes that have prayer rooms built into the designs. They are doing this so that they can have a solitary place to pray. Please, it is important to have a solitary quiet prayer place. It is in the quiet times that you can truly hear Him call your name and hear Him speak to you. Find a quiet time and a quiet place in which you can pray. Jesus had a place where He could be by Himself, pray, get in touch with His Heavenly Father, and replenish Himself spiritually. Don't we all need this? Do it and I promise you that you will be glad that you did.

Sometimes we're called to a private place to pray and be alone with God

April 15th

Matthew 14:22-24-"Immediately Jesus made the disciples get into the boat and go on ahead of Him to the other side, while He dismissed the crowd. After He had dismissed them, He went up on a mountainside by Himself to pray. When evening came, He was there alone, but the boat was already a considerable distance from land, buffeted by the waves because the wind was against it."-NIV

How powerful! The Son of God, Himself, was praying while the things of this hectic and chaotic world were constantly pressing in on Him. Jesus, the Son, was surrendering to God the Father. Jesus, the Son, was realizing that He had no power apart from the Father. Jesus, the Son, was openly admitting to Himself and the world at large that prayer is the answer. Jesus was displaying that total and utter abandonment to God is the only way to win; through complete and total surrender. This amazing truth is personified within this very act of Jesus. How sacred a moment was this? How powerful was this act for all the world to see? It was a time where the world was allowed to see the humility of Jesus, where He was submitting to His Father God. It was a time in the history of the world where Jesus displayed, through this act, how we are to commune with God.

Jesus humbling Himself to the Father is the ultimate demonstration to us on how humble we need to be. He made a decision to humble Himself to the His Father. Shouldn't we be doing the same? Shouldn't we realize the power inherent in going to God on our knees? Let's do it right now. Take some time and drop to your knees in prayer right now and ask God to come into your life and to forgive you of your sins. Right now as you're reading this devotional, drop to your knees and cry out to God. Don't wait. We all need to get back to the basics. We need to get back into prayer. God could use this very book to bring you back to Him.

When I go skiing, I can't help but to turn around on the chair lift and look back to see the entire mountain as I'm approaching the top of the peak. Thousands of feet high I can see back over everything. I feel connected to God's creation during these moments. His reality is present. Powerful! Awesome! Awakening! To think that this isn't even an inkling and glimmer of how insurmountable our God is. He's created the galaxies, let alone the mountain slopes. He's created the sun, the moon, the stars, the oceans, every land and sea creature and every human being. He's created it all. Everything!!

Imagine Jesus walking on earth with the revelation of God existing within Him, leading Him, guiding Him and working through Him. Jesus knew what He had to do. He knew it was a big task, but He was up for it. Jesus was called to it. If you presently cannot see this for what God would have you to see it as, then pray that He would open your eyes to His greatness. Friend, you need no other but Jesus. Once you have Him, you have it all. You're blessed!

April 16th

Matthew 14:25-27-"During the fourth watch of the night Jesus went out to them, walking on the lake. When the disciples saw Him walking on the lake, they were terrified. "It's a ghost," they said, and cried out in fear. But Jesus immediately said to them: "Take courage! It is I. Don't be afraid.".-NIV

God is calling Christians to be radical and revolutionary in placing their complete faith and trust in Him. God says don't fear anything within this world. Don't fear man, no matter how powerful or wealthy he is. Fear only God, for this is the beginning of wisdom. Proverbs 1:7; **"The fear of the LORD is the beginning of knowledge; fools despise wisdom and instruction."** Wise Christians place their entire faith in God without doubting Him. He wants to inculcate His power, His glory, His personhood, His salvation, His light, and His love within us. He wants us to truly be able to say, "Jesus is our God and we are His people."

God is calling us to be courageous warriors. He wants us to fight the good fight of faith. 1 Timothy 6:12; **"Fight the good fight of the faith. Take hold of the eternal life to which you were called and about which you made the good confession in the presence of many witnesses."** In a world that only believes in the tangible, the things seen, the material things, and the physical things, we need to put our faith in something that is real, even though we might not be able to see them with our naked eyes we can see them with our spiritual eyes. Jesus Christ and His Father God are real, have faith in that.

Faith flies in the face of the Scientific Method, Darwinism, and the Theory of Evolution. The believers in these theoretical perspectives would never in a billion years believe that Jesus walked on water, let alone that He was, is, and always will be, the Son of God. Faith is the antithesis of man's reason and goes against his intellect. God Himself said, "The intelligence of the intelligent I will frustrate". 1 Corinthians 1:19; **"I will destroy the wisdom of the wise, and the discernment of the discerning I will thwart."** God explained to us that we must come to Him as babes and as children. Luke 18:17; **"Truly, I say to you, whoever does not receive the kingdom of God like a child shall not enter it."** He shared that it would be those having the faith of a child who would be able to see the Kingdom of God, not the learned, the intelligent, and the scholars of this Dark Age.

Fear of anything this world
throws at us? Never!

April 17th

Matthew 14:28-"Lord, if it's you," Peter replied, "tell me to come to you on the water." "Come," he said."-NIV

Peter was taking a step of faith. He believed in his heart that it was Jesus. He didn't really doubt that it was Jesus like the rest did. The others were thinking that it was a ghost of Jesus or something thereof. Peter was going to go out and meet Jesus halfway. With His walking on the water Jesus was demonstrating that He was Lord of all creation, weather included. He ruled the weather, the storms, everything. Jesus truly was and is the King of Kings and Lord of Lords. He is the Ruler of all.

God knows that doubt is a natural human condition. He also knows that faith is a choice. One can choose to doubt, or one can choose to have faith. We need to believe in the supernatural power of God. God calls us to have Faith in Him, faith with complete and total abandonment to the cross of Christ. There is to be no looking back.

Ask yourself a question, if Jesus appeared to you, would you believe that it was Him, or would you doubt the fact that He could or would come to you? What is your answer? Jesus can appear to whomever He wants anytime He chooses. He is God. Why would you doubt that fact? Do you feel that you are not worthy of a visit from Him?

Have you ever watched a farmer plowing his field? Notice how he looks while he plows, he looks ahead. If he were to look back you would see that his row would veer to either the left or the right. Jump on your bicycle and ride down a dirt road and look over your shoulder, you would notice your tire marks in the dirt going crooked. The same applies to our walk. We are to trust in Christ and not look back. Why? It is because if we looked back we would go off the path that God has chosen for us. We have the choice to stray off, but if we do there would be consequences, just as the farmer who goes off his path would have an ugly crop and he would have a very difficult time reaping his harvest.

As sure as the chair that I'm sitting in while writing this book supports my body, how much more is God meeting and supporting all of my needs in Christ Jesus! I need to keep my focus on Him and trust that He will guide me and not lead me astray. He has my back; I don't have to be looking over my shoulder. Amen, Amen, and Amen!

Put your hand in the hand of God!

April 18th

Matthew 14:29-30-"Then Peter got down out of the boat, walked on the water and came toward Jesus. But when he saw the wind, he was afraid, and beginning to sink, cried out, "Lord, save me!"-NIV

By walking on water in a furious storm, Jesus demonstrated that He indeed is the Lord over all creation, and so there was no need to be afraid or doubt His existence. The only fitting response is to worship Jesus and to acknowledge that truly he is the Son of God, which is the only time in Matthew that the disciples use this full title to address Jesus, as the Son of God.

Peter was walking on water with his faith in Jesus Christ. Doubt and fear crept in and consumed the faith that he had in Jesus. The physical came into view more that the supernatural, unseen faith of his heart, mind, soul, and spirit, in Christ. The significance of the wind seen by Peter's natural eye drained every ounce of faith that He was placing in the power of Jesus. His focus was taken off Jesus and placed on nature. The creation came to be feared more than the Creator. To Peter, a mere wave prevailed in having more significance than Jesus, the Son of God.

In a sense, Peter, without faith, hit rock bottom. Peter came to the realization that He needed Jesus is the midst of His storm. He needed the saving power that only God can give. How often has this same thing happened to us? How many times have we had Jesus in mind and then we allowed the focus to be shifted onto our own situations and circumstances and we have allowed the focal point to shift from Him to us?

I was involved in a serious motorcycle accident some years ago in Alabama. At the time I was vacillating in my belief in God. It was after the accident that I talked to the people who were assisting me at the accident scene that they said I kept repeating over and over "Oh my God." How true that even the unbeliever calls on the name of God when the going gets tough. Think about it, they don't call on any other name under Heaven but the one that really matters. Acts 4:12; **"And there is salvation in no one else, for there is no other name under heaven given among men by which we must be saved."** It is when we're weak that we're made strong in God. God's power is made perfect in our weakness. 2 Corinthians 13:9; **"For we are glad when we are weak and you are strong. Your restoration is what we pray for."**

With God, all things are possible!

April 19th

Matthew 14:31-"Immediately Jesus reached out his hand and caught him. "You of little faith," He said, "why did you doubt?"-NIV

Doubt can have disastrous consequences. When we as believers doubt, one could say that we're merely having a human emotion, feeling, or thought. As a child of God, doubt can also be perceived as not placing ones complete trust, obedience, and reliance, in God. God means what He says. He's going to carry out what He says He's going to carry out when He wants to, how He wants to, and where He wants to. He's God!

God doesn't need to ask man for permission to perform miracles, to perform healings, to bless someone, to save someone, to deliver someone, or to do anything thing He wants to do on His earth. He's omniscient, omnipresent, and omnipotent. He's the reason we exist. He has breathed all creation into existence. No one but God is all knowing and can be everywhere at once. Can anyone in God's creation tell the Creator of the universe how to act? Where to act? What to do? When to do it? The answer is no. God chooses when, how, and where He's going to act. His ways are above our ways. Isaiah 55:8-9; **"For my thoughts are not your thoughts, neither are your ways my ways, declares the LORD. For as the heavens are higher than the earth, so are my ways higher than your ways and my thoughts than your thoughts."**

Faith is the seed that will lead us to the path that God has prepared for His people. Faith is the unseen blueprint that shall lead us onward, upward, and to victory. Hebrews 11:1; **"Now faith is the assurance of things hoped for, the conviction of things not seen."** When Jesus asked Peter, "Why did you doubt?" could He have wanted Peter to do some introspection? Human beings are creatures of habit, encompassed by their natural selves, and they are living in a natural world. Human beings are born into sin with their first earthly breath. Humans are born again into a spiritual birth that can only be found in accepting Jesus Christ as their personal Lord and Savior.

Let us ask ourselves why we doubt God. Let us ask ourselves why we don't think God is going to do what He says He's going to do. Let us ask ourselves why we don't have the faith we should have. Let us ask ourselves why we're not experiencing miracles within our lives. Let us ask ourselves why we're not experiencing healings, deliverances, salvation within our families and amongst our loved ones, friends, and acquaintances. Is it God's fault or ours? Should we take the blame or should we blame God? Of course God isn't to blame. We need to seek God as if He's a hidden treasure and then the manna from Heaven will open up and blessings will flow upon and into our lives, supernatural blessings far greater than we could ever imagine.

Faith provides us with the capacity to look beyond ourselves and to look beyond the limitations placed upon mankind. With faith we can look beyond our intellect and our own created being. Faith allows us to connect with God on His terms, not our own. God has established terms to our relationship with Him built upon the premise of faith. God desires that we trust in Him. Trust is a difficult commodity in today's world. Distrust is prevalent everywhere as people have become suspicious of the motives of others. People have become distrustful toward family members, religious leaders and politicians, and even toward God. Some of this distrust is justified, the rest is simply paranoia.

A healthy, secure relationship with others and even with God cannot be established, maintained, and nourished, without faith and trust. These two ingredients go hand in hand.

People are walking around with such distrust and lack of faith in their fellow human beings that this is carrying over into their relationship or lack thereof with God.

Divorce is up. Adultery is up. Crime is up. Abuse and neglect toward children is up. Financial problems are up. Incarcerations are up. The breakdown of the American Family is up. Satanism is up. Cults are up. Witchcraft is up. False religions are up. The worship of pagan gods is up. Materialism is up. Suicides are up. Homicides are up. Mental health issues are up. Abortions are up. Unwanted pregnancies are up. Alcohol and drug abuse is up. Taking of prescription medications for depression, anxiety, sleep, hallucinations, conduct, attention, stress, behavior and every other mental and emotional problem is up. Psychiatric visits are up. Counseling visits are up. Poverty is up. Homelessness is up. Psychiatric hospitalizations are up. Anger is up. Teen sex is up. Sex out of wedlock is up. Sexually transmitted diseases are up. AIDS is up. Violent video games are up. Pornography is up. The buying and distributing of weapons is up. The only thing that seems down is my bank account.

Jesus says that if we humble ourselves He will lift us up and heal our land. James 4:10; **"Humble yourselves before the Lord, and he will exalt you."** Jesus wants us to humble ourselves and surrender our thoughts, our will, our emotions, our dreams and ambitions, our goals, our desires, and ultimately our lives, to Him. We're now living in a humanistic culture that isn't centered on God. Our culture is now centered on self and our own selfish interests. This humanistic shift was subtle but pervasive. Our once Christian colleges and universities throughout the country have taken a shift to humanism. Once one had to proclaim that he or she had a belief in Jesus Christ as their Personal Lord and Savior in their application for higher education. Isn't it time we brought faith back into the picture? Isn't it time that Christians take a stand for their faith? Collectively, the Christian community can make change happen. There is power in numbers. We have to give of our time, our talents, and our treasures in order for this to happen.

Doubt isn't an option!
Have faith!

Matthew 14:32-33-"And when they climbed into the boat, the wind died down. Then those who were in the boat worshiped him saying, "Truly you are the Son of God."-NIV

Seeing is believing. Some will doubt unless they see it for themselves. Jesus calmed the wind and then they believed. Thomas doubted until he placed his hand into the side and his fingers into the nail holes of Jesus Christ. When a newborn infant comes into the world, the infant doesn't hesitate, stop and think, or doubt, the process of birth. They're born with an intrinsic faith in others, a childlike faith. They gladly welcome the hands of the doctor or the nurse midwife as they enter the world. They don't care what the doctors or nurses training is, what they look like, or even whether or not they know them, at that moment in time, they trust without a seconds thought. We need to be as a child with their innocent trust and faith when we come to trust in God, Jesus Christ, and His Holy Spirit.

As we grow older, many people have let us down in life. We have been let down by our family members, mothers, fathers, siblings, friends, acquaintances, employers, coaches, teammates, teachers, and our own selves. We carry this distrust and displace it upon God, when it wasn't God that let us down at all. God never tells anyone to break a trust, a confidence, or to destroy a relationship. We don't serve a God of destruction. We serve a God of love. People make choices and decisions that have far reaching consequences both upon them and others. People become hurt, scared, angry, resentful, and even bitter. Let's let Jesus restore our broken lives and our fractured and hurting relationships. Life is too precious to waste time on the negative things. Let's accentuate the positives. Let's trust and love God with all of our trust, faith, hope, and heart. Joshua 24:14-15: **"Now therefore fear the LORD and serve him in sincerity and in faithfulness. Put away the gods that your fathers served beyond the River and in Egypt, and serve the LORD. And if it is evil in your eyes to serve the LORD, choose this day whom you will serve, whether the gods your fathers served in the region beyond the River, or the gods of the Amorites in whose land you dwell. But as for me and my house, we will serve the LORD."**

Choose this day
whom you shall
serve!

April 21st

Matthew 14:34-36-"When they had crossed over, they landed at Gennesaret. And when the men of that place recognized Jesus, they sent word to all the surrounding country. People brought all their sick to Him and begged Him to let the sick just touch the edge of His cloak, and all who touched Him were healed."-NIV

Do we recognize Jesus? Are we anointed and walking in the Holy Spirit and able to be discerning of the day and age in which we live? Do we just exist on the fringe of Christianity looking in, or are we actively involved in God's Kingdom? Recognition means a lot. Some of the ways in which we can recognize those that we're closest to is by their physical features and their voices. People can even use their natural eye to distinguish identical twins one from the other. Parents know who their children are and what separates them from others. Sheep recognize their shepherd's voice and flock to it. Can God distinguish us from the unsaved ones of the world? Can our fellow Christians? Do we recognize the Shepherds voice? We are His sheep after all aren't we?

God knows His children and is able to differentiate those that are His from those that aren't. All that are His have His Holy Spirit living within them. God's own blood has ransomed those saved from death and destruction, His sheep, and God knows who those people around the world are. They represent every language, every tongue, every tribe, every culture, every social group, every country around the globe, and are of different political parties. People from all walks of life have put their faith in Jesus Christ as their Personal Lord and Savior. Talk about diversity, multiculturalism, and representing the melting pot of the world. Christians represent the most diversified group of worshippers in the history of the world. Religions of this world are not at all diversified culturally, racially, ethnically, and socially, as is Christianity. Why? Because God has called Christians into the world to preach the Gospel of Christ to all across the entire globe. Matthew 28:19-20; **"Go therefore and make disciples of all nations, baptizing them in the name of the Father and of the Son and of the Holy Spirit, teaching them to observe all that I have commanded you."** The Church of Jesus Christ has been expanding since the birth of Christ. God would want that none perish, but for all to have everlasting life. 2Peter 3:9; **"The Lord is not slow to fulfill his promise as some count slowness, but is patient toward you, not wishing that any should perish, but that all should reach repentance."**

Why is the Christian Church expanding? This is God's will that people would come to salvation in Him. 1 Timothy 2:1-4; **"First of all, then, I urge that supplications, prayers, intercessions, and thanksgivings be made for all people, for kings and all who are in high positions, that we may lead a peaceful and quiet life, godly and dignified in every way. This is good, and it is pleasing in the sight of God our Savior, who desires all people to be saved and to come to the knowledge of the truth."** People of all nations, tribes, and tongue are being called into His family. John gave this prophecy to John in Revelation 7:9 as to a vision of Heaven and those taken up in the Tribulation; **"After this I looked, and behold, a great multitude that no one could number, from every nation, from all tribes and peoples and languages, standing before the throne and before the Lamb, clothed in white robes, with palm branches in their hands."**

God sends His Holy Spirit when called through prayer and He moves within the hearts and minds of people. God is a gentleman and He only comes when and where He is invited. God wishes to send a revival all across the world that would invigorate, empower, enlighten, and most importantly, bring, people into the saving grace of God. What God has to give is free. No one has to pay for it. It's free! Salvation has already been paid by the blood bought crucifixion and resurrection of Jesus Christ. Salvation comes through the blood bought purchase of our lives. Acts 20:28; **"Pay careful attention to yourselves and to all the flock, in which the Holy Spirit has made you overseers, to care for the church of God, which he obtained with his own blood."**

No matter who we are or what we have done, we can run to Jesus and experience His healing power, His redemption, forgiveness, restoration, and above all else, His salvation. All we have to do is reach out to Him. When we are at the end of our rope there is no better place we could possibly be. Remember my friends, when we are at the end of our rope, we are at the beginning of His. We need to be dead to ourselves in order to be alive in Christ. Jesus Christ poured out Himself for us, we need to rid ourselves of pride and self-will in order to live in Him and His glory.

Reach out to Jesus and
He will reach back to you!

April 22nd

Matthew 15: 1-2 –"Then some Pharisees and teachers of the law came to Jesus from Jerusalem and asked, "Why do your disciples break the tradition of the elders? They don't wash their hands before they eat!"-NIV

Traditions of the elders were basically interpretations of Scripture handed down from esteemed rabbis over several centuries and generations. The Disciples of Christ did not wash their hands and this had upset the Pharisees. Priests were required to wash their hands and feet prior to performing their duties. The Pharisees made this a matter of ceremonial purity and, in their desire to meticulously avoid any possibility of becoming unclean, applied it to all Israelites.

Are we to honor traditions over Jesus? Never! This is an example of how human rules and regulations have taken precedence over a personal relationship with God, due to lack of understanding and relationship with the things of God. This above mentioned scripture gives reference to good hygiene, however this isn't the intent of what this scripture is meant to truly convey. The Pharisees were very rigid religious leaders that represented the religious power structure of the time. God wants relationship with us, not religion. Religion is manmade, relationship is Godly ordained.

Even today people have traditions that have blocked and hindered their ability to get a glimmer of who God is. Let's not ever let anything, especially a tradition, interfere with the reality of Jesus Christ and the Holy Spirit within our lives.

One day, all of us will be lying in our coffins and our time will have run out. By the time we pass on, it will be too late to be radically sold out for Jesus and revolutionary for Him. Let's get fired up now! Let's get radically sold out to Jesus and win some souls for the Kingdom of God. When our God given earthly bodies are six feet under, it'll be too late so let's use all of our talents for God. Let's give it all to Him. Let's not hold back anything. Take it all Jesus. You own it. You're the very reason why I live and breathe.

We need to be careful not to follow traditions, religions, wrong ideologies, false gods, vain philosophies, or anything that is not readying us for the Kingdom and our meeting with God. Remember, Jesus is about relationship. God has always longed for relationship with you. That is why He created us. He wanted relationship with His creation. He wanted a relationship with you.

We are His creation.

April 23rd

Matthew 15:3-9-"Jesus replied, "And why do you break the command of God for the sake of your tradition? For God said, "Honor your father and mother" and "Anyone who curses his father or mother must be put to death." But you say that if a man says to his father or mother, "Whatever help you might otherwise have received from me is a gift devoted to God," he is not to honor his father with it. Thus you nullify the word of God for the sake of your tradition. You hypocrites! Isaiah was right when he prophesied about you: "These people honor me with their lips, but their hearts are far from me. They worship me in vain; their teachings are but rules taught by men.".-NIV

Jesus makes a clear distinction between the Old Testament, which was the very commandment of God, and the Pharisaic tradition, which consisted of merely human authoritative opinions and their own personal interpretations of the Word. When they speak of the command of God, they speak of a formal vow, or "Corban", which is a technical term for the formal vow. This type of vow allowed a person to be released from other responsibilities, such as caring for aging parents. This is a man-made ruling.

What the Pharisees did was they made void the word of God with their traditions and rulings: anyone who broke a vow (human law) in order to help needy parents (God's law) would have committed a serious transgression, according to the Pharisees. They made their rulings higher than God's. Pharisees were hypocrites for two reasons: (1) their actions are merely external and do not come from their hearts and (2) their teachings are not from God but reflect human tradition. We need to be cautious of the message we are sending to the public. We are not God and the rules we impose need to match up with the commandments of God and His Word, if they don't it becomes Pharisaical and legalism.

In today's society, we see vast amounts of youths that have absolutely no respect for their parents or adults in general. Many youth don't even respect themselves. Some parents have even been murdered by their children. An increased number of youth throughout the United States are being diagnosed with; Conduct Disorder, Oppositional Defiant Disorder, many are involved in the court system, the criminal justice system, and are involved in gangs. Many of these youth are oppositional and defiant to perceived authority. Many factors come into play in causing this escalation with youth. The outcome and prognosis for these youth are similar no matter what the cause of their issues. A rebelliousness and disobedience to God, their parents, school rules, societal laws, and social norms is ruining society. Many of these youth engage in criminal behaviors at a very young age. Many of these youth have criminal records before even getting out of their teen years.

If a child's own parents aren't being honored within the home, more often than not; teachers, school officials, probation officers, police officers, and others in positions of power and authority won't be respected either. The spirit of rebellion can only be truly altered and changed by another Spirit, The Holy Spirit which God provides.

The Holy Spirit works from the inside out. A change of heart, mind, spirit, and soul, can happen with an encounter of the Holy Spirit. There is a rebelliousness that is happening among our youth in America that even the ungodly are shaking their heads at in disbelief. Just reflect for a moment on the school shootings and other violent acts that have been carried out by youth in America. Where is God in all of this mayhem? God has been removed from many stations in society, and with neglecting God, society falls. We need to reflect on God and His ways and we can turn society once again towards God. We need to open more churches, clubs, youth centers, sports camps, Christian schools, and other Christian based organizations, in order to take back the youth and save them from this God forsaken culture.

Sodom and Gomorrah could have been spared if there were only ten believers in God. Read the record in Genesis 18 and 19. Ten believers were all that were needed but they couldn't be found. We have believers throughout our neighborhoods and cities if we only sought them out. We can take back our cities and communities if we only spoke out and sought out other believers. There is power in numbers my friends.

There are Joshua marches being held all over the country where people are trying to reclaim their children's schools and neighborhoods from the gang violence and drugs that have permeated our society. There are people who are sick and tired of having innocent lives lost to domestic violence due to drugs and gang violence. People are pouring their hearts out to God for intercession and He is answering their prayers. How is your prayer life working out for you? Are you crying out to Him?

Give it all to God,
He's waiting.

April 24th

Matthew 15:8-9-"These people honor me with their lips, but their heart are far from me. They worship me in vain; their teachings are but rules taught by men."-NIV

The expression that one can talk the talk but not walk the walk is so true. God would like for us to know that there is a huge difference between head knowledge and heart knowledge. The transformational power of God is involved in a changed heart. Many can use their words to project an image of who they think they are, or how they would like to be perceived. God is more concerned about what is taking place on the inside than what is taking place on the out. What is a man or a woman's thought life? What are their motives? What do they truly believe? What is their attitude? Do they really care? Remember your thoughts will lead to actions, your actions will lead to behaviors, and your behavior will lead to who you will become. God doesn't want success, He wants commitment. It is the world that wants success. Remember 1 John 4:4; **"Little children, you are from God and have overcome them, for He who is in you is greater than He who is in the world."** We are not of the world, we are from God. We need to remember that when we are faced with the temptation to give in and give up. God is greater than the world.

Our physical heart was knit together by God Himself. He knit it together while we were still in our mother's womb. He fashioned it to pump blood to keep us alive so that we can do His will. God doesn't care to knit something as complex as the heart and then let it beat to a different drummer. He wants the human heart which He created to beat to Him alone. He's the inventor, the creator, and the originator.

Our walk with God is all about heart. It takes a heart to beat after Jesus Christ and to run the race of the Christian. Just think that every single heart beat is another beat which Jesus has allowed us to have. Shouldn't we reciprocate in the acknowledgement of this? Shouldn't we give our life to God as a living and loving sacrifice? With every beat of the heart shouldn't we be drawing closer to God? If we're not, we've lost our perspective. It's about God and God alone.

I made a conscious effort to exercise weekly and my heart rate went from eighty beats a minute to sixty beats a minute so now I know that my heart doesn't have to work as hard as it did previously. I accomplished this through cardio vascular exercise. I primarily played racquetball and tennis. Can you imagine if we discipline our heart life with Christ the changes we could see in our world. It would be radical, revolutionary, and transformational. He desires that our hearts steadfastly beat after Him. My desire is that all sixty beats per minute belong to Him. I want the Lord to have all of my heart, not just a portion, but the whole thing.

April 25th

Matthew 15:10-11-"Jesus called the crowd to him and said, "Listen and understand. What goes into a man's mouth does not make him unclean, but what comes out of his mouth, that is what makes him unclean."-NIV

These two verses piggy back with Mark 7:20-23; **"What comes out of a person is what defiles him. For from within, out of the heart of man, come evil thoughts, sexual immorality, theft, murder, adultery, coveting, wickedness, deceit, sensuality, envy, slander, pride, foolishness. All these evil things come from within, and they defile a person."** Powerful words to ponder? You bet. We are what we speak.

Jesus is both warning and educating us on the importance that words are powerful. Words have the capacity to tear down or build up. Words can heal and words can destroy. Words are the means that we as human beings have in communicating what is in our heart. Words are the external means that we can share what's on our heart, our mind, and also in our soul. Words come from within. Words are a mirror of our insides. We have the power to bless others and also the power to hurt and destroy them with our words. The choice is ours to make on how we use our words.

We pray to God with our words, either out loud, quietly to ourselves, or in our thoughts. We use words to disclose, uncover, and convey, to God our deepest hopes, dreams, fears, and needs. Jesus is attempting to convey that words supersede food in determining whether a man has a clean heart or a dirty heart.

We have all felt the sting of sharp, thoughtless, words spoken to us at one time or another in our life. We all know the pain associated with those words can last a lifetime. I'll bet that you can still remember hurts from your childhoods that were caused by the careless use of another's words. That saying about sticks and stones and broken bones is a lie, words can and do hurt. We need to tame our tongues with the help of God. James 3:8; **"No human being can tame the tongue. It is a restless evil, full of deadly poison."** The Bible says no human being can tame his tongue, which is true. We can't, but He can. We need to pray for His help and His grace in overcoming the obstacle of our tongue. Philippians 4:13; **"I can do all things through Him who strengthens me."** Let's put that verse into practice the next time we get ready to say something we will regret later.

We can't, but He can!

April 26th

Matthew 15:12-"Then the disciples came to him and asked, "Do you know that the Pharisees were offended when they heard this?"-NIV

The Disciples were concerned that the Pharisees were offended by the words of Christ. People, we cannot be concerned with how people might be offended when they hear of Jesus Christ. If, like the Pharisees, they get offended, then they are not of God. The Word says that this will happen. We are to press onward and upward. Not everyone will accept the teachings as we did. We cannot take their rejection as a personal insult.

The Bible is clear on what to do when the Word is rejected or if the messenger is rejected. Matthew 10:14; **"And if anyone will not receive you or listen to your words, shake off the dust from your feet when you leave that house or town."** Again in the New Testament it is mentioned in the Book of Mark what to do if either we or the Word are rejected. Mark 6:11; **"If any place will not receive you and they will not listen to you, when you leave, shake off the dust that is on your feet as a testimony against them."** Rabbinic sources note that Jews who returned from Gentile regions were to shake off the dust that is on their feet as a form of cleansing. Here it also serves as a sign against them. The act of shaking off the dust is an illustration of the fact that their rejection of God's message leaves the people and the town accountable to God. It is not left up to us to decide their fate, that decision is God's. We just have to do our part in spreading and teaching the Word and God will do the rest.

The people that were wrapped up in their traditional way of perceiving the world around them had a problem with Jesus. People will continue to feel offended by Jesus Christ until the end of the age and His ultimate return to Earth. Jesus even says that those that aren't with Him are against Him. Matthew 12:30; **"Whoever is not with me is against me, and whoever does not gather with me scatters."** Either the Lord Jesus Christ is the ruler of your life, or, the ruler of your life is the ruler of the kingdom of the air and this dark world. This is a straightforward, cut to the chase, bottom line truth and an undeniable scriptural fact. Either your God is God the Father armed with angels, or your god is Satan armed with his minions of demons. Satan is really no god at all, he is a fallen angel. There is no middle of the road or arguable scriptural truth that points to any other alternative.

Look around you. At work, at school, within your family, your social network, among friends, acquaintances, and even in some cases, within your church. People are offended if you are radically sold out for Jesus Christ. Lukewarm Christians even have a hard time interacting, associating with, communicating, being around, and definitely understanding Christians that are radically transformed and outspoken for the things of God. People become easily offended when Jesus is placed on His rightful throne before them. Why? I'll tell you why. It is a natural human condition called sin that prevents people from being all that they can be in God. The Holy Spirit calls His people to be practicing holiness and living lives set apart for God. People will be offended when you don't put them first in your life, when God takes precedence over them.

Some people are the center of their own world. Narcissism is rampant with people today. There is so much self-love out there running around that there is barely any room left for God. People expect themselves to be the center of everyone else's world. Heaven forbid you live your life doing the things of God. Heaven forbid you're attempting to be a light in a very dark world. Heaven forbid you're involved in your local church. Heaven forbid you want to send your children to a Christian school. Heaven forbid you believe that God and the devil are real forces to be reckoned with. Heaven forbid you find fulfillment in your soul (that God created) when you cling to the things of God. Heaven forbid you would be involved in His church with His people in fellowship (brothers and sisters in the Lord), praising and worshipping God on Sundays and every other day that the church door is open. Heaven forbid you give of your income, read the Bible, pray, and praise God.

The answer to why people are easily offended by the things of God is that they haven't given God a place in their lives. This is where the rubber meets the road spiritually. If you don't allow God in, then the creation is in rebellion against their Creator. God says in His word that we are either for Him or against Him. Matthew 12:30; **"Whoever is not with me is against me, and whoever does not gather with me scatters."** Many don't buy this extreme because our worldly system has taught us to be complacent and neutral concerning the things of God. The devil would just love to lull us to sleep while he continues to be on the prowl destroying everything he can. The devil loves to be subtle, to sneak up on people, to tempt, to control, to manipulate, and ultimately, have the power. Who's your power source? Let's be true to God!

Become involved in the things of God.

Make God your focal point.

Matthew 15:13-14-**"He replied, "Every plant that my heavenly Father has not planted will be pulled up by the roots. Leave them; they are blind guides. If a blind man leads a blind man, both will fall into a pit.".-NIV**

The Pharisees were blind to the things of God. The Pharisees had not been planted by the Father; therefore they will be rooted up as the weeds spoken of previously. They were basically blind guides. The Pharisees are both blind to their own hypocrisy and they were blindly leading the people astray because they could not see the true intent of God's will in the Old Testament. God needed to be their foundation of both their faith and their lives and He wasn't made such.

There is no other true foundation other than that of God. Listen to the lesson in Matthew 7:24-27; **"Everyone then who hears these words of mine and does them will be like a wise man who built his house on the rock. And the rain fell, and the floods came, and the winds blew and beat on that house, but it did not fall, because it had been founded on the rock. And everyone who hears these words of mine and does not do them will be like a foolish man who built his house on the sand. And the rain fell, and the floods came, and the winds blew and beat against that house, and it fell, and great was the fall of it."**

All truth exists within God and all of His precepts. A precept is rule or principle prescribing a particular course of action or conduct. God has established a code of conduct from which we are to model our lives. Having God and His truth in our lives is like being a plant that has roots growing deep within the soil that cannot be pulled up. When an individual is in God's Word, allowing the Holy Spirit to operate in them, involved in his church, sharing God with others, and ultimately involved in Kingdom business, a witness of God's root is evident. Christians should be less likely to be swayed by others, the culture of the world, their flesh, demonic oppression, the devil, anxiety, fear, and the lack of hope that is so evident in the world.

Have you ever seen a lukewarm Christian? It's sad isn't it? We need to be all and give all for God. God deserves nothing less from us. We are to be building the kingdom for Him and how can we do that if we are not totally sold out for Him? We can't! Would you want a doctor performing surgery on you if he wasn't on top of his game? Of course you wouldn't. Why would God want someone building His kingdom if they weren't totally committed to Him? He wouldn't. Get serious in your walk! Get fired up for God! Hoo-Rah!!

Get fired up for Jesus!!

April 28th

Matthew 15:15-20-"Peter said, "Explain the parable to us." "Are you still so dull?" Jesus asked them. "Don't you see that whatever enters the mouth goes into the stomach and then out of the body? But the things that come out of the mouth come from the heart, and these make a man unclean. For out of the heart come evil thoughts, murder, adultery, sexual immorality, theft, false testimony, slander. These are what make a man unclean; but eating with unwashed hands does not make him unclean."-NIV

Unless enlightened by the Holy Spirit, man cannot comprehend the things of God. 1 Corinthians 2:6-16; **"Yet among the mature we do impart wisdom, although it is not a wisdom of this age or of the rulers of this age, who are doomed to pass away. But we impart a secret and hidden wisdom of God, which God decreed before the ages for our glory. None of the rulers of this age understood this, for if they had, they would not have crucified the Lord of glory. But, as it is written, "What no eye has seen, nor ear heard, nor the heart of man imagined, what God has prepared for those who love him"— these things God has revealed to us through the Spirit. For the Spirit searches everything, even the depths of God. For who knows a person's thoughts except the spirit of that person, which is in him? So also no one comprehends the thoughts of God except the Spirit of God. Now we have received not the spirit of the world, but the Spirit who is from God, that we might understand the things freely given us by God. And we impart this in words not taught by human wisdom but taught by the Spirit, interpreting spiritual truths to those who are spiritual. The natural person does not accept the things of the Spirit of God, for they are folly to him, and he is not able to understand them because they are spiritually discerned. The spiritual person judges all things, but is himself to be judged by no one. "For who has understood the mind of the Lord so as to instruct him?" But we have the mind of Christ."**

The Holy Spirit allows us to be sharp as a tack with spiritual truths. Apart from the Holy Spirit, we're blind and limited by the physical eye. Physical vision is different from spiritual vision. It's the difference between having binoculars for the daytime and having a pair of night vision goggles for the evening. If you use the regular binoculars for the evening you won't see a thing if there isn't any light in the darkness. If you use the night vision goggles for the daytime you won't be able to see the things in the light. The same applies with a mind that clings to the natural as opposed to one that clings to the supernatural things of God. The Holy Spirit is the One that illuminates the things of God so that we can see them clearly.

I find it amazing how much emphasis Jesus places on the heart. The heart is of crucial importance to God. The heart is the control panel of one's motives. With pure motives flowing from our heart, we have pure intentions, pure thoughts, and ultimately, pure actions. With impure motives flowing from our heart we have impure intentions, impure thoughts, and ultimately, impure actions. We need to give our hearts over to God for His work to be carried out through them.

Giving over our heart to God is crucial in being able to carry out God's divine destiny for our lives. The floodgates of Heaven will be poured out for us to overflowing if we humble ourselves and completely surrender to God and follow His precepts. Malachi 3:10; **"Bring the full tithes into the storehouse, that there may be food in my house. And thereby put me to the test, says the LORD of hosts, if I will not open the windows of heaven for**

144~ The Waging War Within

you and pour down for you a blessing until there is no more need." This is a way of life we should want to live by.

Our prayer should be: "Dear God, forgive me of all of my sins and purify my heart so there is no wicked way within me. Cleanse me of all unrighteousness and take hold of my unclean heart. Pour your Holy Spirit and your power upon me and my family so that we may stand as true Christians during this dark time. May we collectively be a beacon of light that shines and radiate your love in this dark world. May you lead us and guide us in your path of righteousness. May you bless our lives so that we may be a blessing to others. Dear God, forgive me a sinner and turn me from the error of my ways and guide me in your way of truth and everlasting life. Cover me with your blood covering and bind all demonic and satanic strongholds within my life and the life of my family members. Bind all demonic powers within my family of previous, present and future generations. Cast all demonic powers into your thorn of crowns and cover them with your blood. I pray these things in the name of Jesus Christ who shed His blood for me. Empower me to live out my Christian life in your power, glory and splendor. May your glory rest upon me and my family and may you place a hedge of protection upon us. Order our paths in your righteousness and may your plan for our lives be fulfilled. May we be able to be witnesses for you, sharing the love of God to others and leading them to salvation. I ask this in the glorious name of your son, Jesus Christ."

God will undoubtedly honor this prayer from your heart. He desires to cleanse your heart and to lead you into a closer relationship to Him. He doesn't want His church to experience the things of this world culture; evil thoughts, murder, adultery, sexual immorality, theft, false testimony, and slander. He desires for our lives to be blessed and for us to have life and have it more abundantly. John 10:10; **"The thief comes only to steal and kill and destroy. I came that they may have life and have it abundantly."**

Be careful what you speak.
Your future may depend on it.

April 29th

Matthew 15:21-22-"Leaving that place, Jesus withdrew to the region of Tyre and Sidon. A Canaanite woman from that vicinity came to him, crying out, "Lord, Son of David, have mercy on me! My daughter is suffering terribly from demon-possession."-NIV

Demon possession, could it be real? God is clearly educating us that demon possession is a very real thing. People are controlled and manipulated by demonic forces from Satan himself. Read the newspaper and watch the local and world news. Aren't your jaws dropping with the things that are happening? Do you believe that all the killings, rapes, muggings, and other heinous crimes are only human in origin? The reason you can't see into the supernatural is that you're not asking God to provide you with the spiritual lens to see and discern what's going on.

Humanity separated from God gives the enemy of our souls a portal in which to come in and destroy our lives. Why does the Bible speak of putting on the full armor of God so that we can stand against the devil's schemes? Ephesians 6:10-18; **"Finally, be strong in the Lord and in the strength of his might. Put on the whole armor of God, that you may be able to stand against the schemes of the devil. For we do not wrestle against flesh and blood, but against the rulers, against the authorities, against the cosmic powers over this present darkness, against the spiritual forces of evil in the heavenly places. Therefore take up the whole armor of God, that you may be able to withstand in the evil day, and having done all, to stand firm. Stand therefore, having fastened on the belt of truth, and having put on the breastplate of righteousness, and, as shoes for your feet, having put on the readiness given by the gospel of peace. In all circumstances take up the shield of faith, with which you can extinguish all the flaming darts of the evil one; and take the helmet of salvation, and the sword of the Spirit, which is the word of God, praying at all times in the Spirit, with all prayer and supplication."** Is this just a joke or something that He just haphazardly mentioned? Is God providing us with vital information that is essential in protecting us from being inundated by the enemy's forces that exist in the unseen realm? Of course He is.

Church, God is trying to protect us! He's given us spiritual tactics to engage the enemy of our souls in supernatural warfare so that we can withstand the wiles of the devil and his demonic forces from hell. Let's get into the Word of God. Let's pray like never before so that we can withstand the onslaught of the enemy and proactively assault Satan and his demons. We have nothing to fear as long as we're on God's team and a part of His army. For God did not give us a spirit of timidity, but a spirit of power, of love and a sound mind. 2 Timothy 1:7; **"For God gave us a spirit not of fear but of power and love and self-control."**

April 30th

Matthew 15:23-28-"Jesus did not answer a word. So his disciples came to him and urged him, "Send her away, for she keeps crying out after us." He answered, "I was sent only to the lost sheep of Israel." The woman came and knelt before him. "Lord, help me!" she said. He replied, "It is not right to take the children's bread and toss it to their dogs." "Yes, Lord," she said, "but even the dogs eat the crumbs that fall from their masters' table." Then Jesus answered, "Woman, you have great faith! Your request is granted." And her daughter was healed from that very hour."-NIV

The first act of devotion is kneeling and humbling ourselves before Jesus and openly admitting to Him that we are powerless in and of ourselves. This is called humility. God requires a humble heart in a true disciple. Our life isn't about us, it's about God. Our life isn't about having our own hopes and dreams come true, it's about having God's divine destiny for our lives fulfilled and carried out here on earth.

Nothing, absolutely nothing of God can be carried out without faith. It should be comforting for us to know that since the creation of the world, and even prior to being in our mother's womb, God has had a divine destiny for our lives. He desires to prosper us, not to harm us. God will bring us through times of great difficulty where we have to walk in the valley of the shadow of death. God's ultimate plan is to use these tough experiences in the valleys of our lives to refine and mold us into the image of His Son Jesus Christ. God is the potter and we are the clay. Jeremiah 18:1-6; **The word that came to Jeremiah from the LORD: "Arise, and go down to the potter's house, and there I will let you hear my words." So I went down to the potter's house, and there he was working at his wheel. And the vessel he was making of clay was spoiled in the potter's hand, and he reworked it into another vessel, as it seemed good to the potter to do. Then the word of the LORD came to me: "O house of Israel, can I not do with you as this potter has done? declares the LORD. Behold, like the clay in the potter's hand, so are you in my hand, O house of Israel."**

God will test our faith to see if it is one of substance and to see if it is able to withstand adversity. Whether good or bad comes your way, get on your knees and cry out to God and ask Him for an abundance of faith. Our faith will be tried in the fiery furnace of life. Look at Daniel in the lion's den in the Book of Daniel, chapter 6: 1-28. We also have another great example again in the Book of Daniel, chapter 3, verses 8-30 in the story of Shadrech, Meshach, and Abednego when they refused to bow to the image of King Nebuchadnezzar. The three had refused to bow down because they knew that God was the true God and not a mortal man even if he were king of the region. For their refusal they were chucked into a fiery furnace heated to an astronomical temperature that was sure to leave nothing behind of the three. The furnace was so hot that the tenders died from the heat but not a hair was harmed on the head of any of the three Hebrew children. God had their back just as He has ours.

We may feel at times that it's just too hot for us and that we cannot withstand the pressures of life. It is at these times that immense growth between us and God can and will happen. He wants us to press in to Him when we think that we can no longer stand. After all, it is not the mountain top experiences that allow us to grow, it is the times when we are in the valley and we think that we have nothing left to give that we grow the most. We are being refined when we are in the fire. Praise God!

Psalm 34:1 says, **"Praise the Lord always."** It doesn't say to only praise Him only when the going is good. It says "Always." It is when we are at the end of our rope that we are at the beginning of His. It's a good place to be. Amen? Amen brother!

Trust in God

MAY

May 1st

Matthew 15:29-"Then He went up on a mountainside and sat down."-NIV

How powerful to think that Jesus went up on a mountainside to pray. How profound of a portrayal of Jesus and His willingness to draw nigh to the Father. How connected, how telling and what an example for us as His disciples did He set for us to follow. I can picture Jesus sitting, resting and taking a time out to draw Himself unto the Father. I can imagine the tenderness and humbleness of His heart on that mountainside. It's in these special moments that we are actually submitting to and allowing God the Father to have His way, to be able to carry out His desires, and ultimately to be more like Him.

Jesus has once again given us a glimpse of His prayer life and I will give you a few more. Matthew 6:5-7; **"And when you pray, you must not be like the hypocrites. For they love to stand and pray in the synagogues and at the street corners, that they may be seen by others. Truly, I say to you, they have received their reward. But when you pray, go into your room and shut the door and pray to your Father who is in secret. And your Father who sees in secret will reward you. And when you pray, do not heap up empty phrases as the Gentiles do, for they think that they will be heard for their many words."** Another example is where He prayed for replenishment in Mark 1:35; **"And rising very early in the morning, while it was still dark, he departed and went out to a desolate place, and there he prayed."** Another is in Spirit and in truth, John 4:23-24; **"But the hour is coming, and is now here, when the true worshipers will worship the Father in spirit and truth, for the Father is seeking such people to worship him. God is spirit, and those who worship him must worship in spirit and truth."** There are multiple examples where Jesus was praying for His Disciples, future believers, for strength to endure, etc...

Let us take some time for ourselves and our relationship with God. Let us ask Him to reveal Himself to our hearts. We can't go up on a mountainside all the time, but we can go to a quiet place in our home or wherever we are and meet with Him. I challenge you to have a quiet place within your home where you can go pray and have quiet time with God. We need alone time with God. The fact of the matter is that no matter where you are, God is there with you. 2 Corinthians 2:14; **"But thanks be to God, who in Christ always leads us in triumphal procession, and through us spreads the fragrance of the knowledge of him everywhere."** He walks with you and talks with you and desires to be your best friend. Have a passion for Him and He will take care of your every need. Pray to Him and you will see His grace poured out in your life.

May 2nd

Matthew 16:1-4 -The Pharisees and Sadducees came to Jesus and tested him by asking Him to show them a sign from heaven. He replied, "You cannot interpret the signs of the times. A wicked and adulterous generation looks for a miraculous sign, but none will be given it except the sign of Jonah." Jesus then left them and went away. –NIV

The Pharisees and Sadducees were both religious leaders at the time but were often bitter opponents of each other. Here they joined forces against Jesus, whom they saw as a threat to their leadership and power. They came to Jesus not out of need or genuine faith but to test him. They were seeking a sign or miracle to use against Him when they were ready and when they wanted to eventually execute Him.

Not a wise decision to put God to the test. There are several verses that tell you not to test God. The way that testing God here is as a bad test. We are told to test God and to see if His Word is true, not the same testing as mentioned here. One is as an act of faith; the other is a conspiracy to cause trouble. Acting in a state of unbelief is sinful. Testing Jesus is not a wise decision. Deuteronomy 6:16; **"You shall not put the LORD your God to the test, as you tested him at Massah."** Matthew 4:7, Luke 4:12 both reiterate the same. God is the ultimate authority and power, I hope we all believe this; if you don't you've failed to understand and comprehend the extent, scope, awesomeness and character of the Creator of Heaven and Earth.

Ephesians 6:17; **"Take the helmet of salvation, and the sword of the Spirit, which is the word of God."** This verse demonstrates the centrality of God's Word in defeating Satan's attacks and temptations by speaking Scripture. We can do this also if we know the Word. We can defeat Satan at his own game. This is why we have to know the Word of God. John 14:6; **"I am the way, and the truth, and the life. No one comes to the Father except through me."**

Never base your belief in God on what you can see, hear and feel. In other words don't base your faith in God on the tangible. John 14:1; **"Let not your hearts be troubled. Believe in God; believe also in me."** We serve God in faith and want, not out of a feeling of fear and obligation. We serve Him because we want to serve Him.

Trust in God and you will not be disappointed.

Matthew 16:6-"Be careful," Jesus said to them. "Be on your guard against the yeast of the Pharisees and Sadducees."-NIV

In contrast to Matthew 13:33; **"The kingdom of heaven is like leaven that a woman took and hid in three measures of flour, till it was all leavened.",** where it meant that it was hidden and able to permeate the kingdom fully, here leaven is a negative metaphor to indicate how the evil of corruption can infiltrate and ruin what is good. We need to be fed the rightly divided Word and then have the Word active in our lives. That is what the Pastor is responsible for, feeding his flock.

Yeast starts off manageable, but then before you know it, it expands and becomes all consuming. Jesus, as He often does throughout the Bible is making a comparison. He's contrasting the rigid religious and traditional beliefs of the day to faith in Him. Jesus is once again attempting to protect His followers from opposing viewpoints. God is warning us that we must guard ourselves from their beliefs. He knows that if we as His followers don't guard ourselves, their beliefs could be like cancer to our souls.

God warns us to be careful and to be on our guard. This is very telling. Jesus is alerting us to the fact that not everyone is following Jesus, that there are religious leaders who are out amongst us that are sowing their own agendas within their flocks. Some people not only don't belong to Jesus, some are diametrically opposed to the very things of God. These leaders will have to answer to God for what they have done.

God is also warning us in 2 Timothy 3:1-5 to guard ourselves against the ways of the worldly people. 2 Timothy 3:1-5; **"But understand this, that in the last days there will come times of difficulty. For people will be lovers of self, lovers of money, proud, arrogant, abusive, disobedient to their parents, ungrateful, unholy, heartless, unappeasable, slanderous, without self-control, brutal, not loving good, treacherous, reckless, swollen with conceit, lovers of pleasure rather than lovers of God, having the appearance of godliness, but denying its power. Avoid such people."**

God wants relationship with us not religion. The Pharisees and Sadducees want religion and laws so that they could hold people into submission. God wants for us to be free in Him, not obligated and prisoner to man's laws. We need to ask ourselves if we are involved in a manmade religion, such as one with the Pharisees and Sadducees making all the rules and laws which hold you into subjection, or a Godly ordained relationship with our Creator. Are you healthy in your relationship with God? I pray that that is what you have with Him. After all, we were created to commune with God.

Religious yeast can be bad.

May 4th

Matthew 16:11-"How is it you don't understand that I was not talking to you about bread? But be on your guard against the yeast of the Pharisees and Sadducees.-NIV

Jesus finds it hard to believe that His followers still didn't comprehend the contrasting comparison or analogy that He was making between yeast and the beliefs of the religious leaders. Jesus knew that the people needed to be educated as to the untruths and the antagonism that the religious leaders had toward Him. They didn't believe that Jesus was who He claimed to be. They would do everything within their power to discredit, disprove and malign Jesus.

Corruption and evil can infiltrate our lives and our thinking if we don't guard ourselves from it. Proverbs 27:17; **"Iron sharpens iron, and one man sharpens another."** We need to stand shoulder to shoulder with other likeminded men and women in this war against the enemy of our souls. Habakkuk 2:1; **"I will take my stand at my watch post and station myself on the tower, and look out to see what he will say to me, and what I will answer concerning my complaint."** Habakkuk was set looking to God for direction. He was upset with all of the evil around him and He complained to God that the evil seemed to be winning.

As citizenry of a way of life which is under attack, we need to keep alert against infiltrators and against others who mean to harm our belief system and our way of life. We would do well to keep on alert regarding the spiritual dangers in these last perilous days. We cannot afford to be caught sleeping on our watch or gain a false sense of security. We need to protect both our body and our soul. Satan is on the prowl. Keeping of our souls is of vital importance. Satan can do us greater harm with his subtleties than if he were to wage a quick onslaught. We need to guard against complacency. We must be vigilant. At night, watchmen must be particularly vigilant.

As the darkness engulfs us, we must be prepared for the battle, for the best time to wage a war is at night. We must not be caught unawares. We are responsible for not only our own souls, but also those who have been entrusted to us. Ezekiel 3: 16-18; **"And at the end of seven days, the word of the LORD came to me: "Son of man, I have made you a watchman for the house of Israel. Whenever you hear a word from my mouth, you shall give them warning from me. If I say to the wicked, 'You shall surely die,' and you give him no warning, nor speak to warn the wicked from his wicked way, in order to save his life, that wicked person shall die for his iniquity, but his blood I will require at your hand."** Ezekiel was assigned the duty as an early warning system for Judah. We are also commissioned with the same task today. We are God's watchmen.

May 5th

Matthew 16:13-"Who do people say the Son of Man is?"-NIV

People back in the days when Christ walked among man as well as people today have all different perspectives as to who the Son of Man is. Some think Jesus was a mere man and some think He was a prophet. Jesus claimed to be God incarnate as He walked the earth in human likeness.

Jesus was and is the Son of God. We need to be clear in our understanding. Jesus Christ was the second Adam. Adam messed things up and sin entered the world. Eve sinned but Adam allowed her to proceed with the act knowing full well that God warned them against it. Adam was the head of their union and as such he was duty bound to stop Eve from sinning and he didn't. Her sin rests on his head. That single act is what brought sin into the world. We have progressed steadily downward from there as a civilization. Jesus came to try to get us back on track and look at what man did to Him. The good news is that Jesus came to become a sacrifice once and for all.

Jesus offered Himself up as a blood sacrifice to atone for our sins. A blood sacrifice was called for as a sin offering by God and Jesus was that sacrifice. He laid down His life for us. He paid the price for our sins. The Son of God died for you and for me. He felt we were worth His sacrifice. That should mean something to you.

Today, Jesus remains at the right hand of the Father interceding for us in Heaven. Acts 7:55; **"But he, full of the Holy Spirit, gazed into heaven and saw the glory of God, and Jesus standing at the right hand of God."** God sent His Son to earth to die for the sins of human kind. John 3:16; **"For God so loved the world, that he gave his only Son, that whoever believes in him should not perish but have eternal life."** Jesus was the ultimate sacrifice for our sins. Isaiah 53:1-12; **"Who has believed what they heard from us? And to whom has the arm of the LORD been revealed? For he grew up before him like a young plant, and like a root out of dry ground; he had no form or majesty that we should look at him, and no beauty that we should desire him. He was despised and rejected by men; a man of sorrows, and acquainted with grief; and as one from whom men hide their faces he was despised, and we esteemed him not. Surely he has borne our grief and carried our sorrows; yet we esteemed him stricken, smitten by God, and afflicted. But he was wounded for our transgressions; he was crushed for our iniquities; upon him was the chastisement that brought us peace, and with his stripes we are healed. All we like sheep have gone astray; we have turned everyone to his own way; and the LORD has laid on him the iniquity of us all. He was oppressed, and he was afflicted, yet he opened not his mouth; like a lamb that is led to the slaughter, and like a sheep that before its shearers is silent, so he opened not his mouth. By oppression and judgment he was taken away; and as for his generation, who considered that he was cut off out of the land of the living, stricken for the transgression of my people? And they made his grave with the wicked and with a rich man in his death, although he had done no violence, and there was no deceit in his mouth. Yet it was the will of the LORD to crush him; he has put him to grief; when his soul makes an offering for sin, he shall see his offspring; he shall prolong his days; the will of the LORD shall prosper in his hand. Out of the anguish of his soul he shall see and be satisfied; by his knowledge shall the righteous one, my servant, make many to be accounted righteous, and he shall bear their iniquities. Therefore I will divide him a portion with the many,** and he shall divide the spoil with the strong, because he poured out his soul to death and was numbered with the transgressors; yet he bore the sin of many, and makes intercession for the transgressors." He was crucified on a cross and has risen from the grave. Mark 15:24-25; **"And they crucified him and divided his garments among them, casting lots for them, to decide what each should take. And it was the third hour when they crucified him."** Matthew 28:5-7; **"But the angel said to the women, "Do not be afraid, for I know that you seek Jesus who was crucified. He is not here, for he has risen, as he said. Come, see the place where he lay. Then go quickly and tell his disciples that he has risen from the dead, and behold, he is going before you to Galilee; there you will see him."** After His burial He experienced a glorious resurrection. We have conquered death, hell, and the grave through Jesus Christ our Lord and Savior. We have the promise that we're in the Lambs Book of Life and that we will live for eternity in Heaven if we follow Him.

So I ask this question; do you know Jesus? I mean do you really know Him? Think about that question. How well do you know Him? He made the ultimate sacrifice for you. He laid down His life and He died for you. What are you willing to sacrifice for Him?

Do you know God?

He wants to know you.

May 6th

Matthew 16:15-"But what about you?" He asked. "Who do you say that I am?"-NIV

Jesus desired to know who people thought He was. This is a crucial theological and relational truth. Who is Jesus? According to the infallible Word of God, Jesus is the Son of God and salvation comes through no other. Salvation cannot be attained through any other means other than accepting Jesus into your heart and life. John 14:6; **"Jesus said to him, "I am the way, and the truth, and the life. No one comes to the Father except through me."**

There isn't a second, a minute, an hour, a day, a month or a year that goes by up until my physical death that I won't want to draw closer and closer to my one and only Savior Jesus Christ. When my physical body is placed in a coffin I want to know Jesus and only Jesus. I want to leave a divine destiny to my children that I was sold out for Jesus Christ. I want to leave my children a Heavenly divine destiny. I want people to know that there was a man that loved Jesus Christ! The divine destiny that I want to leave my children to remember and reflect upon is this; "Dad was a man that loved Jesus, loved us and mom." He was committed to Jesus and his family.

When we stand before God, we should desire to be able to say to Jesus, "Jesus you're God and I accepted you as my Personal Lord and Savior." Jesus will in turn say to me, "Welcome to my Heavenly Kingdom." **"Come in thy good and faithful servant."**, as in Matthew 25:14-30 which is the parable of the master and the servant with the talents. I will then enter my reward. I will be at peace with my God and my fellow believers forever and ever in a place that was promised to me. Jesus has promised us that we will live in complete peace in His Heavenly dwelling.

What about you? Do you believe beyond a shadow of a doubt that Jesus is who He said He is? Do you really believe that Jesus is God? Do you believe that salvation comes through no other? Do you believe in heaven and hell? Do you believe that once you accept Jesus that you are then written in the Lambs Book of Life? Eternity is in the balance my friend, eternity! Let's not waiver in our beliefs people. Let's not doubt or allow the enemy to cause us to question the Lord Jesus Christ. He is who He said He is. He's God. Let's not let **The Waging War Within** infiltrate, penetrate and twist our belief in Jesus Christ. Remember, Satan is a crafty snake.

Satan is crafty. Beware of his ways!

May 7th

Matthew 16:16-"Simon Peter answered, "You are the Christ, the Son of the living God."-NIV

Belief is key. Faith and trust in God is the impetus in which all can say with their mouths and believe in their hearts that Jesus Christ is the Son of the living God. Romans 10:9-10; **"If you confess with your mouth that Jesus is Lord and believe in your heart that God raised him from the dead, you will be saved. For with the heart one believes and is justified, and with the mouth one confesses and is saved."** We're to believe with our hearts and to confess with our mouths that Jesus Christ is Lord. By believing and confessing, we're declaring that there is no other God under Heaven whereby man shall be saved. Acts 4:12; **"And there is salvation in no one else, for there is no other name under heaven given among men by which we must be saved."**

Who you believe Jesus is determines your salvation. If you believe that Jesus, as the Bible declares, is God and that salvation comes through Him then you're capable of living in right relationship with God. If you think something other than this you are unsaved, deceived or just plain ignorant of God's Word. God is clear in who He is. In fact you can't get any clearer.

My friends please remember this more than anything else I've written in this devotional, Jesus says in Romans 10:9-10 that if you confess with your mouth and believe in your heart that Jesus Christ is the Son of God and that He was raised from the dead for your justification and salvation then you will be saved. All you have to do is say the following and believe in faith;

Dear Jesus, I'm a sinner and I accept you as my Personal Lord and Savior. Come into my life and save my soul from the pit of hell so that I might enter your Heaven for eternity. Transform me, save me and rejuvenate me with the power of your Holy Spirit. I surrender my life to you and may your will be done in my life. May you give me the strength to follow you for the rest of my days here on Earth, with your perfect divine destiny being fulfilled in my life. In Jesus' name I pray. Amen.

Matthew 16:17-19-Jesus replied, "Blessed are you, Simon son of Jonah, for this was not revealed to you by man, but by my Father in Heaven. And I tell you that you are Peter, and on this rock I will build my church, and the gates of Hades will not overcome it. I will give you the keys of the kingdom of Heaven; whatever you bind on earth will be bound in Heaven, and whatever you loose on earth will be loosed in heaven."-NIV

This is a widely divisive section of Scripture. It has been interpreted in several ways. It does undoubtedly refer to Peter and the future of believers. Does it mean that Peter is above the others? Emphatically no! We see Peter sent out later by others. He is rebuked by Jesus, Paul, and he disappears from the Gospels later. He is not held higher than the others. They all had their jobs to do and they did them. When it speaks of building His church on this rock it speaks of the Word and the belief that Jesus was the Son of God, not Peter. There was no church back then, it was a synagogue. Jesus was predicting that He will build a community of believers who would follow Him. This "called out" community would soon become known as "the church," a separate community of believers, as described in the book of Acts. He was speaking of believers who would live by the example laid out for them by Him, not Peter.

Jesus is speaking of the war between Heaven and hell. Heaven and hell are two kingdoms, warring factions if you will. The keys of Heaven are given to those who believe and put their trust and faith is Jesus Christ. We have the power that is inherent within Jesus Christ. Jesus has given us all power and all authority in His name while we're here on earth. We have been given the keys by God to take rule and dominion here on earth. God has placed us here on earth to rule it, conquer it and subdue it with two divine destinies in mind. One is to lift up the name of Jesus and secondly to win souls to Christ. Isaiah 45:23; **"By myself I have sworn; from my mouth has gone out in righteousness a word that shall not return: To me every knee shall bow, every tongue shall swear allegiance."** Philippians 2:9-11; **"Therefore God has highly exalted him and bestowed on him the name that is above every name, so that at the name of Jesus every knee should bow, in heaven and on earth and under the earth, and every tongue confess that Jesus Christ is Lord, to the glory of God the Father."**

Jesus is the key to Heaven. Every lock has a key that will open it. Heaven's key is Jesus Christ. The only way to enter Heaven is to accept Jesus Christ as your Personal Lord and Savior. Jesus then will save you and give you the keys to conquer death, hell and the grave. The key is the Spirit of the Living God. The Holy Spirit will come upon you providing you with God's saving grace. This enabling of the Holy Spirit's power will save your soul from hell, allow you to enter the Kingdom of Heaven, and transform you, providing you continue to grow in God's grace. The keys of the Kingdom of Heaven will allow you to overcome death, hell and the grave with the supernatural working of God in your life. Just think of all we've been given in Jesus. We've been given it all. The question is what are we now going to do with this knowledge? What are we going to do with this truth? How are we going to live our lives while here on earth? The Word tells us what to do with our lives in the Great Commission in Matthew 28:19-20; **"Go therefore and make disciples of all nations, baptizing them in the name of the Father and of the Son and of the Holy Spirit, teaching them to observe all that I have commanded you."**

We stand on the Rock. The Rock is our fortress, our redeemer, our protector and our Savior. The Rock is Jesus Christ. The gates of hell no longer have dominion over us after we've accepted Jesus Christ. We've been delivered from hell. We still have to make a determined effort daily to put on the full armor of God to withstand the devil and His legion of demons. **Ephesians 6:10-18** tells us to put on the full **Armor of God**. In order to combat **The Waging War Within** we must be aware of Satan's schemes. This comes with the discernment that only God can give. John 10:2-5; **"But he who enters by the door is the shepherd of the sheep. To him the gatekeeper opens. The sheep hear his voice, and he calls his own sheep by name and leads them out. When he has brought out all his own, he goes before them, and the sheep follow him, for they know his voice. A stranger they will not follow, but they will flee from him, for they do not know the voice of strangers."** This discernment takes place when you allow the Holy Spirit to let you see things from His vantage point and not merely through our own limited viewpoint. Galatians 5:16-25; **"But I say, walk by the Spirit, and you will not gratify the desires of the flesh. For the desires of the flesh are against the Spirit, and the desires of the Spirit are against the flesh, for these are opposed to each other, to keep you from doing the things you want to do. But if you are led by the Spirit, you are not under the law. Now the works of the flesh are evident: sexual immorality, impurity, sensuality, idolatry, sorcery, enmity, strife, jealousy, fits of anger, rivalries, dissensions, divisions, envy, drunkenness, orgies, and things like these. I warn you, as I warned you before, that those who do such things will not inherit the kingdom of God. But the fruit of the Spirit is love, joy, peace, patience, kindness, goodness, faithfulness, gentleness, self-control; against such things there is no law. And those who belong to Christ Jesus have crucified the flesh with its passions and desires. If we live by the Spirit, let us also walk by the Spirit."** Do you recognize the voice of the Shepherd? Are you discerning His voice?

Listen to the
Shepherds voice.

May 9th

Matthew 16:20-Then He warned His disciples not to tell anyone that He was the Christ.-NIV

The reason Jesus said to tell no one that He was the Christ was that often times the people couldn't grasp the concept that He was the Messiah, the Son of God. Often His own disciples couldn't grasp the concept so He didn't expect the regular citizenry of catching on to who He truly was.

Jesus frequently warned His disciples when necessary, but did they accept His warnings? Do we accept His warnings today? God continues to warn us to protect us. Today, He tells us as His disciples to preach the Gospel in and out of season and to be witnesses to all men sharing the Good News of the Gospel of Christ. 2 Timothy 4:1-5; **"I charge you in the presence of God and of Christ Jesus, who is to judge the living and the dead, and by His appearing and His kingdom: preach the word; be ready in season and out of season; reprove, rebuke, and exhort, with complete patience and teaching. For the time is coming when people will not endure sound teaching, but having itching ears they will accumulate for themselves teachers to suit their own passions, and will turn away from listening to the truth and wander off into myths. As for you, always be sober-minded, endure suffering, do the work of an evangelist, fulfill your ministry."** Do we do this? Sadly enough, the answer is often times no. Did you notice that there were 9 verbs between verses 2 and 5? There are 9 verbs because the verse is stressing that it is imperative we carry out the order He gave us. If we don't pass the Word on to others, the Word will die with us.

I know that my life has changed dramatically since I have come to know Christ. I have found a peace that I have never known before. Granted, I still have challenges in my life, but I have a peace when I am confronted with obstacles that would have at a previous point been insurmountable. I have come to know the peace of God and I want for nothing more than to be able to pass that peace on to others. If I don't pass it on, I feel that I am both cheating others and God. It would mean to me that Jesus would have laid His life down for nothing. It would have been as if He would have been a sacrifice for no other reason than to have something to do. I can't live my life knowing He died for all and no one else would have the benefit of knowing Him.

If we respect the positional power of men, how much more should we respect Jesus and His position being seated at the right hand of the Father? We need to respect the warnings from our Heavenly Father as He protects us and guides us while we're still here on earth. When God tells us or warns us of something, we must heed His advice. He's only telling us to protect, to guide, to prosper, to bless and ultimately inform us so that we may prevail in this clear and present darkness.

May 10th

Matthew 16:21-From that time on Jesus began to explain to his disciples that he must go to Jerusalem and suffer many things at the hands of the elders, chief priests and teachers of the law, and that he must be killed and on the third day be raised to life.-NIV

Jesus knew of His mission and He was now gearing up to finish it. The words "from that time" mark the conclusion of Jesus' Galilean ministry and the beginning of his journey to Jerusalem to face His death on the cross. This is the first of four references in which Jesus predicts His arrest and ultimately His death. The other references are in Matthew v. 16:21; 17:22–23; 20:17–19; 26:2.

Jesus communicated with His disciples and explained to them the things He must undergo. The religious leaders of the time were on the brink of putting to death Jesus Christ. This was being completely controlled by God the Father. The Father planned that Jesus would die this kind of death. Jesus didn't want any of His disciples to be left in the dark about what must transpire. 1 John 5:13; **"I write these things to you who believe in the name of the Son of God that you may know that you have eternal life."** Jesus was raised from the dead so we to will be raised with Him to Heaven and experience eternity with Him. Today God is sitting at the right hand of the Father, interceding for His Church.

We need to be diligent with our calling and election. We need to be reliable, unwavering in our Christian walk, and firm in our belief. God has called us through His Gospel in order that we can know the truth in Him and pass it on to future generations of believers. 2 Thessalonians 2:14; **"To this he called you through our gospel, so that you may obtain the glory of our Lord Jesus Christ."** We have been chosen by God for this mission we are on. Ephesians 1:3-5; **"Blessed be the God and Father of our Lord Jesus Christ, who has blessed us in Christ with every spiritual blessing in the heavenly places, even as He chose us in Him before the foundation of the world, that we should be holy and blameless before Him. In love He predestined us for adoption through Jesus Christ, according to the purpose of His will."**

You have a purpose
in Christ!

May 11th

Matthew 16:33-Jesus turned and said to Peter, "Get behind me, Satan! You are a stumbling block to me; you do not have in mind the things of God, but the things of men."-NIV

Jesus made it clear regarding the differentiation of the business of God and the business of men. Jesus was able to draw the line in the sand and unequivocally make this distinction. In fact he went a step further and commanded Peter, "Get behind me, Satan!" Satan can get himself purposefully entangled within the things of men. Even when men are supposedly doing things in the name of God, Satan has a way of getting involved with his destructive schemes and strategies.

Satan will make men fall no matter who they are or what profession they're in. No matter how much power or money they have or what their family heritage is. Satan is a common foe to all people groups worldwide. God warns us of this frequently. Look at all of the so called mighty men of God who have fallen due to their allowing Satan to get a foothold in their lives. 1 Peter 5:8; **"Be sober-minded; be watchful. Your adversary the devil prowls around like a roaring lion, seeking someone to devour."**

What does it mean to have the things of God in your mind and not the things of men? This is an interesting point to ponder. God's ways are above our ways, Isaiah 55:8-9. How do we entertain the things of God within our mind? Getting into the Word of God would be a start. God longs to take hold of our heart and mind with His Word. God can protect us from the infiltration of Satan, if we absorb His Word allowing the Holy Spirit to take precedence in enlightening us. Are we willing to draw the line in the sand with both how the things of God and of men can impact our individual and families lives? Do we have the; commitment, devotion, willingness, relationship, fellowship, discernment and love for Christ that will allow us to draw this line in the sand?

Are you willing to follow Jesus no matter the cost? Are there people, things, issues or circumstances in your life right now that are coming in the way of you following Jesus? Luke 9:60, Matthew 8:22; **"Leave the dead to bury their own dead. But as for you, go and proclaim the kingdom of God."** Many things have to be done away with when you truly follow Jesus Christ. Mark 8:34, Luke 9:23; **"If anyone would come after me, let him deny himself and take up his cross daily and follow me."** He requires a true disciple to be focused, disciplined, and passionate toward the things of God and His Kingdom. There are sacrifices that will have to be made if we plan on following Jesus and living our lives for Him. There are certain habits which will have to be done away with. We may have certain things which we enjoy that may not be pleasing to God which we will have to forgo. Life is not always fun and games.

Are you guarding your mind from **The Waging War Within?** God requires that we have the mind of Christ. Philippians 2:5-11; **"Have this mind among yourselves, which is yours in Christ Jesus, who, though He was in the form of God, did not count equality with God a thing to be grasped, but made Himself nothing, taking the form of a servant, being born in the likeness of men. And being found in human form, He humbled himself by becoming obedient to the point of death, even death on a cross. Therefore God has highly exalted Him and bestowed on Him the name that is above every name, so that at the name of Jesus every knee should bow, in Heaven and on earth and under the earth, and every tongue confess that Jesus Christ is Lord, to the**

glory of God the Father." We have to be in God's Word, attending church and fellowshipping with the saints, we need to do supplemental readings in order to know more of God and His will, we need to attend Sunday School classes and we need to be in constant prayer. God might even lead us to get involved in specific ministries within the church that require our gifts, abilities and resources.

Let's look onward and upward toward the goals that God has set out for us in Jesus Christ. We need never to wallow in the past. Be reflective and learn from it, but move on, don't dwell on it. God would have put our eyes in the back of our heads if He had meant for us to walk backwards through life. The past is history, tomorrow is a mystery, so stay in today as it is enough for us to handle. When you bring up the past with God He says "What are you talking about?" You see, He has already forgiven us of our past. We are on a new path through life. It is a path with Him as our guide.

God has you on
a new path in your life.
Let Him
be your guide.

Matthew 16:24-28-Then Jesus said to his disciples, "If anyone would come after me, he must deny himself and take up his cross and follow me. For whoever wants to save his life will lose it, but whoever loses his life for me will find it. What good will it be for a man if he gains the whole world, yet forfeits his soul? Or what can a man give in exchange for his soul? For the Son of Man is going to come in his Father's glory with his angels, and then he will reward each person according to what he has done. I tell you the truth, some who are standing here will not taste death before they see the Son of man coming in his kingdom." -NIV

Time is short! The kingdom of God is at hand. God is conveying a sense of urgency. He is giving a wakeup call to His Church, His body of believers. How profound this passage is. In a world that is consumed with materialism and having more of everything, God says to turn from it and deny yourself. Let's face it, self is a pretty powerful entity. Thinking about our own self, if we're to be honest, takes up too much of our existence. What should I eat for breakfast, lunch or dinner? What activities should I involve myself in? What people should I associate with? What aspect of church should I participate in? It's not easy to think outside the box of **SELF!** We need to get over the self-hurdle if we are to be used to our full potential in His Kingdom. When we are consumed with self it shows in our ego, and what is ego? It is Edging God Out. Get it? Get rid of it. Our creator who has given us life is telling us to; give our lives away, to deny self-interest, to think about others first, to cling to God and take up His cross daily. Instead of finding ourselves, God wants us to focus on Him and to abandon our egos at the cross of Christ.

The bottom line and where the rubber meets the road is, "Are we living for Jesus?" Are we living life as if He could come back at any moment? Do we truly believe that He's coming back for His Church? Matthew 24:1-31; **"Jesus left the temple and was going away, when his disciples came to point out to him the buildings of the temple. But he answered them, "You see all these, do you not? Truly, I say to you, there will not be left here one stone upon another that will not be thrown down." As he sat on the Mount of Olives, the disciples came to him privately, saying, "Tell us, when will these things be, and what will be the sign of your coming and of the close of the age?" And Jesus answered them, "See that no one leads you astray. For many will come in my name, saying, 'I am the Christ,' and they will lead many astray. And you will hear of wars and rumors of wars. See that you are not alarmed, for this must take place, but the end is not yet. For nation will rise against nation, and kingdom against kingdom, and there will be famines and earthquakes in various places. All these are but the beginning of the birth pains. "Then they will deliver you up to tribulation and put you to death, and you will be hated by all nations for my name's sake. And then many will fall away and betray one another and hate one another. And many false prophets will arise and lead many astray. And because lawlessness will be increased, the love of many will grow cold. But the one who endures to the end will be saved. And this gospel of the kingdom will be proclaimed throughout the whole world as a testimony to all nations, and then the end will come. "So when you see the abomination of desolation spoken of by the prophet Daniel, standing in the holy place (let the reader understand), then let those who are in Judea flee to the mountains. Let the one who is on the housetop not go down to take what is in his house, and let the one who is in the field not turn back to** take his cloak. And alas for women who are pregnant and for those who are nursing infants in those days! Pray that your flight may not be in winter or on a Sabbath. For then there will be great tribulation, such as has not been from the beginning of the world until now, no, and never will be. And if those days had not been cut short, no human being would be saved. But for the sake of the elect those days will be cut short. Then if anyone says to you, 'Look, here is the Christ!' or 'There he is!' do not believe it. For false christs and false prophets will arise and perform great signs and wonders, so as to lead astray, if possible, even the elect. See, I have told you beforehand. So, if they say to you, 'Look, he is in the wilderness,' do not go out. If they say, 'Look, he is in the inner rooms,' do not believe it. For as the lightning comes from the east and shines as far as the west, so will be the coming of the Son of Man. Wherever the corpse is, there the vultures will gather. "Immediately after the tribulation of those days the sun will be darkened, and the moon will not give its light, and the stars will fall from heaven, and the powers of the heavens will be shaken. Then will appear in heaven the sign of the Son of Man, and then all the tribes of the earth will mourn, and they will see the Son of Man coming on the clouds of heaven with power and great glory. And he will send out his angels with a loud trumpet call, and they will gather his elect from the four winds, from one end of heaven to the other." Belief is a very important aspect of our Christian Faith. Have we lost ourselves in God's Word, allowing Him to take hold of us? Have we pushed ourselves out of the way allowing God to subdue us with the power of His Holy Spirit? The Holy Spirit is a gentlemen and He will never push Himself onto anyone. The Holy Spirit will move unto us and open up our lives to Him.

We live in a culture where the lies of Satan will tell us that we need to have; more of everything in order to be content, to feel worthwhile, to be accepted by others and to have a heightened sense of self-worth. Meanwhile, as we're chasing all of this materialism and living this illusion we're growing numb to the things above and to all of the blessings that God has surrounded us with. People have become programmed by the consumer culture in which we live. Buy me, have more, you need this, the newer model, out with the old in with the new. These expressions permeate the radio waves, the television, the magazines, the internet and the media. People have become discontent and on the proverbial course of gaining more tangible possessions to fill this void. God is warning us, that this doesn't satisfy the inner man's needs to fill the soul, only He can do this.

Let God fill the
Void in your life

May 13th

Matthew 17:1-2- After six days Jesus took with him Peter, James and John the brother of James, and led them up a high mountain by themselves. There he was transfigured before them. His face shone like the sun, and his clothes became as white as the light.-NIV

The supernatural power of God revealed! Wow! Fantastic! Unbelievable! We all are in need of a mountain top experience every now and again. Men and woman's retreats are times where we can climb that mountain to a spiritual high. As long as we grasp what God is revealing to our hearts on the mountaintop and carry it over into our daily lives, they serve their purpose. What a blessing. This however, wasn't just a mountaintop experience, this was God incarnate being transfigured, whereby His face and His clothes became radiant to a degree like no other. Talk about God's glory. Think of the looks on the faces of Peter, James and John as they looked at Jesus being transfigured. Astonishment, surprise, shock and awe and maybe even disbelief took them over. Something supernatural that could be seen with their natural eye was taking place before them. This was truly shock and awe at its finest hour.

The supernatural presence of God is awesomely spectacular. I don't know about you, but I desire Jesus to move within my life more than ever before. I desire this same supernatural power that transfigured Jesus to operate in my life on a daily basis. God has the power to fill us with this power and to gird up our heart and our mind with the things of God. I desire to be transfigured when Jesus returns. All I want is Jesus. If Jesus came today it would be just wonderful. Good bye. I'm ready to go with Him and meet Him in the air with all of His angels and the other saints. I will not allow **The Waging War Within** this temporal world culture to take hold of me, thus stamping out the working power of Jesus Christ within my life. I desire the light that was displayed here in the transfiguration of Jesus to be displayed, inculcated and absorbed in my own life and the life of my family. Nothing less will ever do. Nothing will do other than the supernatural working of God. Is it that way with you? It really ought to be.

I can only imagine the awesome rush of meeting Jesus face to face. Think about it all. You will be standing with The Creator. You can ask Him all the questions you couldn't find answers to when you were here on earth. You can ask Him anything and everything. Won't that be great? Just abide in Him and this too will come to pass.

Just believe!

May 14th

Matthew 17:5-8- While he was still speaking, a bright cloud enveloped them, and a voice from the cloud said, "This is my Son, whom I love; with him I am well pleased. Listen to him!" When the disciples heard this, they fell facedown to the ground, terrified. But Jesus came and touched them. "Get up," he said. "Don't be afraid." When they looked up, they saw no one except Jesus.-NIV

Not only was the transfiguration of Jesus something that could be seen, it was something that could be heard. Fear gripped them to the point where they attempted to hide instantly, dropping to the ground. In the midst of their fear, Jesus stepped in and communicated to them to calm the storm they were experiencing. God can calm any storm, at any time, in any place, of any magnitude and in an expedient manner.

When your focus is on Jesus, everything else grows dim. When Jesus becomes real to your heart, soul and mind, nothing in our temporal world can compare. Jesus was meant to fill that vacuum in our soul that nothing else but the Creator of the soul can fill. If you're not satisfied with your existence as a Christian, I have to question what you're filling the vacuum of your soul with. Is it materialism? Is it humanism? Is it work? Is it buying a larger house? Is it buying a better car, motorcycle or boat? Is it an airplane or helicopter? How about a mansion on a hill? How about increasing your stocks, bonds, or your bank accounts?

Maybe you should try Jesus. God Himself will fill your soul with something the world cannot give you if you would only call on Him. He will completely satisfy the desires of your heart. Become a spiritual man, not a man of this world. Give your life to the service of others. Give your life over to serving Jesus, feeding the hungry, clothing the needy and walking the earth as Jesus did. Let's hold fast to Jesus for His grace to make our marriages work, our relationships with our children grow, and our work ethic to bring forth fruit. Let us be a beacon of light in the workplace, our community and to those that don't know Jesus. Let's be the best we can be in Christ Jesus. Amen. Remember, Jesus said, "Fear not, I have overcome the world." John 16:33; **"I have said these things to you, that in me you may have peace. In the world you will have tribulation. But take heart; I have overcome the world."**

In any and all situations I want to see Jesus. I never want to lose focus of the One that saved me, brought me into His Kingdom and cultivated a blessed life within me. Praise God. To Him I give the glory and to no other. To Him and only Him I will live for and die in. I desire to live for Christ and die in Christ. I desire to be an over comer!

Be an overcomer

May 15th

Matthew 17:14-18- When they came to the crowd, a man approached Jesus and knelt before him. "Lord, have mercy on my son," he said. "He has seizures and is suffering greatly. He often falls into the fire or into the water. I brought him to your disciples, but they could not heal him."

"O unbelieving and perverse generation," Jesus replied, "how long shall I stay with you? Bring the boy here to me." Jesus rebuked the demon, and it came out of the boy, and he was healed from that moment. -**NIV**

Belief is a key. Faith is a key. However, belief and faith in Jesus are keys that will unlock all the supernatural power in God Himself. Do we realize the power that we have in Jesus Christ? John 14:12; **"Truly, truly, I say to you, whoever believes in me will also do the works that I do; and greater works than these will he do, because I am going to the Father."** We need to truly believe this. We should see a lot more healings, experiencing revival, witnessing deliverances and ultimately be walking in the power and blessings of God. All we should want to do as Christians is to have Jesus become more and more real to us. God longs to work through His people. Have you given your life over to God? Have you honestly surrendered? Or are you just going through the motions and playing out your Christianity before man?

If we walk in the power of God we will see miracle after miracle occur in our lives and the lives of others. Blessing after blessing will flow to us, within us and through us. We will be the anointed Christians that God is looking for. He's longing for a people whose heart beats after Him with no other idol taking precedence. Nothing but Jesus matters. We are to be relying on Jesus for everything to meet our needs. Think about it. Do you want to rely on the creature or the creator of the creature? Do you want to rely on the temporal or the eternal? Do you want to rely on a theoretical perspective or the truth? Do you want to rely on an idol or the Godhead in deity? Do you want to rely on what can only be seen or the unseen? If you have faith as a mustard seed you shall have more than enough. Matthew 17:20-21, Luke 17:6; **"For truly, I say to you, if you have faith like a grain of mustard seed, you will say to this mountain, 'Move from here to there,' and it will move, and nothing will be impossible for you."** Mulberry tree or mountain, semantics, the point is that we need to expand our faith.

In faith we as Christians should believe that upon acceptance of Him, we have all power, all things, all blessings and all the greatness of God. Acceptance of Jesus requires that we become less and that He becomes **EVERYTHING!** What road are you going to travel down? Are you going to be a lukewarm Christian, a Christian riding the fence or a Christian that is radically sold out to the things of God and one that is living in right relationship with Him? Decide this very moment. You cannot afford to vacillate.

May 16th

Matthew 17:19-20-Then the disciples came to Jesus in private and asked, "Why couldn't we drive it out?" He replied, "Because you have so little faith. I tell you the truth, if you have faith as small as a mustard seed, you can say to this mountain, 'Move from here to there' and it will move. Nothing will be impossible for you."-NIV

With faith in Jesus all things are possible. Nothing is impossible with God. He might choose to answer our prayer at times, and in ways, that aren't exactly how we had envisioned things going or coming to pass. When God's in control you can rest assured that everything will be done correctly. God has plans to prosper Christians.

We have to remember that all prayer is answered, just not necessarily the way we might want or in the timeframe we may want it to. God is our Father and like all good dads not everything we may want will He give to us. There may be things we desire that may not be good for us, or perhaps if we had it, it may pull us away from God or maybe it will harm us. God only wants what's best for us. Could you imagine what you would be like if you got everything you ever wanted? I know I would most likely be a spoiled brat and I probably wouldn't be walking with God right now, so I thank Him for not giving me everything I ever prayed for. We can rest assured that all prayer is answered, it is just that sometimes the answer is no. We need to have faith and trust in God.

With faith we can move mountains that seemingly linger in our way. Luke 17:6; **"If you had faith like a grain of mustard seed, you could say to this mulberry tree, 'Be uprooted and planted in the sea,' and it would obey you."** We can commit things to prayer and pray them through. It might not be as quickly at times as we would like it and other times it might be quicker than we expected. I wouldn't want to even exist on this present day planet without the precious faith I have in my Lord and Savior Jesus Christ. Colossians 1:13-14; **"He has delivered us from the domain of darkness and transferred us to the kingdom of his beloved Son, in whom we have redemption, the forgiveness of sins."** Acts 26:15-18; **"And I said, 'Who are you, Lord?' And the Lord said, 'I am Jesus whom you are persecuting. But rise and stand upon your feet, for I have appeared to you for this purpose, to appoint you as a servant and witness to the things in which you have seen me and to those in which I will appear to you, delivering you from your people and from the Gentiles— to whom I am sending you to open their eyes, so that they may turn from darkness to light and from the power of Satan to God, that they may receive forgiveness of sins and a place among those who are sanctified by faith in me.'"**

He delivered us from the clutches of the enemy and has saved us from death, hell and the grave. We have unlimited power in prayer. Nothing can defeat the Christians who commit themselves to prayer. Jesus has overcome every aspect of what this sin ridden world and Satan himself could throw at Him. Jesus prayed before every hardship He faced. He was in constant contact with God His Father. We need to follow His example.

With God we're no longer doing it alone or with the help of faltering men, we're living with the bright and wonderful expectation that God is working in our lives. He's doing His supernatural working power and making things that weren't come into full existence. He's blessing us in ways far above that which we could ever imagine.

Challenge yourself today, within your spiritual lives to lay it all down so that the divine destiny that God has for you can be made manifest within your very lives. Give everything you have to Jesus and move forward in Christ. Don't look back, to the right or the left, just straight ahead. Luke 9:62; **"No one who puts his hand to the plow and looks back is fit for the kingdom of God."**

Philippians 3:13-14; **"Brothers, I do not consider that I have made it my own. But one thing I do: forgetting what lies behind and straining forward to what lies ahead, I press on toward the goal for the prize of the upward call of God in Christ Jesus."** Give God all the hopes and dreams that you have. In Him you can rest assured that He has your back and your future too. He will answer you in His time and in His way. One thing is for sure, He will shower blessing after blessing into your life. You won't know how to contain all the blessings that God desires to give you. Your life will be overflowing with beautiful blessings from above that the world will never even know how to explain. Have faith friend! Hebrews 11:1; **"Now faith is the assurance of things hoped for, the conviction of things not seen."**

**Put all of your faith
and
all of your trust
in God.**

May 17th

Matthew 17:22-23- When they came together in Galilee, he said to them, "The Son of Man is going to be betrayed into the hands of men. They will kill him, and on the third day he will be raised to life." And the disciples were filled with grief.-NIV

Jesus informs His disciples that He is about to be betrayed. He had informed them earlier of His impending death, but here He gave them more information. They were deeply distressed by this new twist. They couldn't believe one of their own would betray any of them let alone Him.

We need to remember that man was born and he was born into sin. Romans 5:12; **"Therefore, just as sin came into the world through one man, and death through sin, and so death spread to all men because all sinned."** Man, apart from God, is a fallen creature. Ephesians 2:13; **"But now in Christ Jesus you who once were far off have been brought near by the blood of Christ."** Romans 6:6; **"We know that our old self was crucified with him in order that the body of sin might be brought to nothing, so that we would no longer be enslaved to sin."** Humankind separated from God is inundated with sin, sinful thoughts, sinful acts and a continual lust for more. The flesh cannot be conquered apart from the power of the Holy Spirit. God is the only surgeon on the earth that can make His creation whole. On acceptance of Jesus Christ man can be made whole as he or she gives them self over to the restoring power inherent within God.

Of course man in his sinful state was going to betray God. Man cannot begin to follow God without being empowered by the risen Christ. Man will never be able to follow God without the filling and indwelling power of Jesus Christ working in their lives. Christians are often attacked throughout the world just as Jesus Himself was attacked. This is because the Spirit of the Living God is within the Christian and the spirit of this world, the anti-christ spirit comes against us.

Remember that if you're not following God your father is Satan. Satan is nothing but a liar, a deceiver, a destroyer, an enemy, and a cold blooded killer. Satan can sometimes be blatant and sometimes subtle. It's very important to know your enemy. It's very important to know Satan's manipulative strategies to kill and destroy. In order to wage a war you must try to know and understand the tactics of your enemy. This is rule number one when it comes to combat and it is no different than the war we are fighting right here and now. We are in a war; don't kid yourself into believing any different. We may not be able to see our enemy with our physical eyes, but he is present none the less. The scheming devices of Satan have to be exposed by the power inherent within God. John 1:5; **"The light shines in the darkness, and the darkness has not overcome it."** John 3:20; **"For everyone who does wicked things hates the light and does not come to the light, lest his deeds should be exposed."** John 8:12; **"Again Jesus spoke to them, saying, "I am the light of the world. Whoever follows me will not walk in darkness, but will have the light of life.""** 1 Corinthians 4:5-6; **"Therefore do not pronounce judgment before the time, before the Lord comes, who will bring to light the things now hidden in darkness and will disclose the purposes of the heart."** The Holy Spirit can move in ways that we cannot.

We must always remember that our battle is not against flesh and blood; our battle is a war in the spiritual world. Ephesians 6:12; **"For we do not wrestle against flesh and blood, but against the rulers, against the authorities, against the cosmic powers over this present darkness, against the spiritual forces of evil in the heavenly places."** This kind of battle can only be won with much prayer, at times fasting and complete devotion to the Word of God. Our battle must never be fought within the physical world of carnality. It doesn't need to be carried out on this level. We have a relationship with the Creator of the universe, who will gladly fight the battle for us. In fact the major battle has already been won. One died for all on the Cross of Calvary. One shed His blood for the sins of the world. One died and rose again. Through the One, salvation was bought and paid for. Through the One, eternal life is begotten.

Our battle isn't
Against flesh and blood

May 18th

Matthew 18:1-4- At that time the disciples came to Jesus and asked, "Who is the greatest in the kingdom of heaven?" He called a little child and had him stand among them. And he said: "I tell you the truth, unless you change and become like little children, you will never enter the kingdom of heaven. Therefore whoever humbles himself like this child is the greatest in the kingdom of heaven."-NIV

Matthew 18:1; **"Who is the greatest in the kingdom of heaven?"** The disciples completely misunderstood what greatness meant. They mistook it in terms of human endeavor, accomplishment, and status. Jesus meant it in terms of humility and servant hood. The humility of a child consists of childlike trust, vulnerability, and the inability to advance his or her own agenda apart from the help, direction, and resources of a parent. Jesus was the ultimate example of humility. He was God in the flesh yet He was a servant to all.

James 4:10; **"Humble thy self in the sight of the Lord and He shall lift you up."** God works through the humble. He works through a humble heart. When one submits himself or herself to God, God moves mountains both spiritually and sometimes physically. God can both figuratively and literally move things in people's lives. From the addiction that needs to be overcome to the house that needs to be purchased, God provides and moves in people's lives.

There are some that don't know or understand the things of God. Look at little children and see how innocent and precious they are. People of the world say how uncorrupted children are. The world hasn't yet got a hold of them. God expects His children, no matter their age, to come to Him like little children, with a childlike faith. Matthew 19:14; **"Let the little children come to me and do not hinder them, for to such belongs the kingdom of heaven."** Luke 18:15-17; **"Now they were bringing even infants to him that he might touch them. And when the disciples saw it, they rebuked them. But Jesus called them to him, saying, "Let the children come to me, and do not hinder them, for to such belongs the kingdom of God. Truly, I say to you, whoever does not receive the kingdom of God like a child shall not enter it.""** We need a faith in which Christians can trust their Heavenly Father without hesitation and without compromise.

My children know that I take care of them and provide for them alongside with my wife. They know that they can trust us to take them across the busy, dangerous traffic of life, safely to the other side. They know that they can grab our hands and we will lead, direct and bring them to safety. If earthly man is capable of this, how much more is God? God is able to bring us safely through the complexities of life without being bruised, scathed, or scarred. Much depends on us. How are we living? Are we allowing sin to creep up on us? Are we submitting ourselves to ungodly lifestyles that are ruining and destroying our Christian testimonies and lives? If so, then we can never blame God for the pervasive and destructive forces that will prevail within our lives. God has warned us repeatedly throughout the Word of God, how to think and how to live.

As our children can rely on us, so to we can rely on our Heavenly Father all the more. He has us in the palm of His hands and is upholding us, never to let us fall. We will only fall if we make sinful choices and decisions that destroy our spiritual connection with the Father. Joshua 24:15; **"And if it is evil in your eyes to serve the LORD, choose this day whom you will serve, whether the gods your fathers served in the region beyond the River, or the gods of the Amorites in whose land you dwell. But as for me and my house, we will** serve the LORD." God or man, the choice is yours? Let's allow God to conquer **The Waging War Within.**

Humble yourself in the sight
of the Lord
and He
will lift you up

May 19th

Matthew 18:5,6- "And whoever welcomes a little child like this in my name welcomes me. But if anyone causes one of these little ones who believe in me to sin, it would be better for him to have a large millstone hung around his neck and to be drowned in the depths of the sea.-NIV

God paints a clear picture here of how much He values little children. God warns us that little children are to be treated with Godly respect and Godly care. He warns us of the punishment that will transpire to people who mistreat, neglect or abuse children. He uses the analogy of having a millstone tied around ones neck if they mistreat children. Children are a blessing from the Lord Jesus and are created by Him to carry out God's will and divine destiny here on earth. Children are part of God's divine destiny. The Creator looks with adoration upon His creation and we in turn should turn our hearts upon God crying out with praise, prayer, adoration for our loving Heavenly Father and the blessing that is ours in His son Jesus Christ.

We're God's children. Upon acceptance of Jesus Christ, He made us His children. Do we realize every waking moment that we're the King's kids? Do we realize every beat of our heart what we have in Christ Jesus? Do we know with every breath that we take what God has done for us in Christ Jesus? If we have absorbed and digested these truths, then what are we doing with it? Are we still living as we once did in the drudgery of our daily existence, or are we living renewed in our minds and our hearts with a transformational power that has never been seen before? Romans 12:1-2, **"I appeal to you therefore, brothers, by the mercies of God, to present your bodies as a living sacrifice, holy and acceptable to God, which is your spiritual worship. Do not be conformed to this world, but be transformed by the renewal of your mind, that by testing you may discern what is the will of God, what is good and acceptable and perfect."**

God desires to protect His children from the things within the world; the ungodly, Satan and his demonic kingdom. Nothing can come between the believer and God unless we allow it. If we continue to live to please our sinful nature then we will reap total destruction. If we live to please the spirit man within us we will live a life full of blessing from above. We don't want to gratify the earthly carnal desires of the flesh. Let's watch what we say, what we do, what we think and how we live. Let's never curse others, but bless others. Let's live to bring out the best in ourselves and the best in others.

Be the best you can possibly be.

Do it for God.

Matthew 18:7-9- "Woe to the world because of the things that cause people to sin! Such things must come, but woe to the man through whom they come! If your hand or your foot causes you to sin, cut it off and throw it away. It is better for you to enter life maimed or crippled than to have two hands or two feet and be thrown into eternal fire. And if your eye causes you to sin, gouge it out and throw it away. It is better for you to enter life with one eye than to have two eyes and be thrown into the fire of hell.-NIV

God speaks of sin and hell and the importance of avoiding both. We can always turn to God for forgiveness when we fail and fall short. God does warn us of sin and it is very clear that it carries negative consequences. We must ask God to enlighten our spiritual eyes to the negative consequences associated with sin. Sin is a destructive force and will eventually kill our spiritual life if we continually engage in things that are contrary to God's Word.

God warns of how deadly sin is for our spiritual lives. God is making a statement of how important it is to focus on the eternal rather than the temporal. Philippians 2:12; **"Therefore, my beloved, as you have always obeyed, so now, not only as in my presence but much more in my absence, work out your own salvation with fear and trembling."** Sin is a destructive entity that can become all-consuming and pervasive, even to the point of causing someone premature death.

People today have difficulty believing or acknowledging that there exits an eternal hell. Hell isn't even really preached from the pulpit today. Many pastors, evangelists and teachers avoid speaking of hell for many different reasons. A sinful and wayward life can ultimately lead one to live in Hell for eternity. Romans 6:23; **"For the wages of sin is death, but the free gift of God is eternal life in Christ Jesus our Lord."** This is why it's so important to accept Jesus Christ as your personal Lord and Savior. Our lives should be living examples of God's saving, changing and enlightening power. Titus 2:11-14; **"For the grace of God has appeared, bringing salvation for all people, training us to renounce ungodliness and worldly passions, and to live self-controlled, upright, and godly lives in the present age, waiting for our blessed hope, the appearing of the glory of our great God and Savior Jesus Christ, who gave himself for us to redeem us from all lawlessness and to purify for himself a people for his own possession who are zealous for good works."** People should be able to look at us and through what they see acknowledge that we're living differently. We should not be living as the world at all. Remember, God sees and hears all.

Remember,
God sees and hears all.

May 21st

Matthew 18:10,11- "See that you do not look down on one of these little ones. For I tell you that their angels in heaven always see the face of my Father in heaven.- NIV

Our Heavenly Father uses angels to care for his children. Hebrews 1:14; "Are they not all ministering spirits sent out to serve for the sake of those who are to inherit salvation?" The terms **"their angels"** does not imply that each disciple has one assigned "guardian angel" though. There are angels all around us. These angels do, however, have continuous and open communication with God.

God has angelic beings that protect His children. These angels are able to see the face of our Heavenly Father. We're considered God's children. God promises to take care of us, clothing us, feeding us, sheltering us and ultimately providing for us in every way, shape and form. Philippians 4:19; **"And my God will supply every need of yours according to his riches in glory in Christ Jesus."** If we, as mere humans, can show children love and care, how much more does God show us, His children? His love and care are demonstrated through the sacrifice of His Son. He longs to shower us with blessing after blessing. Remember, all good things come from God. James 1:17; **"Every good gift and every perfect gift is from above, coming down from the Father of lights with whom there is no variation or shadow due to change."**

Blessed comes from the Latin term *"beatus" which means* "blessed, or happy". More than a temporary or circumstantial feeling of happiness, blessed infers a state of well-being in relationship to God that belongs to those who respond to Jesus' ministry. The poor in spirit are those who recognize they are in need of God's help. When Jesus spoke of theirs being the kingdom of heaven, He meant those who were broken before Him and those who confessed their spiritual bankruptcy. We today still have that opportunity to confess our sins and the ability to ask Him for forgiveness.

James 1:12; **"Blessed is the man who remains steadfast under trial, for when he has stood the test he will receive the crown of life, which God has promised to those who love him."** The crown of life refers not to the jewel encrusted ruler's crown but to the laurel wreath given to winners in athletic games and victorious emperors. 1 Corinthians 9:25; **"Every athlete exercises self-control in all things. They do it to receive a perishable wreath, but we an imperishable."** The reward for faithful perseverance is eternal life, with all its abundant blessings. We can enjoy eternity with God.

Enjoy eternity with God.

May 22nd

Matthew 18:12-14- "What do you think? If a man owns a hundred sheep, and one of them wanders away, will he not leave the ninety-nine on the hills and go to look for the one that wandered off? And if he finds it, I tell you the truth, he is happier about that one sheep than about the ninety-nine that did not wander off. In the same way your Father in heaven is not willing that any of these little ones should be lost.- NIV

People are often referred in the Bible as sheep. The references are both for the lost unbeliever and the believer. The above verses are a reference to a believer who lost his way and strayed from the path of Jesus and was found by Him once again. This is a time for celebration in the realm of Heaven.

God rejoices when one soul is saved and brought into His Kingdom. Luke 15:7; **"I tell you, there will be more joy in heaven over one sinner who repents than over ninety-nine righteous persons who need no repentance."** Luke 15:10; **"I tell you, there is joy before the angels of God over one sinner who repents."** Let's never forget this. If we pray, God will use everything at His disposal to bring a soul into His Kingdom. Everything is at God's disposal. Let's never doubt the power of God to act when we pray. It's not whether or not He hears our prayers. God always hears our prayers. We must never lose heart, never lose faith and we must always believe that God is working on our behalf. The same God that hears, sees, and knows all, will act upon our prayers as He sees fit.

God will go after what man cannot see. God will save what man cannot save. God's ways are above our ways. Isaiah 55:8-9; **"For my thoughts are not your thoughts, neither are your ways my ways, declares the LORD. For as the heavens are higher than the earth, so are my ways higher than your ways and my thoughts than your thoughts."** Man will always have just a glimmer of the power inherent within God but he will never know the fullness of God because our mind cannot grasp the entirety of Him. God doesn't want one to perish, but all to have ever lasting life. 2 Peter 3:9; **"The Lord is not slow to fulfill his promise as some count slowness, but is patient toward you, not wishing that any should perish, but that all should reach repentance."**

God will seek out
the lost at any
cost

Matthew 18:15-17- "If your brother sins against you, go and show him his fault, just between the two of you. If he listens to you, you have won your brother over. But if he will not listen, take one or two others along, so that 'every matter may be established by the testimony of two or three witnesses.' If he refuses to listen to them, tell it to the church; and if he refuses to listen even to the church, treat him as you would a pagan or a tax collector."-NIV

Go and tell him his fault, between you and him alone. If a matter can be settled without getting others involved, do it. If you keep it quiet that will keep rumors and misunderstandings from getting blown up and out of proportion. Proverbs 25:9; **"Argue your case with your neighbor himself, and do not reveal another's secret."** The ultimate objective is the restoration of the offending brother or sister to the fold.

Now if one chooses not to listen and repent with the one who was offended then you are to bring one or two others with you. This follows the guideline laid out in Deuteronomy 19. Deuteronomy 19:15; **"A single witness shall not suffice against a person for any crime or for any wrong in connection with any offense that he has committed. Only on the evidence of two witnesses or of three witnesses shall a charge be established."** This refers to witnesses of the second confrontation described in this verse, not necessarily eyewitnesses to the original offense mentioned in the previous verse.

If the original offender will not repent even after the matter has been brought before the entire congregation, then he or she is to be removed from the fellowship and be treated as an unbeliever. This is not to hurt the offender, it is done in order to have them think on their offense and hopefully repent of it. Gentiles and tax collectors are described as people who were deliberately being rebellious against God.

Conflict and confrontation even within the church is going to be a natural part of life. We are all in need of a savior no matter how many years we've been following the Lord and no matter what position or title we have. Let's face it; human beings are prone to have problems with other human beings. God knew this and this is why He laid out a plan for us within the church when difficulties arise between brothers and sisters in Christ.

We need to always blanket things with prayer. What we cannot conquer, God sure can with the power of His Holy Spirit operating in our lives. God longs for people to live in unity, in love, and in fellowship with each other and especially with Him.

Blanket things with prayer

May 24th

Matthew 18:18- "I tell you the truth, whatever you bind on earth will be bound in heaven, and whatever you loose on earth will be loosed in heaven."-NIV

Peter's foundational authority which was granted to him in Matthew 16 is extended to the entire community of disciples, giving them the authority to declare the terms under which God forgives or refuses to forgive the sin of wayward disciples. Matthew 16:19; **"I will give you the keys of the kingdom of heaven, and whatever you bind on earth shall be bound in heaven, and whatever you loose on earth shall be loosed in heaven."** Peter is given the authority to admit entrance into the Kingdom through preaching the Gospel, an authority that is subsequently granted to all who are called to preach and proclaim the Good News. This is what happens when you are operating within the parameters of which God has laid out for us.

We need to know that God is operating in our affairs here on earth. God sees everything here on our planet from His Throne. Prayer is the direct, immediate way we can communicate and access God. Picking up and dialing a phone, cell phone, a text or email messaging device allows us to communicate quickly, bridging the gap between space and time. How much more powerful and immediate is our communication with our living Heavenly Father. We're bound to get a crystal clear connection every time from His end. Let's be sure that our connection to Him continuously has service, unlike the times when we deal with frustration with technology when we are denied phone access in rural areas. God never hangs up or screens His calls as people often do.

We have no problem believing that these technological devices will do what's expected of them, however sometimes we lack the faith to believe that God will act upon our communication with Him. The truth of the matter is that this is because human beings often rely on their five senses as opposed to their faith in God. Americans especially have an easier time believing in something that is tangible than something that is intangible. This is why faith is a key in our communication with God. What we ask for we will receive from God. The timing and the manner in which we think God might provide could be vastly different than the way we think He will provide. God has this prerogative, after all He is God.

Faith is the key

May 25th

Matthew 18:19,20- "Again, I tell you that if two of you on earth agree about anything you ask for, it will be done for you by my Father in heaven. For where two or three come together in my name, there am I with them."-NIV

Imagine the awesome power of God. Christians may not be receiving answers to their prayers the way they want them answered because they're not asking in detail. God loves specifics. He longs to pour out His blessings of a spiritual, relational, financial, physical and material kind. God is the great provider. All things are possible with God. God blesses those that follow after Him, seek Him, and ultimately give their lives to Him as a living sacrificial offering.

When two or three believers are gathered in His name, He is in their midst. Jesus affirms that He will be divinely present among His believers as they seek Him in their decision making. Jesus has given His word that He will answer our call to Him which reiterates His ability to be omnipotent and it also affirms His deity.

It should be of great comfort to us to know that God is with us and desires to have a close and personal relationship with us. God is also showing us in His Word that there is power in numbers. When we come together in corporate worship there is a power that is present, and that power is the Holy Spirit. A unity in the bond between the Holy Spirit, God the Father and Jesus His Son, accomplishes things that cannot begin to be divined through our mortal minds. When we pray and worship together we usher in the Holy Spirit and things begin to happen. When Christians display a unity and love for each other in prayer, worship, and fellowship God will respond. God created believers for fellowship both with each other and with Him. He longs to fellowship with us so that we can draw to Him and He to us.

Where my people gather in my name, I am in their midst

Matthew 18:21-22- Then Peter came to Jesus and asked, "Lord, how many times shall I forgive my brother when he sins against me? Up to seven times?" Jesus answered, "I tell you, not seven times, but seventy-seven times.-NIV

Forgiving someone three times was sufficient in the practice of Judaism. Job 33:29-30, Amos 1:3, 2:6 demonstrate this. Peter thought he was demonstrating great generosity with seven times as a response. A true believer in Christ is one who will repeatedly forgive, hence the seventy times seven. This is a reversal of Genesis 4:24 where Lamech was boasting of revenge. Genesis 4:24; **"If Cain's revenge is sevenfold, then Lamech's is seventy-sevenfold."** This also ties in with the teaching of Matthew 5:39. Matthew 5:39; **"But I say to you, Do not resist the one who is evil. But if anyone slaps you on the right cheek, turn to him the other also."**

God forgave us and we in turn should always forgive our brothers and sisters when we're wronged. We can enter the very portals of Heaven, experiencing the forgiveness that God has freely given, if we have a penitent heart. If we're allowing God to flow into our lives, we should be able to have a surplus of forgiveness for our brothers and sisters in the Lord when they have accidently wronged us.

Let's not be surprised as Christians that God expects us to forgive others completely. We should never carry a grudge, or harbor bitterness toward another believer in Jesus Christ. If we do, we should always go to the other we're in conflict with and make an attempt at amends. We should always ask for forgiveness if we have wronged another.

Now as for revenge, God has also made it clear that we are not to go out seeking vengeance. Deuteronomy 32:35-36; **"Vengeance is mine, and recompense, for the time when their foot shall slip; for the day of their calamity is at hand, and their doom comes swiftly.' For the LORD will vindicate his people and have compassion on his servants, when he sees that their power is gone and there is none remaining, bond or free."** Hebrews 10:30; **"For we know him who said, "Vengeance is mine; I will repay." And again, "The Lord will judge his people.""** And again in Romans 12:19; **"Beloved, never avenge yourselves, but leave it to the wrath of God, for it is written, "Vengeance is mine, I will repay, says the Lord.""** As you can all see, we don't have to worry about getting even with anyone because God has our back.

Don't worry, God has your back

May 27th

Matthew 18:23-25- "Therefore, the kingdom of heaven is like a king who wanted to settle accounts with his servants. As he began the settlement, a man who owed him ten thousand talents was brought to him.
Since he was not able to pay, the master ordered that he and his wife and his children and all that he had be sold to repay the debt.-NIV

Here we have Jesus instructing His disciples as to the kind of community life that will be used to characterize their relationships with one another and with the world as a whole. We all need to be able to commune and worship together with one another. We need to know that we can count on one another to meet the needs of the community.

A talent, when referred to in the Bible as a monetary unit, was valued at approximately 20 years' worth of wages, roughly $600,000.00. This would equate to roughly 6 billion dollars in today's dollar system. This was a great deal of money owed to the king. It was a common practice to sell the families of someone who owed a debt and could not pay it back. It was often used as a form of punishment to the debtor.

Grace sometimes happens with man, but always happens with God. 2 Corinthians 12:9; **"But he said to me, "My grace is sufficient for you, for my power is made perfect in weakness." Therefore I will boast all the more gladly of my weaknesses, so that the power of Christ may rest upon me."** God's grace is sufficient and abundant in nature. God's very nature is to give. He gave His own Son for our sins. Colossians 1:13-14; **"He has delivered us from the domain of darkness and transferred us to the kingdom of his beloved Son, in whom we have redemption, the forgiveness of sins."** His sacrificial offering has allowed us to live life with a divine destiny in our lives empowered from above. John 10:10; **"The thief comes only to steal and kill and destroy. I came that they may have life and have it abundantly."**

We have been redeemed in Jesus Christ. Redemption is deliverance or liberation, emphasizing that believers have been delivered and have received forgiveness of their sins. Jesus' promise of abundant life, which begins in the here and now, brings to mind Old Testament prophesies about abundant blessings. (Ezek. 34:12-15, 25-31). Jesus calls His followers, not to a dour, lifeless, miserable existence that squashes human potential, but to a rich, full, joyful life, one overflowing with meaningful activities under the personal favor and blessing of God and in continual fellowship with His people.

God's grace
is sufficient for me

May 28th

Matthew 18:26, 27- "The servant fell on his knees before him. 'Be patient with me,' he begged, 'and I will pay back everything.' The servant's master took pity on him, canceled the debt and let him go.-NIV

The amount of the man's debt would amount to over 6 billion dollars in today's monetary system. This is an astronomical amount in anyone's time. If man can show pity on others, how much more can God display His grace and mercy towards mankind?

Let's draw nigh to God, so He can show us what He longs to do in our lives. He desires to bless us abundantly. If God can forgive mankind for all the wrongs they have committed with the execution of His Son, how much more is He willing to forgive us?

We need to examine our hearts. Do you harbor ill will? Think hard and be honest with yourself. Now think of how insignificant that wrong was when you measure it with what was done to Jesus, when He did nothing to deserve the treatment that was shown Him. It seems pretty measly doesn't it? How is it that we can't forgive someone when they call us names, talk behind our backs, spread a false rumor, whatever the case may be, when God forgave those who killed His Son? We need to reexamine our hearts my friends. I have been guilty myself when I speak of these things.

Let's clean the slate. People often hurt others and they forget all about it shortly after the wrong is committed. I have talked to people who have wronged me from my past and they honestly can't even remember the act whereas I kept the feelings inside me for several years and carried them over to my adulthood. Silly isn't it? We have to forgive the past in order to progress on into our future.

Matthew 7:2; **"For with the judgment you pronounce you will be judged, and with the measure you use it will be measured to you."** Pretty serious stuff when you think about it isn't it. Measure your heart my friends. If you walk around harboring ill will towards others you are wasting a lot of time and effort you can be using in your walk for God.

Examine your heart

May 29th

Matthew 18:28- **"But when that servant went out, he found one of his fellow servants who owed him a hundred denarii. He grabbed him and began to choke him. 'Pay back what you owe me!' he demanded.-NIV**

This is typical of so many people. It is human nature to want forgiveness of something yet the same one who was forgiven doesn't extend the same forgiveness. This man had an insurmountable debt forgiven him and yet he will not forgive a debt that is mere pennies compared to what he owed the other king. This man's debt equals about 12 thousand dollars today. The same servant that was given pity from a multi-billion dollar debt went out and didn't have pity on another servant that owed him far less. He began to choke him for his money. This shows the evilness in a man's heart.

Man is a strange animal isn't he? Greed is an evil that has led to tremendous pain in so many ways. False prophets are spoken of in 2 Peter 2:3; **"And in their greed they will exploit you with false words."** Greed of money is spoken of in 1 Timothy 6:10; **"For the love of money is a root of all kinds of evils. It is through this craving that some have wandered away from the faith and pierced themselves with many pangs."** Greed in any form is wrong. Matthew 6:24; **"No one can serve two masters, for either he will hate the one and love the other, or he will be devoted to the one and despise the other. You cannot serve God and money."** You cannot worship God and money, or whatever else it is you crave, you must choose which one you will serve. Ephesians 5:3; **"But sexual immorality and all impurity or covetousness must not even be named among you, as is proper among saints."** Greed is something we can ill afford.

If you are in constant want of something, your focus is pulled away from God and semi-focused on an object of your affections. God wants your full attention, nothing less. He is a jealous God. As one reads through the major prophets of the Old Testament we see that God is jealous. He is intolerant of rivalry or unfaithfulness. When it comes to our relationship to Him, He does not desire to share the worship of His people with anyone or anything else. He must be preeminent or first in every part of our lives. Exodus 34:12-17; **"Take care, lest you make a covenant with the inhabitants of the land to which you go, lest it become a snare in your midst. You shall tear down their altars and break their pillars and cut down their Asherim (for you shall worship no other god, for the LORD, whose name is Jealous, is a jealous God), lest you make a covenant with the inhabitants of the land, and when they whore after their gods and sacrifice to their gods and you are invited, you eat of his sacrifice, and you take of their daughters for your sons, and their daughters whore after their gods and make your sons whore after their gods. You shall not make for yourself any gods of cast metal."**

Matthew 18:29-31- "His fellow servant fell to his knees and begged him, 'Be patient with me, and I will pay you back.' "But he refused. Instead, he went off and had the man thrown into prison until he could pay the debt. When the other servants saw what had happened, they were greatly distressed and went and told their master everything that had happened."-NIV

Remember that we said that he owed about $12,000 in today's money. This was still a large amount, but compared to the debt that the wicked servant himself owed, roughly $6 billion, it's really a relatively small amount. The servant's unwillingness to forgive even this amount, though having been forgiven his own massive debt, revealed his lack of character and that he had not in fact been transformed by the forgiveness that his master had extended and shown toward him.

True mercy doesn't happen much among people. Look around you even today with the litigious society we live in. Everyone seems to be suing each other today. People sue when they feel they've been wronged and some even when they are the one clearly in the wrong. Some are out there trying to look for someone to sue so that they won't have to work to make a living. People are suing as a full time job.

1 Timothy 6:10; **"For the love of money is a root of all kinds of evils. It is through this craving that some have wandered away from the faith and pierced themselves with many pangs."** Money can't buy happiness. I know you have heard this before. Look at all the people who have a great deal of money and what do you see? There are few who are not concerned with where they will be getting their next dollar. I have known literal billionaires and several millionaires and every one of them are majorly concerned with where their money is in the market. They don't have fun with their money, they are a slave to it. Look at all of the people who have hit the lotto big, the vast majority of them will say that they regret hitting big. They are miserable.

God is the one who will supply our needs, not the almighty dollar. Philippians 4:19; **"And my God will supply every need of yours according to his riches in glory in Christ Jesus."** God and Jesus Christ are the only ones I need. They will take care of me when I have a need. With them in my corner, I don't need anything else. They are my provider and the Ones I seek when in need of anything.

God will provide

May 31st

Matthew 18:32-34- "Then the master called the servant in. "You wicked servant,' he said, 'I canceled all that debt of yours because you begged me to. Shouldn't you have had mercy on your fellow servant just as I had on you?' In anger his master turned him over to the jailers to be tortured, until he should pay back all he owed.-NIV

The reference of being turned over to the jailers is a metaphorical reference to eternal punishment. This is a warning to us that we are to forgive as we have been forgiven. If you harbor anger in your heart, it will destroy you eventually.

Once you allow anger into your life, forget it. Anger just makes a mess of things all the more. When people are angry they do things and say things that they wouldn't do normally. God says in His Word that anger resides in the lap of a fool. Ecclesiastes 7:9; **"Be not quick in your spirit to become angry, for anger lodges in the bosom of fools."** Anger changes even the chemistry of the brain and body. The heart can start to beat faster and the endorphins pumping throughout our body increase exponentially. Physiological changes result when one gets angry. The words start flying and everything is magnified and intensified.

There are times when we get angry and the cause is vanity and pride. We all want to look good in front of people and if someone snubs us or makes a joke at our expense we get angry. This is a natural response. In the case of the wicked servant being ugly to the one who owed him money and the response he showed him, the lack of compassion, this was wrong. When it came to the master after the other servants briefed him on the actions of the one, he had justifiable anger after he erased the debt of the one. Anger is an emotion and they are not wrong, it is how we handle them that distinguish them from being right or wrong. We cannot be trying to justify a wrong response and try to place the blame for our poor actions on another either.

Have you forgiven
as you have been forgiven?

JUNE

June 1st

Matthew 18:35- "This is how my heavenly Father will treat each of you unless you forgive your brother from your heart."-NIV

A transformed heart has to result in a changed life. It can't help but change a life. With this change comes a displaying of mercy and forgiveness, just as we have been shown by God. God understands our sufferings and He longs to have us be an integral part of His life. He has shown us great mercy and forgiveness, the same as He did the Jewish children when they were in exile in Babylon. Isaiah 40:2; **"Speak tenderly to Jerusalem, and cry to her that her warfare is ended, that her iniquity is pardoned, that she has received from the LORD's hand double for all her sins."** Someone who does not grant forgiveness to others shows that his own heart has not experienced God's forgiveness. Throughout Scripture, the heart refers to the center of one's being, their core, including one's reasoning, their emotions, and their will.

God has required us to forgive our brothers and sisters. He warns that unless we forgive each other that He will treat us the same. It's of the utmost importance that we learn to forgive and make this a priority in our lives. God first forgave us, so we in turn should forgive others that have wronged us in some way.

Forgiveness is a conscious decision that we have to make as it relates to the lives of others. With forgiveness we can build a bridge toward others and break down the walls that bolster spiritual shackles and chains. The best way to allow forgiveness to flow in our hearts is to always keep in mind what God has done for us in giving Jesus Christ and to live in a state of constant repentance before God.

We have to display the same grace that God has shown to us. There is not a "should" mentioned, it is a must. You know that turn the other cheek thing? God meant that.

Forgive, as I have forgiven you. (God)

June 2nd

Matthew 19:1,2- When Jesus had finished saying these things, he left Galilee and went into the region of Judea to the other side of the Jordan. Large crowds followed him, and he healed them there.-NIV

Jesus' fame was growing all over the region. One reason was the healings that He was performing. When someone sees a person day after day and they are either sick or infirmed in some way and then all of a sudden they are healed by a touch, the word gets around. Jesus was healing the people who were societal outcasts, the lepers, the lame, people with blood issues, etc… He was raising the dead. He was the real deal. The healings were witnessed by many and they were irrefutable.

Jesus Christ has a huge church body all around the globe. The Church of Jesus Christ is a people from all over the world, all different cultures, ethnic groups, languages and traditions. As in the past, even today God longs to save everyone. This results in people worldwide hearing of and responding to Jesus.

From the television evangelist to large mega churches, to large sports stadiums packed with people, to the fields in Africa where thousands of people gather to praise Jesus Christ and have services, people are worshipping God. When we hear of and respond to the call of Jesus, the angels rejoice. Luke 15:7; **"I tell you, there will be more joy in heaven over one sinner who repents than over ninety-nine righteous persons who need no repentance."** Large crowds are still following and being led to the Lord Jesus Christ and the angels are partying hearty in Heaven.

It's not uncommon in Africa for people to walk miles to get to the place where they have church. They are worshiping, praising and honoring Jesus Christ. Thousands of people will meet together seeking God. Sometimes they stand praising, worshiping, and praying to God for hours and hours. I have been told that the movement of the Holy Spirit is powerful. People are literally crying out to God seeking Him and all He has for us.

It's hard for Americans to imagine this kind of gathering, because for the most part it doesn't typically happen in our culture. We travel by car once or twice a week to our local community church where we gather together. We typically sit near the same people in the same pew week after week. We can turn to the left, the right, look in front of us and back of us and basically know everyone. The important thing is that God is still leading large crowds of people from all over the world to Himself.

Seek God and all
that He has for you

June 3rd

Matthew 19:3-6- Some Pharisees came to him to test him. They asked, "Is it lawful for a man to divorce his wife for any and every reason?" "Haven't you read," he replied, "that at the beginning the Creator 'made them male and female,' and said, 'For this reason a man will leave his father and mother and be united to his wife, and the two will become one flesh'? So they are no longer two, but one. Therefore what God had joined together, let man not separate."-NIV

God obviously takes unity in marriage seriously. God's perspective on marriage is the opposite of the philosophy that is being propagated in the world today. Marriage is an institution created by God. He actually unites the male and the female making them one flesh. The two shall become one in marriage. In marriage, despite the fact of having two separate individuals, the two individuals have become one. All kinds of philosophies and ideologies are present today that go against and counter to God's created institution of marriage.

God is very clear about marriage. It is a covenant, a promise, a pact, made with God and each other regarding the unity of the two individuals making them one. The only things that are acceptable in breaking this covenant are infidelity, abandonment, or death. Genesis 19: 4-8; It is man that separates and divides, not God. God desires people to live in unity and love. Mankind and Satan love to conquer and divide. These two forces are at odds with God and rebellious toward Him. Once Satan can destroy the family, He can dominate and control the culture. Once Satan dominates and controls anything, He ultimately will destroy the fabric of our society. All hell will break loose forging a satanic attack on God's institution, the family. America could wind up like another Sodom and Gomorra. Genesis 19:24-25; **"Then the LORD rained on Sodom and Gomorrah sulfur and fire from the LORD out of heaven. And he overthrew those cities, and all the valley, and all the inhabitants of the cities, and what grew on the ground."** If this eventually becomes the case, American families better be on guard.

We need to protect our families and beliefs with every fiber of our being. Satan and his minions are sneaky and they will stop at nothing to destroy our familial unity and serenity. We must be on guard. We can stand on the Word of God and use it to fight the wily ways of the evil one. You can't use it if you don't know it though. We need to read and heed the Word in order for it to work.

The Creator made them male and female

June 4th

Matthew 19:7-9- **"Why then," they asked, "did Moses command that a man give his wife a certificate of divorce and send her away?" Jesus replied, "Moses permitted you to divorce your wives because your hearts were hard. But it was not this way from the beginning. I tell you that anyone who divorces his wife, except for marital unfaithfulness, and marries another woman commits adultery."-NIV**

The Pharisees had asked why Moses commanded divorce, but Jesus corrected them, showing that divorce is not what God intended from the beginning, and that even when it is allowed, it is permitted only on very specific grounds but never required. From the beginning it was not so, points back to God's original intent that marriage would be a lifelong condition, not one easily cancelled when the going got tough.

Jesus is clear on the sanctity of marriage and the importance of fidelity. Christians need to be in God's Word to understand God's truths and to apply them to their lives. Just going to church once a week doesn't cut it, if you plan on standing for God and obeying all of His precepts you need to be surrounded by like-minded people. If Christians believe that the Bible is God's inspired Word, then Christians need to start reading it. So many Christians today are getting divorced for petty reasons. I realize that there are multifaceted and complex reasons, circumstances and life situations that surround a divorce, however let's start getting back to the fundamentals of how to live, and how to love God's way.

Christians are under attack today, more than ever. The multi-dimensional platform of the media is pervasively relegating Christian values, ethics, morals, political ideologies and agendas to the prehistoric age. Christians are being perceived and portrayed as being close minded, shallow, racist, fascist, nonintellectual and rigid. There exist a host of other negative adjectives to describe Christians.

We have to stay sharp, remain well read, and be well educated on all fronts if we're going to combat these discriminatory and negative forces. We have to know what we're up against and **The Waging War Within** that exists in the hearts and minds of the American People. Christians have to be willing to dedicate themselves to understanding the complex and ever changing world that we're in. In order to have a strong offense or defense we as Christians must be able to strategize our lives with an up-to-date playbook. Our playbook will never be outdated if it's the Word of God. Let's allow God to take us to new uncharted territory in the realm of our future here in America and around the world. To maintain an equal playing field, we need to continue to become leaders within the fields of medicine, history, sciences, technologies, human services, politics, Biblical studies, law, business and the field of education.

No matter what field we go into professionally, we must always hold the truths of the Bible to be the fundamental truths we live by. We cannot let the value structure of the world permeate our minds, our hearts, our souls and our spirit. We as Christians need to be staunch adherents to the Word regardless of the world and its values or lack thereof.

Decisions determine destiny and decisions stem from our value structure. If not from God, where are the values we live our lives by coming from? Hopefully our value structure comes from God's Word which is His truth revealed to mankind. Be careful that you don't start minimizing the power of reading God's Word, no matter how long you've been a Christian. If you start this downward spiral you might wind up as a mere statistic as it relates to your marriage and other important facets of your life. If we let the worldly culture water down God's Word and dictate to us the insignificance of the traditional Christian family, Christian marriage and the raising of Christian children, then we're through. If it ever comes to this we've lost **The Waging War Within** our culture for the hearts and minds of generations to come. What you believe, what you think, and what values you hold onto passionately, set you apart as a Christian. They show who you are and whom you have become once coming to Christ. God's Word is His bond. Let your word be your bond.

Decisions determine destiny

Matthew 19:10-12- The disciples said to him, "If this is the situation between a husband and wife, it is better not to marry." Jesus replied, "Not everyone can accept this word, but only those to whom it has been given. For some are eunuchs because they were born that way; others were made that way by men; and others have renounced marriage because of the kingdom of heaven. The one who can accept this should accept it."-NIV

God understands that we're all cut out of a different cloth. He understands that there are many differences within the human race as it relates to marriage, as well as other aspects of our existence. He does convey that whether we're married or single we should devote our lives to Him and His service. Men and women were created by God to do His will. Mark 16:15; **"Go into all the world and proclaim the gospel to the whole creation."** Luke 24:47; **"Repentance and forgiveness of sins should be proclaimed in his name to all nations, beginning from Jerusalem."** John 20:21; **"As the Father has sent me, even so I am sending you."** Acts 1:8; **"You will receive power when the Holy Spirit has come upon you, and you will be my witnesses in Jerusalem and in all Judea and Samaria, and to the end of the earth."** We are told that once we have come to know Christ that we are forgiven of our past sins and we start with a new slate. This is why we should want to go and spread the Word to all we come into contact with. 2Corinthians 5:17; **"Therefore, if anyone is in Christ, he is a new creation. The old has passed away; behold, the new has come."**

Gods will is different for every one of us. He's called some into the market place and some to the ministry. He's called some to marry and some not. It's up to us to draw close to our Creator and to determine what His will is for our lives. This direction that God has for us is between God and ourselves. God gives us specific dreams, hopes, visions, gifts, abilities and opportunities. Not all are called to the same profession. Not all are called to marriage. God realizes these differences that we all possess, because He's the One that created us. No matter what direction we take in remaining single, getting married or in what we do professionally, God wants us to remain focused on Him and to be eternally not temporally minded. Let's remember not to be so heavenly minded we're no earthly good. God gave us all the Great Commission to go out and share His Word no matter profession or marriage status. Matthew 28:19-20; **"Go therefore and make disciples of all nations, baptizing them in the name of the Father and of the Son and of the Holy Spirit, teaching them to observe all that I have commanded you."**

Make disciples of all nations!

June 6th

Matthew 19:14,15- Jesus said, **"Let the little children come to me, and do not hinder them, for the kingdom of heaven belongs to such as these."** When he had placed his hands on them, he went on from there.**-NIV**

Matthew 18:4; **"Whoever humbles himself like this child**." The humility of a child consists of childlike trust, vulnerability, and the inability to carry out their agendas apart from the help, direction, and the resources of a parent. The little ones who are called to Him refer to Christ's disciples, past, present, and future. God loves the heart of a child as it is uncorrupted, so much unlike that of an adult.

God has a profound love for little children. He longs for the adults in His Kingdom to come to Him as little children. Not as gullible, not as infantile, not as susceptible to manipulation, not as ignorant and not as helpless. God wants us to have faith in Him as a child should be able to place his or her faith and trust in the adults taking care of them. Children should be able to trust their mother and father. Children should be able to trust and place their faith in knowing that their caretakers are going to make good and sound choices, not to harm but to help them. God takes special joy in the faith of children and He uses their faith as an example of which Heaven belongs to.

In the Bible, children often are used as a metaphor of the humility and innocence necessary for entrance into the Kingdom of Heaven. We need the uncorrupted faith and trust possessed by children and the only way we will be able to attain the innocence and incorruptibility is through our surrendering of our wills and our lives to Christ. Once this is done, our pasts are erased.

God loves us and He demonstrated that love by sacrificing His only Son, Jesus Christ, on a cross so that He paid the blood sacrifice necessary for us to gain entrance into Heaven. Jesus loved us so much that He willingly took on the cross for us. How much more of a demonstration is required to get the point across? I pray that you can see the love He has for us.

Let God love you

June 7th

Matthew 19:17- "Why do you ask me about what is good?" Jesus replied. "There is only One who is good. If you want to enter life, obey the commandments."- NIV

Only in understanding God as infinitely good can anyone discover that performing good deeds cannot earn eternal life. Jesus is not teaching that good works can earn eternal life for we all far short, He is teaching that falling short of adhering to the two greatest commandments, Matthew 22:36–40; **"You shall love the Lord your God with all your heart and with all your soul and with all your mind. This is the great and first commandment. And a second is like it: You shall love your neighbor as yourself. On these two commandments depend all the Law and the Prophets."** But obedience to the law is also an expression of belief in the truly good God who is the source of all good, including eternal life. Scripture elsewhere clearly affirms that salvation is a gift of God's grace received through faith, and not by works. Ephesians 2:8-10; **"For by grace you have been saved through faith. And this is not your own doing; it is the gift of God, not a result of works, so that no one may boast. For we are his workmanship, created in Christ Jesus for good works, which God prepared beforehand, that we should walk in them."**

If we were good then we wouldn't have been born into sin and we certainly wouldn't be in need of a Savior. If we were good we wouldn't be saved by God's grace but we would be saved by what we do and our own performance. The only way we can live by the commandments is if we're empowered by the Holy Spirit, otherwise we're going to fall short every time. This is one of the reasons why God says to seek first the Kingdom of God and His righteousness. Matthew 6:33; **"But seek first the kingdom of God and his righteousness, and all these things will be added to you."** God knows that our righteousness is as filthy rags to His. Isaiah 64:6; **"We have all become like one who is unclean, and all our righteous deeds are like a polluted garment."**

We are all dirt bags apart from God and His divine ways. A pastor friend used to say, "I am a low down, dirty rotten, stinking, filthy sinner." We all are apart from God. We need to repent of our sins daily and make a serious effort to stay away from our old sinful ways. As soon as we open our eyes for the day we should offer up a prayer of thanks and then we should ask God for the strength to make it through the day. God will grant our prayer if we are sincere in the asking.

Obey God's Commandments!

June 8th

Matthew 19:18,19- Jesus replied, " 'Do not murder, do not commit adultery, do not steal, do not give false testimony, honor your father and mother, and love your neighbor as yourself."-NIV

These are powerful commandments, especially in the darkness of today's world. We see these commandments being broken across the board. Murder rates are up in several areas of the country. Felonies related to armed robberies are up in many places. People lying and being dishonest seems to be at an all-time high. Children that are defiant and disrespectful to their parents seem to be pervasive and many neighbors don't even associate with each other. This is a sad state of affairs.

The prison system seems to be about the only business that is booming. America cannot build enough prisons. The amount of people incarcerated in America is growing at an astronomical rate. What I find bewildering is that some people still don't, even after being in prison, come to an understanding that apart from God we're nothing. Isn't something amiss when you can't live by the laws of the land and function above board in our society?

When someone is incarcerated, they have to be confined like a caged animal behind bars, away from their loved ones, living in isolation from the free world. If you can't find God in prison when you hit rock bottom, when will you find Him? Where will people have to go to begin to understand that self isn't the answer? How much of human depravity will one have to endure before he or she humbles them self before God? How much self-destruction will one have to put them self through before dropping down on their knees and crying out to God for help?

This all starts within the home. Honoring your father and mother is a big part of this equation. Parents are the authority figures that God places in our lives to direct us, mold us, guide us and lead us. With more and more children rising up and defying parental authority, the repercussions for our society are going to be monumental. Many children are growing up in single parent households due to their bio-fathers or mothers being incarcerated or out of the picture for one reason or another. Many grandparents are raising their grandchildren today because of the destructive forces that are destroying the family unit. People are trying to raise families without God.

God specifically states in His Word that He created the family. Genesis explains the family formation and unit. Why would anyone not choose the designer of the family to be the centrality of their family? The answer is found in **The Waging War Within which** is permeating our society. This war is gripping the minds and hearts of people. As God is moved further out of society and out of the home, the further into the abyss we will go as a people. We see it happening daily as we watch the evening news.

Matthew 19:21- Jesus answered, "If you want to be perfect, go, sell your possessions and give to the poor, and you will have treasure in heaven. Then come, follow me."-NIV

Jesus knows the man's wealth has become his means to personal identity, power, and his sense of meaning. To many, it has become the idolatrous god of his life. Jesus' strategy is to turn this man from focusing on his outer relationship with his peers and society dealing with his money, to examining his heart, revealing his ruling god. The man had no doubt given some money to the poor, as the giving of alms was considered a pious duty, especially among the Pharisees. But Jesus calls him to give everything he owns away, exchanging the god of wealth for the eternal treasure found in following Jesus as the one true God. Jesus' ultimate answer to the question, "What ... must I do to have eternal life?", is to follow Him.

Jesus is right to the point and clear in what He thinks is important. God is talking about giving to others and not living a greedy life, not letting your possessions be the reason why you're living. God wants us to be aware of the fact that we all came into the world with nothing and we will be leaving it with nothing. Where our treasure is, so is our heart. Luke 12:34; **"For where your treasure is, there will your heart be also."** God wants us to focus on things from Him. Colossians 3:2; **"Set your minds on things that are above, not on things that are on earth."** This present world is no match for the things from above. The things of earth are not even comparable to the riches and glory that belong to us in and through Christ Jesus.

We need to pursue a deeper knowledge of Jesus Christ and all that belongs to living with and for Him. Philippians 3:10; **"That I may know him and the power of his resurrection, and may share his sufferings, becoming like him in his death."** Seek first the Kingdom of God and live a life worthy of Him who has called us. Matthew 6:33; **"But seek first the kingdom of God and his righteousness, and all these things will be added to you."** Colossians 1:10; **"so as to walk in a manner worthy of the Lord, fully pleasing to him, bearing fruit in every good work and increasing in the knowledge of God."** Colossians 2:6; **"Therefore, as you received Christ Jesus the Lord, so walk in Him."** Christ is seated at the right hand of the Father where He can intercede on our behalf. Psalms 110:1; **"The LORD says to my Lord: "Sit at my right hand, until I make your enemies your footstool.""**

Give it all away
and follow Jesus

June 10th

Matthew 19:22- When the young man heard this, he went away sad, because he had great wealth.-NIV

Even though the young man wants eternal life, he cannot bring himself to stop worshiping the ruling force in his life, his great wealth and possessions. This is so true of many people throughout history. We cannot place our eternity in the comfort of wealth.

Many people that are rich by the standard of this world are spiritually destitute in the eyes of God. Wealthy people often have a difficult time truly following Jesus Christ because their focus is on the material possessions they have. Their focus is misplaced on the riches and possessions that this world has to offer and not on Jesus Christ where it should be. They have become tantalized by the things that this world has to offer and in some cases they are even seduced by them. Their soul has become captive to their sinful desires of never having enough. They want and want and want. Their soul is never satisfied because the soul can only be quenched by the Holy Spirit and the One True Living God, Jesus Christ.

We must not become mesmerized by an idolatrous god, wealth. We need to focus on the one true God, and focus on Him alone. We need to change our focus if it is aimed at anything other than our relationship with Jesus Christ. The prevailing force of Jesus will help us in winning **The Waging War Within**.

Never choose earthly wealth over Heavenly gain

June 11th

Matthew 19:23,24- Then Jesus said to his disciples, "I tell you the truth, it is hard for a rich man to enter the kingdom of heaven. Again I tell you, it is easier for a camel to go through the eye of a needle than for a rich man to enter the kingdom of God."-NIV

Wealth was equated with favor and blessings from God. Deuteronomy 28:1-14; "And if you faithfully obey the voice of the LORD your God, being careful to do all his commandments that I command you today, the LORD your God will set you high above all the nations of the earth. And all these blessings shall come upon you and overtake you, if you obey the voice of the LORD your God. Blessed shall you be in the city, and blessed shall you be in the field. Blessed shall be the fruit of your womb and the fruit of your ground and the fruit of your cattle, the increase of your herds and the young of your flock. Blessed shall be your basket and your kneading bowl. Blessed shall you be when you come in, and blessed shall you be when you go out. The LORD will cause your enemies who rise against you to be defeated before you. They shall come out against you one way and flee before you seven ways. The LORD will command the blessing on you in your barns and in all that you undertake. And he will bless you in the land that the LORD your God is giving you. The LORD will establish you as a people holy to himself, as he has sworn to you, if you keep the commandments of the LORD your God and walk in his ways. And all the peoples of the earth shall see that you are called by the name of the LORD, and they shall be afraid of you. And the LORD will make you abound in prosperity, in the fruit of your womb and in the fruit of your livestock and in the fruit of your ground, within the land that the LORD swore to your fathers to give you. The LORD will open to you his good treasury, the heavens, to give the rain to your land in its season and to bless all the work of your hands. And you shall lend to many nations, but you shall not borrow. And the LORD will make you the head and not the tail, and you shall only go up and not down, if you obey the commandments of the LORD your God, which I command you today, being careful to do them, and if you do not turn aside from any of the words that I command you today, to the right hand or to the left, to go after other gods to serve them." Rich men can be converted as the examples of Joseph of Arimathea in Matthew 27:57; "When it was evening, there came a rich man from Arimathea, named Joseph, who also was a disciple of Jesus." Another example is Zacchaeus in Luke 19:9-10; "Today salvation has come to this house, since he also is a son of Abraham. For the Son of Man came to seek and to save the lost."

God warns that entering the Kingdom of Heaven isn't easy for the rich of this earth. God uses a physical example because He knows that we're visual creatures. He paints the picture of the impossibility of a camel going through the eye of a needle. The needles eye referred to here is not a literal needles eye; it was a reference to a home's gateway which was shaped like a needles eye. In order for a camel to enter the gateway it would have had to kneel down and crawl. This was near impossible for a camel to do. Those of us in comparison that have threaded needles realize that it is difficult, however not impossible to put a thin thread through an eyelet. It may take many times before we get it through. It's absurd to even think a camel could go through the eye of a needle. The rich should take notice. What's God saying? I think it's time to make some radical changes, don't you? We are running out of time.

If you have your loyalties placed anywhere else but with God you had better make a change. God is the only one who can save your soul from eternal damnation. All you have to do is ask Jesus to come into your heart. Jesus died for the remission of your sins so that you and I can enjoy eternity with Him. He died on the cross as atonement for our sins and He rose again on the third day. If you believe this you are saved. It is not rocket science, but it can be hard to grasp. That is where faith comes in. We need to trust somebody and that somebody is Jesus Christ.

Where are your loyalties?

Put them in the right place.

June 12th

Matthew 19:25,26- When the disciples heard this, They were greatly astonished and asked, "Who then can be saved?" Jesus looked at them and said, "With man this is impossible, but with God all things are possible."-NIV

With God all things are possible, nothing is impossible with God. The Creator of the Universe is able to do all things. Man cannot do what God can do. Can man rotate the earth or put the planets into place? Can man put the stars in the universe? Can man create black holes and constellations? Can man create the sun to heat the earth? Can man create the moon to light the night? Can man create a universe that goes on and never ends? Can man create another man? Can man create the animals of the land and the fish of the sea? No! Look at Psalms 8:4-5; **"What is man that you are mindful of him, and the son of man that you care for him? Yet you have made him a little lower than the heavenly beings and crowned him with glory and honor."**

The power of God is absolute power! There is no other power that is so great in all the world. God is so powerful that not even a sparrow can drop from the sky and hit the earth without Him knowing it. Matthew 10:28-31; **"And do not fear those who kill the body but cannot kill the soul. Rather fear him who can destroy both soul and body in hell. Are not two sparrows sold for a penny? And not one of them will fall to the ground apart from your Father. But even the hairs of your head are all numbered. Fear not, therefore; you are of more value than many sparrows."** God is the Creator of everything, both great and small. He created the speck of sand at the bottom of the sea, as well the biggest mountain overlooking the sea. He's created the smallest insect and the largest mammal. He's created every human being on every part of the planet.

The next time that we think we can't accomplish something let's turn our eyes upon Jesus. We can accomplish all things with God. Philippians 4:13; **" I can do all things through him who strengthens me."** Anything and everything is possible with God. With our relationship and friendship with God we should never become defeated. We can climb the highest mountain, complete the marathon and conquer anything we set our minds to do.

With God all things are possible

June 13th

Matthew 19:28-30- Jesus said to them, "I tell you the truth, at the renewal of all things, when the Son of Man sits on his glorious throne, you who have followed me will also sit on twelve thrones, judging the twelve tribes of Israel. And everyone who has left houses or brothers or sisters or father or mother or children or fields for my sake will receive a hundred times as much and will inherit eternal life. But many who are first will be last, and many who are last will be first.-NIV

The term renewal refers to looking forward to the future end-time renewal of the world. In this new world, the Disciples of Jesus Christ will participate in the final establishment of His Kingdom of God on earth. Now those who have given up the god of their lives to follow Jesus will receive an abundant reward and they will inherit eternal life. Eternal life (which is a gift) is an inheritance, not an earned reward.

God's ways are above our ways. Isaiah 55:9; **"For as the heavens are higher than the earth, so are my ways higher than your ways and my thoughts than your thoughts."** Following God requires sacrifice. God was the example when He sacrificed His son Jesus Christ for the sins of the world. God rewards those that give up things to follow Him. Hebrews 11:6; **"And without faith it is impossible to please him, for whoever would draw near to God must believe that he exists and that he rewards those who seek him."** God knows who has stepped out in faith and trusted Him to provide. A missionary leaves a home, a family, and material possessions to go off to a faraway land to follow Him. This comes with sacrifice, faith, trust and desire. We need to develop a passion for the things of God.

God promises to bless those who follow Him and that they will inherit eternal life. God doesn't look at things the way man does, His perception and perspective is much different. God isn't controlled by the culture. He doesn't have the limited point of view of man. God knows all.

Have you made your sacrifice?

June 14th

Matthew 20:16- "So the last will be first, and the first will be last."-NIV

We, as Disciples of Christ, should not measure our own worth by comparing it to the sacrifices and accomplishments of others around us. We are here to serve with a gracious heart, all the while seeking God's grace. God's generosity is far above that of the world. Jesus was not denying degrees of reward in heaven. 1 Corinthians 3:14–15; **"If the work that anyone has built on the foundation survives, he will receive a reward. If anyone's work is burned up, he will suffer loss, though he himself will be saved, but only as through fire."** Jesus is affirming that God's generosity is far more abundant than anyone would expect: all the laborers except the very first got more than they probably deserved. This is also a warning that Jesus' early followers (such as the Twelve) should not despise those who would come later as we are all His disciples and workers of His Kingdom and we are all entitled to entrance into eternity with Him.

This is the antithesis of what we learn in our culture. Our culture teaches that those that come in first are winners and those that come in last are losers. In America and the world over, most people enjoy winning. In business, in education, in sports and many other aspects of life, it's all about winning. If you win you're looked upon as being a success, and if you lose you're looked upon as being a failure. Who won the race? What place did they finish? Did they score? Did they beat the other team? Did they run faster? Were they stronger? Did they have more money? Did they have a bigger and more expensive house? Did they have a bigger car? Was he taller? The list goes on and on.

In the Kingdom of God it's about the heart. God knows the motives and inclinations of the heart. He knows what is in the heart of each and every human being on earth. He knows the reasons and motives of why people do what they do. God knows if we're doing things for Him or if we're doing it for selfish motives. Following God needs to be a matter of the heart, a heart for God and doing His will in our lives. Living out our walk with Christ here on earth is of crucial importance.

Heavenly perspective is different from the perspective of this world

June 15th

Matthew 20:17-19- Now as Jesus was going up to Jerusalem, he took the twelve disciples aside and said to them, "We are going up to Jerusalem, and the Son of Man will be betrayed to the chief priests and the teachers of the law. They will condemn him to death and will turn him over to the Gentiles to be mocked and flogged and crucified. On the third day he will be raised to life!"-NIV

This is the third of four predictions that Jesus gave as to His arrest and crucifixion. The others were in Matthew 16:21, 17:22-23, and the forth will be in 26:2. Here we also have references to Jerusalem, the religious leaders, and the Gentiles which heighten the drama; for the first time in the narrative, Jesus gives additional clues about his betrayal and who will carry out his arrest and crucifixion.

Jesus was condemned to death, mocked, flogged and crucified. This was such a deadly combination. This is the most poignant display of compassion ever given to the world. It's one thing if a man intentionally dared to die such a death for another. I don't think you'd see many people willingly go to the cross for another person. God willingly sent His Son to the Cross of Calvary, despite the fact that He knew what would transpire. This was God's perfect supernatural divine destiny. This was the ultimate gift for us. He sacrificed His Son to save us. He sacrificed His Son so He could call us His children. He sacrificed His Son so He could conquer death, hell and the grave on our behalf. He had to condemn Himself so that He might rise again to life, to impart to us salvation and the gift of eternal life. How awesome is that?

God found us worthy to be called His children; sons and daughters of the Most High God. We need to act accordingly, not with our noses in the air where we would drown if it rained, but as servants of Jesus Christ. We should want to live lives worthy of God.

You are a son or daughter of the Most High God.

Are you acting like it?

Matthew 20:20-24- Then the mother of Zebedee's sons came to Jesus with her sons and, kneeling down, asked a favor of him. "What is it you want?" he asked. She said, "Grant that one of these two sons of mine may sit at your right and the other at your left in your kingdom." "You don't know what you are asking," Jesus said to them. "Can you drink the cup I am going to drink?" "We can," they answered. Jesus said to them, "You will indeed drink from my cup, but to sit at my right or left is not for me to grant. These places belong to those for whom they have been prepared by my Father." When the ten heard about this, they were indignant with the two brothers.- NIV

Salome, the mother of the sons of Zebedee, was also in all probability the sister of Mary, Jesus' mother, so that James and John were in fact Jesus' cousins. She was among the women who stayed with Jesus at the cross and later witnessed the empty tomb. Now Salome shows respect to Jesus as her messianic Master by kneeling down in front of Him honoring His position as the Son of God, but she also hoped to use her earthly kinship with Jesus to her sons' advantage. Salome's petition was likely inspired by Jesus' remarks in Matthew 19:28, where he had announced the Twelve's reign with Him in His future kingdom. She heard that the Twelve would be judging the twelve tribes and she naturally wanted her son's to join them. It is only natural for a mother to want the best for her children, but Salome missed the point of Jesus' message.

The cup spoken of in Scripture is symbolic of one's divinely determined destiny, whether blessing (Psalms 16:5) or disaster (Jeremiah 25:15), salvation (Psalms 116:13) or wrath (Isaiah 51:17). Here in this verse it refers to Jesus' forthcoming suffering and the foreknowledge that the Twelve would also die premature deaths; Judas at his own hand and all of the others but John were martyred. When Jesus said that they would drink His cup, He was letting them know that they were to suffer as He was about to. James became the first apostolic martyr and the rest soon followed with the exception of John, who suffered persecution and exile.

The disciples were perhaps not as upset by the immodesty of the request from Salome as by the brothers' attempt to use their family relationship with Jesus to gain an unfair advantage in obtaining what they themselves also wanted. They all wanted the position of honor at Jesus' side.

Can you believe having the gall and tenacity of asking the Son of God to sit at His left and right in the Kingdom of Heaven? Jesus didn't have the authority to grant such a thing. Jesus realized that His Father in Heaven determines these things. Jesus realized that His Father was the determiner of who sits on His left and the right in the Kingdom of Heaven. Are you prepared to drink from the cup which Christ drank?

June 17th

Matthew 20:26-28- Not so with you. Instead, whoever wants to become great among you must be your servant, and whoever wants to be first must be your slave- just as the Son of Man did not come to be served, but to serve, and to give his life as a ransom for many."-NIV

In Jesus' day, a servant was a hired worker who maintained the master's household, and a slave was someone forced into service. These were two distinctly different also two of the lowest positions in Jewish society, yet Jesus reverses their status in His circle and in the community of His disciples to indicate both prominence and greatness. Jesus said that the Son of Man came not to be served but to serve. Jesus himself was the primary example of servant hood.

How different from the kings, royalty, people of prestige, dignitaries, princes, queens and princesses of this world. You see the gigantic castles, mansions, materialism and the decadent life styles they live. They live large. They're rich and famous. They have servants, butlers, nannies and people to care for their grounds, cars, yachts, and planes. They have homes all over the world. Billionaires have more money than third world countries. Many do wonderful things for the world in which they live and give back to society by creating jobs, creating new industries and technology and ultimately helping our economy, but do they serve the will of God? Probably not. Their god is the almighty dollar.

It is clear that God created us in His image so we could serve others. As God gave, He wants us to give of ourselves in service to His Kingdom. When God, who created the heart, sees the pure motives of our hearts as we carry out His service to others He is pleased. His grace abounds in love when we're living out His will and divine destiny for our lives. 2 Corinthians 1:5; **"For as we share abundantly in Christ's sufferings, so through Christ we share abundantly in comfort too."**

When serving others we have to be humble before our Lord and Savior. God works powerfully through a humble heart, a heart brought into total and complete subjection to the Creator of the universe. God realized that there would be no greater joy we could experience in our lives than when we give of ourselves to others. Much joy and contentment happens as we walk with Christ giving of ourselves selflessly in His service.

God has called us
to serve others

June 18th

Matthew 20:29-34- As Jesus and his disciples were leaving Jericho, a large crowd followed him. Two blind men were sitting by the road side, and when they heard that Jesus was going by, they shouted, "Lord, Son of David, have mercy on us!" The crowd rebuked them and told them to be quiet, but they shouted all the louder, "Lord, Son of David, have mercy on us!" Jesus stopped and called them. "What do you want me to do for you?" he asked. "Lord," they answered, "we want our sight." Jesus had compassion on them and touched their eyes. Immediately they received their sight and followed him.-NIV

Isn't it something that even in the face of the rejection by His own people, and the impending betrayal as He enters Jerusalem, Jesus still continued to show compassion to those in need. Jesus always seemed to put the needs of others above His own. How many of us would be thinking about others suffering when we know that we are about to die one of the most agonizing deaths known to man? Jesus did it on a regular basis. Here He healed two blind men due to their faith in Him.

Faith. What a marvelous entity that has been freely given to us. What a price God paid. What a sacrifice. Many of us place our faith in many things. Anything that we place our faith in before God is an idol. When something becomes an idol in our lives we've lost perspective. Today many things have become idols for us as Americans. It's time we get back to our Christian heritage and our roots. If not, our homes will be ransacked by divorce, financial ruin, domestic turmoil and unbelief in God.

We don't have to conjure up anything to get close to God. He's right here, right now. You will never pray enough, you will never read the Word enough, you will never lead enough people to Christ and you will never give enough to God. You will never be mister or misses perfect spiritually. You will never arrive to a spiritual plain to be good enough for God. You already are where you need to be if you've accepted Jesus Christ as your Personal Lord and Savior. Jesus was the only perfect sacrificial offering that could be counted toward our reconciliation with God. We're only accepted into God's Kingdom because of Jesus. It's about Him, not us. What He did, not what we can do. Let's not lose perspective.

We don't have to feel in our spiritual life that we're on some perpetual treadmill based on our performance. Let's take our eyes off ourselves and what we can do and look to God. God lives and operates within us now, in the present and in our current need. He longs for us to drop to our knees and to cry out to Him now. Not later. Immediately! Surrender! God wants to work in our live this very minute, not one second later.

June 19th

Matthew 21:1-5- As they approached Jerusalem and came to Bethphage on the Mount of Olives, Jesus sent two disciples, saying to them, "Go to the village ahead of you, and at once you will find a donkey tied there, with her colt by her. Untie them and bring them to me. If anyone says anything to you, tell him that the Lord needs them, and he will send them right away." This took place to fulfill what was spoken through the prophet: "Say to the Daughter of Zion, 'See, your king comes to you, gentle and riding on a donkey, on a colt, the foal of a donkey.'"-NIV

As he enters Jerusalem, Jesus is proclaimed as the Messiah; but He enters humbly, riding on a donkey. Matthew specifies that Jesus' entrance into Jerusalem upon a colt fulfills the prophecy of Zechariah 9:9; **"Rejoice greatly, O daughter of Zion! Shout aloud, O daughter of Jerusalem! behold, your king is coming to you; righteous and having salvation is he, humble and mounted on a donkey, on a colt, the foal of a donkey."** Jesus' action was an open declaration that He is the righteous Davidic Messiah, for the prophecy says, **"your king is coming to you."**

Now when Christ rode in on the donkey colt He also reiterated the verses in Genesis which prophesized about a kingly descendant of Judah whose rule would extend to all the nations. Genesis 49:8-12; **"Judah, your brothers shall praise you; your hand shall be on the neck of your enemies; your father's sons shall bow down before you. Judah is a lion's cub; from the prey, my son, you have gone up. He stooped down; he crouched as a lion and as a lioness; who dares rouse him? The scepter shall not depart from Judah, nor the ruler's staff from between his feet, until tribute comes to him; and to him shall be the obedience of the peoples. Binding his foal to the vine and his donkey's colt to the choice vine, he has washed his garments in wine and his vesture in the blood of grapes. His eyes are darker than wine, and his teeth whiter than milk. Zebulun shall dwell at the shore of the sea; he shall become a haven for ships, and his border shall be at Sidon. Issachar is a strong donkey, crouching between the sheepfolds."**

Our King came on a donkey humbly before the world and the world knew Him not. On a donkey! Please! This is God? This is the savior of the world? Can it be? In today's day and age when people are driving around in expensive cars, it's amazing to think that Jesus road on a donkey. The Son of God entered on a donkey, not on a horse or a chariot or a horse drawn carriage, but a donkey? Jesus wanted people to know that the wealth He offered was from above and not of this world. This world could not produce the inheritance that Jesus Christ has given to us by dying on the cross. God Himself chose to ride on a donkey! This is a powerful statement to us all.

June 20th

Matthew 21:12-13- Jesus entered the temple area and drove out all who were buying and selling there. He overturned the tables of the money changers and the benches of those selling doves. "It is written," he said to them, "My house will be called a house of prayer,' but you are making it a 'den of robbers."-NIV

Jesus is a leader, taking a stand for His church. God, in a righteous anger and indignation, overturned the tables. Jesus stated clearly and concisely that His church is a house of prayer, not a place to buy and sell. God certainly got the attention of those buying, selling and making money; let this be a lesson for us as Christians, about the profound importance of having right motives of heart before the Lord and understanding what His church is all about. It's about spiritual things, things from above and things of the heart. It's about the internal, not the external. It's about renewing ourselves before the living true God of the universe.

Let this be a lesson about leadership. When a Godly leader expresses righteous indignation concerning a dynamic of what should be happening within the church that ruffles a few feathers and maybe even your own feathers, don't altogether discount it. Don't throw the baby out with the bath water. God uses men of God to give a hard message. It could be on tithing, fasting, repentance, church involvement, gossip, sin, hell, dying to self or many other difficult to confront issues that we as Christians face within the church.

Proverbs 27:17; **"As iron sharpens iron, so one man sharpens another."** We have to go through the fiery furnace to mature in the Lord. Nothing good and worthwhile has ever been accomplished without blood, sweat and tears. Jesus Himself wept. Jesus was nailed, stabbed in the ribs, crucified and hung on a cross. Nails were placed in His feet and hands. A crown of thorns was placed on His head. In all these occurrences, His flesh was pierced to the bone and blood was shed in all directions. Imagine the agony, the pain, the devastation and this journey that our Lord took for both you and me. Nothing is comparable to this sacrificial offering made on our behalf.

Are you a leader after God's own heart? How are you leading your family? How are you leading your children? How are you leading at church, at home and at work? Are you leading by example or are you leading with words and no action? How do you want to be remembered here on earth? Are you a Christian that just goes through the motions of playing church? To lead is a conscious decision and choice that we all have to make before God. We need leaders my friends, not followers. We are all servants, but we are called to be God heads wherever we are.

June 21st

Matthew 21:16-17- "From the lips of children and infants you have ordained praise?" And he left them and went out of the city to Bethany, where he spent the night.-NIV

Hosanna to the Son of David! Jesus acknowledged the children's praise and likens it to **Psalms 8:2; "Out of the mouth of babes and infants, you have established strength because of your foes, to still the enemy and the avenger."** The religious leaders saw the praises and the rejoicing that accompanied the entrance of Jesus into the city and they should have known that this scenario applied such praises to God, which confirmed that Jesus was the divine Messiah, but instead they grew angered by it.

Why is it that children can often times see and know things that we as adults miss? I believe they have an inner sense which tells them whom they can trust and whom they can't. I have seen children watch adults interact with each other and know when there is tension without even hearing the words. You can watch them and use them as a barometer to measure the scene. They just seem to know when someone is safe to be around or if there is a sense of danger. Want to see if you have a good pastor for your kids, watch the children around him. If the children run up to them and give them hugs, trust their judgment.

Think of your own children when they were infants. Infants have total faith in their parents to hold them, care for them and do the right thing by them. Infants and children have only been in the world a short time in comparison with us as adults. Their faith has not yet been tarnished or thwarted by the world, except of course if the child or infant is abused and neglected, and then of course there are a host of other issues that come into play. Unfortunately these issues are beyond the control of the abused or neglected child.

God frequently wants us as to look at things with an enlightened mind. When we look at children through the eyes of God we can begin to see the blessing that infants and children are in the world in which we live. God would like us to have the faith of an infant and a child. Mark 10:15; **"Truly, I say to you, whoever does not receive the kingdom of God like a child shall not enter it."** Ephesians 3:17-19; **"That Christ may dwell in your hearts through faith—that you, being rooted and grounded in love, may have strength to comprehend with all the saints what is the breadth and length and height and depth, and to know the love of Christ that surpasses knowledge, that you may be filled with all the fullness of God."** Children trust their mother and father to make the right decisions and choices in their care and well-being. God would like us to trust Him as our infants and children trust us.

Have a trust of God just like a child

June 22nd

Matthew 21:21- Jesus replied, "I tell you the truth, if you have faith and do not doubt, not only can you do what was done to the fig tree, but also you can say to this mountain, 'Go, throw yourself into the sea,' and it will be done. If you believe, you will receive whatever you ask for in prayer."-NIV

Moving a mountain was a common metaphor in Jewish tradition as doing what was seemingly impossible. Jesus is telling us that anything is possible in prayer. God will answer us. Yes He will. God knows our needs. He wants what is in our best interest. God hears us and knows our heart. God enjoys when we pray and petition Him in our prayer time. It just takes faith, a simple faith in Him. God doesn't require us to be super spiritual prayer warriors, even though there is nothing wrong with being a prayer warrior. God desires us to place our needs before Him in prayer with a childlike belief and faith in Him. Have you ever seen and heard a child pray before. Children have simple prayers that they offer up to God, nothing complex, flashy or profound. Their prayers are right from their heart! They're real, sincere and wholesome. We can learn a lot from a child when they pray.

When we pray, we need to speak to God from our hearts. We need to speak to Him as we would to each other. We don't need to pray in the King James English; you don't speak that way do you? Pray to Him from your heart. Speak to Him as you would love to speak to your parents. Parents love to hear from their kids and God loves to hear from us. Talk to Him and let Him know what is going on in your life.

Faith is our weapon against the warfare that bombards our homes, our marriages, our churches, our schools, our families and our children. When we pray, God desires more than anything for us to have an unwavering passionate faith in Him. Prayer is what binds and solidifies our faith with God. Faith is the glue that holds everything together. Faith is the secret weapon that God requires of us to combat **The Waging War Within.** With faith we can draw closer to God, accomplish His will for our lives and ultimately attain our divine destiny in Jesus Christ. As long as God is in it, it's a done deal, sealed, rock solid, and as good as gold.

Belief and faith from God's perspective are the foundational truths that make our personal relationship with Jesus Christ so powerful. When we communicate with God, we have to have faith that He hears us. We cannot see Him with our physical eyes or hear Him with our physical ears so it takes faith to believe. Put your trust and your confidence in God, especially because we cannot see Him. Just because Jesus cannot be seen doesn't mean that He doesn't exist or that He has never lived. God is real. People we once knew that have died and have gone on to be with the Lord were real too. Just because you can no longer see them, doesn't mean you cannot treasure the memory you have of them. You can remember the times spent with them, the type of person that they were and the profound positive impact they had on your life.

God has given us His Word for us to look upon to determine what kind of God He was while living on this earth. God has given us His Word to guide and teach the path of living a righteous life before Him. God has shared with us many aspects of His life and His personality through the Word of God.

You probably have example after example of how God has provided a way for you through prayer. I can't even count the ways God has provided for me in prayer! It's been unlimited. I can make lists of many, many ways God has blessed my life through prayer. God longs to bless His people in ways beyond what we can ever imagine. He longs to bless His children spiritually, physically, financially, occupationally, relationally and within every aspect of their lives. With faith all this is possible. Mark 9:23; **"All things are possible for one who believes."** Pray and believe in faith. Bring you desire, your concerns and the brokenness of your life to Jesus. God will respond in ways more beautiful than we can ever imagine. He desires to fulfill the longings of our heart. Cry out to God in faith. He never wanted you to do it alone. He desires to be more than just a friend, He desires to be your everything. Give Him everything you are and everything that you have within you. I mean everything. God will answer in His time, in His way and as He sees fit. Trust and obey. Place your faith in Him. Who better to place your faith in? Who is more worthy than Jesus?

Are you in need of a physical healing? Call on God. Are you in need of a healing spiritually? Call God. Are you in need of healing in a relationship? Seek God. Are you in need of God's will for your life to unfold in you? Seek God. Are you in need of a closer relationship with God? Call on God. Are you in need of a spiritual breakthrough? Call God. Are you in need of the miraculous in your life? Call God. Are you in need of anything? Call on God? If it's God's will in your life, God will provide a way for it to happen. Your faith is the key ingredient that completes God's recipe for success!

I am convinced that we don't realize half of the power that we have in Jesus Christ. We need to increase our passion for Him and seek Him with an unwavering intensity like nothing that we've ever been after before in our lives. We have to be in prayer, in His Word, in worship and fellowship with other believers otherwise we won't reach our maturity with the Lord. Our whole reason for being has to be our faith in Christ and everything else has to be secondary. With this type of tenacity we will know the blessings of God. Pray ceaselessly and rejoice always. 1 Thessalonians 5:15-22; **"See that no one repays anyone evil for evil, but always seek to do good to one another and to everyone. Rejoice always, pray without ceasing, and give thanks in all circumstances; for this is the will of God in Christ Jesus for you. Do not quench the Spirit. Do not despise prophecies, but test everything; hold fast what is good. Abstain from every form of evil."**

June 23rd

Matthew 21:23-25- Jesus entered the temple courts, and, while he was teaching, the chief priests and the elders of the people came to him. "By what authority are you doing these things?" they asked. "And who gave you this authority?" Jesus replied, "I will also ask you one question. If you answer me, I will tell you by what authority I am doing these things. John's baptism-where did it come from? Was it from heaven, or from men?" They discussed it among themselves and said, "If we say, 'From heaven,' he will ask, 'Then why didn't you believe him?'-NIV

The religious leaders were trapped. As religious leaders they must now show their ignorance. If they do not know whether John was from God, how can they judge whether Jesus is? They are showing the true intent of their hearts.

They were trying to trap Jesus, what a shame. Here we have mere human beings attempting to trap and defame the Living God, Jesus Christ. This shouldn't be a surprise that it happened, it is still happening today. Men are still attempting to accuse Jesus of being a fake and a phony and not being who He claimed Himself to be. Man is still elevating the creation above the Creator. Man is still looking to elevate themselves to a place above God. This has always been and will always be the case. This is the internal struggle of **The Waging War Within.**

Man will always be attempting to set themselves on a platform above God. Mere man cannot fathom the things of the Holy Spirit. 1 Corinthians 2:14; **"The natural person does not accept the things of the Spirit of God, for they are folly to him, and he is not able to understand them because they are spiritually discerned."** Man continues to be in rebellion to what God has intended him to be. Men that aren't filled with the Holy Spirit can only be in rebellion to God and to the things of God. If man isn't filled with the Holy Spirit and born again they're filled with the spirit of this world, Satan, the father of lies. Man doesn't believe that there is a false spirit, the anti-christ, which is controlling and manipulating this entire world. They don't know the complexities of the battle because they don't realize the spiritual nature of our existence.

The minds and hearts of men need to be brought under the authority of the one true God, Jesus Christ. Man cannot even begin to see the things of God without accepting him as our Creator. Our eyes, our souls, our spirits and our hearts have to be enlightened by God, in order for us to understand the things of God.

God is the ultimate authority. Acts 4:12; **"And there is salvation in no one else, for there is no other name under heaven given among men by which we must be saved."** Salvation comes through none other than Jesus Christ and Him crucified. He shed His blood for the world. John 3:16; **"For God so loved the world, that he gave his only Son, that whoever believes in him should not perish but have eternal life."**

Matthew 21:26,27- But if we say, 'From men'-we are afraid of the people, for they all hold that John was a prophet." So they answered Jesus, "We don't know." Then he said, "Neither will I tell you by what authority I am doing these things.-NIV

God desires us to use our minds in our belief in Him. He realized that the religious leaders of His day weren't going to believe Him. It certainly didn't prevent Him from sharing the truth and nullifying what they believed and said. Jesus stood His ground with the best of them. He didn't back away. He certainly wasn't a coward or fearful of what they might do. He realized that His Heavenly Father was in charge, the ultimate authority and that He knew what He was doing in carrying out the divine destiny.

Man still attempts to distort, misconstrue, nullify and relegate the Word of God to something it isn't. Someone without Salvation and who doesn't have God operating in their lives cannot begin to unlock the spiritual truths of Jesus. You must be born again, born of the Spirit. You need to be born from above, not from this world. One must have the second birth to see the things of God. John 3:1-7; **"Now there was a man of the Pharisees named Nicodemus, a ruler of the Jews. This man came to Jesus by night and said to him, "Rabbi, we know that you are a teacher come from God, for no one can do these signs that you do unless God is with him." Jesus answered him, "Truly, truly, I say to you, unless one is born again he cannot see the kingdom of God." Nicodemus said to him, "How can a man be born when he is old? Can he enter a second time into his mother's womb and be born?" Jesus answered, "Truly, truly, I say to you, unless one is born of water and the Spirit, he cannot enter the kingdom of God. That which is born of the flesh is flesh, and that which is born of the Spirit is spirit. Do not marvel that I said to you, 'You must be born again.'"** Having faith in the ultimate authority of God is a key that will unlock any and every door in your life. The Lion of the Tribe of Judah will always prevail. Revelation 5:5; **"And one of the elders said to me, "Weep no more; behold, the Lion of the tribe of Judah, the Root of David, has conquered, so that he can open the scroll and its seven seals."**

Behold Jesus,
the Lion of the tribe of Judah!

June 25th

Matthew 21:31-32- Jesus said to them, "I tell you the truth, the tax collectors and the prostitutes are entering the kingdom of God ahead of you. For John came to you to show you the way of righteousness, and you did not believe him, but the tax collectors and the prostitutes did. And even after you saw this, you did not repent and believe him.-NIV

Jesus associated with the seemingly unsociable. Jesus went to the downcast, the people that were castaways, those that didn't fit in. He went to those that were outside of the norm of society, what we would call abnormal. He went to the wayward, those that were off course. If we read the Word we would see that all of those which Jesus associated with were the outcasts of society. This includes the Twelve. He associated with the lepers, the women with blood issues, the illiterate, the sick and the crippled, the blind and deaf, and the people like you and like me. He wanted those that no one else wanted.

This is Gregg writing here. I was once on a mission's trip to Panama to build a school for Latin American Child Care. While on that trip we went to a local church to worship with the people. One aspect of the visit is praying for the local populace. We finished the main part of the service and then we were asked to pray for those that needed prayer. We went to different areas of the church and the people came forward for prayer. I had a man approach me that was obviously mentally challenged and poor and also in dire need of not only prayer but also a bath. This man was repulsive to my sense of smell. I didn't want to lay hands on him or pray for him. I didn't want to even be near him because he was extremely dirty and nasty and smelly. Well I had to pray for him and as I began he grabbed my hand and placed it on his head. I thought I was going to be sick.

As soon as this happened I was touched in my spirit. I was placing myself on a higher plane than I was this man. I was placing myself in the judgment seat and passing sentence on this man. I was determining that this man was not worthy of my prayer time. I was crushed with the realization that I had placed myself in God's seat. Who am I that I shouldn't pray for that man? When did God go on leave and place Gregg Kretschmer in charge? He didn't. I immediately started to cry with a reality check on my soul and spirit. I apologized to God and also to that man. I prayed a prayer for forgiveness of my sin and I prayed a prayer of healing and prosperity on that man. I finished that prayer by giving that man a bear hug with a heart of repentance. I now look for the people not only in third world countries, but also at any church I go to who are looked down upon by the people attending service and I sit with them, I talk with them, and I ask if I can pray with and for them. That trip changed my life forever. I pray this confession touches someone who reads it. It wasn't a proud moment in my life but it was a learning experience which I will never forget.

Hebrews 13:2; **"Do not neglect to show hospitality to strangers, for thereby some have entertained angels unawares."** I don't think that the man mentioned above was an angel, but he could have been for all I know. That is not the point. The point I am trying to make is that we do not have the right to pass judgment on anyone. We are called to be servants and what kind of a servant was I being if I was only going through the motions of praying for someone without the heart accompanying the prayer? I was being a fake and I am ashamed to say that I had done that before that time. Confession time my brothers and sisters. I felt that God took me to the woodshed that night.

I have no right to deny anyone prayer. None of us do. My actions that night were not a mistake. A mistake is something you do wrong and you repeat the action again and again. What I had was a learning experience. A learning experience is one in which you take a valuable lesson from the error made and you apply it to your life so that you don't repeat the action again. I took a look at my walk that night and I made some drastic changes to it. I thank God for revealing how dirty and disgusting my heart was that night. That man was so squeaky clean compared to me. I was the dirty one. I repented heartily that night and I pray that I never judge anyone like I did that night again.

God's Word makes it understood that belief and repentance are the key aspects of the Christian Faith and in following the ways of Jesus. Belief and repentance can determine your eternal destiny, not just your temporal existence. What do you believe in? Do you believe in God? Have you repented before Him?

Lord, please forgive me.
Please Lord, work in me
and through me.

June 26th

Matthew 21:42-44- Jesus said to them, "Have you never read in the Scriptures: "The stone the builders rejected has become the capstone; the Lord has done this, and it is marvelous in our eyes? "Therefore I tell you that the kingdom of God will be taken away from you and given to a people who will produce its fruit. He who falls on this stone will be broken to pieces, but he on whom it falls will be crushed."-NIV

The cornerstone is the stone of ultimate importance. It is the stone that is dated and often it often holds the hidden treasures throughout the ages. Jesus Christ is the Cornerstone of our faith. The rejected Son of God received the highest honor. He is the Stone in which we build our faith and shape our foundation.

Jesus was conveying through this parable the Kingdom of God wasn't a physical temple made of stone, but that He was the finishing stone of God's Kingdom. Religious leaders were rejecting Jesus because they couldn't comprehend or understand Him. Jesus wasn't about religiosity, He was about relationship. He taught things never taught before here on earth. He was perplexing to the religious leaders of the day. The religious leaders were so indoctrinated in their religious traditions that they couldn't relinquish their cultural and religious indoctrination.

A struggle, a **Waging War Within** still wages today amidst the very worldly religions, its leaders and that of Christianity. Either Jesus was who He said He was or we're all being deceived. My faith, my belief, my trust, my hope and my life are placed in God's hands. I trust God, His Word and His salvation message. Choose this day who you will serve. Joshua 24:15; **"And if it is evil in your eyes to serve the LORD, choose this day whom you will serve, whether the gods your fathers served in the region beyond the River, or the gods of the Amorites in whose land you dwell. But as for me and my house, we will serve the LORD."**

Make Jesus the Cornerstone
of your faith

June 27th

Matthew 22:1-3- Jesus spoke to them again in parables, saying: "The kingdom of heaven is like a king who prepared a wedding banquet for his son. He sent his servants to those who had been invited to the banquet to tell them to come, but they refused to come.-NIV

This "feast" represents us enjoying fellowship with God in His kingdom, and coming to the feast represents entering the Kingdom of Heaven. To refuse a direct invitation from a king would be an extreme insult and a dangerous affront to his authority. When we refuse to abide by God's authority and live in His ways is a slap in the face to Him as our Lord and Creator. We break His heart.

Let's not be perplexed when individuals within our own families, our social circles, people of the world and those in other religions don't accept God's message of salvation. **A Waging War Within** exists within their souls. A battle is going on right now at this very minute for our very eternal existence. Some refuse to come to God, to surrender and accept His free offer of salvation. Many factors prevent people from coming into a heartfelt relationship with God. Pride, sin, false doctrines and religions, atheism, self and certain philosophical and scientific theories prevent people from accepting the salvation truths of Jesus.

Many the world over will refuse to follow Jesus and to accept His plan of salvation for their lives. Hundreds of millions have come and hundreds of millions will come to Jesus accepting His message of truth. There are presently hundreds of millions of Christians all over the world representing different cultures and different languages. Praise God! God's desire is to bring people from every walk of life into a relationship with Him and for them to experience the supernatural free gift of salvation. Salvation is free to us, but costly to God. Jesus paid with His very life. John 3:16; **"For God so loved the world, that he gave his only Son, that whoever believes in him should not perish but have eternal life."** Romans 4:5-8; **"And to the one who does not work but trusts him who justifies the ungodly, his faith is counted as righteousness, just as David also speaks of the blessing of the one to whom God counts righteousness apart from works: "Blessed are those whose lawless deeds are forgiven, and whose sins are covered; blessed is the man against whom the Lord will not count his sin.""** Psalms 32:1-2; **"Blessed is the one whose transgression is forgiven, whose sin is covered. Blessed is the man against whom the LORD counts no iniquity, and in whose spirit there is no deceit."** What does salvation cost us? Nothing really. For us it is a win-win situation. We win eternal life with God and all of our sins are forgiven.

Are you right with God?

June 28th

Matthew 22:8-10- **"Then he said to his servants, 'The wedding banquet is ready, but those I invited did not deserve to come. Go to the street corners and invite to the banquet anyone you find. So the servants went out into the streets and gathered all the people they could find, both good and bad, and the wedding hall was filled with guests.-NIV**

The wedding invitation which was given to those who were not previously invited anticipates the spread of the Gospel to the Gentiles. The spread of the Gospel allowed the Gentiles to learn about and accept Jesus Christ as their Savior. This was good news to all who believed but weren't of the Jewish faith. This is also the reason you and I can count us among the saved.

As Christians we're expected to be partakers with God in **The Waging War Within.** God wants us to go out and evangelize and lead people, the unsaved to Him. God doesn't want us to keep silent with His message of salvation. He wants all to come to Him. He desires the salvation of all upon this earth. He doesn't want anyone to perish, but all to come to have everlasting life. 2 Peter 3:9; **"The Lord is not slow to fulfill his promise as some count slowness, but is patient toward you, not wishing that any should perish, but that all should reach repentance."** 1 Timothy 2:4; **"who desires all people to be saved and to come to the knowledge of the truth."** Romans 2:4; **"Or do you presume on the riches of his kindness and forbearance and patience, not knowing that God's kindness is meant to lead you to repentance?"** He wants us to go out on the highways and byways of life bringing anyone and everyone into His Kingdom. Matthew 28: 19-20; **"Go therefore and make disciples of all nations, baptizing them in the name of the Father and of the Son and of the Holy Spirit, teaching them to observe all that I have commanded you."** He doesn't want us to be closet Christians. In a war you don't stay in the foxhole to die. You get out of it to fight, to battle the enemy and to get the victory! In the same fashion we must be warriors, bringing down strongholds and leading others to Jesus.

When an army destroys an enemy stronghold, the first thing they have to do is find the enemies supply routes and their supply lines. Then they set about a plan to destroy the routes and lines to effectively cut off all sustenance and ammo. This will isolate the stronghold, starve the enemy, and effectively cut off the enemies head. The next plan of action would be to fortify your new position. You wall it off, seal it from the outside forces, and place a guard all around it. We as Christians have to do the same thing with our new position in life. We need to cut off our old lifeline and reinforce our new one.

Next time you're at a wake or funeral ask yourself the question, "Did I lead that person to Jesus?" If not, why not?

June 29th

Matthew 22:13-14- "Then the king told the attendants, 'Tie him hand and foot, and throw him outside, into the darkness, where there will be weeping and gnashing of teeth.' "For many are invited, but few are chosen."-NIV

Many are called means that many people have been invited to the wedding feast. But not all those who have been invited will actually be the ones who are supposed to be there, because the Word says that few are actually chosen. This has been described as the doctrine of a "general calling": the gospel is proclaimed to all people everywhere, both those who will believe and those who will not. When the Gospel is proclaimed, only some are effectively called, those who are the elect, who respond with true faith. 1 Corinthians 1:24-28; "**but to those who are called, both Jews and Greeks, Christ the power of God and the wisdom of God. For the foolishness of God is wiser than men, and the weakness of God is stronger than men. For consider your calling, brothers: not many of you were wise according to worldly standards, not many were powerful, not many were of noble birth. But God chose what is foolish in the world to shame the wise; God chose what is weak in the world to shame the strong; God chose what is low and despised in the world, even things that are not.**" This is Jesus' statement that "few are chosen," for the ones "chosen" are "the elect," a term used by Jesus to refer to His true disciples.

This parable displays for us the consequences of poor decisions. We are given an opportunity to accept Jesus as our Lord and Savior. Many are called but few are chosen refers to us. Are we going to accept the invitation or are we going to reap the consequences of our bad choice? We need to decide. Hell is very real. Matt. 8:12, 13:42, 50, 22:13, 24:51, 25:30, all verify the "gnashing of teeth" analogy. Be one of the few, the proud, and the chosen. Accept the invitation to the feast before it is too late. Please I pray, make a wise choice.

The reality is that you will only be forgiven of your sins and chosen for the Kingdom of Heaven if you accept Jesus Christ as your Personal Lord and Savior. A heavy price will be paid if you and others don't accept Jesus. I am not basing this on feeling, my hunch, my opinion, the opinion of others, but on the Truth in God's Word.

We need to have a sense of urgency in leading others to Jesus Christ. We cannot remain complacent. We have to be on fire and radically transformed with Jesus. Ask God to reveal to you the spiritual truths associated with life and death. God will make it real to you. He can show you **The Waging War Within** that exists and the importance of the salvation message.

Have you answered the call?

Matthew 22:15-22- Then the Pharisees went out and laid plans to trap him in his words. They sent their disciples to him along with the Herodians. "Teacher," they said, "we know you are a man of integrity and that you teach the way of God in accordance with the truth. You aren't swayed by men, because you pay no attention to who they are. Tell us then, what is your opinion? Is it right to pay taxes to Caesar or not?" But Jesus, knowing their evil intent, said, "You hypocrites, why are you trying to trap me? Show me the coin used for paying the tax." They brought him a denarius, and he asked them, "Whose portrait is this? Whose inscription?" "Caesar's," they replied. Then he said to them, "Give to Caesar what is Caesar's, and to God what is God's." When they heard this, they were amazed. So they left him and went away.- NIV

Jesus knows your thoughts. He could read minds and hearts then and He still can today. God knows the intentions and motives of His creation. He knit the heart and mind together. Don't you think He knows what's going on in them? He's God!

As attempts were made to trap God, so attempts will be made to trap and destroy Christians. As His followers, we have the Holy Spirit living within us. Ezekiel 36:26,27; "**And I will give you a new heart, and a new spirit I will put within you. And I will remove the heart of stone from your flesh and give you a heart of flesh. And I will put my Spirit within you, and cause you to walk in my statutes and be careful to obey my rules.**" The Holy Spirit and the spirit of the anti-christ are at odds with each other. The Spirit of God confounds the spirit of the world, in **a Waging War Within.** 1 Corinthians 1:27; "**But God chose what is foolish in the world to shame the wise; God chose what is weak in the world to shame the strong.**" Did you know that "Holy" means set aside for a special purpose? The Holy Spirit is "the Breath of God" That is, He is set aside as the Source of Life, and also to guide and direct you and I along the path of righteousness.

We should not be shocked when the people of this world system attack us, battle us and try to trap us. These people are fearful of Christians because we have the Holy Spirit living within us. The Holy Spirit convicts the unsaved of sin within their own lives. John 16:8; "**And when he comes, he will convict the world concerning sin and righteousness and judgment.**"

Let's not fall prey for the ungodly of this world and to their traps and attempts at maligning our relationship with the Lord Jesus Christ.

Jesus knows your thoughts

JULY

July 1st

Matthew 22:29-32- Jesus replied, "You are in error because you do not know the Scriptures or the power of God. At the resurrection people will neither marry nor be given in marriage; they will be like the angels in heaven. But about the resurrection of the dead- have you not read what God said to you, I am the God of Abraham, the God of Isaac, and the God of Jacob'? He is not the God of the dead but of the living."- NIV

The Word teaches that marriage as we know it will no longer exist in Heaven. We will be residing in Heaven as angels without a commitment to one person. We don't have to be bummed out about this. We will surely know our loved ones in Heaven. Matthew 8:11; "**I tell you, many will come from east and west and recline at table with Abraham, Isaac, and Jacob in the kingdom of heaven.**" Luke 9:30; "**And behold, two men were talking with him, Moses and Elijah.**" Luke 9:33; "**And as the men were parting from him, Peter said to Jesus, "Master, it is good that we are here. Let us make three tents, one for you and one for Moses and one for Elijah"**" Our love in Heaven will be even greater than our love here on earth was. God is able to establish relationships of far greater proportions than He did for us here. The Word teaches us that the eternal glories awaiting us will be more splendid than anyone could ever imagine. 1 Corinthians 2:9; "**But, as it is written, "What no eye has seen, nor ear heard, nor the heart of man imagined, what God has prepared for those who love him"** Ephesians 3:20; "**Now to him who is able to do far more abundantly than all that we ask or think, according to the power at work within us.**"

Jesus will take His Church people that are living in the Rapture and those that have died with Him in His resurrection. God is coming back to take us to live with Him forever and ever. He didn't create us to be bound to this earth, but He created us to be one with Him for eternity. God promises that He will be back to transfigure His Church to glory and the paradise that He has created for us that have accepted Him. This truth is paramount to our way of thinking as Christians. We're no longer bound by the things of this world, because our focus is on eternity.

Know the
power
of God

July 2nd

Matthew 22:34-40- Hearing that Jesus had silenced the Sadducees, the Pharisees got together. One of them, an expert in the law, tested him with this question: "Teacher, which is the greatest commandment in the Law?" Jesus replied: "Love the Lord your God with all your heart and with all your soul and with all your mind." This is the first and greatest commandment. And the second is like it: 'Love your neighbor as yourself.' All the Law and the Prophets hang on these two commandments."-NIV

We need to battle it out in the culture in which we live. Daily we need to spend quality time with God. Communication with our Savior is key to not just surviving, but winning **The Waging War Within.** We will be tested by the people of the world and by God Himself. Testing with God will provide us with refinement. God uses tests to mold us more into His image. He will allow testing to refine and buff our rough edges. God will allow certain people to come in and out of our lives in order to mold us and to draw us closer to Himself. Just as with Lot, God knows our limits and He tests us with them. 1 Peter 1:6-7; **"In this you rejoice, though now for a little while, if necessary, you have been grieved by various trials, so that the tested genuineness of your faith—more precious than gold that perishes though it is tested by fire—may be found to result in praise and glory and honor at the revelation of Jesus Christ."**

The most important thing is to have a pervasive passion for Jesus Christ. Seeking God through prayer, worship, praise, reading of the Bible and fellowship should take precedence over every other aspect of our lives. We need to have passion for Christ in a disciplined fashion.

You know the fervor in which you cheer on your favorite sports team, be it the Boston Red Sox or the Green Bay Packers, we need to generate that same enthusiasm with our Lord and savior Jesus Christ. He deserves nothing less. Don't you agree?

Look at all that Jesus Christ has done for you and then think of what a sports figure has done for you. There is no sports figure that has really done anything for me personally except for a few that have spoken at Prayer Breakfasts or Promise Keeper events where their talks have touched my heart. Jesus Christ died so that we might have life. John 10:10; **"The thief comes only to steal and kill and destroy. I came that they may have life and have it abundantly."** Think about that the next time you watch a ball game and get excited when your team hits a home run or scores a touchdown.

Have life abundantly

July 3rd

Matthew 23:8-12- "But you are not to be called 'Rabbi,' for you have only one Master and you are all brothers. And do not call anyone on earth 'father,' for you have one Father and he is in heaven. Nor are you to be called 'teacher,' for you have one Teacher, the Christ. The greatest among you will be your servant. For whoever exalts himself will be humbled, and whoever humbles himself will be exalted.-NIV

How powerful! We as Christians have one Master. We're all called brothers and sisters. We have One Heavenly Father, God, and we have One Teacher and He is called Jesus Christ. The greatest among us will be our servant. Whoever puffs himself up will be demoted and whoever demonstrates humility will be lifted up. Does this not go against the current of the world? We as Christians are like salmon going up stream. The world system is the antithesis of this. The world says be the best at any cost. The end justifies the means. It doesn't matter how you get there, just get there anyway you know how. Stomp over people, lie, cheat, steal and conquer others. It's the survival of the fittest. No ethical or moral standard seems to be a compass for guidance. The world slogan is if it feels good, do it. Do unto others then split. Just do it! Lift yourselves up by your proverbial boot straps and do it. Our Christian community and lives are being negatively inundated by **The Waging War Within.**

We as Christians are to be servants to each other. Christ is our example. He came to serve others, not to be served. Mark 10:43-45; "**But it shall not be so among you. But whoever would be great among you must be your servant, and whoever would be first among you must be slave of all. For even the Son of Man came not to be served but to serve, and to give his life as a ransom for many.**" He gave of Himself whole heartedly; He gave the ultimate price, His life. Jesus Christ is our everything! He's our Master and our teacher. Without Christ we wouldn't have salvation. John 14:6; "**I am the way, and the truth, and the life. No one comes to the Father except through me.**"

Jesus Christ is our existence. He is the Giver of Life. We live because He lived. 1 John 4:13-16; "**By this we know that we abide in him and he in us, because he has given us of his Spirit. And we have seen and testify that the Father has sent his Son to be the Savior of the world. Whoever confesses that Jesus is the Son of God, God abides in him, and he in God. So we have come to know and to believe the love that God has for us. God is love, and whoever abides in love abides in God, and God abides in him.**" God loved us so much that He sacrificed His Son's life so that we might live.

July 4th

Matthew 23:13-14- **"Woe to you, teachers of the law and Pharisees, you hypocrites! You shut the kingdom of heaven in men's faces. You yourselves do not enter, nor will you let those enter who are trying to.-NIV**

Happy Independence Day!! Watch out and beware of false teachers. Watch out for they will try to lead you astray from your faith in Christ. **A Waging War within** is on for the eternal destiny of your soul. Religious leaders, even some considered the elect of the church will be leading the flock away in the last days. Don't let anything come between you and Jesus Christ. He's the reason that your heart is even beating. With every step you take on earth Jesus should be at the center of your life. With every breath you take, Jesus should be on your mind. With every beat of your heart, Jesus should be your hearts cry. He's the reason we have life and even exist.

Many even today are manipulative hypocrites. They will distract you from your high calling in Jesus Christ. Don't ever let this happen. God has a divine destiny for your life. Don't ever let anyone prevent you from fully answering this high calling you have on your life and the race that God desires you to run with a passion not of this world. Be ready and vigilant. 1 Peter 5:8; **"Be sober-minded; be watchful. Your adversary the devil prowls around like a roaring lion, seeking someone to devour."** Be strategic in your thinking. Believe God not men in their deceitful scheming. God does everything He can to lead people to Himself, it's the people that turn their backs on Jesus. These same individuals don't understand and comprehend **The Waging War Within** that's being carried out in the supernatural and natural worlds alike.

Remember that accepting Jesus Christ is the key that unlocks the door for eternity in Heaven for us. Jesus Christ is The Way, The Truth and The Life. John 14:6; **"I am the way, and the truth, and the life. No one comes to the Father except through me."** We need to believe this verse with our whole heart. If we forget everything else, this we need to remember, our eternity rests on it.

Beware of false teachers!

Be sure of what you preach.

July 5th

Matthew 23:15,16- "Woe to you, teachers of the law and Pharisees, you hypocrites! You travel over land and sea to win a single convert, and when he becomes one, you make him twice as much a son of hell as you are. "Woe to you, blind guides! You say 'If anyone swears by the temple, it means nothing; but if anyone swears by the gold of the temple, he is bound by his oath.'-NIV

Jesus wasn't angered by the fact that the Pharisees were trying to win converts, He was angered by the fact that they were trying to enforce all of their extra biblical traditions. The Pharisees made a habit of focusing on traditions and on swearing the wrong oaths. They missed the whole reason that Jesus Christ came to earth, to sacrifice Himself for mankind so that they could have eternal life with Him. They focused on sacrifices but not The Sacrifice, Jesus. We swear by Christ and His sacrifice.

Don't let anyone mess around with your soul, your spirit, your mind, your heart, your life and your eternal reward that God has given you as a Christian who believes in Him. The destructive forces within our world culture will try to bring you down and so will Satan himself. Satan and his demonic forces will try to annihilate you and bring you to hell. Satan will strategize anyway he can to do this. He will bring people to manipulate you, to turn you from the faith you have in Christ. Satan will use subtle strategies and tactics for combat and sometimes he will use pervasive ones. Never let down your guard and always keep in prayer, asking for the blood covering of Jesus Christ.

Don't allow the things of this world to distract you from your road to your Heavenly calling and destiny. As Saint Bernard of Clairvaux said, "Individuals may do bad things even though they intend the results to be good." This is another way of saying that the ends justify the means. The road to hell is paved with good intentions. Procrastination is an enemy to us all. How often do we intend to do good things only to put them off until later? We cannot afford to do this with our surrendering of our lives to God and His Son Jesus Christ. We need to act and act now.

We need to be radically sold out for Christ. Let's not teeter-totter around planning to surrender later. We need not be resting on a lukewarm fence. Vacillating is not Godly. We need to make a decision and stand on it. Let's stand on the side of God.

Stand on the side of God!

Matthew 23:17-22- You blind fools! Which is greater: the gold, or the temple that makes the gold sacred? You also say, 'If anyone swears by the altar, it means nothing; but if anyone swears by the gift on it, he is bound by his oath. You blind men! Which is greater: the gift, or the altar that makes the gift sacred? Therefore, he who swears by the altar swears by it and by everything on it. And he who swears by the temple swears by it and by the one who dwells in it. And he who swears by heaven swears by God's throne and by the one who sits on it. –NIV

We are accountable to God and His Son, Jesus Christ. Our accountability is an ongoing thing. It is for each and every moment of each and every day. Our yes is to be yes and our no is to be no. We are bound by our word, not an oath.

Spiritual blindness still exists today. If you're drawing closer to Jesus Christ, don't expect others to be able to see what you see spiritually. Not everyone has the passion to draw unto God and to allow the Holy Spirit to enlighten them. 1 Corinthians 2:9-11; "**But, as it is written, "What no eye has seen, nor ear heard, nor the heart of man imagined, what God has prepared for those who love him"— these things [20]God has revealed to us through the Spirit. For the Spirit searches everything, even the depths of God. For who knows a person's thoughts except the spirit of that person, which is in him? So also no one comprehends the thoughts of God except the Spirit of God.**" Some people don't feel the need. They're comfortable with their lives. They have everything they want and they don't see the need of a Savior. Especially in America, people can begin to become complacent due to having so much. How much does one rely and trust in God when they have so much materialism? People by nature, when comfortable, don't stretch themselves too much.

God equates spiritual blindness with hypocrisy, and many are highly educated and quite intelligent by the world's standards, yet before God they are spiritually blind and foolish. John 12:35; "**The light is among you for a little while longer. Walk while you have the light, lest darkness overtake you. The one who walks in the darkness does not know where he is going.**" In order to have the blinders removed, one must realize that God is our sacred gift and that fear in Him is the beginning of wisdom. Proverbs 1:7; "**The fear of the LORD is the beginning of knowledge; fools despise wisdom and instruction.**" Proverbs 9:10; "**The fear of the LORD is the beginning of wisdom, and the knowledge of the Holy One is insight.**" We need to be wise in all that we say and all that we do. Folly brings ruin whereas wisdom brings joy.

We are accountable to God

Matthew 23:23,24- "Woe to you, teachers of the law and Pharisees, you hypocrites! You give a tenth of your spices- mint, dill and cumin. But you have neglected the more important matters of the law- justice, mercy and faithfulness. You should have practiced the latter, without neglecting the former. You blind guides! You strain out a gnat but swallow a camel.-NIV

Jesus was not Biblical. He wanted them to continue this practice of tithing, but He also wanting them to concentrate on the much larger matters. The Pharisees used to strain the impurities out of the temple wine and they would overlook the entire unbiblical goings on taking place in their own personal lives. They needed to concentrate on the sanctity in which they lived them. God clearly has expectations that need to be met on every front. He confronted the Pharisees and called them hypocrites.

God elevates the importance of justice, mercy and faithfulness. In the fullness of time God expects these important internal Godly traits to be practiced and carried out in our own lives. He doesn't appreciate and He downright frowns on those that talk one thing and do another. He doesn't like when we just talk the talk. He expects us to walk the walk. He wants us to focus on the important things. We need to keep our focus on what God sees as important and key in our relationship with Him. Let's not be like the Pharisees of the past. He doesn't like duplicity!

Notice the religious leaders were primarily focused on the outward appearance of things. Things are not always as they appear to the naked eye. Jesus is attempting to get the Pharisees to realize that internal qualities relating to justice, mercy and faithfulness are of primary importance to God and His followers. These are matters of the heart. He wants us to practice these Godly internal principles, while at the same time carrying out the outward fundamental aspects of our faith in God.

Justice, mercy and faithfulness

July 8th

Matthew 23:25-28- "Woe to you, teachers of the law and Pharisees, you hypocrites! You clean the outside of the cup and dish, but inside they are full of greed and self-indulgence. Blind Pharisee! First clean the inside of the cup and dish, and then the outside also will be clean. "Woe to you, teachers of the law and Pharisees, you hypocrites! You are like whitewashed tombs, which look beautiful on the outside but on the inside are full of dead men's bones and everything unclean. In the same way, on the outside you appear to people as righteous but on the inside you are full of hypocrisy and wickedness.-NIV

Let's look at the motives of our own hearts. Jesus is using this example of the Pharisees and how they were so focused on self and satisfying their own needs. We can learn from these key scriptures. The same applies to us today. Are we consumed with our own interests beyond those of others? Are we so focused on our self that we cannot even begin to see the needs of others? We need to change our focus from self and place the focus on others.

To clean ourselves from within we must repent and draw unto God and allow His Holy Spirit to cleanse and rid us of the filth within. Let's not think of ourselves more highly than we ought. Apart from God we're nothing. With God we're everything we need to be. We're children of the King of Kings. We are sons and daughters of The Most High God. We need to hold our heads high, all while not being overcome with wrongful pride.

Let's not be hypocritical in our Christian Faith. We represent Jesus Christ and Him crucified. We need to be vigilant in how we live and with every aspect of our lifestyle. When you have God operating in your life, you shouldn't do the things that the world does. You should be living differently. This difference should be evident as the Holy Spirit works in our lives. I truly believe that our witness to the world in most cases is lifestyle evangelism. It's all about how we live, how we act, how we treat our families, how we treat each other, what we say and do. Out of the heart a man acts and speaks. Matthew 15:18-19; "But what comes out of the mouth proceeds from the heart, and this defiles a person. For out of the heart come evil thoughts, murder, adultery, sexual immorality, theft, false witness, slander." Luke 8:12; "The ones along the path are those who have heard. Then the devil comes and takes away the word from their hearts, so that they may not believe and be saved." Romans 12:2; "Do not be conformed to this world, but be transformed by the renewal of your mind, that by testing you may discern what is the will of God, what is good and acceptable and perfect."

What is the will of God for your life?

July 9th

Matthew 23:29-32- "Woe to you, teachers of the law and Pharisees, you hypocrites! You build tombs for the prophets and decorate the graves of the righteous. And you say, 'If we had lived in the days of our forefathers, we would not have taken part with them in shedding the blood of the prophets. So you testify against yourselves that you are the descendants of those who murdered the prophets. Fill up, then, the measure of the sin of your forefathers!-NIV

Jesus showed the true hearts of the Pharisees that in their complicity to have Him killed, they were just as guilty as their forefathers were in having the prophets killed and persecuted. We need to watch the intentions of our hearts. We also need to be watchful in what we do and insure that we are not involved in the schemes of the dark one.

Jesus takes a bold stance and conveys His unlimited authority with the Pharisees. He doesn't back down from the religious leaders of the time. He pursues them speaking in parables and with authority. He speaks with the ultimate authority. He confounded the religious leaders. He confounded the wisdom of that present age. He challenged the religious establishment with His speech. He was articulate and passionate. When He spoke they listened, however they didn't understand because their hearts were hardened and spiritually shackled.

Jesus didn't mince words. He was right to the point. Jesus conveyed a righteous anger towards the hypocrisy that the religious leaders were living. Jesus raised the standard and thought that their practices were detestable and deplorable. Jesus was a strategist in engaging the Pharisees in **The Waging War Within.**

Don't ever
back down
in your faith

July 10th

Matthew 23:33-36- "You snakes! You brood of vipers! How will you escape being condemned to hell? Therefore I am sending you prophets and wise men and teachers. Some of them you will kill and crucify; others you will flog in your synagogues and pursue from town to town. And so upon you will come all the righteous blood that has been shed on earth, from the blood of righteous Abel to the blood of Zechariah son of Berekiah, whom you murdered between the temple and the altar. I tell you the truth; all this will come upon this generation.-NIV

When Jesus speaks of sin, it would be best if we heeded His words. Here we have Jesus speaking of Abel's murder and how he was the very first murder victim and then He mentioned Zechariah who was the last murder victim mentioned in 2 Chronicles, which is the last book of the Jewish canon. By Jesus calling the Pharisees snakes, He was emphasizing the guilt of the religious leaders. Jesus demonstrated a righteous anger. Anger is not a bad thing as long as it is controlled. Feelings are not right or wrong, they are natural. It is what we do with our feelings that make them right or wrong.

God is speaking of sin. He refers to the religious leaders of the time as snakes and tells them that they will be condemned to hell. Jesus speaks to the killing, crucifying and flogging they will do of the prophets, wise men and teachers. God spoke in His righteous anger against the things the religious leaders were doing and would do in the future.

As Christians today, shouldn't we have a righteous anger toward the atrocities that are happening around our world? We should be at the forefront in combating **The Waging War Within** that's transpiring at various fronts around the world. As believers we should be up in arms at the injustices that are happening. We should be the ones starting all the leading organizations to combat poverty, abortion, death and destruction, the divorce rate, the demise of the traditional family, unwed pregnancies, teen pregnancy, the homeless situation and the political agenda of the ungodly.

Let us be bold as we engage the culture of this unsaved world with the agenda of God. God has a way of doing things that are far above the world's ways. 1 Corinthians 2:10-11; "**God has revealed to us through the Spirit. For the Spirit searches everything, even the depths of God. For who knows a person's thoughts except the spirit of that person, which is in him? So also no one comprehends the thoughts of God except the Spirit of God.**" Let us strategize, engage, educate and work toward changing for the better our society and culture. Let us promote and lift up God and His Word and put it all into action. God wasn't, and He currently isn't, a coward. We've been created in His image. Genesis 1:27; "**God created man in his own image, in the image of God he created him; male and female he created them.**"

July 11th

Matthew 23:37-39- "O Jerusalem, Jerusalem, you who kill the prophets and stone those sent to you, how often I have longed to gather your children together, as a hen gathers her chicks.-NIV

When Jesus spoke of Jerusalem, He was actually referring to all of Israel. Israel turned her back on Jesus and the truths He preached and He grieved deeply for her. He begged the Jews to listen to His Word but they wouldn't.

The Jewish leaders led their people toward destruction. All of the Jewish religious authority collapsed with the destruction of the temple in AD 70. Great judgment befell Israel and I believe it is still falling till this present day. God doesn't play games. What He says He will do, He will do. When God takes you to the woodshed it is not a pleasant visit. His punishment can be and is severe. Just look at Sodom and Gomorrah. Genesis 18:22-19:29 for an example.

When the religious leaders were killing the prophets a **Waging War Within** was being initiated. A turf war, if you will, was ensuing between the Pharisees and the prophets sent of God. The Pharisees refuted the words from Jesus and thought that every word of teaching that came out of His mouth was from the realm of the demonic. They even thought the miracles that Jesus performed were due to power that He received from demonic forces. **A Waging War Within** was being carried out, the battle cry for the souls of mankind was beginning to be initiated between the forces of the antichrist and God.

Despite the devastation and the destruction that was being initiated by the religious leaders toward Jesus Christ, God still displayed His love for Jerusalem and it's children. He longed to reach out and help the children of Jerusalem, but the religious leaders of the day were holding Jerusalem in bondage. The people were shackled, held hostage and bound in false teachings taught by men imprisoned in their traditions.

What God says He will do,
He will do.

July 12th

Matthew 24:1-2- Jesus left the temple and was walking away when his disciples came up to him to call his attention to its buildings. "Do you see all these things? He asked. "I tell you the truth, not one stone here will be left on another; everyone will be thrown down."-NIV

Jesus was speaking of the destruction of Jerusalem in AD70 when the Roman army laid siege to Jerusalem and the Temple. That was the consequence that Jerusalem paid their denying God and Jesus as the Son of God. How many of us have turned our backs on God and His commandments for us at some point in our lives? I know it has happened to a great many people and we still have today to turn back and rededicate our lives to Him once again. Why not rededicate our lives to Him anew even if we haven't turned? It is a good time here and now and it's not too late to get right with God.

The gates of hell will not be able to stand against Jesus Christ and the building of His true church. Jesus came to conquer and to build His church. God came to conquer the enemy and He did. He paid the price for the sin of humanity on the Cross of Calvary. It's finished. The debt for the sins of mankind has been paid. One died for all, so that all might live for eternity. God desires creating a people that uncompromisingly will follow Him, wherever He leads them. He's not in the business of putting up buildings, even though He might use people to do that. He's more interested in your heart, your mind, your soul, your spirit and the inner workings of who you are in Him. He's in the business of transformation. He longs to bring you to new levels and uncharted territory with Him. Be all you can be in Jesus Christ. Belong to Jesus Christ and Him alone. Seek only the Kingdom of God and everything else will fall into place.

Get right with God
before it's too late to do so.

July 13th

Matthew 24:3- As Jesus was sitting on the Mount of Olives, the disciples came to him privately. "Tell us," they said, "when will this happen, and what will be the sign of your coming and of the end of the age?"-NIV

Jesus' disciples had questions as we all do pertaining to the future of mankind. We would all like to be able to know of future events so that we can plan accordingly. The reason we don't have the answers is that we are to be prepared regardless of the coming events. We need to live today as if it were our last day here on earth. Ghandi said "Live as if you were to die tomorrow. Learn as if you were to live forever." He may not have been Christian but he sure hit the nail on the head. We need to live for Christ as if we were being called home tomorrow and we need to learn His Word as if our lives depended on it because they do. Matthew 24:36; **"But concerning that day and hour no one knows, not even the angels of heaven, nor the Son, but the Father only."** Mark 13:32; **"But concerning that day or that hour, no one knows, not even the angels in heaven, nor the Son, but only the Father."** Notice this is mentioned more than once in the Word? Maybe emphasis was placed on it for a reason. We are being warned that we must be prepared at all times.

The disciples longed to know when the end of the age would transpire. Most likely the disciples lost sleep over this and constantly had this on their mind. When would their Master be coming back once He leaves? The disciples wanted to know the signs of the times, when would they know and how would they tell He was coming again. They were human as we are. Jesus was also. He is the only one to be 100% Divine and 100% human. He was taught things as we all were when we were growing up. He grew up as we all did. Luke 2:52; **"And Jesus increased in wisdom and in stature and in favor with God and man."** Hebrews 5:8; **"Although he was a son, he learned obedience through what he suffered."** He hurt as we all hurt and He laughed as we do also. Jesus grew in wisdom and knowledge as He grew up for He was the Son of God. John 2:25; **"He needed no one to bear witness about man, for he himself knew what was in man."** John 16:30; **"Now we know that you know all things and do not need anyone to question you; this is why we believe that you came from God."** John 21:17; **"He said to him the third time, "Simon, son of John, do you love me?" Peter was grieved because he said to him the third time, "Do you love me?" and he said to him, "Lord, you know everything; you know that I love you." Jesus said to him, "Feed my sheep."** Jesus was and is God. He has called us to feed His sheep. Let's get to it shall we?

Let's get busy shall we?

July 14th

Matthew 24:4-8- Jesus answered: "watch out that no one deceives you. For many will come in my name, claiming, 'I am the christ.' and will deceive many. You will hear of wars and rumors of wars, but see to it that you are not alarmed. Such things must happen, but the end is still to come. Nation will rise against nation and kingdom against kingdom. There will be famines and earthquakes in various places. All these are the beginning of birth pains.-NIV

Since the resurrection of Christ, there have been people proclaiming to be Him. We need to guard ourselves from such heresies. Jesus warns us not to be deceived by false prophets and those claiming to be the Christ. During these times we will hear of warfare going on around the world. Kingdoms will be rising against other kingdoms and there will be famines and earthquakes. I think that all these things have already started and with the era of terrorism things seem to have intensified. In my life time never have I personally felt the traumatic effects of a 911 hitting American soil. Never before in my life did I watch two of the largest buildings in the world located on American soil tumble down due to a terrorist regime with a pervasive hatred toward America.

I was doing administrative responsibilities as a counselor only to have a colleague come into my office stating that the twin towers have been hit by planes and the United States is under attack. I remember that I literally had goose bumps on my arms. I could not believe that warfare was happening on American soil. This was the onslaught of the enemy, the thrust of a terrorist plot and the scheme of Satan to **Wage a War Within** our borders. The taking of innocent American lives by an enemy that went virtually undetected and unseen until they turned a means of transportation into weapons of destruction.

God has warned of **The Waging War Within** that will be interfacing on the world scene. God doesn't want us to be alarmed as if He hasn't warned us that these things are to happen. These things are a sign of the times and they will happen before He arrives to take His church. All of creation has been groaning as if mourning for centuries. Romans 8:22-23; **"For we know that the whole creation has been groaning together in the pains of childbirth until now. And not only the creation, but we ourselves, who have the first fruits of the Spirit, groan inwardly as we wait eagerly for adoption as sons, the redemption of our bodies."** We are all seeing this. There has been pain and anguish since sin entered the scene in the Garden of Eden. Isaiah 13:8; **"They will be dismayed: pangs and agony will seize them; they will be in anguish like a woman in labor. They will look aghast at one another; their faces will be aflame."** Isaiah 21:3; **"Therefore my loins are filled with anguish; pangs have seized me, like the pangs of a woman in labor; I am bowed down so that I cannot hear; I am dismayed so that I cannot see."** Isaiah 42:14; **"For a long time I have held my peace; I have kept still and restrained myself; now I will cry out like a woman in labor; I will gasp and pant."** Jeremiah 30:5-7; **"Thus says the LORD: We have heard a cry of panic, of terror, and no peace. Ask now, and see, can a man bear a child? Why then do I see every man with his hands on his stomach like a woman in labor? Why has every face turned pale? Alas! That day is so great there is none like it; it is a time of distress for Jacob; yet he shall be saved out of it."** Hosea 13:13; **"The pangs of childbirth come for him, but he is an unwise son, for at the right time he does not present himself at the opening of the womb."** We will witness great suffering and cry out as a woman with birth pains. Isaiah 26: 17-19; "Like a pregnant woman who writhes and cries out in her pangs when she is near to giving birth, so were we because of you, O LORD; we were pregnant, we writhed, but we have given birth to wind. We have accomplished no deliverance in the earth, and the inhabitants of the world have not fallen. Your dead shall live; their bodies shall rise. You who dwell in the dust, awake and sing for joy! For your dew is a dew of light, and the earth will give birth to the dead." Isaiah 66:7-11; "**Before she was in labor she gave birth; before her pain came upon her she delivered a son. Who has heard such a thing? Who has seen such things? Shall a land be born in one day? Shall a nation be brought forth in one moment? For as soon as Zion was in labor she brought forth her children. Shall I bring to the point of birth and not cause to bring forth?" says the LORD; shall I, who cause to bring forth, shut the womb?" says your God. "Rejoice with Jerusalem, and be glad for her, all you who love her; rejoice with her in joy, all you who mourn over her; that you may nurse and be satisfied from her consoling breast; that you may drink deeply with delight from her glorious abundance."** Jeremiah 22:23; "**O inhabitant of Lebanon, nested among the cedars, how you will be pitied when pangs come upon you, pain as of a woman in labor!**" Micah 4:9-10; "**Now why do you cry aloud? Is there no king in you? Has your counselor perished, that pain seized you like a woman in labor? Writhe and groan, O daughter of Zion, like a woman in labor, for now you shall go out from the city and dwell in the open country; you shall go to Babylon. There you shall be rescued; there the LORD will redeem you from the hand of your enemies.**" This is not a pretty picture is it?

God will obtain the attention of His creation one way or another. Unfortunately for some, it will be of loss, due to war, famine, home, country, loved ones, whatever the means necessary to get their attention. I can remember how full the churches around America were after one of America's darkest hours when the Towers fell. They didn't remain full for very long did they? The event captured the people's attention for only a little while. He wants our attention for all time, not momentarily. What will it take to get it? How much more pain and anguish must we suffer?

How much does it take?

July 15th

Matthew 24:9-14- then you will be handed over to be persecuted and put to death, and you will be hated by all nations because of me. At that time many will turn away from the faith and will betray and hate each other, and many false prophets will appear and deceive many people. Because of the increase of wickedness, the love of most will grow cold, but he who stands firm to the end will be saved. And this gospel of the kingdom will be preached in the whole world as a testimony to all nations, and then the end will come.-NIV

America will be hated because of its Christian Faith. Jesus says that we will be hated by all nations because of Him. We will be persecuted, put to death and hated by other nations. We all know that history repeats itself. 911 was evidence of things that will happen before the coming of Jesus Christ. Countries that harbor terrorists operating in the guise of religious zealots will be a threat to our country.

Some Christians will grow cold in their faith and will turn against one another. False prophets will arise on the scene teaching deception. There will be an increase in wickedness and evil. We're already witnessing the evil that is happening within our country and around the world. Human depravity seems rampant and on the rise.

God says that we who stand firm will be saved. Mark 13:13; "**And you will be hated by all for my name's sake. But the one who endures to the end will be saved.**" We cannot let **The Waging War Within** our worlds deter us from our salvation, living for God and carrying out His Divine Destiny for our lives. We must study, analyze, strategize and ultimately deter the enemy proactively from attack on our souls. We must stand our ground and realize that God wants us to spread His Word using means that are ethical, moral and worthy of His name. Ephesians 6:10-20 is the "Armor of God" chapter. With this we are prepared for battle. We have been given the "Armor of God" to use so that we can withstand the darts of the enemy. There is only one offensive weapon, the Sword of the Spirit, God's Word. All of the other pieces are defensive. In verses 10-13 we have the **Lord's Strength**. Ephesians 6:10-13; "**Finally, be strong in the Lord and in the strength of his might. Put on the whole armor of God, that you may be able to stand against the schemes of the devil. For we do not wrestle against flesh and blood, but against the rulers, against the authorities, against the cosmic powers over this present darkness, against the spiritual forces of evil in the heavenly places. Therefore take up the whole armor of God, that you may be able to withstand in the evil day, and having done all, to stand firm.**" Verses 14-17 are our charge to **Stand Firm**. Ephesians 6:14-17; "**Stand therefore, having fastened on the belt of truth, and having put on the breastplate of righteousness, and, as shoes for your feet, having put on the readiness given by the gospel of peace. In all circumstances take up the shield of faith, with which you can extinguish all the flaming darts of the evil one; and take the helmet of salvation, and the sword of the Spirit, which is the word of God,**" Verses 18-20 is our instruction to **Be Constant in Prayer**. Ephesians 6:18-20; "**praying at all times in the Spirit, with all prayer and supplication. To that end keep alert with all perseverance, making supplication for all the saints, and also for me, that words may be given to me in opening my mouth boldly to proclaim the mystery of the gospel, for which I am an ambassador in chains, that I may declare it boldly, as I ought to speak.**"

Paul closes Ephesians with a blessing being offered up for all believers who will

236~ The Waging War Within

follow him in their walks. "Peace be to all the brothers, and love with faith, from God the Father and the Lord, Jesus Christ. Grace be with all who love our Lord Jesus Christ with love incorruptible." This is beautiful. Paul had a heart for God seldom seen. He started out as a persecutor of Christians and he saw that many were even put to death for their beliefs. God got his attention one day and we see the beautiful and miraculous transformation that took place. I believe that the greatest miracle is a transformed heart. I know what God has done in my life and the lives of many and this to me is more powerful than a healing from an illness or sight given to the blind. A transformed heart is a witness to all and it is one that can change the world given the chance.

Paul's life is a witness of the power of God. If He can get Paul to lay down his life for Him, imagine what He can do for us. What a letter Paul left for us all. We need to take his words to heart. When we have God on our side, we can withstand anything. Romans 8:31; "**If God is for us, who can be against us?**" Amen and Amen.

If God is for us, who can be against us?

July 16th

Matthew 24:23-25- at that time if anyone says to you, 'Look, here is the christ! Or, 'there he is!" do not believe it. For false christs and false prophets will appear and perform great signs and miracles to deceive even the elect-if that were possible. See, I have told you ahead of time.-NIV

Open God's Word and read for yourself the warnings that He has given us. Presently there are people on the world scene that are claiming to be the Christ and others that are claiming to be prophets sent of God. God is warning His Church of **The Waging War Within** that will potentially have devastating consequences on the church and His believers.

Know God's Word. Know the Scriptures and your footing and foundation will be sure. The only way to combat the enemy is with the Word of God. The Bible has the truth within its pages to reveal to you the truth and armor of God. (Ephesians 6:10-20). God wants you to be equipped to win the war spiritually. He desires that your mind, heart and your entire being become saturated with the Word of God. We have to be girded up with the truth inherent within the pages of the Bible.

When God reveals that even the elect of His Church will be subject to the infiltration of the enemy shouldn't we take serious warning? We need to be vigilant, steadfast, disciplined and passionate about our Christian Faith. More than ever before, we need to cling to Jesus.

The Word of God tells us to "test the spirits". Matthew 7:15-20; **"Beware of false prophets, who come to you in sheep's clothing but inwardly are ravenous wolves. You will recognize them by their fruits. Are grapes gathered from thorn bushes, or figs from thistles? So, every healthy tree bears good fruit, but the diseased tree bears bad fruit. A healthy tree cannot bear bad fruit, nor can a diseased tree bear good fruit. Every tree that does not bear good fruit is cut down and thrown into the fire. Thus you will recognize them by their fruits."** 1 John 4:1; **"Beloved, do not believe every spirit, but test the spirits to see whether they are from God, for many false prophets have gone out into the world."** We are not to be gullible of spirits. We need to observe their doctrine and conduct and see for ourselves if they match up with God's Doctrine, His Word. We have been given spiritual discernment so that we are not led blindly by every whim and deceiver that comes along. False prophets have been around since Christ first appeared. We need to be wise in all that we do. Proverbs 13:20 says **"Whoever walks with the wise becomes wise, but the companion of fools will suffer harm."** Let's be wise my friends.

July 17th

  Matthew 24:27-29- for as lightning that comes from the east is visible even in the west, so will be the coming of the son of man. Wherever there is a carcass, there the vultures will gather. "Immediately after the distress of those days "the sun will be darkened, and the moon will not give its light; the stars will fall from the sky, and the heavenly bodies will be shaken."-NIV

  Don't be caught unaware. You don't want the buzzards circling overhead waiting to devour your carcass. You want to be ready for His triumphant return. So prepare yourself for the coming of Jesus Christ. Matthew 24:36; "But concerning that day and hour no one knows, not even the angels of heaven, nor the Son, but the Father only." God will be coming soon. No one knows the hour or the time, but He will be coming to claim His church. God will come back as lightning to take us. Keep yourself close to God. This is all that matters. No one but God satisfies. Nothing within this world compares to God and the love that we have found in Jesus Christ. The next time you're tempted to sin remember that Jesus has the power to keep you, to sustain you and cover you with His supernatural blood covering. Call on the name of Jesus. We call on the name of Jesus to save us, but we can call on the name of Jesus at any time for any need that we have. When we're in need Jesus is there.

  Do not let anything separate you from the love of God or to take away from your witness in Him. When He comes back you want to be found doing God's business and nothing else. You want to be found in right relationship to God when Jesus comes back on the scene. You don't want Him to cast you aside. You'll want to be with Him for eternity. Count the cost and pay the price it takes to follow God. Luke 14:25-35; "Now great crowds accompanied him, and he turned and said to them, "If anyone comes to me and does not hate his own father and mother and wife and children and brothers and sisters, yes, and even his own life, he cannot be my disciple. Whoever does not bear his own cross and come after me cannot be my disciple. For which of you, desiring to build a tower, does not first sit down and count the cost, whether he has enough to complete it? Otherwise, when he has laid a foundation and is not able to finish, all who see it begin to mock him, saying, 'This man began to build and was not able to finish.' Or what king, going out to encounter another king in war, will not sit down first and deliberate whether he is able with ten thousand to meet him who comes against him with twenty thousand? And if not, while the other is yet a great way off, he sends a delegation and asks for terms of peace. So therefore, any one of you who does not renounce all that he has cannot be my disciple. "Salt is good, but if salt has lost its taste, how shall its saltiness be restored? It is of no use either for the soil or for the manure pile. It is thrown away. He who has ears to hear, let him hear."" Don't look to the right or the left. Proverbs 4:27; "Do not swerve to the right or to the left; turn your foot away from evil." Just look straight to Jesus and stay the course. When He returns He will be pleased with your faith in Him. You'll win the prize He's called you heavenward in Jesus for and He will say to you, "well done thy good and faithful servant." Matthew 25:23; "His master said to him, 'Well done, good and faithful servant. You have been faithful over a little; I will set you over much. Enter into the joy of your master."

July 18th

Matthew 24:30-31- "at that time the sign of the son of man will appear in the sky, and all the nations of the earth will mourn. They will see the son of man coming on the clouds of the sky, with power and great glory. And he will send his angels with a loud trumpet call, and they will gather his elect from the four winds, from one end of the heavens to the other.-NIV

There will be great moaning in the lives of the many that were left behind. Could you imagine what it would be like if you were left behind? How sad. Knowing you could have been one of the elect and you passed up the opportunity in order to party another day with your friends must be one of the most heart wrenching feelings known to man. I pray you make the right decision. If you haven't made the decision yet to give your life to Christ, you're not too late. Act now, you don't want to miss out, you want to see the Son of God return in all His glory don't you?

Talk about being heavenly minded. All I want is Jesus. Think about this Scripture. Jesus is coming back with His angels and will be gathering up His church. There should be nothing that we desire as much as this. Nothing! I will be rejoicing at the coming of Jesus, because I'm saved and going to live with Him for eternity. I will not be mourning, because I will be going with Him. Praise God! Decisions determines destiny. You should emphatically make the choice and decision to live every waking moment as if He could come back any second and take you with Him.

At any moment Jesus could come back and take you if you've accepted His free gift of salvation. Jesus could come while you're working, you're vacationing, you're getting married, and you're sleeping in or whatever you're doing. Jesus could come when you least expect it. Ephesians 1:4; **"He chose us in him before the foundation of the world, that we should be holy and blameless before him."** He desires you to lift up His name on this side of Heaven. He has a specific divine destiny planned from the beginning of the world for you. He has singled you out for something beautiful and He desires to bless your life beyond belief. Don't look back, just forward at what Jesus has called you for while living out the life that He gave you

Acts 4:29; **"And now, Lord, look upon their threats and grant to your servants to continue to speak your word with all boldness."** Acts 4:29 says that we are to "speak your Word with all boldness", and it is followed up with verse 30; **"while you stretch out your hand to heal, and signs and wonders are performed through the name of your holy servant Jesus."** This is how I want to be remembered.

Matthew 24:33-35- even so, when you see all these things, you know that it is near, right at the door. I tell you the truth, this generation will certainly not pass away until all these things have happened. Heaven and earth will pass away, but my words will never pass away.-NIV

God's Word is eternal. Our soul is eternal. Our heavenly reward is eternal. Our destiny with God has always been determined by Him to never end. He never intended for us to die. He intended for us to live eternally. He made the eternal soul to carry out His will here on earth. The physical body only lasts for our earthly life, however then we will put on our heavenly bodies that are eternal and supernatural. We have hope with Christ here on earth and even after His coming! Psalms 34:22; **"The LORD redeems the life of his servants; none of those who take refuge in him will be condemned."** Praise God! Don't you think it's about time we started to look at things through the lens of Scripture? If you suffer physically, the good news is that we will have new bodies when we pass on into eternity. We will have bodies that are uncorrupted with maladies and pain.

Jesus could be right at the door ready to make His move to earth with speed and finality. He has warned us, His people to live as if you're ready for the rapture. We must have a sense of urgency in our spiritual lives. This is of critical importance. We must be focused on Christ with a tenacity that this world cannot even comprehend. When we're saved and have the Holy Spirit operating in our lives, the old is gone and the new has come. Old things have passed away and we are born again into His Supernatural Kingdom. The war still exists for us; however God has given us the Holy Spirit to fight **The Waging War Within.** With the Holy Spirit we will have victory.

My friends, let's be wise in all of our decisions. We need to seek Him and follow Him fully. Proverbs 27:11; **"Be wise, my son, and make my heart glad, that I may answer him who reproaches me."** Isaiah 55:6; **"Seek the LORD while he may be found; call upon him while he is near."** Joel 2:32; **"And it shall come to pass that everyone who calls on the name of the LORD shall be saved. For in Mount Zion and in Jerusalem there shall be those who escape, as the LORD has said, and among the survivors shall be those whom the LORD calls."** Answer His call.

God's Word
will never
pass away!

July 20th

Matthew 24: 36-41- "no one knows about that day or hour, not even the angels in heaven, nor the son, but only the father, As it was in the days of Noah, so it will be at the coming of the son of man. For in the days before the flood, people were eating and drinking, marrying and giving in marriage, up to the day Noah entered the ark; and they knew nothing about what would happen until the flood came and took them all away. That is how it will be at the coming of the son of man. Two men will be in the field; one will be taken and the other left. Two women will be grinding with a hand mill; one will be taken and the other left.-NIV

I'm pretty sure you don't want to be left behind here on earth when Christ reappears. I know I certainly don't. I have committed my life to Jesus and walked uprightly with God now for years. Ever since I accepted Jesus Christ as my Personal Lord and Savior I've been radically on fire for the Lord Jesus with no turning back. I've intensely, for years sought Him in prayer. I have sought Him for His will in my life. I have sought Him to draw me closer into a relationship with Him. I have sought Jesus to bless my family so that we can be a blessing to others and to touch the world for Jesus Christ. Most importantly I have specifically asked God to captivate, conquer and control my life with His Holy Spirit. I've asked God to keep me pure and living righteously while here on earth. God has answered every single one of my prayers. God's way may not necessarily be the way I wanted all of my prayers answered, but none the less they were answered according to His will for my life. He is never late in answering my prayer, always on time and always in His way.

Christ is coming soon, of that I have no doubt. Just as Christ wishes, I too pray that none should perish. John 3:15-16; "**That whoever believes in him may have eternal life. For God so loved the world, that he gave his only Son, that whoever believes in him should not perish but have eternal life.**" It speaks in 1 Thessalonians 5 of the imminent second coming and it says how we need to be sober minded and prepared for that awesome day. 1 Thessalonians 5:1-6; "**Now concerning the times and the seasons, brothers, you have no need to have anything written to you. For you yourselves are fully aware that the day of the Lord will come like a thief in the night. While people are saying, "There is peace and security," then sudden destruction will come upon them as labor pains come upon a pregnant woman, and they will not escape. But you are not in darkness, brothers, for that day to surprise you like a thief. For you are all children of light, children of the day. We are not of the night or of the darkness. So then let us not sleep, as others do, but let us keep awake and be sober.**" Are you ready? Christ is coming soon. Praise God!!

Matthew 24: 42-44- "therefore keep watch, because you do not know on what day your lord will come. But understand this: if the owner of the house had known at what time of night the thief was coming, he would have kept watch and would not have let his house be broken into. So you also must be ready, because the son of man will come at an hour when you do not expect him.-NIV

Be ready! Be ready! God is coming back at an hour and a time when you least expect it. Wow! Do you believe this? I sure hope so. I know that I don't want to be left behind when God comes back. See you, I'm out of here. I'm just passing through. I've believed and put my faith in God, not man or man's philosophies or ideologies. For me the Kingdom of God has become of paramount importance above and beyond the culture of this world.

I can't wait. It can't come soon enough for me. My wife and my three children have accepted Jesus Christ as their Personal Lord and Savior and are out of here at the coming of our Lord and Savior, Jesus Christ. We've had the opportunity to live together here in our temporary temporal existence, but onward and upward we will go to our heavenly reward. Praise God! Hallelujah. Amen. Tell it like it is!

We need to have God enlighten us to the reality of His return. This will transform our earthly lives with a much clearer focus to the reality of Jesus Christ and our lives here on earth. Our focus will be clearer and our Christian Living will be more fruitful if we live with this at the forefront of our lives. Our passion for Christ and Christian living is radically renewed when our focus is on His return. This return will be sudden.

Shouldn't we be bringing people into the fold, into a relationship with Jesus Christ? Shouldn't we be asking ourselves from the time we get up to the time we go to bed, "What we can do for Jesus today?" God has predestined a divine destiny for our lives since the foundation of the world. Shouldn't we be seeking out His divine destiny for our lives? You know we should.

Have you ever had your house broken into? I have. It's not a good feeling to know that someone was in your house while you were sleeping upstairs. That is what happened to me. I was working and my wife Maria was sleeping upstairs when someone broke into our home. She called me at work and said "Gregg, someone broke into the house while I was upstairs sleeping." We were caught unaware. That is how it is going to be when Christ makes His triumphant return. We will be unaware of the day or the hour. Are you ready? If not, you better get your life right.

No-one knows the day or hour

July 22nd

Matthew 25:31-33- "When the son of man comes in his glory, and all the angels with him, he will sit on his throne in heavenly glory. All the nations will be gathered before him, and he will separate the people one from another as a shepherd separates the sheep from the goats. He will put the sheep on his right and the goats on his left.- NIV

The Lord Jesus will come back and take His chosen people from every tribe, every kindred and every nation. Matthew 28:19; "**Go therefore and make disciples of all nations, baptizing them in the name of the Father and of the Son and of the Holy Spirit.**" Jesus will take His church from every country, from every socio-economic group and from every people group around our globe. He owns it all! Every last ounce of the world, He owns. He created it. He's the Creator of everything. Everything that we can see, as well as the things we cannot see. He's the Creator of the world.

God will cast out all of the people that haven't put their trust in Him and He will gather up to glory all the people that have humbled themselves to salvation through Him. Matthew 7:21-23; "**Not everyone who says to me, 'Lord, Lord,' will enter the kingdom of heaven, but the one who does the will of my Father who is in heaven. On that day many will say to me, 'Lord, Lord, did we not prophesy in your name, and cast out demons in your name, and do many mighty works in your name?' And then will I declare to them, 'I never knew you; depart from me, you workers of lawlessness.'**" Matthew 13:40-43; "**Just as the weeds are gathered and burned with fire, so will it be at the close of the age. The Son of Man will send his angels, and they will gather out of his kingdom all causes of sin and all law-breakers, and throw them into the fiery furnace. In that place there will be weeping and gnashing of teeth. Then the righteous will shine like the sun in the kingdom of their Father. He who has ears, let him hear.**" God's grace saves. Salvation can only be obtained from God through His grace. These things are spiritually discerned and people that are shackled in sin have a difficult time understanding the things of God. Isaiah 55:8-9; "**For my thoughts are not your thoughts, neither are your ways my ways, declares the LORD. For as the heavens are higher than the earth, so are my ways higher than your ways and my thoughts than your thoughts.**" Romans 8:5-6; "**For those who live according to the flesh set their minds on the things of the flesh, but those who live according to the Spirit set their minds on the things of the Spirit. To set the mind on the flesh is death, but to set the mind on the Spirit is life and peace.**" 1 Corinthians 2:14; "**The natural person does not accept the things of the Spirit of God, for they are folly to him, and he is not able to understand them because they are spiritually discerned.**" A majority of the time adults have to hit rock bottom in their addictions, meaningless existence, false religious beliefs and their sin before they begin to understand the salvation message that is within the pages of the Gospel of Jesus Christ. Let's not hit rock bottom before we realize the fact that God exists. He created us. We're in need of salvation and a relationship with Him to fulfill our God given divine destiny here on this planet. This is no joke. Billions of people all over the world are asking themselves, "What is the meaning of my existence?" Billions of people are searching for the answer. This is why it is of critical importance that the Gospel message be preached all over the world. Matthew 28:16-20; "Now the eleven disciples went to Galilee, to the mountain to which Jesus had directed them. And when they saw him they worshiped him, but some doubted. And Jesus came and said to them, "All authority in heaven and on earth has been given to me. Go therefore and make disciples of all nations, baptizing them in the name of the Father and of the Son and of the Holy Spirit, teaching them to observe all that I have commanded you."

All of the nations
will be gathered
before Him

July 23rd

Matthew 25: 34-36- "then the king will say to those on his right, 'Come, you who are blessed by my father; take your inheritance, the kingdom prepared for you since the creation of the world. For I was hungry and you gave me something to eat, I was thirsty and you gave me something to drink, I was a stranger and you invited me in, I needed clothes and you clothed me, I was sick and you looked after me, I was in prison and you came to visit me.'-NIV

We're the representatives for Jesus Christ while here on earth, nothing else. We weren't created to live to ourselves and gratify our own desires. We were created to live out God's divine destiny for our lives. God knit us together, we're His handy work. Like gasoline powers and propels an engine, so The Holy Spirit empowers and propels us as Christians living here on earth. He is the Potter, we are His clay. Jeremiah, 18:1-11; **"The word that came to Jeremiah from the LORD: "Arise, and go down to the potter's house, and there I will let you hear my words." So I went down to the potter's house, and there he was working at his wheel. And the vessel he was making of clay was spoiled in the potter's hand, and he reworked it into another vessel, as it seemed good to the potter to do. Then the word of the LORD came to me: "O house of Israel, can I not do with you as this potter has done? declares the LORD. Behold, like the clay in the potter's hand, so are you in my hand, O house of Israel. If at any time I declare concerning a nation or a kingdom, that I will pluck up and break down and destroy it, and if that nation, concerning which I have spoken, turns from its evil, I will relent of the disaster that I intended to do to it. And if at any time I declare concerning a nation or a kingdom that I will build and plant it, and if it does evil in my sight, not listening to my voice, then I will relent of the good that I had intended to do to it. Now, therefore, say to the men of Judah and the inhabitants of Jerusalem: 'Thus says the LORD, behold, I am shaping disaster against you and devising a plan against you. Return, everyone from his evil way, and amend your ways and your deeds.'"**

Look around at the needs that exist within our world, our society, our cities, our towns, our communities, our churches and our families. Then let's point the proverbial finger at ourselves. What am I doing? How can I help? What need can I meet? How can I give? What would God have me to do? If we pray, He will give us an answer. Seek Him and His counsel.

God says that when we help those that need our help, we've done it for Him. Matthew 25: 31-46; **"When the Son of Man comes in his glory, and all the angels with him, then he will sit on his glorious throne. Before him will be gathered all the nations, and he will separate people one from another as a shepherd separates the sheep from the goats. And he will place the sheep on his right, but the goats on the left. Then the King will say to those on his right, 'Come, you who are blessed by my Father, inherit the kingdom prepared for you from the foundation of the world. For I was hungry and you gave me food, I was thirsty and you gave me drink, I was a stranger and you welcomed me, I was naked and you clothed me, I was sick and you visited me, I was in prison and you came to me.' Then the righteous will answer him, saying, 'Lord, when did we see you hungry and feed you, or thirsty and give you drink? And when did we see you a stranger and welcome you, or naked and clothe you? And when did we see you sick or in prison and visit you?' And the King will answer them, 'Truly, I** say to you, as you did it to one of the least of these my brothers, you did it to me.' "Then he will say to those on his left, 'Depart from me, you cursed, into the eternal fire prepared for the devil and his angels. For I was hungry and you gave me no food, I was thirsty and you gave me no drink, I was a stranger and you did not welcome me, naked and you did not clothe me, sick and in prison and you did not visit me.' Then they also will answer, saying, 'Lord, when did we see you hungry or thirsty or a stranger or naked or sick or in prison, and did not minister to you?' Then he will answer them, saying, 'Truly, I say to you, as you did not do it to one of the least of these, you did not do it to me.' And these will go away into eternal punishment, but the righteous into eternal life." He looks down from Heaven with favor for those of us that seek direction from Him. Our guidance must come from above. Our vertical relationship must come first before the earthly horizontal relationship with our world can be carried out within the umbrella of God's divine destiny for our lives. We must seek first His Kingdom and everything else will unfold in God's timing and with God's divine destiny in the midst. Matthew 6:33; "**But seek first the kingdom of God and his righteousness, and all these things will be added to you.**"

We need to keep our focus on God and not on the world. Matthew 6:24; "**No one can serve two masters, for either he will hate the one and love the other, or he will be devoted to the one and despise the other. You cannot serve God and money.**" You cannot serve both God and whatever it is that is keeping you from Him. It's one or the other, the choice is yours.

Since the
creation of
the world,
He has known you

July 24th

Matthew 25: 37-39- "then the righteous will answer him, 'Lord, when did we see you hungry and feed you, or thirsty and give you something to drink? When did we see you a stranger and invite you in, or needing clothes and clothe you? When did we see you sick or in prison and go to visit you?"-NIV

Jesus Christ and the Gospel have a profound impact on those that truly hear the word. Take it to heart and actually apply it within your life. The gospel doesn't return void on good soil. Isaiah 55:11; **"So shall my word be that goes out from my mouth; it shall not return to me empty, but it shall accomplish that which I purpose, and shall succeed in the thing for which I sent it."** The Holy Spirit moves when God's Word is preached to both the righteous and the unrighteous. The righteous will grow in God's word. Proverbs 2:1-5; **"My son, if you receive my words and treasure up my commandments with you, making your ear attentive to wisdom and inclining your heart to understanding; yes, if you call out for insight and raise your voice for understanding, if you seek it like silver and search for it as for hidden treasures, then you will understand the fear of the LORD and find the knowledge of God."** Proverbs 4:4; **"Let your heart hold fast my words; keep my commandments, and live."** Proverbs 4:20-24; **"My son, be attentive to my words; incline your ear to my sayings. Let them not escape from your sight; keep them within your heart. For they are life to those who find them, and healing to all their flesh. Keep your heart with all vigilance, for from it flow the springs of life. Put away from you crooked speech and put devious talk far from you."** Proverbs 7:1; **"My son, keep my words and treasure up my commandments with you."** The unrighteous will come to salvation through the preaching of the Holy Bible.

Our communities are profoundly positively impacted on this side of Heaven, within our temporal existence, with the eternal message. Christians have throughout the ages started and maintained Christian organizations that helped the poor, the hungry, the sick and the downtrodden. These organizations have been throughout the United States and around the world. Church related and Para church organizations have been extended to the communities as an extension of Jesus Christ to the world. Even today many of these organizations continue to do good works in the name of our Lord and Savior Jesus Christ.

When we as Christian believers enter the Kingdom of Heaven, God will say to us, Matthew 25:23; **"Well done thy good and faithful servant, you can enter your reward, the Kingdom that I have prepared for you."** I myself have found that as I draw closer and closer to Jesus Christ, He's become a supernatural extension of who I am. It's not me that can do things for God, but Christ within me. Despite all my faults He uses me. I have found that I am led by the Holy Spirit to do good works for Him, in the name of the Father, the Son and the Holy Ghost. All I want is Jesus to work through me on this side of Heaven, before I go on to my eternal reward. The meaning of my life and the fulfillment that I find is only found in one, Jesus Christ. When the faithful enter the Kingdom we will supernaturally have led our lives to help those that were in need, in the name of the Lord Jesus. God will acknowledge this before His angels in Heaven. James 1:25; **"But the one who looks into the perfect law, the law of liberty, and perseveres, being no hearer who forgets but a doer who acts, he will be blessed in his doing."** Ephesians 2:1-10 explains that there is nothing that we can do to earn our way into Heaven. It is not works that allow us entry, but faith. Ephesians 2:1-10; **"And you were dead in the trespasses and sins in which you** once walked, following the course of this world, following the prince of the power of the air, the spirit that is now at work in the sons of disobedience— among whom we all once lived in the passions of our flesh, carrying out the desires of the body and the mind, and were by nature children of wrath, like the rest of mankind. But God, being rich in mercy, because of the great love with which he loved us, even when we were dead in our trespasses, made us alive together with Christ— by grace you have been saved— and raised us up with him and seated us with him in the heavenly places in Christ Jesus, so that in the coming ages he might show the immeasurable riches of his grace in kindness toward us in Christ Jesus. For by grace you have been saved through faith. And this is not your own doing; it is the gift of God, not a result of works, so that no one may boast. For we are his workmanship, created in Christ Jesus for good works, which God prepared beforehand, that we should walk in them."

**It is not by works,
it is by faith
that we are admitted
into Heaven.**

July 25th

Matthew 25:40-43- "the king will reply, 'I tell you the truth, whatever you did for one of the least of these brothers of mine, you did for me.' "Then he will say to those on his left, 'depart from me, you who are cursed, into the eternal fire prepared for the devil and his angels. For I was hungry and you gave me nothing to eat, I was thirsty and you gave me nothing to drink, I was a stranger and you did not invite me in, I needed clothes and you did not clothe me, I was sick and in prison and you did not look after me.'-NIV**

We are called to take care of the least just as Jesus' disciples were. There are needy among us as there were then. We are called to take care of any and all needy that are in legitimate need, not just those in the body of believers. If we follow through on this order we will be blessed. The Word cannot be any clearer on this point.

The opposite will be true for those on this side of Heaven that didn't carry out God's Will by giving to those that were in need. The fact of the matter is that when Jesus Christ is indwelling within you, you just want to spend the time that God has given you living for Him and helping others to see Christ in you whether by His works operating in you or His heart in you. One thing that naturally flows by the power of the Holy Spirit through us is giving of ourselves to others. All we want to do is spread God's Word and bless others with what Jesus Christ has given to us. Let others see God working through us to reach the world and to build up others in the faith. God desires that His Gospel Message would be shared freely. He would want us to use as many modalities as possible to get His Word spread around the globe. Matthew 28: 19-20; "**Go therefore and make disciples of all nations, baptizing them in the name of the Father and of the Son and of the Holy Spirit, teaching them to observe all that I have commanded you.**" He desires that every human being would have the opportunity to make a decision for His salvation message. 1 Timothy 2:3-4; "**This is good, and it is pleasing in the sight of God our Savior, who desires all people to be saved and to come to the knowledge of the truth.**"

In this passage we see that those that are disobedient on this side of Heaven will receive the due penalty of not accepting, following and living out the message of Jesus Christ. Literally, there will be hell to pay. A struggle, **The Waging War Within** and a battle is ensuing for the souls of man. Upon acceptance of Jesus Christ, the Holy Spirit comes to live in us and to work through us. Hebrews 2:4; "**God also bore witness by signs and wonders and various miracles and by gifts of the Holy Spirit distributed according to his will.**" 1 Corinthians 2:4-5; "**My speech and my message were not in plausible words of wisdom, but in demonstration of the Spirit and of power, that your faith might not rest in the wisdom of men but in the power of God.**" 1 Corinthians 2:10; "**These things God has revealed to us through the Spirit. For the Spirit searches everything, even the depths of God.**" Those that haven't accepted Jesus Christ in many instances are operating out of the flesh. Look what I can do. People that are humanistic in orientation are operating on a level where they're lifting themselves up, instead of God and God's Word. Self-aggrandizement is big for those that don't know Jesus, because they're operating out of the spirit of the flesh. Remember, man cannot save himself from the eternal judgment. God is the one that judges the hearts, the motives and lives of people. Ecclesiastes 3:16-17; "**Moreover, I saw under the sun that in the place of justice, even there was wickedness, and in the place of righteousness, even there was wickedness. I said in my heart, God will judge the** righteous and the wicked, for there is a time for every matter and for every work." The Creator judges the creation. We're accountable to God and God alone at the eternal judgment call. Jesus received fulfillment in carrying out the Father's will. John 4:34; "**My food is to do the will of him who sent me and to accomplish his work.**" This is a great example to follow, don't you agree?

I can't begin to express the sense of fulfillment when I am knowingly following the will of God. There is a sense of peace that is so far beyond words. When you are walking in the will of the Father you will know beyond a shadow of a doubt that you are on the right track. If you don't know what that will for your life is, ask Him and He will let you know. Ask Him what He has for you to do the next time you pray, and remember, prayer is proportional to your ears and your mouth. God gave us two ears to listen twice as much as we talk.

**Ask God what His
will for your life is.
He won't leave you
hanging for an answer.**

Matthew 25:44-46- "they also will answer, 'Lord, when did we see you hungry or thirsty or a stranger or needing clothes or sick or in prison, and did not help you?' "He will reply, 'I tell you the truth, whatever you did not do for one of the least of these, you did not do for me.' "Then they will go away to eternal punishment, but the righteous to eternal life."-NIV

The sheep will inherit the Kingdom of God and the wolves will inherit the Kingdom of Hell. They who carried out the will of God cared for the lost sheep and the wolves just laid in waiting for them so that they could hurt and devour them. They will get their just do when they stand in judgment before God.

When we accept Jesus Christ we begin to realize that we're not the center of the universe. We're not it. Our attention is no longer focused on self, our feelings and what we think we need to do. We become focused on God and what His Will is for our lives. God's Will takes precedence over our own will, our own needs, wants and desires. We become focused on others and the needs of others.

These are very strong words by the prophets of old. This is definitely reality therapy! Listen, this is a wake-up call to the world. Let's get busy with the things of God. The time is short and He is going to come back shortly and take His Church. John 14:3; "**And if I go and prepare a place for you, I will come again and will take you to myself, that where I am you may be also.**" Let's be ready, doing the things that the Lord would have us to do in the last days. We need to have vigilance about our work for the Lord Jesus Christ. Right now as you read this book, the world is vigilant in spreading their message, whatever that might be. As Christians, we need to take our Christian message to the entire world. Matthew 28:19-20; "**Go therefore and make disciples of all nations, baptizing them in the name of the Father and of the Son and of the Holy Spirit, teaching them to observe all that I have commanded you.**" The world is a competitive place and the world longs for power, prestige and presence. We must allow the Holy Spirit to flow through us. 1 Corinthians 12:4-12; "**Now there are varieties of gifts, but the same Spirit; and there are varieties of service, but the same Lord; and there are varieties of activities, but it is the same God who empowers them all in everyone. To each is given the manifestation of the Spirit for the common good. To one is given through the Spirit the utterance of wisdom, and to another the utterance of knowledge according to the same Spirit, to another faith by the same Spirit, to another gifts of healing by the one Spirit, to another the working of miracles, to another prophecy, to another the ability to distinguish between spirits, to another various kinds of tongues, to another the interpretation of tongues. All these are empowered by one and the same Spirit, who apportions to each one individually as he wills. For just as the body is one and has many members, and all the members of the body, though many, are one body, so it is with Christ.**" Ephesians 4:11-16; "**And he gave the apostles, the prophets, the evangelists, the pastors and teachers, to equip the saints for the work of ministry, for building up the body of Christ, until we all attain to the unity of the faith and of the knowledge of the Son of God, to mature manhood, to the measure of the stature of the fullness of Christ, so that we may no longer be children, tossed to and fro by the waves and carried about by every wind of doctrine, by human cunning, by craftiness in deceitful schemes. Rather, speaking the truth in love, we are to grow up in every way into him who is the head, into Christ, from whom** the whole body, joined and held together by every joint with which it is equipped, when each part is working properly, makes the body grow so that it builds itself up in love." We must allow His complete and unbridled power to unleash the gifts and abilities that He has given us to reach the world with His Truth. No compromise. This comes with a cost, but the reward is great. Luke 5:11; "**And when they had brought their boats to land, they left everything and followed him.**" Luke 9:57-62; "**As they were going along the road, someone said to him, "I will follow you wherever you go." And Jesus said to him, "Foxes have holes, and birds of the air have nests, but the Son of Man has nowhere to lay his head." To another he said, "Follow me." But he said, "Lord, let me first go and bury my father." And Jesus said to him, "Leave the dead to bury their own dead. But as for you, go and proclaim the kingdom of God." Yet another said, "I will follow you, Lord, but let me first say farewell to those at my home." Jesus said to him, "No one who puts his hand to the plow and looks back is fit for the kingdom of God."**" Luke 14:25-33; "**Now great crowds accompanied him, and he turned and said to them, "If anyone comes to me and does not hate his own father and mother and wife and children and brothers and sisters, yes, and even his own life, he cannot be my disciple. Whoever does not bear his own cross and come after me cannot be my disciple. For which of you, desiring to build a tower, does not first sit down and count the cost, whether he has enough to complete it? Otherwise, when he has laid a foundation and is not able to finish, all who see it begin to mock him, saying, 'This man began to build and was not able to finish.' Or what king, going out to encounter another king in war, will not sit down first and deliberate whether he is able with ten thousand to meet him who comes against him with twenty thousand? And if not, while the other is yet a great way off, he sends a delegation and asks for terms of peace. So therefore, any one of you who does not renounce all that he has cannot be my disciple.**" All must come to know Him! We must find our calling and then work at it with an uncompromising tenacity.

Leave everything behind
and follow Me!

July 27th

Matthew 26:40-41- then he returned to his disciples and found them sleeping. "Could you men not keep watch with me for one hour?" He asked Peter. "Watch and pray so that you will not fall into temptation. The spirit is willing, but the body is weak."-NIV

We have to realize our own weaknesses. We're weak in the flesh, but strong with the Holy Spirits power invigorating us to carry out His Will for our lives. Apart from God we can do nothing. Humility has to be present within our spiritual lives. We have to acknowledge on a second by second, minute by minute basis where our strength comes from. It comes from above. It comes from God.

God gives us endurance and perseverance so we will be able to make it through persecution. Hebrews 10:32-36; "**But recall the former days when, after you were enlightened, you endured a hard struggle with sufferings, sometimes being publicly exposed to reproach and affliction, and sometimes being partners with those so treated. For you had compassion on those in prison, and you joyfully accepted the plundering of your property, since you knew that you yourselves had a better possession and an abiding one. Therefore do not throw away your confidence, which has a great reward. For you have need of endurance, so that when you have done the will of God you may receive what is promised.**" God gives us confidence. Hebrews 3:6; "**Christ is faithful over God's house as a son. And we are his house if indeed we hold fast our confidence and our boasting in our hope.**" Hebrews 4:16; "**Let us then with confidence draw near to the throne of grace, that we may receive mercy and find grace to help in time of need.**" Hebrews 10:19; "**Therefore, brothers, since we have confidence to enter the holy places by the blood of Jesus.**" God gives us endurance. Hebrews 12:1; "**Therefore, since we are surrounded by so great a cloud of witnesses, let us also lay aside every weight, and sin which clings so closely, and let us run with endurance the race that is set before us.**" We need to be practicing God's will. Hebrews 13:21; God will "**equip you with everything good that you may do his will, working in us that which is pleasing in his sight, through Jesus Christ, to whom be glory forever and ever.**" We need to be practicing God's will with the goal of inheriting the promised salvation. Hebrews 4:1; "**Therefore, while the promise of entering his rest still stands, let us fear lest any of you should seem to have failed to reach it.**" Hebrews 6:12; "**so that you may not be sluggish, but imitators of those who through faith and patience inherit the promises.**" Hebrews 8:6; "**But as it is, Christ has obtained a ministry that is as much more excellent than the old as the covenant he mediates is better, since it is enacted on better promises.**" Hebrews 9:15; "**Therefore he is the mediator of a new covenant, so that those who are called may receive the promised eternal inheritance, since a death has occurred that redeems them from the transgressions committed under the first covenant.**"

The disciples couldn't even keep watch for Jesus an hour. He warned the disciples about the weakness of their fleshly existence. He is warning the disciples of **The Waging War Within** that is being fought out in the realm of our physical and spiritual existences. Temptations are of the devil. God doesn't tempt His Church or anyone. Our own fleshly desires, the devil, his demonic forces and our sinful nature throw us into the turmoil of temptation.

We must keep alert on our own spiritual journey with Jesus Christ. We must keep Him at the center of our universe, in clear focus and as our priority in every aspect of our lives. We must acknowledge the truth in His return and what this means to our lives. Matthew 24:31; **"And he will send out his angels with a loud trumpet call, and they will gather his elect from the four winds, from one end of heaven to the other."** 1 Corinthians 15:51-52; **"Behold! I tell you a mystery. We shall not all sleep, but we shall all be changed, in a moment, in the twinkling of an eye, at the last trumpet. For the trumpet will sound, and the dead will be raised imperishable, and we shall be changed."** With His return at the forefront of our existence we should live differently, with a clearer vigilance in our Christian walk and with an all-consuming fire igniting our Christian life and our existence as a whole.

Jesus will be returning
with the blast of a mighty trumpet.

Are you ready?

July 28th

Matthew 26:42- He went away a second time and prayed, "My father, if it is not possible for this cup to be taken away unless I drink it, may your will be done."- NIV

Jesus set a great example for us to emulate when He prayed to His Father. We need to be in constant prayer. We need most of all to pray that His will be done in our lives and that we set our own will aside. If we pray this and obey His will for us, we will be on a solid footing.

Like those Christians of old, we will have to go through times of great trial and suffering. Even in times of great difficulty we must pray that God's will be done and carried out in our lives. We must remain in constant prayer. Luke 21:36; "**But stay awake at all times, praying that you may have strength to escape all these things that are going to take place, and to stand before the Son of Man.**" Another thing we need to do is we need to give praise. Here is something that will probably come as a shock to a few people. Ephesians 5:20; "**Give thanks always and for everything to God the Father in the name of our Lord Jesus Christ.**" Did you notice that it said always, not just in the good times or when things are going our way? It said to give praise always and for everything. Our focus has to be brought back into subjection to Him and only Him. When Christ is at the forefront, He will be exalted no matter what happens in our temporal existence. Sometimes, even as Christians we will feel like we just can't continue the race set before us. Some of us will combat spiritual, physical, psychological/mental and other types of traumatic things that will come against us. We must in faith and belief continue to lift our eyes up to Jesus to give us strength in our time of need. Ultimately, we're trusting in Jesus, no matter what. Come life, or death or great persecution we're to trust God for deliverance and the wherewithal to stand for Him.

May the will of God always be done in our lives. We should always pray that the will of God be done in our lives. On all occasions, under all circumstances and in all situations we should be seeking God for His will in our lives. Whether we're in the valley or on the mountaintop, we should be asking God to supernaturally carry out His divine destiny in our lives. We should never settle for less than the constant seeking of His will to unfold within our precious life which God has breathed into existence. No other matter, beside the salvation of souls is more important to God then to have His divine destiny to take place within our lives. He specifically knit us together with His grand supernatural divine destiny to be carried out in our natural lives.

May God's will always be done in our lives

July 29th

Matthew 26:43-46- When he came back, he again found them sleeping, because their eyes were heavy. So he left them and went away once more and prayed the third time, saying the same thing. Then he returned to the disciples and said to them, "are you still sleeping and resting? Look, the hour is near, and the son of man is betrayed into the hands of sinners. Rise, let us go! Here comes my betrayer!"-NIV

The disciples were weary. They were exhausted and couldn't stay vigilant at the request of Jesus. We need to stay vigilant in our Christian walk for the Lord Jesus Christ. Matthew 25:13; **"Watch therefore, for you know neither the day nor the hour."** There is no other way. We need to keep our focus and place a concerted effort into the things of God. We must be disciplined, far beyond those of the world if we're going to combat the enemy. Our flesh is a weakness that sometimes gets the better of us. Matthew 26:41; **"Watch and pray that you may not enter into temptation. The spirit indeed is willing, but the flesh is weak."** Whether it's just being tired, frustrated, depressed, angry, or unconfident our flesh will lead us astray from the divine destiny that God has for our lives. We shouldn't rely on our natural selves to lead us on our spiritual journey. We need to be sensitive to the Will of God when He tells us something. Acts 9:6; **"Watch and pray that you may not enter into temptation. The spirit indeed is willing, but the flesh is weak."** Psalms 32:8; **"I will instruct you and teach you in the way you should go; I will counsel you with my eye upon you."** Psalms 37:23-24; "The **steps of a man are established by the LORD, when he delights in his way; though he fall, he shall not be cast headlong, for the LORD upholds his hand."**

Christians cannot afford to sleep in a day and age like today. We're experiencing a **Waging War Within** that is attacking our very existence. Forces are coming against the Christian believer like no other time in history. We must continue to battle to keep God on the throne and to lift up His name as the ultimate authority. Man will continue to fight against God for His position. Man wishes to place himself at the forefront of everything. Man likes to exalt himself in the places of power and authority. Let's pray that God would give us strength at a day and hour like this. We need to have a supernatural covering of protection against Satan and his demonic forces, so that we can be vigilant in God's divine destiny for our lives. Let's not grow weary. Galatians 6:6-10; **"One who is taught the word must share all good things with the one who teaches. Do not be deceived: God is not mocked, for whatever one sows, that will he also reap. For the one who sows to his own flesh will from the flesh reap corruption, but the one who sows to the Spirit will from the Spirit reap eternal life. And let us not grow weary of doing good, for in due season we will reap, if we do not give up. So then, as we have opportunity, let us do good to everyone, and especially to those who are of the household of faith."** Let's walk with the empowerment God gives.

When Jesus returned to His disciples after praying for the third time He was disappointed to find them sleeping once again. Jesus was attempting to get the disciples activated, ignited and vigilantly aware that He was going to be betrayed into the hands of sinners. The disciples were anything but vibrantly engaged at this point. Jesus expressed with importance and exclamation that His disciples should be warned what was about to take place. He warned them of the things to come. He has warned us in His written Word, but are we really heeding the warning of the coming calamity for those caught unprepared?

257~ The Waging War Within

How many times were we told of Jesus and we did not respond? Several people responded right away, some were even brought up in the faith, but there are those who have been told time and again with them still not responding. The spirit is willing but the flesh is weak. Matthew 26:41; **"Watch and pray that you may not enter into temptation. The spirit indeed is willing, but the flesh is weak."** We cannot afford to be caught sleeping at the wheel. We need to be ready for the glorious return of our Savior. There is much to do now. We have to get the Word out. We are running out of time my friends.

Have you been boldly presenting the Word to those you associate with? Are you living out the Word in all that you do? Are you ashamed or embarrassed to speak of Jesus to your inner circle of influence? If the answer to the last question I just presented is yes, why? Jesus is the Son of God. If you bought a new car you would show it off to your friends no question about it. Isn't Jesus more precious than a new car? You know He is. Why aren't we bragging about the awesomeness of Jesus like we do when we buy a new car or when we move into a new house? I don't understand this.

My friends, let's change our attitudes and start getting the Word out into the streets before it is too late. Let's put the Word into action. Let's get fired up for God. Let's start today.

Let's get fired up for Jesus!

Let's get the Word out!

Matthew 26:47-54- While he was still speaking, Judas, one of the twelve, arrived. With him was a large crowd armed with swords and clubs, sent from the chief priests and the elders of the people. Now the betrayer had arranged a signal with them: "the one I kiss is the man; arrest him." Going at once to Jesus, Judas said, "greetings. Rabbi!" and kissed him. Jesus replied, "Friend, do what you came for." Then the men stepped forward, seized Jesus and arrested him. With that, one of Jesus' companions reached for his sword, drew it out and struck the servant of the high priest, cutting off his ear. Put your sword back in its place," Jesus said to him, "for all who draw the sword will die by the sword. Do you think I cannot call on my father, and he will at once put at my disposal more than twelve legions of angels? But how then would the scriptures be fulfilled that say it must happen in this way?"-NIV

The betrayal of Jesus had now taken place with a kiss. A kiss typically is an acknowledgement of affection, but here it was a demonstration of betrayal and a trap for Jesus. Have you ever been betrayed? Have you ever been bewildered by the trap of a supposed friend? Jesus knew what was going to happen. Jesus knowing what would be carried out, told the men to do what they came for even before they acted.

Jesus knew that He could call on His angels in Heaven and that they would be at His side at once, a whole army of angels sent by the Father. Jesus knew **The Waging War Within** that existed and that this was part of God's Divine Plan. Jesus knew that the scriptures must be carried out and that God's providence was allowing all this to take place.

Jesus told His companion to put back his sword and not to use it. He realized that the fight was not within the physical world, but against the principalities and powers of this dark world. Ephesians 6:12; "**We do not wrestle against flesh and blood, but against the rulers, against the authorities, against the cosmic powers over this present darkness, against the spiritual forces of evil in the heavenly places.**" He knew that the fight had to take place with Him on His knees to His Father. Jesus also knew that He was the center of **The Waging War Within.** Jesus knew that He had to go to the cross, be crucified and to rise again for the sins of the world so that we might have eternal life with Him. It was a sacrifice He was willing to make.

He sacrificed Himself for us.
What have you sacrificed for Him?

July 31ˢᵗ

Matthew 26:55-56- at that time Jesus said to the crowd, "am I leading a rebellion, that you have come out with swords and clubs to capture me? Every day I sat in the temple courts teaching, and you did not arrest me. But this has all taken place that the writings of the prophets might be fulfilled." Then all the disciples deserted him and fled. Those who had arrested Jesus took him to Caiaphas, the high priest, where the teachers of the law and the elders had assembled. But Peter followed him at a distance, right up to the courtyard of the high priest. He entered and sat down with the guards to see the outcome.-NIV

A Waging War Within was being carried out. Jesus was left by His disciples. They took off like they never knew Him. Jesus questions His adversaries, "am I leading a rebellion, that you have come out with swords and clubs to capture me?" He knew that all of this must take place, there was no other way. The road that Jesus walked was predestined and preordained from the foundation of the world. Jesus was the center of the divine plan. He was and is The Way, The Truth and The Life.

Don't ever follow Jesus from a distance. Jesus needs to be the center of our lives, a reflection of who we are and the ultimate salvation of our souls. Following Jesus will come with a cost, a high price, but will end in Heavenly glory and eternal peace. Matthew 10:16-31; "Behold, I am sending you out as sheep in the midst of wolves, so be wise as serpents and innocent as doves. Beware of men, for they will deliver you over to courts and flog you in their synagogues, and you will be dragged before governors and kings for my sake, to bear witness before them and the Gentiles. When they deliver you over, do not be anxious how you are to speak or what you are to say, for what you are to say will be given to you in that hour. For it is not you who speak, but the Spirit of your Father speaking through you. Brother will deliver brother over to death, and the father his child, and children will rise against parents and have them put to death, and you will be hated by all for my name's sake. But the one who endures to the end will be saved. When they persecute you in one town, flee to the next, for truly, I say to you, you will not have gone through all the towns of Israel before the Son of Man comes. "A disciple is not above his teacher, nor a servant above his master. It is enough for the disciple to be like his teacher, and the servant like his master. If they have called the master of the house Beelzebub, how much more will they malign those of his household? "So have no fear of them, for nothing is covered that will not be revealed, or hidden that will not be known. What I tell you in the dark, say in the light, and what you hear whispered, proclaim on the housetops. And do not fear those who kill the body but cannot kill the soul. Rather fear him who can destroy both soul and body in hell. Are not two sparrows sold for a penny? And not one of them will fall to the ground apart from your Father. But even the hairs of your head are all numbered. Fear not, therefore; you are of more value than many sparrows." We have to count the cost of following Jesus. The cost doesn't even come close to the outweighing of the benefit though. Rest assured there is a cost. Don't you think that if the Christian life was easy everyone would be a Christian? Luke 14:28; "For which of you, desiring to build a tower, does not first sit down and count the cost, whether he has enough to complete it?" Jesus accepted the cost of Christianity with laying down His life. Are you willing to do the same if it came to that? Some have paid with their very lives. Giving of your very life is the greatest price in counting the cost of following the Master.

Romans 15:20-21; "**I make it my ambition to preach the gospel, not where Christ has already been named, lest I build on someone else's foundation, but as it is written, "Those who have never been told of him will see, and those who have never heard will understand.**" We are to speak and preach the Gospel of Christ. 2 Timothy 4:5; "**As for you, always be sober-minded, endure suffering, do the work of an evangelist, fulfill your ministry.**" We are to do the work of an evangelist and get the Word out. Are you holding up your end of the bargain? John 3:36; "**Whoever believes in the Son has eternal life; whoever does not obey the Son shall not see life, but the wrath of God remains on him.**" I am getting the Word out everywhere I go. I am proud to be called a son of God, a son of the Most High God. How about you? I pray that you answer yes. Let's get busy and answer our mission to get the Word to all those who are lost. It is not up to us to drag them to church, but it is up to us to expose them to the Word. What they do with the invitation is between them and God.

Are you spreading the Word?

Are you answering
your call to duty?

Let's get busy!

AUGUST

August 1st

Matthew 26:59-63- **The chief priests and the whole Sanhedrin were looking for false evidence against Jesus so that they could put him to death. But they did not find any, though many false witnesses came forward. Finally two came forward and declared, "this fellow said, 'I am able to destroy the temple of god and rebuild it in three days.' Then the high priest stood up and said to Jesus, "are you not going to answer? What is this testimony that these men are bringing against you?" But Jesus remained silent. The high priest said to him, "I charge you under oath by the living god: tell us if you are the Christ, the Son of God."-NIV**

The Sanhedrin had gathered and tried to find false witnesses who would credibly testify that Jesus had violated the law, so that they could find him guilty as quickly as possible. They were desperate to have Him out of their way as He was disrupting their way of life. The whole Council that gathered was not necessarily all 70 members of the Sanhedrin, it was most likely those who were roused to get their plan of having Jesus crucified well under way.

When Jesus was said to have been quoted where He said I am able to destroy the temple of God and rebuild it in three days was misquoted and taken out of context. John 2:19; **"Jesus answered them, "Destroy this temple, and in three days I will raise it up."''** This quote was easily distorted by Jesus' opponents.

The silence of Jesus was a fulfillment of Isaiah 53:7; **"He was oppressed, and he was afflicted, yet he opened not his mouth; like a lamb that is led to the slaughter, and like a sheep that before its shearers is silent, so he opened not his mouth."** This silence of Jesus places the responsibility for His death squarely on his accusers. When they asked Jesus to tell them if He was the Christ, Caiaphas wanted Jesus to admit to this charge so that He could be accused of insurrection against Rome and tried before Pilate for treason. This was their ticket to execute Him.

The accusations were flying around. The religious leaders wanted to catch Jesus. **The Waging War Within** was at its pinnacle! They all wanted to get and eliminate Jesus. How dare Jesus claim that He's the Christ. How dare Jesus claim that He's sent of God. How dare Jesus take man off the pedestal of power. Jesus remained silent as the slanderous remarks and accusations were slung at Him. How powerful was it that He remained silent in the midst of **The Waging War Within!** At the hands of those who were against Him and ultimately the one's that would crucify Him He remained silent. Jesus' silence is a powerful statement. He didn't have to prove Himself. He was and is God.

Matthew 26:64- 68-"Yes, it is as you say," Jesus replied. "But I say to all of you: In the future you will see the Son of Man sitting at the right hand of the mighty one and coming on the clouds of Heaven. Then the high priest tore his clothes and said, "He has spoken blasphemy! Why do we need any more witnesses? Look, now you have heard the blasphemy. What do you think?" "He is worthy of death," they answered. Then they spit in his face and struck him with their fists. Others slapped Him and said, "Prophesy to us, Christ. Who hit you?"-NIV

Jesus infuriated the Jewish leaders. He had declared that He was not only the Messiah but also the divine Son of Man. Daniel 7:13-14; "I saw in the night visions, and behold, with the clouds of heaven there came one like a son of man, and he came to the Ancient of Days and was presented before him. And to him was given dominion and glory and a kingdom, that all peoples, nations, and languages should serve him; his dominion is an everlasting dominion, which shall not pass away, and his kingdom one that shall not be destroyed." He said that He would sit at the right hand of His Father, God, and also that He would come again on a cloud to reign over the entire earth. Psalms 110:1-2; "The LORD says to my Lord: "Sit at my right hand, until I make your enemies your footstool." The LORD sends forth from Zion your mighty scepter. Rule in the midst of your enemies!" This statement enraged the High Priest so much so that he tore his cloths. This was normally forbidden but here it seemed to be an appropriate response. They felt that if Jesus was lying about the claim that He was divine then indeed He deserved death from the standpoint of the Jewish law. Leviticus 24:16; "Whoever blasphemes the name of the LORD shall surely be put to death. All the congregation shall stone him. The sojourner as well as the native, when he blasphemes the Name, shall be put to death. " The ironic thing here is He was to be executed for telling the truth.

The Jewish leaders' physical abuse of Jesus and their mocking question, "Who is it that struck you?" demonstrated their disbelief in His prophetic gifts. They felt that the abuse being meted out to Jesus was just for His claims to divinity. Jesus was up front and to the point with everything pertaining to His second coming and of who He indeed was. Jesus warned them that He was indeed the Son of God but they still mocked Him and abused Him. He knew that the religious leaders were going to look upon what He had said as blasphemy and He also knew that all of the events taking place needed to happen to fulfill His Divine Destiny.

After hearing Jesus tell of what was to happen, the high priest and the religious leaders tore His clothes and explained that He had spoken blasphemy. They answered that He is worthy of death. Jesus' whole life was a **Waging War Within**.

August 3rd

Matthew 26:69-74-"Now Peter was sitting out in the courtyard, and a servant girl came to him. "You also were with Jesus of Galilee," she said. But he denied it before them all. "I don't know what you're talking about," he said. Then he went out to the gateway, where another girl saw him and said to the people there, "This fellow was with Jesus of Nazareth." He denied it again, with an oath: "I don't know the man." After a little while, those standing there went up to Peter and said, "Surely you are one of them, for your accent gives you away." Then he began to call down curses on himself and he swore to them, "I don't know the man!" Immediately a rooster crowed."-NIV

Peter was sitting outside in the courtyard. This took courage for Peter to sit in the courtyard considering what was happening in the volatile area around the trial of Jesus, but his courage failed to show itself when his own personal safety was threatened. I am sure he would not be the lone man in the boat if this trial took place today. It is normal for one's self-preservation to reign when faced with danger and/or harm.

The oath that Peter took was not profanity but calling upon something sacred, especially God's name, to guarantee that what he said was true was not a good thing to do. Jesus warned us against making such oaths because what they did was they called into question the givers truthfulness and their integrity. Matthew 5:33-37; "**Again you have heard that it was said to those of old, 'You shall not swear falsely, but shall perform to the Lord what you have sworn.' But I say to you, Do not take an oath at all, either by heaven, for it is the throne of God, or by the earth, for it is his footstool, or by Jerusalem, for it is the city of the great King. And do not take an oath by your head, for you cannot make one hair white or black. Let what you say be simply 'Yes' or 'No'; anything more than this comes from evil.**" Now what Peter was doing was wrong because he was lying. He was one of the Disciples and he was from Galilee. All of Jesus' disciples, with the exception of Judas, were from Galilee, and Judeans in Jerusalem had often looked down on Galileans.

Peter denied Jesus. Imagine denying Jesus Christ after you were His disciple and you witnessed the miraculous healings, teachings and life of Jesus Christ. Peter denied Jesus. Imagine that. After everything they went through together. Peter thought he was ultimately preserving himself by denying Jesus, however in the end it led to his destruction. Peter denies Jesus a second time. He says that he doesn't know the man with exclamation. He again outright denies knowing Jesus. Jesus had prophesied that this would take place. He had said that Peter would deny Him three times and that a rooster would crow the third time and it did.

August 4th

Matthew 26:75-27:1-2-"Then Peter remembered the word Jesus had spoken; "Before the rooster crows, you will disown me three times." Then he went outside and wept bitterly. Early in the morning, all the chief priests and the elders of the people came to the decision to put Jesus to death. They bound him, led him away and handed him over to Pilate, the governor."-NIV

After Peter's denial of Jesus occurred, he wept. He had felt the horrible sting of guilt. When morning came on Friday, all the chief priests and the elders of the people assembled with a majority assembly so that they could give a more formal accounting of their earlier judgment set against Jesus during the early morning hours. After their meeting they bound Him over to Pilate, who was the governor of Judea and the Roman prefect under Emperor Tiberius. In order to maintain ultimate control over the Jewish populace, the Romans kept the death penalty under their own jurisdiction and reserved the right to intervene in any case they deemed necessary.

It was decided that Jesus should indeed be put to death. The religious authorities decided that Jesus had to die due to the accusations He was making and how they felt He was leading a rebellion against their religious rule. Just think, the religious leaders had no idea of the significance of putting Christ to death. They had no idea that they were actually unlocking the secrets of the Kingdom for mankind. They had no idea that once Jesus was dead, He would rise again providing a way to Heaven for all of mankind.

Could you imagine Jesus going on trial today? The mindset of modern man doesn't seem that far off from what it was then. People are infuriated at the mention of the name Jesus Christ. It is illegal to pray in a public gathering corporately and out loud as someone might get upset and feel that their rights are being infringed upon. You can't pray at high school sporting events or in public school at all as it has been ruled unconstitutional yet every session of Congress is opened with prayer. Does that seem hypocritical to you? It does to me. We as Christians have been stripped of our rights and nothing seems to be being done about that. We need to really start praying and developing the knees like a camel that Paul was said to possess due to his constant prayer. Paul's knees developed calluses due to his being down on them before the Lord.

Let's get the knees of a camel

August 5th

Matthew 27:3-5- "When Judas, who had betrayed him, saw that Jesus was condemned, he was seized with remorse and returned the thirty silver coins to the chief priests and the elders. "I have sinned," he said, "for I have betrayed innocent blood." "What is that to us?" they replied. "That's your responsibility." So Judas threw the money into the temple and left. Then he went away and hanged himself."-NIV

Judas's feelings of remorse and his attempt to return the blood money are recorded only by Matthew. Judas had changed his mind but it was too little too late. Judas experienced feelings of great regret and remorse and even attempted to give back the money he received for his betrayal, but this is less than "repentance". Judas really didn't have a true change of heart. With Judas showing no sign of repentance, he hanged himself rather than face his crushing guilt. He betrayed the Son of God, how could anyone live with that? His attempt at giving the money back was only a surface attempt to rid himself of his sense of guilt, not a true repentance of the heart.

Judas knew that he had nothing and that he was nothing without Jesus Christ. He knew that he had turned on Jesus and Jesus had known that he would. Judas went mad. When you turn your back on God you eventually will go mad. Our Creator is just that, our Creator. When creation turns on the Creator, eventually madness, insanity and utter chaos will take over. Look at our world today if you don't believe that.

Judas lost his mind. He knew that what he had done was inexcusable. He knew that it was too late for him and that he would have to pay for his betrayal. He had turned on Jesus. He had renounced the Son of God, Jesus Christ. He didn't know what to do and he saw no hope so he took his own life. His world was full of darkness. He saw no way out. His life with Jesus had ended due to his betrayal. Life as he knew it was no more. He took his life, a life that God had given him. Don't ever deny Jesus. We need to stand up for whom and what we believe in, even if it means death!

We are nothing
without Jesus

Matthew 27:11-14- "Meanwhile Jesus stood before the Governor and the Governor asked him, "Are you the king of the Jews?" "Yes, it is as you say," Jesus replied. When He was accused by the chief priests and the elders, He gave no answer. Then Pilate asked him, "Don't you hear the testimony they are bringing against you?" But Jesus made no reply, not even to a single charge-to the great amazement of the governor."-NIV

The Jewish religious leaders lacked the final authority to impose the death penalty on anyone. The charge of blasphemy against Jesus was insufficient for a death sentence under Roman rule so the Jewish leaders sent Him to the Roman governor, Pilate, to stand trial. Jesus gave no answer to the question posed to Him as to whether He heard the testimony brought against Him. Jesus had answered Pilate's original question as to whether He was the King of the Jews though, and there was nothing more to say that would change Pilate's mind. Pilate was greatly amazed at Jesus' refusal to defend himself even though He knew He would die. This is as recorded in Isaiah with the death of the servant. Isaiah 53:7; "**He was oppressed, and he was afflicted, yet he opened not his mouth; like a lamb that is led to the slaughter, and like a sheep that before its shearers is silent, so he opened not his mouth.**"

Can you imagine being Jesus Christ, having people come against you and not responding to your message? Probably the answer you have is an emphatic, "no I can't". Jesus could call upon the Angels of Heaven to deliver Him. He was God incarnate! He knew that all of this had to take place. He knew that He had to sacrifice Himself, the Perfect Lamb, on the altar for all of humanity so that we could reside in Heaven with Him! Only God could do this. We would try and save ourselves, wouldn't we? With ought a doubt we wouldn't be able to carry this great act out. I know I sure wouldn't be able to do it. I'm not God. I'm just a mere man in need of a Savior named Jesus Christ. I'm a child of God. I'm created in His image. Remember, don't ever forget, we all are mere men, women and children. From dust we come and to dust we return. Genesis 3:19; "**By the sweat of your face you shall eat bread, till you return to the ground, for out of it you were taken; for you are dust, and to dust you shall return.**" We're absolutely nothing without Jesus, none of us are.

He gave no response

August 7th

Matthew 27:15-20- "Now it was the governor's custom at the feast to release a prisoner chosen by the crowd. At that time they had a notorious prisoner, called Barabbas. So when the crowd had gathered, Pilate asked them, "which one do you want me to release to you: Barabbas, or Jesus who is called Christ?" He knew it was out of envy that they had handed Jesus over to him. While Pilate was sitting on the judge's seat, his wife sent him this message: "Don't have anything to do with that innocent man, for I have suffered a great deal today in a dream because of Him." But the chief priests and the elders persuaded the crowd to ask for Barabbas and to have Jesus executed"-NIV

The Jews had a custom of releasing a prisoner at the feast which was brought on by Pilate in order to will favor with the citizenry of Jerusalem. Barabbas was a notorious criminal who had committed a variety of crimes including robbery, as well as murder and insurrection. He may have belonged to one of the area guerilla bands that victimized the wealthy upper class people of Israel, as well as the Romans, and the bandits were often very popular with the common people. They were like Robin Hood and his gang and therefore kind of revered by the people because they rebelled against the Romans.

Pilate knew that the high priest and the Sanhedrin were not concerned with the threat to Roman rule; rather, they are envious of Jesus' popularity and therefore they felt threatened by his authoritative ministry. They felt that they were losing power every time that Jesus preached and taught at the temple. The leaders knew that their power was slipping every day that Jesus was free. They knew the only way they could retain their power was to have Jesus put to death and they knew that their time had come.

The Romans often viewed dreams as omens and Pilate knew that his wife having one pertaining to Jesus and His innocence had to have significant meaning. The dream was probably given by God as a sign of Jesus' innocence and Pilate wanted to free Him but the will of the people was to have Barabbas freed. The odd thing was that these very same people only a few days earlier had shouted "Hosanna!" at Jesus' entry and now they were crying "Let him be crucified!"

Envy being a powerful force is such an intense feeling and state of mind that it erodes the truth. Barabbas was clearly in the wrong under the law and he had committed a crime, however, the people were envious of Jesus. How could Jesus claim to be the Christ and put Himself on the same level as God? The chief priests used persuasion to their advantage when they managed to move the masses into believing what they themselves believed. They wanted Jesus executed so badly, yet they also wanted to please the people. They knew that Jesus was the one the people really wanted, not Barabbas, yet envy prevailed once again.

Matthew 27:21-23- "Which of the two do you want me to release to you?" asked the governor. "Barabbas," they answered. "What shall I do, then, with Jesus who is called Christ?" Pilate asked. They all answered, "Crucify him!" "Why? What crime has he committed?" asked Pilate. But they shouted all the louder, "crucify him!"-NIV

Pilate was doing his best to have Jesus set free. He knew that he had to abide with the custom of releasing one prisoner, especially being as he instituted the custom for the feast, therefore he chose Barabbas to go against Jesus. Pilate was sure the people would choose Jesus over a convicted robber and murderer but he was wrong.

All reason went by the wayside and was long gone. This was part of God's divine destiny. God knew that Jesus must die upon the cross of Calvary and so did Jesus. I am sure, by reading all accounts of the Passion of Christ, that Jesus had struggled with the knowledge of His impending death, but He also knew that He would rise on the third day. Obviously God knew what had to take place for His great design of salvation to be imparted to the whole world. All that the crowd wanted was to kill Jesus, thanks to the religious leaders of the day. I am sure the leaders rued the day after His resurrection. Envy stirs anger, hatred, jealously and murderous thoughts. The religious leaders had wanted Jesus dead, because, how dare He say that He's the Christ, the Messiah.

Even after the crowd heard Pilate attempt to question them on what grounds was He being crucified, they still wanted Him killed. Little did they know that Jesus must die so that we might live, and have life more abundantly. John 10:1-10; **"The thief comes only to steal and kill and destroy. I came that they may have life and have it abundantly."** One died for all, so that all might live through Him. The act of Jesus' death, resurrection and ascension into Heaven was so merciful and gracious. We owe Him our very existence.

Who have you chosen?
Jesus, or Barabbas?

August 9th

Matthew 27:24-26-When Pilate saw that he was getting nowhere, but that instead uproar was starting; he took water and washed his hands in front of the crowd. "I am innocent of this man's blood," he said. "It is your responsibility!" all the people answered, "let his blood be on us and on our children!" Then he released Barabbas to them. But he had Jesus flogged, and handed him over to be crucified.-NIV

Now when Pilate washed his hands he wasn't trying to rid himself of sin he was just saying that he found no grounds with which to give Jesus the death penalty. This was just a formal demonstration of his judgment. He was symbolically removing himself from this process and giving the crowd what they desired. The crowd didn't really care due to the religious leaders working them into such frenzy. They didn't shudder or even give a second thought to Jesus' innocent blood being placed upon their heads and the heads of their children. And when the people were chanting let His blood be on our heads and on the heads of our children, this was a common idiom denoting culpability, or accepting blame, for someone's death, here it was the death of Jesus. The people placed the responsibility for Jesus' death and crucifixion directly on their own heads, and they were judged with the destruction of Jerusalem in A.D. 70. At that moment, Pilate could have used his authority to renounce the people. He could have continued to argue the valid point of Jesus' innocence, but instead he succumbed to the public outcry to have Jesus crucified. Public opinion and the want of popularity took precedence over placing an innocent man on the cross.

When the blame was accepted by the Jews the proceedings went on and Jesus was flogged. Roman flogging was a horrifically cruel punishment. Those condemned to it were tied to a post and beaten with a leather whip that was interwoven with pieces of bone and metal, which tore through skin and tissue, often exposing bones and intestines. In many cases, the flogging itself was fatal. 99 lashes was a death sentence. The Romans scourged Jesus nearly to death so that He would not remain alive for long while He hung on the cross.

We should never allow our relationship with Jesus Christ to be swayed, deterred or nullified by peer pressure, acts of injustice, or intolerance or falling for what's politically correct. Our relationship with Jesus should always be the most important aspect of our existence here on earth. Jesus needs to be the reason why we live, breathe and have our being. A relationship with God will foster right choices and decisions. Our lives have the opportunity to have the light shed on them, the light of Christ. The blinders will be removed and we will be able to differentiate light from darkness. **The Waging War Within** ensues.

Matthew 27:27-30- then the governor's soldiers took Jesus into the praetorian and gathered the whole company of soldiers around him. They stripped him and put a scarlet robe on him, and then twisted together a crown of thorns and set it on his head. They put a staff in his right hand and knelt in front of him and mocked him. "Hail, King of the Jews!" they said. They spit on him, and took the staff and struck him on the head again and again-NIV

Now we are at the very heart of what the Gospel is all about. We are now at the point of what Jesus came for, to free and liberate the oppressed, us. He came to become the Ultimate Sacrifice. Jesus was the Suffering Servant. He was the fulfillment of Old Testament prophecies about the suffering servant. Isaiah 42:1-4; "**Behold my servant, whom I uphold, my chosen, in whom my soul delights; I have put my Spirit upon him; he will bring forth justice to the nations. He will not cry aloud or lift up his voice, or make it heard in the street; a bruised reed he will not break, and a faintly burning wick he will not quench; he will faithfully bring forth justice. He will not grow faint or be discouraged till he has established justice in the earth; and the coastlands wait for his law.**" Isaiah 52:13-53:12; "**Behold, my servant shall act wisely; he shall be high and lifted up, and shall be exalted. As many were astonished at you— his appearance was so marred, beyond human semblance, and his form beyond that of the children of mankind— so shall he sprinkle many nations; kings shall shut their mouths because of him; for that which has not been told them they see, and that which they have not heard they understand. Who has believed what they heard from us? And to whom has the arm of the LORD been revealed? For he grew up before him like a young plant, and like a root out of dry ground; he had no form or majesty that we should look at him, and no beauty that we should desire him. He was despised and rejected by men; a man of sorrows, and acquainted with grief; and as one from whom men hide their faces he was despised, and we esteemed him not. Surely he has borne our grief and carried our sorrows; yet we esteemed him stricken, smitten by God, and afflicted. But he was wounded for our transgressions; he was crushed for our iniquities; upon him was the chastisement that brought us peace, and with his stripes we are healed. All we like sheep have gone astray; we have turned everyone to his own way; and the LORD has laid on him the iniquity of us all. He was oppressed, and he was afflicted, yet he opened not his mouth; like a lamb that is led to the slaughter, and like a sheep that before its shearers is silent, so he opened not his mouth. By oppression and judgment he was taken away; and as for his generation, who considered that he was cut off out of the land of the living, stricken for the transgression of my people? And they made his grave with the wicked and with a rich man in his death, although he had done no violence, and there was no deceit in his mouth. Yet it was the will of the LORD to crush him; he has put him to grief; when his soul makes an offering for sin, he shall see his offspring; he shall prolong his days; the will of the LORD shall prosper in his hand. Out of the anguish of his soul he shall see and be satisfied; by his knowledge shall the righteous one, my servant, make many to be accounted righteous, and he shall bear their iniquities. Therefore I will divide him a portion with the many, and he shall divide the spoil with the strong, because he poured out his soul to death and was numbered with the transgressors; yet he bore the sin of many, and makes intercession for the** transgressors."

We also have the fulfillment of Jesus' own predictions about His impending death. Matthew 16:21; **"From that time Jesus began to show his disciples that he must go to Jerusalem and suffer many things from the elders and chief priests and scribes, and be killed, and on the third day be raised."** Matthew 17:22-23; **"As they were gathering in Galilee, Jesus said to them, "The Son of Man is about to be delivered into the hands of men, and they will kill him, and he will be raised on the third day." And they were greatly distressed."** Matthew 20:17-19; **"And as Jesus was going up to Jerusalem, he took the twelve disciples aside, and on the way he said to them, "See, we are going up to Jerusalem. And the Son of Man will be delivered over to the chief priests and scribes, and they will condemn him to death and deliver him over to the Gentiles to be mocked and flogged and crucified, and he will be raised on the third day.""** Matthew 26:2; **"You know that after two days the Passover is coming, and the Son of Man will be delivered up to be crucified."**

The Roman soldiers in Jerusalem were infamous for playing cruel games with condemned prisoners, particularly insurrectionists. They were known to dress them in costumes and then move them around a huge game board as if they were a piece of the game. Still, their actions spoke louder than they knew. The one they dressed and hailed as a king was truly about to become the crucified King. Mark and John describe the cloak that they put on Jesus as a cloak of purple which was a royal color worn by kings and rulers.

Jesus was stripped and made to wear a crown of thorns. He was mocked, spit on and then struck in the head several times by the governor's soldiers. If you truly believe in Jesus Christ and the Living God this is absolutely a powerfully devastating scene. It's heart wrenching to envision this happening to our Lord and Savior Jesus Christ. How could they have done this to our King, our Lord and our Savior? How could the authorities in power do such a thing? They did not know who Jesus was? They did not know what Jesus came to do? They did not know that God ordained from the foundations of the world for them to usher Jesus to the Cross of Calvary.

If we can truly absorb what transpired at the Cross of Calvary nothing should ever faze us. If we allow this road that Jesus took to the cross to filter through into our spirit, mind, soul and heart we will never be stunned again by the horrific things done by man. Jesus carried this divine destiny out for you and me. He suffered these things for the sins of mankind. Every blow was taken for others, not Himself. He surrendered to the point of death on a cross. Jesus paid with His very life.

He paid with His life

Matthew 27:32-36- After they had mocked him, they took off the robe and put his own clothes on him. Then they led him away to crucify him. As they were going out, they met a man from Cyrene, named Simon, and they forced him to carry the cross. They came to a place called Golgotha (which means the place of the skull). There they offered Jesus wine to drink, mixed with gall: but after tasting it, He refused to drink it. When they had crucified Him, they divided up His clothes by casting lots. And sitting down, they kept watch over Him there.-NIV

The Romans were a cruel breed of people who loved to taunt and torment the Jewish populace. They especially liked to inflict great pain and humiliation on the condemned. Their tools of torture and death were famous for their barbarism. The cross was particularly cruel. If you put the cross on the back of one who has been severely lashed with the tools of a skilled flogger the back was torn open with the bones exposed and the muscles shredded. The average cross weighed at least 30-40 pounds. This is on the back of one who was flogged and most likely has internal organ damage and most likely spinal damage as well. Sick!!

The guards offered Jesus wine with gall mixed in. This gall was an herb. It was bitter in taste and it was often poisonous. There are some who say it helped ease the pain of the condemned but this is only speculation. Crucifixion was a horrible death. The condemned would be either nailed or tied to the cross. They would usually suffocate to death. They had a small piece of wood to place their feet on to attempt to stand. Their legs were often severely bruised and often broken after a short while so that their death could be hastened. Their arms were sore and their wrists were torn open with their weight from hanging. It was a miserable death.

Could you imagine Jesus being thrust into this? Imagine Him having to be made by the governor's soldiers to carry the literal cross that would crucify Him. I couldn't imagine it. I find it difficult to even contemplate this. What a horrific situation to be in with no way out. This man Simon didn't know that He was carrying the cross for God. He was just an African come on a pilgrimage to Jerusalem for Passover. He carried the cross for God Himself! This man didn't know that this very wooden cross would be crucial in carrying out God's Divine Destiny of salvation and forgiveness for the entire world. It had to be a horrifying time in the hearts of everyone remotely connected to Christ. Their friend and traveling teacher was soon to die.

He was soon to die

August 12th

Matthew 27:37-42- Above His head they placed the written charge against Him: this is Jesus, the King of the Jews. Two robbers were crucified with Him, one on His right and one on his left. Those who passed by hurled insults at Him, shaking their heads and saying, "you who are going to destroy the temple and build it in three days, save yourself! Come down from the cross, if you are the Son of God!" In the same way the chief priests, the teachers of the law and the elders mocked Him. "He saved others," they said, "but He can't save Himself! He's the King of Israel! Let Him come down now from the cross, and we will believe in Him.-NIV

Written on a plaque above Jesus' head was the King of the Jews sign. The purpose of this taunt was for it to act as a deterrent against any who would even consider rising up against the Roman authority. It was written "in Aramaic, in Latin, and in Greek" so that all traveling for pilgrimage to Jerusalem and also those entering the city would be able to read it and heed the threat.

Nothing more is known about the background of the two men hung on crosses with Jesus. The fact that Jesus was crucified with criminals fulfills the prophecy of Isaiah 53:12. "**Therefore I will divide him a portion with the many, and he shall divide the spoil with the strong, because he poured out his soul to death and was numbered with the transgressors; yet he bore the sin of many, and makes intercession for the transgressors.**"

Hebrews 13:12 says; "**So Jesus also suffered outside the gate in order to sanctify the people through his own blood.**" The place for sacrificing animals was outside the gate, Calvary. Jesus was sacrificed for all of us. We need to appreciate this. The people and priests mocked Jesus' claim of supernatural power. This was alluded to in Psalms 22:7; "**All who see me mock me; they make mouths at me; they wag their heads.**" The high priests and rulers couldn't resist the urge to mock Jesus one last time so they did it at the scene of His death. The religious leaders do not address Jesus directly, but turn to one another as they mocked Him. This fulfilled Psalms 22:7-8; "**All who see me mock me; they make mouths at me; they wag their heads; "He trusts in the LORD; let him deliver him; let him rescue him, for he delights in him!"**"

They were bewildered that Jesus wouldn't save himself, especially since He claimed to be the Christ. Jesus submitted Himself to the perfect will of His Father in Heaven. Jesus submitted to the will of His Father. He was preordained to go to the Cross of Calvary. He knew the path that He must take.

Jesus could have come down from the cross at any moment. He didn't because it wasn't God's Divine Destiny for His life. Jesus was carrying out God's Divine Destiny.

August 13th

Matthew 27:43-44- He trusts in God. Let God rescue Him now if He wants Him, for He said, 'I am the Son of God.'" In the same way the robbers who were crucified with Him also heaped insults on Him.-NIV

The religious leaders of the day didn't want to waste their last opportunity to throw insults at Jesus so they taunted Him one last time while He was suffering and dying on the cross. The religious leaders did not address Jesus directly, but they turned to one another as they mocked Him before the people in attendance. "Let God deliver Him" is what they said. They obviously had no idea of the consequences they were heaping on themselves by following through with their twisted plot sprung up from their jealousy against Jesus. Jealousy is a tool of the evil one, it is not of God.

We need to trust God fully, completely and without reservation. This is easier said than done. The religious leaders and the governor's soldiers all heaped insults at Him. "**Let God deliver Him**" was quoted. This is a lament found in Psalms 22:8 concerning an innocent sufferer. The thieves that were being crucified next to Jesus also heaped insults at Him. The Son of God, Jesus the Christ, was being persecuted while He was actually hung up on the Cross of Calvary. Insult after insult was being shot His way. It wasn't enough torture for the governor's soldiers to see what they thought was a mere man hanging bludgeoned, bloody, with open wounds and at deaths door. They had to increase **The Waging War Within** that was taking place. Physical brutality and punishment wasn't enough to do to an innocent man, they had to harass Him more and say biting comments to Him. They had to verbally persecute Him.

Jesus knew that clinging to God and trusting God the Father took precedence over anything that man could do to Him. He knew that they may kill the body, but they could never kill the Spirit. Jesus also knew that His Heavenly Father had Him in the palm of His hand and that He was working on the divine design that God had predestined from the beginning of the world. What seemed like a hopeless situation to the natural eye was really the crux of our Christian Faith. Jesus Christ paid the price for the atonement of our sins on the Cross.

They may have killed the body but they never touched the Spirit of Jesus. The body without the Spirit is like a car without the driver. Without the driver the car is useless, it is just a bunch of metal and plastic and it is serves no purpose, but give it the driver and great things can and do happen. The driver is the Spirit. This is like us also. The car is our body, the driver is our Spirit and the car with the driver is our soul. We are nothing without the Holy Spirit but a car without a driver. Genesis 2:7; "**Then the LORD God formed the man of dust from the ground and breathed into his nostrils the breath of life, and the man became a living creature."**

Matthew 27:45-53- From the sixth hour until the ninth hour darkness came over all the land. About the ninth hour Jesus cried out in a loud voice, "eloi, eloi, lama sabachthani?"- Which means, "My God, my God, why have You forsaken Me?" When some of those standing there heard this, they said, "He's calling Elijah." Immediately one of them ran and got a sponge. He filled it with wine vinegar, put it on a stick, and offered it to Jesus to drink. The rest said, "Now leave him alone. Let's see if Elijah comes to save Him." And when Jesus had cried out again in a loud voice, He gave up his Spirit. At that moment the curtain of the temple was torn in two from top to bottom. The earth shook and the rocks split. The tombs broke open and the bodies of many holy people who had died were raised to life. They came out of the tombs, and after Jesus' resurrection they went into the holy city and appeared to many people.-NIV

From noon until 3:00 P.M. Josephus says that the ninth hour was the time when Jews offered the daily evening sacrifice. Now the darkness spoken of could not have been a solar eclipse since Passover had occurred during a full moon, and a solar eclipse can occur only during a new moon; what happened was a supernatural act of God, displaying His displeasure and His judgment upon humanity for their crucifying of His Son.

Jesus was in great agony, paying the debt of sin for humanity cries out from the cross to His Father in Heaven. **"Eloi, eloi, lama sabachthani?"** These are perhaps some of the most profoundly mysterious words in the entire Bible. In some ways Jesus had to be cut off from the favor of and fellowship with His Father, God, because He was bearing the sins of His people and therefore enduring God's wrath. And yet, in quoting Ps. 22:1; **"My God, my God, why have you forsaken me? Why are you so far from saving me, from the words of my groaning?"** Jesus probably had in mind the remainder of the psalm as well, which moves on to a cry of victory. Psalms 22:21–31; **"Save me from the mouth of the lion! You have rescued me from the horns of the wild oxen! I will tell of your name to my brothers; in the midst of the congregation I will praise you: You who fear the LORD, praise him! All you offspring of Jacob, glorify him, and stand in awe of him, all you offspring of Israel! For he has not despised or abhorred the affliction of the afflicted, and he has not hidden his face from him, but has heard, when he cried to him. From you comes my praise in the great congregation; my vows I will perform before those who fear him. The afflicted shall eat and be satisfied; those who seek him shall praise the LORD! May your hearts live forever! All the ends of the earth shall remember and turn to the LORD, and all the families of the nations shall worship before you. For kingship belongs to the LORD, and he rules over the nations. All the prosperous of the earth eat and worship; before him shall bow all who go down to the dust, even the one who could not keep himself alive. Posterity shall serve him; it shall be told of the Lord to the coming generation; they shall come and proclaim his righteousness to a people yet unborn, that he has done it."** Jesus expresses faith, calling God "my God." I am sure He knew why He had to die. The whole purpose of Christ coming to earth was for Him to die for us and our transgressions. His cry, uttered with a loud voice, was Him expressing not confusion at His plight, but a witness for the bystanders and through them to the world, that He was experiencing God-forsakenness not for anything in Himself but for the salvation of others. Jesus' torment, despite His preparation for it in the garden of Gethsemane, was most assuredly incomprehensible. The governor's soldiers continue to watch Jesus on the cross,

276~ The Waging War Within

even at the ninth hour. Some of the onlookers were still wondering if Jesus would be delivered by Elijah because they thought that the first part of His quote was a call to the prophet Elijah. All in all Jesus had hung on the cross for approximately six hours until He succumbed to death.

Even in death, Jesus maintained total control over His destiny. "His spirit" means His human spirit. While Jesus' body remained on the cross and was then placed into the tomb, His spirit went into the presence of God His Father, and in this way He became the pattern for believers who would die after Him.

The curtain spoken of in the temple, the one between the Holy Place and the Most Holy Place, was an elaborately woven fabric of 72 twisted plaits of 24 threads each. It was 60 feet high and 30 feet wide. No one was allowed to enter the Most Holy Place behind the curtain except for the high priest, and he only did this once a year, on the Day of Atonement. Being torn in two signifies the removal of the separation between God and His people.

As for the earth shaking, Palestine sits on a major seismic rift, so earthquakes were not uncommon, but the splitting of rocks and the opening of tombs makes this a major testimony to the meaning of Jesus' resurrection. There were many strange and mysterious events taking place all at once which really got the attention of the people. There was little if any doubt that an innocent man, one who was most assuredly the Son of God, was executed unjustly that day. And can you imagine the dead coming out of their tombs? There were prophets of old walking out of their tombs and other Old Testament figures and godly intertestamental Jews, re-embodied to witness to the new order of things that was now in the process of dawning. This shows that the resurrection of people who died looking forward to the Messiah depends on Christ's actual death and resurrection, just as we depend on His having suffered, died, and also His glorious resurrection in order for us to enjoy eternity with Him.

From His physical death on the cross to His supernatural resurrection of His spirit to eternity in Heaven. Amen!

August 15th

Matthew 27:54- When the centurion and those with him who were guarding Jesus saw the earthquake and all that had happened, they were terrified, and exclaimed, "surely He was the Son of God!"-NIV

The centurion and his guards were accustomed to seeing crucifixions, but these cataclysmic events, coupled with the extraordinary self-control, purity, and love shown by Jesus in His death, made the centurion realize that Jesus was truly the Son of God.

The centurion and the others that were guarding Jesus had to see the physical signs in order to believe that He was the Son of God. They needed evidence. They needed to see it with their own eyes and hear it with their own ears. This is why controversy has always taken place between faith and science. Here the centurion and others believed that He was the Son of God only because of the earthquake and all the other things that had happened when Jesus gave up His Spirit. Are you one that has to have evidence in order to believe something?

People continue to have a need for verifiable evidence that Jesus existed in order for them to believe. They cannot accept Jesus by faith, because they have not allowed Jesus to penetrate their heart and life. Our God works from the inside out. Faith is being sure of what you hope for and certain of what you do not see. Hebrews 11:1; **"Now faith is the assurance of things hoped for, the conviction of things not seen."** Even though the Bible exists and people from different cultures all over the world believe in Jesus, some are still lost. They haven't yet been able to place their hope, their faith, their trust and ultimately their life into the hands of Jesus. Many people are still searching for answers. This is why there is nothing more important than getting the Gospel Message out to all the people groups in our world. Our ultimate strategic planning for Jesus Christ on this side of Heaven needs to be the spreading of the Gospel, spreading His Word and placing a Bible in everyone's hand in the entire world. Matthew 28:19-20; **"Go therefore and make disciples of all nations, baptizing them in the name of the Father and of the Son and of the Holy Spirit, teaching them to observe all that I have commanded you."**

People can come to faith in Christ by your testimony, how you live your life and you sharing your witness for God. God desires for all to come to know Him and for all to come to have everlasting life with Him in Paradise. He doesn't want for any to perish. 2 Peter 3:9; **"The Lord is not slow to fulfill His promise as some count slowness, but is patient toward you, not wishing that any should perish, but that all should reach repentance."** Our mission as Christians should be to spread the word of God and to share the Gospel that gives hope to all of mankind.

August 16th

Matthew 27:55-66- Many women were there, watching from a distance. They had followed Jesus from Galilee to care for his needs. Among them were Mary Magdalene, Mary the mother of James and Joses, and the mother of Zebedee's sons. As evening approached, there came a rich man from Arimathea, named Joseph, who had himself become a disciple of Jesus. Going to Pilate, he asked for Jesus' body, and Pilate ordered that it be given to him. Joseph took the body, wrapped it in a clean linen cloth, and placed it in his own new tomb that he had cut out of the rock. He rolled a big stone in front of the entrance to the tomb and went away. Mary Magdalene and the other Mary were sitting there opposite the tomb. The next day, the one after preparation day, the chief priests and the Pharisees went to Pilate, "sir," they said, "we remember that while he was still alive that deceiver said, 'after three days I will rise again.' So give the order for the tomb to be made secure until the third day. Otherwise, his disciples may come and steal the body and tell the people that he has been raised from the dead. This last deception will be worse than the first." "Take a guard," Pilate answered. "Go; make the tomb as secure as you know how." So they went and made the tomb secure by putting a seal on the stone and posting the guard.-NIV

When it spoke of the women who had accompanied Jesus as His disciples had, they were witnesses of Jesus' crucifixion, and they will also be the first witnesses to His glorious resurrection. What an awesome blessing that must have been.

Now when we hear of Joseph here, Joseph was a member of the Sanhedrin who did not consent to the actions which were taken against Jesus. His high standing within the Jewish religious community gave him special access to Pilate. The location of the region of Arimathea is uncertain. Perhaps it is Ramathaim in the hill country of Ephraim, which is about 20 miles northwest of Jerusalem. Joseph had asked Pilate for the body of Jesus. Jewish custom dictated that crucified bodies should be taken down before evening, especially before the Sabbath, which began at sundown on Friday.

Joseph had cut a new tomb for himself and he offered to have Jesus' body placed in it. The tomb was a rectangular chamber cut into rock. It was accessed through a low entry room and blocked with a stone that could be rolled back and forth, mainly to protect the body from wild animals. The use of a rich man's tomb fulfills Isaiah 53:9; **"And they made his grave with the wicked and with a rich man in his death, although he had done no violence, and there was no deceit in his mouth."**

In verse Matthew 27:61 it speaks of the other Mary. This was most likely the mother of Joses; he was probably the same person referred to as "Joseph" throughout the gospels.

Jesus was referred to as a deceiver by the Pharisees and the Chief Priests. They had remembered that the deceiver had said that He would rise again after three days. They thought maybe the disciples of Jesus would come and steal the body of Jesus and then claim that He had been raised from the dead. They had the tomb sealed to avoid this from taking place. The Pharisees and the Chief Priests were attempting to prevent this last deception from occurring. They even convinced Pilate to place a guard on the tomb. This was no ordinary guard either. It was Pilate's own Palatial Guard.

To think about this is absolutely powerful. Contemplate how this dynamic can carry over to today, as a believer in Jesus Christ. Those that are not of the faith think that we are deceived in believing in Jesus Christ. They think that we're brain washed.

279~ The Waging War Within

The deceiver, Satan has the sole goal of twisting things and preventing people from experiencing salvation. Satan operates hell with his demonic forces. Hell is for eternity. Heaven is for eternity. One offers eternal punishment and the other offers eternal reward. Deception from the master of deceit always attempts to lead people away from Jesus Christ. Satan will do anything in his power to lead people astray with manipulation, lies and untruths. He will twist lies and make it look like the truth. He will pervert the truth and make it look like lies. He manipulates the mind, the will and the flesh. He'll also manipulate your feelings, your thoughts and your emotions. John 10:10; **"The thief comes only to steal and kill and destroy. I came that they may have life and have it abundantly."** Don't let the devil steal your life and your joy in the journey. Get on the side of God and enjoy eternity with Him. Please.

Christ has become real in our lives. We know in whom we trust. We've experienced His power in our lives. We've experienced the cleansing power of the blood of the lamb. We've experienced a radical life change in the way in which we now live our life. We're seeking and submitting to the things from above. We're no longer focused on living for our self for now we live for Him. Every day we live for God and God alone. Nothing in the entire world even comes close to living life for Jesus. We die to ourselves daily in order to live for Him. Why don't you join us? Be a part of instead of a part from. If you are already a member of the God team, why not recommit your heart to Him anew?

Join the God team
and be a part of
instead of a part from!

August 17th

Matthew 28:1-4- After the Sabbath, at dawn on the first day of the week, Mary Magdalene and the other Mary went to look at the tomb. There was a violent earthquake, for an angel of the lord came down from heaven and, going to the tomb, rolled back the stone and sat on it. His appearance was like lightning, and his clothes were white as snow. The guards were so afraid of him that they shook and became like dead men.-NIV

There was an earthquake on that Sunday morning that had either occurred as soon as the angel of the Lord appeared or it may have possibly been an instrument used by the angel by which the rock covering the cave was rolled away, either way the angel was there and the rock was rolled away. The appearance of the angel caused great fear to run through the battle hardened guards and they shook with freight for they had never seen anything remotely close to their encounter with this angel.

When an angel appeared from Heaven they were terrified, they shook in their boots and suddenly they appeared like dead men, they were frozen stiff. The guards were stunned; they had never in all their lives seen anything like this. The supernatural being appeared simultaneously with an earthquake. The angel had an appearance like that of lightning and his clothes were white as snow. This was definitely something that they would never forget.

I often wonder what it would be like to see an angel. Who knows I may already have seen one and not known it. Hebrews 13:2; **"Do not neglect to show hospitality to strangers, for thereby some have entertained angels unawares."** You may have had an encounter with an angel and not known it either. We really need to be alert as to how we treat others. This encounter may have brought those soldiers to Christ, we don't know. What did it take for you to come to Christ? We need to be Ambassadors for Christ always. Not just on Sunday mornings while we are at church but twenty four hours a day seven days a week.

We need to be alert as to how we are coming off to others. We don't need to be standing on a soapbox reciting Scripture so everyone says "What a nice Christian boy." That doesn't please God. We need to preach always and when necessary use words. In other words, we need to be an example through our actions. People should see God through the way that we walk and the way that we talk. We need to be the light always.

Be an example for all to follow.

August 18th

Matthew 28:5-7- The angel said to the women, "Do not be afraid, for I know that you are looking for Jesus, who was crucified. He is not here; He has risen, just as He said. Come and see the place where He lay. Then go quickly and tell His disciples: 'He has risen from the dead and is going ahead of you into Galilee. There you will see Him.' Now I have told you."-NIV

Jesus had risen. Halleluiah! Praise the Lord! What a triumphant day that was. Could you even begin to fathom the elation these women must have felt? First they met an angel of the Lord and then they found out that Jesus had indeed risen from the dead.

The majestic angel spoke and explained to the women that they would find Jesus in Galilee. The angel explained that Jesus had risen from the dead. Jesus had done what He had promised to do. The grave could not hold Him. If the grave held Him captive we would not have a Christian Faith and our Jesus would be a phony, which we indeed know He isn't. He would've promised something that He didn't deliver. Jesus is not this way. Whatever He promises, He will come through on. Don't trust me, trust Him!

The grave couldn't hold Him.

He is risen!

Praise the Lord!

Matthew 28:8-10- So the women hurried away from the tomb, afraid yet filled with joy, and ran to tell His disciples. Suddenly Jesus met them. "Greetings," He said. They came to Him, clasped His feet and worshiped Him. Then Jesus said to them. "Do not be afraid. Go and tell my brothers to go to Galilee; there they will see me."- NIV

When they spoke here of Jesus' Disciples, they were most likely referring to Eleven. He said for them to go to Galilee. Galilee was the central location of Jesus' earthly ministry and here it continued in its importance during His post-resurrection ministry. The whole traveling done by Jesus and His Disciples was roughly a thirty mile area.

When the women had taken hold of His feet this was both out of reverence as well as a display that He was indeed there in the flesh and no mere vision or hallucination. Jesus had indeed a physical resurrection. By allowing this act of worship, here and in verse 17, Jesus accepted the acknowledgment of His deity. He allowed the worship of Him as only He is to be worshiped.

When in verse 10 He spoke of His brothers He was possibly referring to the Eleven, but more likely He was referring to the larger group of disciples who had been following Jesus.

The women held onto the feet of Jesus. They grabbed onto His feet and they worshipped Him. They, the women, were fearful in seeing Jesus after He had been resurrected from the dead. Jesus tells them not to be afraid. When the supernatural happens, it's much more than just a normal occurrence. These women must have been totally overwhelmed with mixed feelings of sorrow at Jesus' death, fear from not only seeing an angel but also Jesus risen, and exultation with the realization of Christ's return from the grave. Wow.

The women clasped His feet and worshipped Him.

Matthew 28:11-17- While the women were on their way, some of the guards went into the city and reported to the chief priests everything that had happened. When the chief priests had met with the elders and devised a plan, they gave the soldiers a large sum of money, telling them, "You are to say, 'His disciples came during the night and stole Him away while we were asleep.' If this report gets to the governor, we will satisfy him and keep you out of trouble." So the soldiers took the money and did as they were instructed. And this story has been widely circulated among the Jews to this very day. Then the eleven disciples went to Galilee, to the mountain where Jesus had told them to go. When they saw Him, they worshiped Him; but some doubted.-NIV

Here we once again have the religious leaders conspiring and lying in order to preserve their places in society with their religious and political standings. They didn't want to face the reality that Jesus was and is the Son of God, and when faced with the truth that He rose, they lied. Now the soldiers faced possible execution for allowing Jesus' followers to steal His body, which as we all know wasn't the case, He rose. Their offense was dereliction of duty, one of the most severe offenses while occupying foreign territory. While cooperating with the Jewish religious leaders, the soldiers at least have a chance to save themselves.

Just as with the nay-sayers, some of the disciples still doubted that Jesus had risen. Doubt is the opposite of belief and faith. Faith and belief in something or someone will drive us forward in life, especially if we have faith in our belief in God. Hebrews 11:1; "**Now faith is the assurance of things hoped for, the conviction of things not seen.**" Doubt is stagnant. It stays still with no movement. Doubt is a pessimistic way of looking at things, tainted with negativity and a mixture of negative feelings, emotions and thoughts. Doubt usually has a negative outcome. Faith in something breeds positive belief, positive feelings, positive thoughts, positive emotions and typically positive outcomes. Faith, belief and doubt typically have self-fulfilling prophecies attached to them.

Faith and belief in Christ takes place in the supernatural and natural worlds. We serve a supernatural God. He displayed His magnificence in the natural world with His creation, while at the same time performing the supernatural acts of; salvation, restoration, conviction, answered prayer, protection, and healing. Faith in God is a decision that has supernatural consequences. God's supernatural answers to prayer can impact our physical worlds. We just need to believe.

Believe!

Matthew 28:18-20- Then Jesus came to them and said, "All authority in heaven and on earth has been given to me. Therefore go and make disciples of all nations, baptizing them in the name of the Father and of the Son and of the Holy Spirit, and teaching them to obey everything I have commanded you. And surely I am with you always, to the very end of the age."-NIV

In his risen state, Jesus exercises absolute authority throughout heaven and earth, this shows His deity. His authority has been given to Him by the Father, which indicates that Jesus still remains subject to the Father. We all answer to someone who holds a higher position than we do. We ultimately answer to God in everything we have done and in everything we will do.

The imperative to make disciples means to call individuals to commit their lives to Jesus as their Lord and Master. This is the main objective of the Great Commission. We are to go, baptizing and teaching wherever we go. We are called to go "Into the entire world." Jesus' ministry was in Israel, ours will be wherever we are planted. We are to proclaim Jesus to not only the Jew but also to the Gentile. He died for all. We are to baptize them in the name, which is singular, not plural, of the Father, the Son, and the Holy Spirit.

We are to teach the disciples to be more like Christ. This is an ongoing process which we will never complete until we pass on and reside with Him. We are to obey all of His precepts. Jesus Christ has laid out a plan for our lives and He has called us to follow that plan. We are continually transformed in our walks in order to become more like Christ. Jesus concluded His Commission with the important reminder that He is with us always. This is a great comfort to me.

All authority has been given to Jesus Christ. No authority supersedes Jesus. He's on the top rung. Nothing and no one has more power than God. Men and women will attempt to elevate themselves, however they will never surpass God, no matter how much fame and fortune, privilege, money, wealth, riches they may accrue.

We're born into the world with our ultimate divine destiny as laid out by God in Heaven. Heaven should always be in sight. When Heaven's in sight, we'll live differently, or at least we should, because we'll always have Jesus and His Kingdom in our minds sight. Let's have our Creator in mind with everything we do.

We're called to go into the world to preach the Gospel and to make disciples in every nation, from continent to continent. We need to get out of our churches and our back yards and preach the Good News. We're to baptize in the name of the Father, the Son and the Holy Spirit. This is also referred to as the Trinity. Three in One! Praise God!

If only we spent every waking moment, whether at home, church, work or play with a humble heart, a prayer like attitude and a spirit of thankfulness, our lives would be revolutionized and changed. We would be connected to our Creator, in an authentic relationship and ultimately more aware of His presence in our lives. This would be a life changing attitude if we would only do this. Imagine a world where everyone focused on God instead of the almighty self. What a great place we would live in.

God desires that His Word be spread all over the world; from the biggest cities, to the smallest towns, from the richest neighborhoods to the poorest section of town, from the most urban area to the most rural of places, and from America to distant lands, from the valley to the highest mountain top. God desires that we use every medium possible to share His

Word in these last days. The time is short my friends. We need to have a sense of urgency and get motivated; we need a fiery passion and an overwhelming sense of focus to make this happen. We need to use all of our resources to carry this mission through to completion. All of our money, all of our time, all of our gifts and all that we own belong to our Lord and Creator. All of it belongs to God! Nothing is ours and we certainly cannot take it into eternity with us so why not share it?

PRAY!!

What is a disciple? *Vine's Expository Dictionary of New Testament Words* describes a disciple as "not only a pupil, but an adherent...spoken of as imitators of their teacher." Disciples did not simply acquire knowledge from their teacher; rather, they learned to be like him. Timothy was a disciple of Paul. He exemplified Paul and in doing such, Jesus.

The Bible tells us how to be disciples. John 8:31; **"If you abide in My word, you are My disciples indeed"**. Those who follow His Word as a way of life are His disciples. Paul, a disciple of Christ, urged all of the Corinthians to follow his example. 1 Corinthians 11:1 says to **"Be imitators of me, as I am of Christ."** Paul led by example just as we all should.

We are called to be disciples of God, not disciples of man. We must exercise caution with whom we choose to sidle up with and have as a mentor. They must be seasoned in their walk and they also must study the Word of God. We can follow the example of others as long as it agrees with the example of Christ, but our ultimate goal must be to follow Jesus. 2 Peter 3:18; **"But grow in the grace and knowledge of our Lord and Savior Jesus Christ. To Him be the glory both now and to the day of eternity. Amen."**

A disciple lives solely for Jesus Christ and for Him alone. A true disciple realizes that everything good flows from God. God is the sole fuel a true disciple runs on. With this He will light our path. The reading and following of God's Holy Bible is key. Enclosed within the pages of The Holy Bible are the treasures of God. Many books have been written but nothing compares to The Holy Scriptures. God has placed all authority within His Word. A true disciple follows Jesus no matter the cost. The cost could even ultimately be your very life. Philippians 1:21-23; **"For to me to live is Christ, and to die is gain. If I am to live in the flesh, that means fruitful labor for me. Yet which I shall choose I cannot tell. I am hard pressed between the two. My desire is to depart and be with Christ, for that is far better."** Physical death seems final here on earth, but from God's eyes it's only the beginning of our eternal reward. God never intended for our true being, our internal spirit man to die. We were meant to live on and on forever. How great and wonderful it is to die in Christ! Eternity is promised to all who follow His instruction. Heaven's home is a declaration from God that He will fulfill.

All I want is to live in the authority and power that Jesus Christ has given me. I don't know the day or the hour I will depart this world, but one thing I want is to be walking right before the Lord. Don't you? If we ask, we will receive freely from Jesus Christ. He will empower us with His Holy Spirits power that will enable us to walk with Him. He longs to bless us, His people that believe in Him.

Many voices. So called authorities are speaking and having an impact on your minds, your will and your emotions. What voice is going to lead you? Your own, your family members, a person you respect, your husband, your wife, your children, your boss, your pastor, the president of the United States or God Himself? The latter is the One true voice that will guide us in our dealings here on earth. The path of life, not death. The path of blessing, not eternal punishment. The path of restoration, not brokenness. The path of hope not despair. The path of captured dreams; not broken would've, could've or should've beens.

One voice we can listen for and trust is that of the Holy Spirit. The Holy Spirit can and does speak. Acts 8:29; " **And the Spirit said to Philip, "Go over and join this chariot."**" Another example is a voice from the Holy Spirit speaking to Peter in Acts 11:12; **"And the Spirit told me to go with them, making no distinction. These six brothers also accompanied me, and we entered the man's house."** And yet again in Acts 13:2; **"While they were worshiping the Lord and fasting, the Holy Spirit said, "Set apart for me Barnabas and Saul for the work to which I have called them."**" This is an occurrence which can and does happen regularly even today if you are willing to listen. We need to be silent and in the silence we can hear the voice of God. God gave us two ears and one mouth to use proportionately. Pray and see for yourself how soon it will be before you too can hear the voice of God.

As disciples we need to be obedient to our relationship with our Lord Jesus Christ. Following Jesus Christ is not a cause; it's a relationship with God. God sent Jesus Christ to connect us to the One True Living Jesus, who can bring us into relationship with God. He can bring us into a relationship on this side of Heaven that will guide us and lead us down the right path. This relationship will help us in our temporal existence, but one day will supernaturally transcend our mortal world bringing us into the presence of God and His eternal Kingdom.

What voice are you going to follow?

August 24th

One day we will hear the words spoken in Matthew 25:21,23; "**Well done thy good and faithful servant.**" When God says, "Why should I let you enter my kingdom?" Our reply will be because I have accepted Jesus Christ as my personal Lord and Savior. I didn't come to enter Heaven in my own authority but that of God's, through His Son Jesus Christ. It's only Jesus that could have provided the way. Jesus was the perfect sin offering to God. Jesus was without sin while He was here on earth, not me nor anyone else in all of history was ever without sin, except our Lord Jesus Christ. This was all part of God's master plan.

The truth is that much of our existence is based on what we want to do both for ourselves and for others. Self is a great obstacle which we need to overcome. **The Waging War Within** is primarily fought on the battlefield of self. We have to let the Father, the Son and the Holy Spirit penetrate and take over the me, myself, and I aspect of our self-seeking personalities. This can only be done with the empowerment of the Holy Spirit. Remember my friends that ego is Edging God Out and easing ourselves into the driver's seat. If you have God as your co-pilot, try trading seats with Him. He is far better equipped to take the controls of our lives than we are. I know I can make a mess out of my life if I retake the reins. I am far better off when God is in control of my life.

Selfishness can and will ruin a life quicker than you may think. Look at the life of King Saul in the Books of Samuel. He was the King the people wanted. They wanted to be like the Jones' and they had God removed as their King so that they could have an earthly king like all of the other lands around them. Their earthly desires brought them ruin. Read the books for yourself and see if I am wrong. When we let ourselves get in the way of God's plan for our life, we bring all kinds of unwanted pressures and problems and circumstances down upon our heads and then when they get to be so bad we cry out for God to clean up our mess. Be honest and tell me if you have done this. I know I have. I have to be on guard against this kind of bad behavior. God is far better equipped to run my life than I am. I make it a point to pray daily that His will be done in my life and for me to be able to step back and allow Him to work both in and through me.

Let go and let God!

August 25th

Matthew 28:20; **"And behold, I am with you always, to the end of the age."** It is comforting that Jesus will be with us always and even until the end of the age. God will never leave us, nor forsake us. His love for us as Christians is powerful. His entire desire is to use us to bring others into the Kingdom. He gave us a command in Matthew 28:19-20; **"Go therefore and make disciples of all nations, baptizing them in the name of the Father and of the Son and of the Holy Spirit, teaching them to observe all that I have commanded you."** Are you following through on His command?

I realize with every stroke of the pen and every tap of the computer keyboard in writing this book that God is using me as a mere vessel and catalyst in the spreading of His Word. My hope and prayer is that His Church would be built up and that many would come to know Him as Lord and Savior through this mighty endeavor. God can and does use us wherever He has us planted. He is using children in elementary school and executives in the mighty institutions of industry. Wherever we are we are to be Ambassadors of Christ. We need to blossom where He has planted us. I know of a small Assemblies of God church in Noble, Oklahoma which took a group of young people to Milwaukee, Wisconsin to do street ministry and witness to the people up north. How awesome is that! You don't have to go overseas to some foreign land in order to witness to the lost. We have plenty of lost right here in our own backyard.

We need to remember that God is with us wherever He has us. He doesn't ever leave us or forsake us. Hebrews 13:5; **"I will never leave you nor forsake you."** John 6:37-39; **"All that the Father gives me will come to me, and whoever comes to me I will never cast out. For I have come down from heaven, not to do my own will but the will of him who sent me. And this is the will of him who sent me, that I should lose nothing of all that he has given me, but raise it up on the last day."** John 10:28-29; **"I give them eternal life, and they will never perish, and no one will snatch them out of my hand. My Father, who has given them to me, is greater than all, and no one is able to snatch them out of the Father's hand."**

Others may leave,
but Jesus won't bail on us.

August 26th

The divine destiny of God behind **The Waging War Within** is to draw me and you into a closer spiritual depth in our relationship with Him. I started this book with the desire of drawing unto Him and having God reveal His divine destiny for my life at forty years old. I desired God more and more. I desired Him more than ever before in my life. God spoke to my heart and this is how this book was birthed. It was given by the movement of the Holy Spirit within my life. This book started with me kneeling and crying out to God to use my gifts for His divine glory. I desired God to fulfill His divine destiny. God definitely took me outside the dots of my life. Does He want you to think outside the dots? What direction does He want you to go? What is His call on your life? What part of yourself can you give to God that you haven't already given to Him? What ability and gift does God desire to birth within you? Whatever it is, give it up to God and He will bless it, ten, a hundred and a thousand fold!

Jason asked me to take a look at this work and for some practical insight and we decided to work together on it. I was honored to lend a hand to this devotional as I love God and all that He has done for me in my life. I came to have a relationship with Him 12 years ago. Today I am working on my Masters of Divinity at Gordon-Conwell Theological Seminary. God has moved in me mightily and I desire to see everyone have a relationship with Him like I do. He has a purpose for all of us; we just need to discover what that purpose is. God has called me from a life of drug and alcohol addiction and tremendous pain and abuse to a life where He has me in the position of Director of Men's Ministry at Bethany Assembly of God in Agawam, Massachusetts. I never in a million years would have ever thought I would be working on a book for fellow Christians hoping to draw them into a closer relationship with Christ. I never would have thought that He would have me speaking to men at gatherings telling them of what He has brought me through. God has certainly stretched me and He can stretch you too. God has a plan for your life. I pray you find it and use it to your greatest potential.

What is God's purpose for your life?

If you don't know, ask Him.

August 27th

Living in God's Will, with His authority in our lives is a blessing beyond all of our hopes and dreams. Our prayer should be that God let us do our part in His Kingdom. What direction do you want me to go God? What do you want me to do? Lead me God by your Holy Spirit to do Your will in my life. Help me to be obedient to Your Holy Word and Your Ten Commandments. God please uncover me from the rubble of my life. Lift me up and lead me onward. Lord, lead me onward and upward to Your higher ground. Oh how I long to soar with wings like eagles and to be able to run and never grow weary. Teach me! Lead me! Guide me! Fill me with Your Holy Spirit! Restore me! Protect me! Provide for me and speak to my heart Lord!

Are you seeking God in all you do? Are you praying with specifics in mind? Do you pray that God will give you a plan and the ability to carry it out? Are you seeking Him in all that you do? When you pray are you listening for His response? How is your prayer life? Is it a healthy prayer life or is there room for improvement?

I find today that there are too many people who don't know how to pray. There are people praying formal prayers instead of praying from the heart. My friends, God wants to hear your heart. He wants to hear what makes you tick. He wants to hear what you have to say. Don't try to dazzle Him with some artsy-fartsy prayer, let Him hear your heart pouring out to Him. Get real with Him. He created you and He called you out to be a part of His family, don't you think He has earned the right to hear your heart. I do.

God is the reason we are. Talk to Him like He is your friend. Look at the Our Father prayer example Jesus gave us in Matthew 6:9-13; **"After this manner therefore pray ye: Our Father which art in heaven hallowed be thy name. Thy kingdom come Thy will be done in earth, as it is in heaven. Give us this day our daily bread and forgive us our debts, as we forgive our debtors and lead us not into temptation, but deliver us from evil. For Thine is the Kingdom, and the power, and the glory, for ever. Amen"** This is an example of how we should pray, it was not intended to be a prayer itself. Jesus was giving us an example of how to pray.

The Lord's prayer is a model prayer that is to be ***prayed through***. It is **"after this manner,"** *in this way, like this*, that you are to pray. Christ was teaching the disciples how to pray. He was giving words, phrases, thoughts that are to be the points of your prayer. You are to develop the points as you pray. An example would be something like this:

- "Our Father ...": "Thank you, Father, that you are our Father—that you have adopted me as a child of God, a son of yours. Thank you for the believers of the world who make up the family of God. Thank you for the church, the body of Christ that gives us the family of God. Thank you for loving me that much." And on and on you are to pray.
- " ...which art in heaven": "Thank you for heaven—that you are in heaven—that you have chosen me to be with you in heaven. Thank you for the hope and anticipation of heaven." And on and on you are to pray.

There are 10 elements to the Lord's Prayer:

1   A personal relationship with God- **"Our Father"**
2   Faith- **"which art in heaven"**
3   Worship- **"hallowed be Thy name"**
4   Expectation- **"Thy kingdom come"**
5   Submission- **"Thy will be done in earth, as it is in heaven"**
6   Petition- **"give us this day our daily bread"**
7   Confession- **"and forgive us our debts"**
8   Compassion- **"as we forgive our debtors"**
9   Dependence- **"and lead us not into temptation, but deliver us from evil"**
10 Acknowledgment- **"for Thine is the kingdom, and the power, and the glory forever."**

Christ taught His disciples to pray "after this manner." When you pray through the Lord's Prayer, you find you have covered the scope of what God wants you to pray. When we pray, we pray to honor God, to seek His perfect will for our lives, to petition for our needs, and we expect His supply and we offer ourselves in service to Him.

My friends, I pray I don't offend anyone here. My intention is not to offend anyone or their way of praying, I am just pointing out a fact. I want for all of us to have a stronger prayer life and one way of doing that is to point out a few things that I hope will draw us all onward and upward. I want for all of us to be able to get all that He has for us and our lives.

Let's all draw onward and upward to our Heavenly Father.

Practical insight in daily devotion

August 28th

Sensing, imagining and feeling what Jesus might have felt on His way to the cross as I was reading and studying scripture in Matthew, I couldn't help to think. He knew He had to walk that road. He could have delivered Himself, but He didn't. He could feel the pain as a common man, but He was completely divine. He could experience all the sadness, pain, suffering and brokenness as a man, but He responded with divinity. He emanated Godliness. He didn't retaliate. He didn't seethe with anger, bitterness and rage at the abuse that He endured.

The pain of many blows of a whip that left open sores down to the bone was most assuredly horrifically excruciating. There must have been blood everywhere. All the while He realized that God the Father's plan was unfolding. We can begin to understand the sacrificial offering of His Son, Jesus Christ. We really have to get this truth into our thinking and into our hearts. The next time we think we can't make it through some difficulty in our lives, let's look to what Jesus not only went through, but what He accomplished on the Cross of Christ. Great things, great feats, great heights and unchartered territory can never be conquered without going through the storm and **The Waging War Within.** Our life is a constant battle ground. All the while, through this war we must move forward and allow the Holy Spirit to work in our lives as He desires.

Let God stretch you far beyond anything you ever imagined.

Get out of your comfort zone and experience all that God has for you.

Jesus says that He will be with us to the end of the age. Hebrews 13:5; "**Keep your life free from love of money, and be content with what you have, for he has said, "I will never leave you nor forsake you."**" Jesus will never leave us. He will always be with His people. He's faithful one hundred percent of the time. God never takes time off from being there for us. God has nothing that He would rather do than be made manifest in the lives of His people. God is all about relationship and connection. That is why He created us, so that we could have relationship with Him. He's the Wonderful Counselor. God knows just how to meet our needs. Are you going through something? One thing is for sure, Jesus can meet your needs. Let's embrace God, seek God, call out to Him, trust Him, have faith in Him and He will respond to us. The Church of God is not alone. Draw unto God and He will draw unto you. James 4:8; "**Draw near to God, and he will draw near to you.**" Ask, seek, knock and the door will be opened. Matthew 7:7; "**Ask, and it will be given to you; seek, and you will find; knock, and it will be opened to you.**" Our relationship with God is paramount. Nothing should take precedence over our relationship with the ultimate authority Jesus Christ. He has to become the core of our lives and then, and only then, will everything fall into place.

We have been created to have a relationship with God. God wanted to hang out with us. Unfortunately sin entered the Garden and destroyed any hope of eternity with Him. That is the reason Jesus came to earth; in order to be the Blood Sacrifice for our sins. God still desires a relationship with us, His created, in spite of our sinful nature. Do you have a good relationship with Him? You can you know? We can't keep beating ourselves up for mistakes from our past. Once we lay them at the foot of the cross they are forgiven and forgotten. We have to let them go. When we bring them up God asks "What are you talking about?" If He can forgive you why can't you? Let it go. It is done and over. Jesus paid the price so you don't have to. If you spend all kinds of time beating yourself up over past sins you are wasting all the time you could be doing positive things for the Kingdom.

We can be our worst enemies. If you have asked for forgiveness for a sin and you are truly repentant you can rest assured you are forgiven, now let it go and don't bring it up again. It's like a dog returning to its vomit. It's nasty, so stop it already. Do some good for the Kingdom with your time and your life.

Let it go!

August 30th

The enemy can come to us from many different directions and in many different situations and circumstances. One thing is certain; God can protect us from this onslaught of the enemy of our souls. God will prevail, if we place Him first in our lives. Nothing can overcome us with the penetrating blood of the Lamb of God and the Holy Spirit on our side. Legions and legions of demons may wage war, but God is greater. A true soldier of Jesus Christ wages war on his knees in prayer. When we bow on bended knee to Jesus He will move Heaven and Earth to help us. His sovereign will always prevails.

The enemy can operate through another believer, an unbeliever, through valley experiences, mountaintop experiences and through common place situations. We have to be aware of how Satan operates and the devices he uses. John 10:10; **"The thief comes only to steal and kill and destroy. I came that they may have life and have it abundantly."** He's a manipulator. He may fill your mind and heart with doubt, fear, anger, hatred, jealously, anxiety, depression and uncertainty. One thing in life is absolutely true, Jesus Christ is God. Psalms 18:31; **"For who is God, but the LORD? And who is a rock, except our God?"** This is the truth that all of humanity is longing to know. Satan is no match for God. Satan knows this. Revelation 12:7-10; **"Now war arose in heaven, Michael and his angels fighting against the dragon. And the dragon and his angels fought back, but he was defeated and there was no longer any place for them in heaven. And the great dragon was thrown down, that ancient serpent, who is called the devil and Satan, the deceiver of the whole world— he was thrown down to the earth, and his angels were thrown down with him. And I heard a loud voice in heaven, saying, "Now the salvation and the power and the kingdom of our God and the authority of his Christ have come, for the accuser of our brothers has been thrown down, who accuses them day and night before our God."**

No substitution for combating **The Waging War Within** exists against the devils schemes other than; reading God's Word, intense prayer, fasting, seeking Godly counsel, fellowship and getting yourself involved in a solid local community Bible believing church and attending that church consistently. This is a key. Getting involved in weekly worship services, healing services and prayer services is an important aspect in combating satanic infiltration.

Know the enemies devices.

If you want to know how someone's spiritual life is, including your own, count how many times you or they attend church. When is the last time you opened a Bible? When is the last time you lead someone to the Lord? When is the last time you spent time in prayer? Consistency is critical in carrying out our Christian Walk. Discipline is also an important ingredient to the recipe of living a consistent Christian Life.

We have to have a heart that is willing to seek after the things of God. Matthew 6:33; **"But seek first the kingdom of God and his righteousness, and all these things will be added to you."** Our passion has to be focused toward His will. He has to literally be our Everything. He must become more and we must become less. It's up to us. If we want more of God, this is left up to us. If we want more of Him we must decide that our desire to live for the things of God is preeminent in our life. One thing is for sure, we cannot do this walk alone.

The Church of Jesus Christ is a living organism. We all need each other. We need to refine, mold, build up, strengthen, encourage and hold each other accountable in the faith. When one falls, we must restore them. The Shepherd and the 99 parable is fitting here. Matthew 18:12-14; **"What do you think? If a man has a hundred sheep and one of them has gone astray, does he not leave the ninety-nine on the mountains and go in search of the one that went astray? And if he finds it, truly, I say to you, he rejoices over it more than over the ninety-nine that never went astray. So it is not the will of my Father who is in heaven that one of these little ones should perish."** The same goes for the parable of the Prodigal Son in Luke 15:11-32. We need to treat people with loving kindness, not a sharp tongue.

We must help people with the Holy Spirit's help to bring out their gifts and abilities in ministry. We must strengthen our relationship with Christ and reach the lost. It's not about us, it's about Him. We need to treat others the way we would want to be treated. Jesus set the example for all of us to follow. He treated everyone with kindness, even His executioners. He was the epitome of kindness. Jesus up till His dying breath offered only kindness to His tormenters. Luke 23:34; **"And Jesus said, "Father, forgive them, for they know not what they do." And they cast lots to divide his garments."** Could you do that? I would be hard pressed to take the kind of abuse He did and still have forgiveness in my heart. We are called to accept abuse and forgive them their sins through Jesus Christ. I pray daily for a heart like Christ. Do you?

Consistency is critical

September

September 1st

Honesty; we must be transparent with God in dealing with our short comings, our faults and our sinful nature. We cannot live a Christian Life if we're living in lies and denial. 1 Peter 2:21-25; **"For to this you have been called, because Christ also suffered for you, leaving you an example, so that you might follow in his steps. He committed no sin, neither was deceit found in his mouth. When he was reviled, he did not revile in return; when he suffered, he did not threaten, but continued entrusting himself to him who judges justly. He himself bore our sins in his body on the tree, that we might die to sin and live to righteousness. By his wounds you have been healed. For you were straying like sheep, but have now returned to the Shepherd and Overseer of your souls."** Our very life needs to be an open book to our Living God. He deserves nothing less than our total and open honesty, after all, He already knows doesn't He? God knows our thoughts and our motives.

We must first acknowledge that no matter where we are in life, we're lost without Him. We all have to long for change, growth and maturity in Him. 1 Corinthians 14:25; **"The secrets of his heart are disclosed, and so, falling on his face, he will worship God and declare that God is really among you."** Despite ourselves, He will lift us up and we will fall on our faces and worship Him. Only He deserves to be exalted. He's the Truth. He's God. He's the True Hero, the True Star, and the True Famous One. He deserves our worship and praise. Look at all He has done for us. Nothing in all the world compares to the love and riches that can be found in Him, in Jesus Christ!

Honesty and Love

September 2nd

All over America and throughout the world people are hungering for truth. From kings to paupers, people are searching for spiritual truth. God is moving and drawing all people unto Him. People are realizing now more than ever that materialism, humanism, Satanism, atheism, false religions, alternative life styles, positions of power and prestige don't bring fulfillment and contentment to the soul. The soul can only be completely satisfied with Jesus Christ. Psalms 73:28; **"But for me it is good to be near God; I have made the Lord GOD my refuge, that I may tell of all your works."** Once you get to know God through a personal relationship with Him, you won't ever want to let that go. God can and will bless you abundantly. He wants to love you like you have never known love before. We just need to let Him.

True love comes from God. After all, God is love. Human beings are looking for love, for someone to care for them and they desire to care for others. People often look for love in all of the wrong places. God has made us to love. He made us this way and has given us this need for love. Without Christ; love, sexuality and our humanity can become distorted. A maddening of the minds of people of the world will happen that deny God's existence. People will become increasingly selfish and sadistic without Christ. The depravity of the mind can become intense without the renewing power of the Holy Spirit. Romans 12:2; **"And do not be conformed to this world, but be transformed by the renewing of your mind, that you may prove what is that good and acceptable and perfect will of God."** Our minds need to be renewed and washed daily with the Word of God and the Blood of the Lamb. The lamb in the Old Testament times was used as a sacrifice offering for sin. Although the blood of a lamb could cover sin, such blood could never actually take away sin. A lamb is not a man, and only a man could die for a man. Only a sinless man could die for a sinful man and Jesus was that man. Jesus was sent to live as a man on the Earth. He was sent to die on a cross and shed His blood on that cross. Jesus' death on the cross was God's answer to the problem of the sinful hearts of man. His blood and healing power was needed to restore man to God's favor. We need the healing and restoring power of God to flow within our lives.

We are all sinners and we have fallen short of the Glory of God. Sure, you can always find someone who is a worse sinner than you yourself are. This is not the point. The point is that, because you have sinned, you are a sinner. Romans 3:23; **"For all have sinned and come short of the glory of God."** With the blood of Jesus covering your sins, your sins are washed away and forgotten. God will never again see your sins and you will not have to go to Hell over them, instead, you will spend eternity in Heaven with Jesus and God His Father.

September 3rd

Our values and morals have to be an extension of who we are and what we believe. We must show the world the power of God through both our words as well as actions. We must live our lives as that of an Ambassador of Christ. We must act as Jesus did while He was walking Earth. We must talk as Jesus did, spreading the Good Word to all inhabitants of the world. We must work as a representative of Christ. We must love as Jesus loved, not as one who doesn't know Jesus. Our priorities must be set to a much higher standard than that of an unbeliever and our monies must be spent accordingly. If we're not living to a standard worthy of God than we are cutting ourselves and Jesus short of that deserved. If we are not living a life that is different then we're not showing the world that being a Christian holds any significance at all.

Christians should be the most well-read people. Christians should be the most educated in both the Word as well as scholastic circles. Christians should hold positions of power. Christians should be the most involved in politics. Just because we are Christians doesn't mean we are to exclude ourselves from the political system. We need to advocate for the underdog, the downtrodden and the excluded; Jesus did didn't He? Christians should be the most involved in their community. Christians should have the lowest divorce rate of all, but unfortunately ours is as high or perhaps even higher. Christians should work the hardest at their jobs and not be influenced by shoddy work ethics being displayed by others. Christians should be the most focused and the most dedicated people on earth. Christians should be the most giving and the most loving individuals the world has ever seen. Despite living in a fallen and broken world, we should be the best we can be in and through Jesus Christ.

We need to set a standard of living and work ethics that does not bring shame on the name of Jesus Christ. Are you doing this? I pray you are. People are watching everything you are doing once they find out that you are a Christian. Is this fair? No it isn't but life as you know isn't always fair. You let it be known that you were a son or daughter of The Most High, through something you either said or did and now you have to live with that fact. Live a life worthy of your position. Please.

Be an example of a son or daughter of the Most High, worthy of His name!

September 4th

Many Christians feel like they're under attack from the very culture in which they live. We feel like this because we are under fire. We sometimes feel like we're surrounded by gunfire, snipers, tanks and grenade launchers. It feels like an all-out nuclear war. The political schema of the United States is changing. A religious war is taking place within our society. It is an all-out war against Christ.

Our country used to hold Christian values and the Protestant Faith in higher esteem than it does today. With the infiltration of eastern religions, witchcraft, Satanism, humanistic philosophies and ideologies, Darwinism, atheism and other false beliefs a distain and even an all-out hatred by some exist toward the Christian God, Jesus Christ. The spirit of the anti-christ has penetrated our infrastructure like never before. Paganism is running rampant in our country. A literal battle is waging for the minds and hearts of the next generation. We must not lose heart over this.

Jesus said that He wouldn't ever leave us didn't He? Hebrews 13:5-6; **"Keep your life free from love of money, and be content with what you have, for he has said, "I will never leave you nor forsake you." So we can confidently say, "The Lord is my helper; I will not fear; what can man do to me?"** We need to fall on our knees and thank the Lord for His promise to always be with us. He hears our hearts cry and He sees our tears. Let Him comfort you. Cry out to Him in your times of desperation. Don't hold back. The Lord has kept His Word safe from destruction for how many thousands of years? Why would He let it or His children perish now? He won't, rest assured. Pray to God for protection for yourself and your loved ones. He will hear you. We are so small before the Lord and so in need of help. We are all doing that which we can do just to stay alive in these dark and troubled times. We need all of the help we can get. We are not a ship of fools throwing our hopes and fears at the feet of nothing. No, we throw our hopes and fears at the feet of our Most High God and He will reciprocate.

We can rest on the promises of God that He will be with us always and forever. I find great comfort in that promise. He is with me each and every moment of the day. Sure I will have problems just like all of you do but that's ok. I know deep down in my heart that I am a son of the Most High God. We were never promised that we would not have problems. We were promised that God would deliver us from them. It is not the mountain top experiences in which we will grow, it is the valley experiences and struggles where we will grow. We must be a grateful people. We are told to give praise always. Ephesians 5:20; **"Give thanks always and for everything to God the Father in the name of our Lord Jesus Christ."** Give praise when? Only in the good times? No! Always! Give praise always. Give praise for the good times as well as the bad times. Remember, diamonds are formed under great pressure, and we are God's jewels aren't we?

September 5th

We all have to ask God how He wants us to get involved in spreading the Gospel and curbing the tide of ungodliness. The only way to combat this cesspool of satanic activity is with the Holy Bible. God expects His people to be active in their churches and communities. We must get into the written Word and study that Word in order to have it not only work for us but for Him also. We need to pray and cry out to God. Ask Him what would you have me to do? Where do you want to send me? What can I do for you? Pray these questions to Him and He will most definitely answer you. Just listen while you pray. Don't just talk to Him and cry out but listen to Him and for Him. He gave us two ears and one mouth to use proportionally.

We have to take back our towns and cities for Jesus Christ. The local church has to get involved in this action. We also have to take back the different media venues. We need more of God and less of the garbage we see filling the airwaves and in print today. Christian television programming has to take place to a greater degree. An increase in Christian radio stations needs to happen. More and more Christians need to get together in establishing Christian businesses and ministries. We need to take back our land people. An increase in Christian schools, at the primary, secondary and college level needs to be put into action. An increase in Christian programs; such as community centers, after school programs, counseling and other agencies to help people that are struggling need to be implemented. Christians need to produce more movies and write more books sharing the Gospel message. More Christian sports and outward bound programs need to happen with a Christian emphasis not secular as we see today.

Why aren't we spending more time at our prayer rails after the altar call is given? The altar call is one of the most important parts of the service. People need to come down and answer the call of Christ, this is a given. Once that is over and the applause has died down, why aren't we running down to the rail and dropping to our knees and crying out to God for His will to be carried out in us and through us? We need to get back to prayer. Prayer is our Lifeline to God. It is essential if we plan to be used to our full capacity for Him. Let's encourage our fellow church members to flood the rails after our services. We can skip the doughnut hour and pray can't we? God supplies all of our needs, not the Donut Dip. Am I right? I thought so. Try it, you'll like it. You'll be glad you did.

Try it, you'll like it!

September 6th

More Christians need to open up their homes and form home prayer, worship and Bible study meetings. Fellowship is a key in building yourself and others up in the Christian Faith. Doing things that lift the name of Jesus up before the world is what is needed in today's day and time. Whatever platform you use, lift the name of Jesus up. Give God the glory. We need to have unity in our community of Christian believers. God moves when there is unity. Unity in our relationship with others is vital. Unity in our churches and homes is a must. Unity between husband and wife is a powerful thing. Unity speaks volumes to the unsaved world. With so much divisiveness happening, unity stands out. There is strength in numbers.

I have been a big proponent of empowering men to be the men that God has called us to be. This is Gregg writing here. Fellas, how is it that the women have been empowered to get the kids off to church and study the Word when that responsibility has been given to us? It is unfair to them. We are the ones who have been given the responsibility of being the priests of our households, work places, communities and our churches, not the women. We need to get ourselves out of bed on Sunday mornings and get down on our knees and offer up thanks to God that He has given us another chance to get it right. Once you realize you are sucking air, praise God for that and then ask Him to strengthen you so that you can carry out your duties and responsibilities to both Him and your families. God has entrusted your wives and children to you. That is a tremendous responsibility given to you. You need Him to help you throughout your day. Once you have done your praying and your readings then get up your family and help your wives out with getting the kids ready for church. You are responsible for more than just having the fun of making them. Accept that fact and champion to it.

Men, we have a role to play in the upbringing of our kids. If you have a son, teach him how to be a man of God. Lead by example. If your son is approaching dating age, show him how to treat a lady. Don't just tell him what to do, show him. Use his mother as an example. Open her door for her. Pull out her chair at the dinner table. Complement her on the time it took her to look beautiful for you. Be a man of God. Teach your sons. If you have a daughter, demonstrate to her what a boy should do when he takes her out on a date. Take your daughter out on her first date. I am serious. Pull up your car to the curb and walk up to the house and ring the doorbell for her. Open the door for her when she goes to exit the house. Open her car door so she doesn't have to. Complement her looks. Do the whole nine yards. Then when the night is over do a march order and let her know that if a boy doesn't do all of those things for her that he is not worthy of her time. I firmly believe that this is one way we can stop the problems plaguing our younger generation today.

September 7th

Our lives need to be blanketed in deep devotional time and prayer to our Lord and Savior Jesus Christ. God moves mightily in a believer that has a consistent, dedicated commitment to devotional time and prayer time. The more time we spend with God on our knees, the more He infuses Himself into our broken lives. Let's allow Jesus to live in us. He works in a people that are walking in humility.

We need to have role models and mentors that are the pillar of the church. Don't settle for less when it comes to men and women whom you aspire to be like. We all need role models of Christian men and women that we can look up to because of their Godly life. Who or what you value is typically who or what you become and determines greatly what road you take in life.

Find Christian leaders locally and around the world whom you respect. Read their books if they are authors, watch their programs if they are pleasing to the Lord, watch how they act and interact, pay attention to how they speak and emulate how they conduct themselves as representatives of Christ. Buy their autobiographies and their life stories. Read about their lives and allow the Holy Spirit to show you things about their lives that you can use in order to be all that He would have you to be.

We all serve as examples in life; it is up to us to choose whether we will be a good example or a bad one. We are all called to let our light shine. Matthew 5:16; "**Let your light shine before others, so that they may see your good works and give glory to your Father who is in heaven.**" We are to give glory to God in all that we do. People are to know we are Christians by the light we let shine through our actions as well as our words. It is not by works or deeds that we get into Heaven, it is a condition of our heart that gets us there. Paul states this in the Book of 2 Timothy 1:8-10; "**Therefore do not be ashamed of the testimony about our Lord, nor of me his prisoner, but share in suffering for the gospel by the power of God, who saved us and called us to a holy calling, not because of our works but because of his own purpose and grace, which he gave us in Christ Jesus before the ages began, and which now has been manifested through the appearing of our Savior Christ Jesus, who abolished death and brought life and immortality to light through the gospel.**" Preach always, and when necessary, use words. Let the people know you care.

It is not by actions that
we are admitted into Heaven
but by the condition of our heart

September 8th

You should attend Christian conferences, events, concerts and retreats whenever you can. These can help in a plethora of ways. They can build you up spiritually as well as emotionally. They can help you broaden your circle of like-minded people. They can introduce you to other avenues of influence. Getting together with other Christians who have a like precious faith is important for your maturity in the Lord.

Involvement in your local church is the most important place for you to be actively participating. Teaching Sunday school, singing in the choir, working within the children's ministries, the women's or men's ministries can all help bring you to a whole other level of exposure to the Word and strengthen your walk as a Soldier of Christ. First and foremost, you need to become a member of a local assembly of Believers in the Lord and make a commitment to the church. Find a church you feel comfortable in. Step out in faith and get involved. Give of your time, talents and treasures. There is really a no more rewarding experience then giving of yourself into God's Kingdom. We all have different talents and abilities and coming together as a body of believers in whatever venue available is a great dynamic. Can you imagine the heart attack you are giving the devil when you gather with other like-minded believers? Too cool!

When you gather with people of like minds you are generating a power that is so mighty. You have an opportunity to praise God when you gather. Psalms 22:22; "**I will tell of your name to my brothers; in the midst of the congregation I will praise you.**" When you gather you give praise to God. Psalms 22:3; "**Yet you are holy, enthroned on the praises of Israel.**" Romans shows where when we gather you have an opportunity to share His name and greatness. Romans 10:17; "**Faith comes from hearing, and hearing through the word of Christ.**" And lastly you have an opportunity for prayer when you gather together. Matthew 18:20; "**For where two or three are gathered in my name, there am I among them.**" Praise God.

How are you
being
built up spiritually?

September 9th

Spend alone time with God. Make sure there is time every day whereby it's you and God. This time can be spent in a time of prayer, contemplation, and journaling, praising, reading of God's Word or listening to Christian music. We all need to be renewed in the faith both frequently and consistently. Make time. It is vital to your existence as a Christian and God relishes that time spent with you.

Do you have a devotional time with your family? You should try it. Having a devotional time is a great way for you to draw nearer to the Lord. This might be with your wife if married and with your children if you have kids or if you so choose, alone. Spending time in prayer, sharing what God is doing in your life and reading scripture will strengthen your family. It is also a great example to pass on to your kid's. What a legacy to leave behind for them.

Prayer and devotion time is vital in keeping your faith strong, not to mention the bountiful blessings it will place on your marriage. I have found that when I pray with my wife that we are drawn closer to each other as well as to the Lord. It also shows my wife that I really do care for her safety and well-being. We need to pray over our loved ones. Psalm 91:1; **"He who dwells in the shelter of the Most High will abide in the shadow of the Almighty."** This is a great passage to ponder. The whole chapter of Psalm 91 is powerful. A great prayer to pray daily with your families is Ephesians 6: 10-20, the Armor of God. It is more than just a passage; it can be made a prayer also. Make it a prayer you pray over your loved ones and also your pastors and their loved ones. You do pray over your pastors don't you?

So many times we neglect to pray for our local pastors and their families. They have a tremendous responsibility on their lives. They are not only responsible for their families but also their congregation as well. How would you like that weight placed on your shoulders? They covet our prayers. Make it a practice to pray over your pastor's daily will you? We at Bethany pray over our service and our pastors before each service in a hallway leading into our sanctuary. It is a very powerful thing to do. I know our pastoral team gathers strength through that prayer. We call the hallway our "Holy Hallway" and we gather the men of the church before each service to pray with the pastoral leadership team. It is an example to the ladies that we are truly the men of God that we have been called to be. I always give out invitations to the men to gather. This is also an invitation to the young men of the church. We lead by example and what better example than praying over our church services and leadership.

Lead by example

September 10th

We should practice being able to inculcate the peace of God in our lives. Try to be able to have a vision of God's presence in your life at all times. Live in His peace while allowing Him to quiet your soul. This will allow you to develop depth and maturity in your relationship with the Lord. The calm assurance of the presence of Jesus even in the midst of conflict and confrontation is what we all need. Practice being reflective with Jesus. Ask Him to open your eyes to all He is and all that He has for you. Be aware of His divine presence in your life and within the lives of others.

God has called you out to be His son or daughter. Are you really grasping that concept? He has called you to be His son or daughter. Take a moment to think about that. Why would He have called you of all people? Remember those days when you felt less than? Do you remember those days where you felt that you were worthless? Don't tell me you never felt that. We all have had those feelings at one time or another. Now think about God calling on you to be His son or daughter. It is pretty humbling isn't it? You have been called out to be the kid of the King of Kings and the Lord of Lords. How awesome is that? Hold your head up and be proud of that fact. Whenever someone calls you worthless remind them that you are a child of the Most High God and mean it.

God has called us to be His. 1 Peter 1:3-5; "**According to his great mercy, He has caused us to be born again to a living hope through the resurrection of Jesus Christ from the dead, to an inheritance that is imperishable, undefiled, and unfading, kept in Heaven for you, who by God's power are being guarded through faith for a salvation ready to be revealed in the last time.**" See, He wants you in Heaven with Him. He has given you a personal invitation through His written Word. God wants to spend eternity with you. If that doesn't make you feel special I don't know what will.

You were created so that you can have a relationship with God. He created you so that you can have relationship with Him, the Most High awe inspiring God. Genesis 2:7; "**Then the LORD God formed the man of dust from the ground and breathed into his nostrils the breath of life, and the man became a living creature.**" God created us so we can enjoy relationship with Him. He made us different from the beasts of the land by giving us a soul. That is where we have our relationship with Him; our soul is our spirit, a place where He resides within us. We didn't come from apes. If we did there would be no apes left, they would have evolved into people. Scientists, supposedly being such smart people, seem to have forgotten that little fact. We aren't apes; we were created in the image of the Almighty God. Genesis 1:27; "**So God created man in His own image, in the image of God He created him; male and female He created them.**" God created us in His image, not in the image of an ape. We are a reflection of God and His awesome love; let's act accordingly.

September 11th

Set short-term and long-term goals for your Christian life. Be sensitive to the direction that God might lead you. He usually taps into your gifts and abilities and gives you gentle nudges in the direction He wishes for you to follow. He desires to use you to edify and build up the body of Christ. He also desires to capture the lost with His Word. God has you to be a reflection of Him and His love by spreading His love to all you come into contact with. The beautiful thing about the body of Jesus Christ, the body of believers, is that everyone is different and we all have various gifts. There are **9 Spiritual Gifts** listed in 1 Corinthians 12:1-14. The Spiritual Gifts listed are **wisdom, knowledge, discerning of various spirits, speaking in tongues, interpretation of tongues, prophecy, faith, working of miracles, and healing.** I know there are some that think that they were just for the first century church but think of this, why would God give us a gift and then take it back? He is the all giving God, not the giving so He can take it away God am I right? I don't understand that train of thought. Nowhere does it say in the Bible that God gave the gifts only for the first century church, nowhere.

God has a divine destiny for your life. He has had a determined divine destiny for you since the foundation of the world. He longs to bless you richly with every blessing inherent within Jesus Christ. Are you ready for your blessings? Are you already receiving them? If not, what are you doing to prepare for them? Are you studying the Word to show yourself approved as in 2 Timothy 2:15? 2 Timothy 2:15; "**Do your best to present yourself to God as one approved, a worker who has no need to be ashamed, rightly handling the word of truth.**" If you hunker down in the written Word of God you will be picking up tender morsels with which you can build a great foundation with.

Have you been praying for direction from God? Do you know what it is He has for you to do with your life? Are you studying the Word? Are you attending church regularly? Do you attend Bible study or are you a member of a small group? Do you teach a Sunday school class? What are you doing with your life? Is God pleased with the man or woman you have become? Are you leading others to Christ? Is your life a reflection of the walk of Jesus? If not, why not? Think of these questions and search your heart diligently for a reply. Be honest with yourself. What are you doing for the Kingdom of God?

What are you doing for the Kingdom of God?

September 12th

      We need to claim and speak Scripture. The enemy shudders when we quote and speak Scripture out loud. It's God's Word! Demons flee and Satan cringes when the Scripture is spoken by a Christian believer. Scripture is a weapon, as is prayer in combating the enemy and fighting **The Waging War Within.** Scripture is called the Sword of the Spirit. Ephesians 6:10-20 is the Armor of God section. Ephesians 6:10-20; **"Be strong in the Lord and in the strength of his might. Put on the whole armor of God, that you may be able to stand against the schemes of the devil. For we do not wrestle against flesh and blood, but against the rulers, against the authorities, against the cosmic powers over this present darkness, against the spiritual forces of evil in the heavenly places. Therefore take up the whole armor of God, that you may be able to withstand in the evil day, and having done all, to stand firm. Stand therefore, having fastened on the belt of truth, and having put on the breastplate of righteousness, and, as shoes for your feet, having put on the readiness given by the gospel of peace. In all circumstances take up the shield of faith, with which you can extinguish all the flaming darts of the evil one; and take the helmet of salvation, and the sword of the Spirit, which is the word of God, praying at all times in the Spirit, with all prayer and supplication. To that end keep alert with all perseverance, making supplication for all the saints, and also for me, that words may be given to me in opening my mouth boldly to proclaim the mystery of the gospel, for which I am an ambassador in chains, that I may declare it boldly, as I ought to speak."** Did you catch it? The Word is the Sword of the Spirit. It is the only defensive weapon in God's arsenal. The rest are for offensive battle.

      When you read Scripture out loud or to yourself, you're hearing and absorbing the Word of God. Getting the Word into your brain, your heart, your soul and spirit is a key to winning the war. God's Word is powerful and is able to pull down the strongholds of the enemy. Hebrews 4:12; **"For the Word of God is quick, and powerful, and sharper than any two edged sword. Piercing even to the dividing asunder of soul and spirit, and of the joints and the morrow. And is a discerner of the thoughts and intents o f the hearts."** You have to know the Word in order to use it effectively. How well do you know it?

How well do you
know the Word?

September 13th

Prayer is a key in fighting a satanic attack. Drop to your knees and call on the Father, the Son and the Holy Spirit for their wisdom giving and their gift of serenity. Allow God and Jesus Christ to enter your prayer time with His power and majesty. Allow God to reveal to you how and what to pray for and be specific in your petitions. Find a quiet place to pray where you won't be distracted. Choose a time to pray when you have the time to get down to business with God. Go to God with everything in your life. Go to Him with every decision, every move and transition. God will lead you and guide you. Set aside a certain time of day and make a concerted effort to pray at that time daily. Make it a discipline.

Have you ever given thought as to what prayer is all about? Why did Jesus pray when He was one of the God-head? What makes up prayer? There are just as many questions about prayer as there are answers. The word pray can be broken down into: **P-Praise, R-Rejoice, A-Ask, and Y-Yield**. This is a great foundational point from which to build your own prayers off of. Now on how to pray, let's take it to the Word for our answers.

We have our example for prayer from Jesus Christ Himself in **Matthew 6:9-13**.
"After this manner therefore pray ye: …

- **Our Father**
- **Which art in heaven**
- **Hallowed be thy name**
- **Thy kingdom come**
- **Thy will be done in earth, as it is in heaven**
- **Give us this day our daily bread**
- **And forgive us our debts, as we forgive our debtors**
- **And lead us not into temptation, but deliver us from evil**
- **For thine is the kingdom, and the power, and the glory, forever. Amen"**

Note the words **"After this manner . . . pray ye."** Now let's look at Luke's account where the disciples asked Jesus to teach them to pray in Luke 11:1-2.

Luke 11:1-4 (ESV)
¹ Now Jesus was praying in a certain place, and when he finished, one of his disciples said to him, "Lord, teach us to pray, as John taught his disciples."
² And he said to them, "When you pray, say: "Father, hallowed be your name. Your kingdom come.
³ Give us each day our daily bread,
⁴ and forgive us our sins, for we ourselves forgive everyone who is indebted to us. And lead us not into temptation."

The prayer was given to show the disciples *how to pray*—how they should go about praying, not the *words* they should pray. There are distinct differences in the wording between the two examples of the Lord's Prayer. However, the meaning is the same. The very context of what Christ had just taught shows this clearly. **Matthew 6:5-8 (ESV)**
⁵ **"And when you pray, you must not be like the hypocrites. For they love to stand and**

pray in the synagogues and at the street corners, that they may be seen by others. Truly, I say to you, they have received their reward.

⁶ But when you pray, go into your room and shut the door and pray to your Father who is in secret. And your Father who sees in secret will reward you.

⁷ "And when you pray, do not heap up empty phrases as the Gentiles do, for they think that they will be heard for their many words.

⁸ Do not be like them, for your Father knows what you need before you ask him.

The Lord's prayer is a model prayer that is to be **prayed through**. It is **"after this manner,"** *in this way, like this*, that you are to pray. Christ was teaching the disciples how to pray. He was giving words, phrases, thoughts that are to be the points of your prayer. You are to develop the points as you pray. An example would be something like this:

- "Our Father …": "Thank you, Father, that you are our Father—that you have adopted me as a child of God, a son of yours. Thank you for the believers of the world who make up the family of God. Thank you for the church, the body of Christ that gives us the family of God. Thank you for loving me that much." And on and on you are to pray.
- " …which art in heaven": "Thank you for heaven—that you are in heaven—that you have chosen me to be with you in heaven. Thank you for the hope and anticipation of heaven." And on and on you are to pray.

There are 10 elements to the Lord's Prayer:

1 A personal relationship with God- **"Our Father"**
2 Faith- **"which art in heaven"**
3 Worship- **"hallowed be Thy name"**
4 Expectation- **"Thy kingdom come"**
5 Submission- **"Thy will be done in earth, as it is in heaven"**
6 Petition- **"give us this day our daily bread"**
7 Confession- **"and forgive us our debts"**
8 Compassion- **"as we forgive our debtors"**
9 Dependence- **"and lead us not into temptation, but deliver us from evil"**
10 Acknowledgment- **"for Thine is the kingdom, and the power, and the glory forever."**

Christ taught His disciples to pray "after this manner." When you pray through the Lord's Prayer, you find you have covered the scope of what God wants you to pray. When we pray we pray to honor God, to seek His perfect will for our lives, to petition for our needs, and we expect His supply and to offer ourselves in service to Him.

Prayer is a two way street. Our Father in heaven yearns to communicate with us. We have been given this wonderful opportunity to have a two-way conversation with our Creator. He already knows our hearts and thoughts, but to express them to Him releases our burdens and desires.

Paul was said to have knees like those of a camel from all the time he spent on them in prayer. What an awesome compliment. Paul knew and trusted in the power of prayer. He is an example we should emulate, not some entertainer who is in the spotlight today and gone tomorrow. Don't you agree? Luke 21:36 gives us a command concerning prayer. Luke 21:36; **"But stay awake at all times, praying that you may have strength to escape all these things that are going to take place, and to stand before the Son of Man."** We have multiple passages in the Word concerning Jesus Christ and His prayer practice. If Jesus was spending time praying to His Father don't you think it would behoove us to do the same?

Let's devote time to prayer.
Pray always!

Let's get the knees
of camels shall we?

September 14th

Prior to speaking, choose the words you're going to say, especially if you're angry. Are they healing or hurtful words? Measure your words. Words are powerful. Words speak things into existence. Words can restore or destroy. Weigh your words carefully. Ask God to give you discernment with the way you speak. Ask God to give you the words when you are in a difficult situation.

Sometimes it's better to keep your words to yourself. Sometimes it's better to listen. If you don't have anything good to say about someone, don't say anything at all. I am sure you have heard all of this advice a million times throughout your life. When we listen, truly listen, we can learn so much about another person. Challenge yourself to do more listening and less talking. This is sage advice worth heeding.

How often did Jesus set the example where He would enter a village or a building and He would sit and listen to the people around Him? He did it quite often. He would ask people what it was that they needed. He would listen most often before He would speak. Let's make an effort to emulate Jesus shall we? We learn so much when we listen. So often people we come into contact with just need to talk and unburden themselves to someone who truly cares. We have all been there ourselves at one time in our lives. Two ears and one mouth are for a reason; to use proportionately. When was the last time you listened to your friend? I mean really listened? How much do you really know about your spouse if you have one? Do you really know what makes them tick? Ask them again what it is that they really love to do, then do it. Have you given up date night just because you are married? Start it again and get to know each other all over again. You have changed in the last number of years haven't you? They have too. Get to know each other all over again. You will be glad you did. I promise.

**Start date night with your spouse
so that you can get to know them all over again.
You'll be glad you did.**

September 15th

Your life is a scale that needs to be balanced in order for it to function properly. Always put your relationship with God first. The order of importance should be God, family and lastly your career. Don't ever let anything or anyone get in the way of your spiritual life. People, especially unbelievers, will sap all the life blood out of you. Be careful and aware of how the enemy uses people. Ask God to give you a sensitively to the Holy Spirit.

God created us to be relational people. He wanted us to enjoy life with others. We are not meant to be alone. Man is to take a wife just as a woman is to take a husband. Genesis 2:24; **"Therefore a man shall leave his father and his mother and hold fast to his wife, and they shall become one flesh."** We are meant to be married. We are not meant to be alone in life. Man is meant to be in a relationship with a woman and a woman is meant to be in a relationship with a man. It is Biblical. Society seems to try to pervert the Word and twist it to meet their agendas but the Word of God stands.

We need to balance our life as well as balance our diet. God has told us to do everything within moderation. Philippians 4:4; **"Let your moderation be known unto all men."** Everyone needs balance in their life. If you put too much into one section of your life the other two sections will be off kilter and it will throw you into a tailspin. We need to keep ourselves balanced.

Have you ever put so much time and energy into something that you forgot to take care of something else that was pressing and you felt like garbage afterwards? I have. I have missed appointments because I got so into something I was doing that I lost track of time and I let others down as a result of my lack of attention. We cannot get so caught up in life that we neglect God, our families or our jobs. If your life is out of balance and you don't know what to do about it try saying no sometime. I have learned this valuable lesson and it really works. I have a Timothy and a Barnabus that help me out now. I got so caught up in ministry that I was starting to neglect my wife. I wasn't aware of it but a dear friend pointed it out to me. Boy did I feel like the dung pile. I have since made adjustments to my life and walk and I have others helping me. I am a perfectionist and I always want everything to be the best it can be. I was trying to do everything myself so that it was right. Wrong way to do things buddy. I was burning myself out for God when He was wanting me to spend time with my helpmate, my wife. I learned a valuable lesson. Learn from me so you don't have to go through the misery I did. God wants balance in your life.

Balance is important!

September 16th

You should take notes when the preacher is preaching. You never know what golden nuggets God wants to drop into your lap. Keep your notes when God speaks to you about something in your life. God uses ministers, teachers, evangelists and other Christians to minister to you through His Word. He may even use a prophet to speak something prophetic over your life. You never know. Be open to the moving of God through your local congregation. Note taking is a great practice to get into if you haven't already started to do it.

I stress to the men that I lead that they really need to take notes for several reasons. Chief among them is that we are called to show ourselves approved. 2 Timothy 2:15; "**Do your best to present yourself to God as one approved, a worker who has no need to be ashamed, rightly handling the word of truth.**" We need to keep our hearts as well as our heads in the written Word of God. It is not up to our Pastor to get us into Heaven for eternity. It is our responsibility to read and research that what he says is the rightly divided Word of God. I love my pastor but it is my job to make sure that what he is preaching is correct. How can I do that if I am not taking notes and researching the message? I can't.

I love note taking. I have multiple notebooks full of notes from messages. I love to research them. Each time I restudy my notes I learn a little bit more. I can look back and see where I have made a note about a prior message and I can hear the Word being spoken all over again. The Bereans were great studiers of the Word. Acts 17:11; "**Now these Bereans were more noble than those in Thessalonica; they received the word with all eagerness, examining the Scriptures daily to see if these things were so.** " Another great passage to ponder is 1 Thessalonians 5:21; "**Test everything; hold fast to what is good.**" We should be following this lead. What a great opportunity to get into the Word even deeper. Let's try it shall we?

Always place God first in your life and study His Word.

September 17th

    Live in the present, learn from the past and look forward to the future. Don't ever let Satan take you back into your past and rake your life over the coals with guilt and shame. We're all a new creation in Jesus Christ. 2 Corinthians 5:17; **"Therefore, if anyone is in Christ, he is a new creation. The old has passed away; behold, the new has come."** When the devil tries to remind us of our past we must remind him of his future. We must look to the past to learn from it, not dwell in it. Never live in the past. We serve a God that desires to move in our lives now and to lead us to a bright future. Living with God in the present is the best place to be. All our sins are washed away. Acts 22:16; **"And now why do you wait? Rise and be baptized and wash away your sins, calling on his name."** God has taken all our guilt and shame on the Cross of Calvary When we are baptized we are going under the water as a symbolic death and rising with all of our sins washed white as snow.

    Don't ever give the enemy a foothold into your life by believing his lies about your past. Reject anything that is condemning and contrary to God's Word for your life. Condemnation is not of God. It's of the enemy or someone's flesh. Their sin nature is at work. God longs to encourage us, build us up and lead us to higher ground.

    The enemy is crafty. He will use whatever tool he can to try to trip you up and get you to believe that you are unworthy for the calling of Christ. Don't fall for his lies. Stand on the truth. The truth is that you are a son or daughter of the Most High God. Don't you ever forget that. God is your Father. You are the bride of Christ. When the devil brings up your past you bring up his future and see how he responds to that. Don't fall for his schemes. Be strong in the Lord. Ephesians 6:10; **"Finally, be strong in the Lord and in the strength of his might."**

When the devil tries to remind you of your past, just remind him of his future!

September 18ᵗʰ

Doubt is not of God. God doesn't promote negativity. He promotes the good within our lives. As you go forward with God, you can bet your bottom dollar that the enemy will use others to try and bring you down and try to deter you from following God's divine destiny for your life. Never allow this to happen. Nothing is worse than not living up to all you can be in and through Jesus Christ. Nothing is more joyous than being all that He has laid out for you to be. God requests that we give Him our all. He is a jealous God that way. He wants you all to Himself. Deuteronomy 4:24; **"For the LORD your God is a consuming fire, a jealous God."** He is not into sharing you with the devil. If you give Him your all, He will pour blessings out on you that will totally fry your mind.

If we do the little that God requires of us He will be sure to do the rest. Isn't that a comfort? That's just like saying that when we are at the end of our rope we are at the beginning of His. That to me is comforting. I can't but He can. The point is that we are not alone in our walk. God is right there beside us. All we have to do when we are in a jam is ask Him for His help and He is right there to take up the slack. Matthew 7:7; **"Ask, and it will be given to you; seek, and you will find; knock, and it will be opened to you."** All we have to do is ask and we will have it. The Word says so. James 4:2; **"You do not have, because you do not ask."** All we need to do is ask. Be specific. Pray Scripture to God. He loves hearing His Word. That lets him know you are reading it and claiming it as your own.

Do you remember when you were a kid and you really wanted something so bad that you begged and pleaded with your parents? Don't do that with God. Just ask Him for what you need, not necessarily what you want. God will meet your needs. He is our Father. He will supply all of our needs. Philippians 4:19; **"And my God will supply every need of yours according to his riches in glory in Christ Jesus."** Don't look at Him like a trip to Toys R Us where you want everything in sight. Do I necessarily need a 1948 Pan Head Harley Davidson? No. Do I want one? I would love one. It is my dream bike. I can't afford one and it is not a priority in my life. I dream of having one someday though, riding up in the hills of Western Massachusetts. It is only a dream. Maria doesn't necessarily share that dream for me though. I think it's a guy thing. Lol.

God supplies
all of our needs

September 19th

Share your faith and witness to others. Almost nothing will enhance your spiritual connection with Jesus like you sharing with others your relationship in Jesus. When you share Jesus something supernatural happens between you and Jesus, as well as between you and the person you're sharing your faith with. Sharing our own faith also reminds us of our own first encounter with Jesus. Reflecting on who led us to the Lord and the events surrounding our own salvation is a profound experience. Pray daily that God would open up opportunities to share His love and the message of His salvation.

Matthew 28:16-20 is the Great Commission. It is God telling us what it is we are here for. Did you know that you are commanded to share your faith? Commanded, not asked. It isn't a suggestion if you feel like doing it. You are to do it. Matthew 28:16-20; **"Now the eleven disciples went to Galilee, to the mountain to which Jesus had directed them. And when they saw him they worshiped him, but some doubted. And Jesus came and said to them, "All authority in heaven and on earth has been given to me. Go therefore and make disciples of all nations, baptizing them in the name of the Father and of the Son and of the Holy Spirit, teaching them to observe all that I have commanded you. And behold, I am with you always, to the end of the age.""** Did you catch that? He said "Go!" He didn't say "If you want to, maybe if you feel like it you could tell them about Me maybe?" He said "Go!" So are you doing it? If not, why not? If you are afraid of saying something wrong, go with a brother or sister who is more seasoned. You can gather ideas from them. Share what God has done for you in your life.

At Bethany, we have a group of fellas that go out every Saturday morning and they hit the streets of the Greater Springfield area sharing the Good News. There are people out there who are hungry for the Word. There are some who have never been exposed to God. How sad is that? God has given us the greatest gift imaginable, eternal salvation. We need to let others share in the greatest gift imaginable. We can't let fear creep in and snuff out our flame. If you are willing, God will use you. The Holy Spirit will give you the words to say. Just be willing to be used by Him. He will be with you every step of the way.

**Let go and let God.
He will be with you
every step of the way.**

September 20th

Practice unity among the Body of Christ. We should all attempt to live peacefully with each other. If we have a disagreement with a fellow believer we should confront our brother in love. Matthew 18:15-20; **"If your brother sins against you, go and tell him his fault, between you and him alone. If he listens to you, you have gained your brother. But if he does not listen, take one or two others along with you, that every charge may be established by the evidence of two or three witnesses. If he refuses to listen to them, tell it to the church. And if he refuses to listen even to the church, let him be to you as a Gentile and a tax collector. Truly, I say to you, whatever you bind on earth shall be bound in heaven, and whatever you loose on earth shall be loosed in heaven. Again I say to you, if two of you agree on earth about anything they ask, it will be done for them by my Father in heaven. For where two or three are gathered in my name, there am I among them."** If we have sinned, we are called to confess our sins. Sin can only come out of the life through the mouth. God commands confession. He doesn't say "If you feel like confessing, you can." He says "Confess!' Acts 17:30; **"The times of ignorance God overlooked, but now He commands all people everywhere to repent."** He has given us the 10 Commandments, not the 10 Suggestions. God commands confession to get rid of sin. Confession will put us on the road to righteousness. Repentance from sin will help get our lives rightfully in balance with God. Unconfessed sin is unforgiven sin. We need to confess our sins.

God puts leadership in positions of authority for a reason. We may need Godly counsel in how to handle a particular matter or sin issue in order to be free of it. Always stay centered on Christ, not on your own hurt feelings or emotions. When Jesus Christ is exalted, the offense, whatever it may be, will seem minimal in most cases. Unity among believers is a witness to the world as to the power that is inherent within Jesus Christ. Disunity exists within the world. When unity is displayed people cannot help but to take notice. We must try everything to live in the bond of peace, Jesus Christ.

Practice unity

Jesus set the example for us to follow throughout the Gospels of the Bible. He constantly consulted with His Heavenly Father through prayer. He was on His knees quietly by Himself in prayer throughout His ministry here on earth. He frequently would go off by Himself and pray. Mark 1:35; **"And rising very early in the morning, while it was still dark, he departed and went out to a desolate place, and there he prayed."** Another example of Jesus praying alone was in the Gospel of Mark again. Mark 6:46; **"And after he had taken leave of them, he went up on the mountain to pray."** Jesus spent a lot of time in prayer. Are you?

I used to ask myself; why would Jesus have to pray when He was God? The answer is because that is where the power is at. Jesus prayed for the power from on high, the power made available through His Father. That is where we gather our power from; God. Jesus would separate Himself from the crowds to be alone with His Father so that He could commune through prayer. We must make every attempt possible to be alone with God.

God is our strength, our refuge and our help in time of trouble. Psalm 46:1; **"God is our refuge and strength, a very present help in trouble."** We're calling upon God and His awesome power when we pray. We're asking Him to descend to meet our needs. Philippians 4:19; **"And my God will supply every need of yours according to his riches in glory in Christ Jesus."** We're humbling ourselves by letting Him know that we cannot make it on our own. As Jesus went up to the mountaintop to pray, so we also must be alone with God. We need to be able to hear His voice in our heart and able to listen clearly to His Holy Spirit's guidance. God's voice was heard all throughout the Bible. Just start in Genesis and follow on throughout the Word. God spoke in Genesis with Adam and Eve in the Garden of Eden. Genesis 3:9; **"But the LORD God called to the man and said to him, "Where are you?"** It wasn't that Adam and Eve were playing peek-a-boo; they had been caught in sin and they were hiding from God. Pray and listen and you will be able to hear His voice. I promise you this.

Whose example
are you following?

September 22nd

Don't be surprised when other Christians turn on you. Many Christians are not walking in the power of the Holy Spirit. Some are walking in their own flesh. Galatians 5:16; **"But I say, walk by the Spirit, and you will not gratify the desires of the flesh."** We need to be guided by the Spirit, not the flesh. Don't be shocked if another believer responds; abruptly, out of character, in a jealous manner, angrily, disgruntled, or even in a malicious fashion. Remember, the church is full of people and just like us; they are a work in progress. Standing in a church makes you no more a Christian than standing in a garage makes you a car. Unfortunately, many Christians have issues that they're dealing with and we have to learn not to take everything personally. This is not an easy thing to do, especially when you're in the ministry and operating from your heart.

We have to be cautious in how we conduct our business both in church and in the world. Be careful that you don't always wear your heart on your sleeve. God even says in the Bible to guard your heart. Luke 21:34; **"Above all else, guard your heart, for it is the wellspring of life."** In certain circumstances and specific situations you have to be careful. I am not saying to be jaded in how you treat people. Treat people with love; just don't make yourself vulnerable to attack. Luke 21:34; **"But watch yourselves lest your hearts be weighed down with dissipation and drunkenness and cares of this life, and that day come upon you suddenly like a trap."** Healthy boundaries are a good thing, not a bad thing. Sometimes we all need our own psychological space.

You have to be wise in what you tell people and how far you let them into your own life. God will guide you in your decision making if you let Him. God has sent us the Helper, the Holy Spirit. If you pay attention you can feel Him give you a gentle nudge when you are about to make a bad decision. He is like another conscience. Pray for His guidance and He will give it to you. Just be open and receptive to His guiding and you will be protected. Remember, God our Father knows best.

Are you open and receptive to God's guidance?

September 23rd

Do not put any man on a pedestal. Never elevate a man above God. Don't ever put any human being, even a church leader on the platform in your life where God should be elevated. If you do, you are certain to eventually be let down. Psalm 146:3; "**Put not your trust in princes, in a son of man, in whom there is no salvation.**" All church leaders are human beings, with faults, short comings and rest assured that they are sure to make their share of mistakes. Only God should be on the perfect platform because He is the only One that is perfect through and through.

Did you realize that when you put a person on a platform we also will be minimizing the importance that God wants to play in our own lives? God is not, nor has He ever been, a respecter of persons. He values all equally in the body of Christ. God has given some specific spiritual gifts, (see below references), however it doesn't mean that He favors any one man over another. He doesn't. Whomever you elevate in your mind becomes your focus and takes your attention away from God. Don't ever let anyone or anything take the place of your attention toward your personal relationship with God.

Here are the Biblical listings of the Spiritual gifting:

Other Gifts	**The 5 (five) Fold Ministry**	**The 9 (nine) Spiritual Gifts**
Romans 12:6-8	**Ephesians 4:11**	**1 Corinthians 12:1-14**
· Prophecy		· Wisdom
· Ministry	· Apostolic	· Knowledge
· Teaching	· Prophetic	· Discerning spirits
· Exhortation	· Evangelical	· Speaking in tongues
· Giving	· Pastoral	· Interpretation of tongues
· Leading	· Teaching	· Prophecy
· Mercy		· Faith
		· Working of miracles
		· Healing

God has given us all gifts from which to operate. Some of you may have multiples and others may have one or two. The number of them is not important; what is important is what you do with them. You have been blessed from above with a spiritual gift. You are entrusted to use that gifting for the betterment of both you and those with whom you come into contact with. God has blessed you with this gift so that your life may be enriched and so that you can further His Kingdom here on earth by walking in faith. We need to get outside of the boxes we have placed ourselves in. We need to trust God and His knowledge of what is best for us and our lives. Go on out and stretch yourself into an area in which you know God wants you to but one in which you have been afraid to operate. Go out and witness to strangers, not just your friends. Go out and talk to your neighbors and your workmates. Talk to a stranger about your faith and how you came to have a personal relationship with God. Why don't you brag about your relationship with Jesus the way you do when you get a new car? Jesus is more important than a new car isn't He? Talk to people about Him. Don't worry; you will be given the words to speak. I know it may make you feel uncomfortable for a bit but God has your back. You know, you might even come to like it.

Have you ever given thought to the mission field? There are people all over the world who have yet to know Jesus. Why aren't we out spreading the Word to everyone we know? We are so selfish with God and letting people know about Him. Why? Why is it that we are so abundantly blessed in so many ways and yet we are the most bankrupt in God knowledge? We have the finest seminaries and theological institutions in the world here in the USA, how is it that we are the most uneducated in our knowledge of God? This is so sad. I can't explain it except that people are embarrassed to speak of the greatest thing in their life, a one on one relationship with God. Let's change that statistic back to the way it was a short century ago shall we? Let's get busy.

Don't put any man on a pedestal. It's not fair to you or them.

September 24th

Remove yourself from the thrown and place God where He belongs for He is far more qualified to sit there than you or I. Don't ever get involved in ministry for selfish reasons because if you do you can rest assured that your true motives will be exposed. Numbers 32:23; **"But if you will not do so, behold, you have sinned against the LORD, and be sure your sin will find you out."** Selfish motives avail us nothing. Mark 8:36-37; **"For what does it profit a man to gain the whole world and forfeit his life? For what can a man give in return for his life?"** James 4:3; **"You ask and do not receive, because you ask wrongly, to spend it on your passions."** The cure for selfishness is found in the Book of Galatians 2:20; **"It is no longer I who live, but Christ who lives in me. And the life I now live in the flesh I live by faith in the Son of God, who loved me and gave himself for me."**

God moves when a person is in humble servant hood within a ministry, whatever ministry it may be. The Holy Spirit's power is poured out into the heart of a person when they are carrying out the Fathers will. When Jesus Christ is truly elevated instead of our egos, everything will go so much better. You can sense, feel and experience when the Holy Spirit is involved in something within the ministry; there is such a sense of peace that it's hard to explain. You have to experience it in order to fully comprehend it.

There is a big difference between the spirit of the flesh and the Holy Spirit's power and anointing. The Holy Spirit's number one goal in your life is to bring you into a closer relationship with Jesus Christ and His Father, God. The Holy Spirit knows that once this happens everything else will take care of itself. When you are operating in the flesh there are no blessings being poured out, for you are operating outside of the will of God. You need to operate within the will of God. You can do this by building up for yourself a solid foundation from which to operate. You can do this by studying the Word, praying ceaselessly, and developing a solid relationship with God. Once you have built a solid foundation in Jesus Christ, you're less likely to be swayed by the cunning and craftiness of men in their deceitful scheming. Matthew 7:26; **"And everyone who hears these words of mine and does not do them will be like a foolish man who built his house on the sand."** You would never build your house on sand would you? If you did you would be a fool. You would want a solid foundation so that your house would last. That is how our foundation with God needs to be, rock solid so that you will stand. The devil will try to shake your foundation like a mighty windstorm. John 10:10; **"The thief comes only to steal and kill and destroy. I came that they may have life and have it abundantly."** Go with God my friends. He has your best interests at heart. God will never let you down.

If you stay in the Word you will have a much happier existence here on earth. You know the old adage, let go and let God. It is true. If you let go of your selfish desires and live for God you will have a much better life. God has our best interests at heart. He knows what we need far better than we do. Could you imagine what your life would be like if you got every little thing you ever prayed for? You would be a spoiled brat that no one would want anything to do with. We need to surrender our will to God and let Him take the wheel. If you say God is my copilot, you need to switch seats and let Him take the controls. Once I did that, my life became a whole lot better.

How do you surrender? You make a conscientious decision every morning when you get up to give your will to God. You walk through your day praying throughout that God will guide your steps and decisions. You act and talk as if Jesus was standing right there beside you throughout your day and you respond accordingly. You pray for God's will to be done in and through your life. You pray for a protective hedge to be placed around you and your loved ones. You thank God for allowing you another opportunity to try to get it right and when you mess up, as you undoubtedly will, you pray for His forgiveness. We are not perfect; we are works in progress. God doesn't expect us to be perfect, He expects us to strive for perfection. That is all we can do. God just wants us to do the best that we can and be all that we can be through Him. We are His created and He loves us and wants the best for us. We just need to love Him back.

**Is your butt on the throne in your life?
If it is, you had better remove it.**

September 25th

We need to know the Word of God. You have to know the Word if you are going to stand on the Word. To do this you must read and study the Bible, God's written Word. That is the only way you are going to defeat the enemy of your soul. Get a concordance and other study materials so that you can be proven to rightly divide the Word of the Lord. We must be as a good Berean. The Berean's were known for their study habits. They would read and study the Scriptures constantly. They were known for their primacy of Scripture. They were scholars with no equal when it came to the knowledge of the written Word. Are you measuring up to their example or could you use a little brush up on your study habits? We must study to show ourselves approved. The Word tells us this. 2 Timothy 2:15; **"Do your best to present yourself to God as one approved, a worker who has no need to be ashamed, rightly handling the word of truth."** When you know the Bible inside and out you're less likely to be taken for a ride with false teachings. Know the Word of the Lord in its entirety, from cover to cover. Take some courses with reputable teachers that you trust.

Some people are called to Bible school or seminary in order to learn the Bible while others will study at home on a consistent basis. Learning to divide the Word of Truth is of critical importance. I myself study God's Word daily. I believe that study will prove a man worthy of the calling God has placed upon his life. Like Moses in Exodus 4, we all have a calling if we are willing to accept it. Moses doubted all that God had for him to do so God proved to Him who He truly was. He has a call on our lives that only we can answer. We need to know God and His Word and we can do this through His written Word. The Holy Scriptures are key to understanding the divine destiny which God has for us. I typically pray that the Holy Spirit would illume my heart and mind before I read God's Word. I find that the Holy Spirit anoints the reading of the Bible when I pray and ask to have my mind and heart open to grasp what is inside the pages and I pray that God will help me to apply it to my life in its entirety.

Are you being
a good Berean?

September 26th

Get yourself involved in Sunday school. Sunday school is an integral aspect of going to church. Sunday school provides you with an opportunity to learn or to teach God's truth's from the Holy Bible. God uses Sunday school lessons to strengthen, edify and build up your faith and knowledge of our Lord and Savior Jesus Christ. In Matthew as we have read Jesus was always teaching others His Way, His Truth and His life. Jesus was always making others think and challenging them to grasp the things of God. Matthew 22:15-22 speaks of rendering the things unto Caesar the things that are Caesar's and to God the things that are God's. Here Jesus was speaking of taxes. Jesus was not attempting to establish a political kingdom in order to oppose Caesar. He had no political agenda what so ever. His goal was to give to the government what was rightfully theirs, i.e. taxes, allegiance, due respect, and obedience to civil laws. There are matters that are civic and there are matters that are matters of the Church which belong to God. The Christian Church as a whole believes in some form of separation between the church and the state. There are other governments that have taken total control of the state, seizing all control in matters of the state and the church. There is no separation in certain Islamic countries; they have total control in all matters civic and church. We see the results of this form of governance on the nightly news with people being flogged, stoned, beheaded, people stripped of all freedoms. Wars have waged over this type of totalitarianism.

Jesus said we are to obey civil laws. He taught us how to live. He would often teach in parables in an attempt to understand the simple yet profound truths He was sharing. Getting involved in Sunday school on some level is a key in developing and maintaining a consistent and healthy Christian walk. Learning and passing on what we know is so rewarding. Paul set the example for us to follow with Timothy and Barnabus. We all need to mentor someone when we are solidly grounded in the Word and we also need a helper, one to assist us so that we don't get burned out by overloading ourselves. We all need to get into the Word.

How are you learning?

September 27th

Take a risk when an altar call is given for healing or for other areas of our life that we're in need of a touch from God. God really moves when we step out in faith. What is faith? Hebrews 11:1; "**Now faith is the assurance of things hoped for, the conviction of things not seen.**" When you get up from the pew and start walking to the front of the church for God to meet a need; that takes faith, trust and belief. These three things are operating in Christians when they take a step away from the pew and get actively involved in what God has in store for them through their faith in Him.

Altar workers are usually right there with you when you step out in faith so that you don't feel alone. They are usually people who have proven their ability to pray for and believe in the power of God to work in and through them. They are usually intercessors and or elders of the Church. Challenge yourself to step out in faith the next time there is an altar call. Take a risk. Next time you're in church, walk to the altar for prayer and see if God doesn't move mountains in your spiritual life. I have personally done just that.

There was a time when I was new to the Word, this is Gregg by the way, and I had a growth which was visible on my jaw. I was told by a doctor that it was a tumor and that it was not good. I didn't understand the whole anointing with oil thing but I stepped out in faith that it would work if I believed. A friend of mine, Pastor Jim Grove, was praying for people this particular night so I went to him and asked him "I don't understand this whole oil deal buddy but can you slap some on? I need prayer." I put my faith in God that night. It was all new to me but I had my heart believing God would deliver me. After the prayer my jaw felt hot. I asked him "What was in that oil, some kind of menthol or something?" He said it was just olive oil; that it was symbolic. God answered my prayer that night. The next day when I awoke my face was normal and the tumor was gone. God can and does hear the cries of His people. All prayers are answered. Proverbs 15:29; "The LORD is far from the wicked, but he hears the prayer of the righteous." I was and still am a sinner but it was my faith and God that delivered me that night. Praise God.

Go ahead and take a risk at an altar call.

Take a step of faith.

September 28th

     Don't be afraid to go to the pastors of your church for guidance, help, prayer and Godly counsel. Don't be intimidated by their position. Pastors are human beings and aren't perfect specimens of God's creation but they have answered a call placed on their lives. They have studied God's Word and they are guiding their flocks in the ways of our Lord Jesus Christ. Many people find pastors intimidating due to their position as a spiritual leader. I have sat with many pastors over the years and I have been pleasantly surprised to find out how down to earth they really are. Many will be transparent and open up about their own lives, even their issues and struggles. Pastors are real people, with real feelings and they aren't specially cut from a different cloth than you or I. They are people who go through the same struggles we all do. Don't put them up on some pedestal. They are just men. It isn't fair to put them up in some exalted position. Don't ever exalt man and ritual above the Word and the Spirit.

     If you've accepted Jesus Christ as your Personal Lord and Savior and are following Jesus than God can use you, just as much as He can use pastors. Pastors are people that have realized the call of God upon their lives, decided to devote themselves to full-time ministry and have typically received Bible training at a college or university. Remember, Jesus deserves the pedestal and no one else. At the beginning of the day, pastors still put their trousers on one leg at a time just as you and I do.

     Are you studying your Word? Are you placing others in exalted positions? Are you being a servant of Jesus? Has God called you to serve in a pastoral capacity? Are you praying for the knowledge of where you are to serve Him and others? God has a place for all of us. Not all are called to be pastors just as not all are called to be missionaries. We all have a calling placed on our lives nonetheless. What is your calling? Pray for the answer.

What has God called you to do?

September 29th

Make sure you get rooted in the fundamental truths of Scripture. This could mean the difference between you knowing, living and walking in the truth and believing a lie. A believer's steadfastness and stability in the Lord is dependent on a firm grasp of the Truth revealed in the Bible. Ephesians 4:13,14; "**We all attain to the unity of the faith and of the knowledge of the Son of God, to mature manhood, to the measure of the stature of the fullness of Christ, so that we may no longer be children, tossed to and fro by the waves and carried about by every wind of doctrine, by human cunning, by craftiness in deceitful schemes.**" Whereas, lack of knowledge leads to backsliding and destruction. Hosea 4:6; "**My people are destroyed for lack of knowledge; because you have rejected knowledge, I reject you from being a priest to me. And since you have forgotten the law of your God, I also will forget your children.**" This is not something we would ever want to happen to us or our loved ones.

Here are a few examples of false beliefs; the belief of once saved always saved, or that you can gain salvation by works and not by God's grace. For you to be on a firm foundation spiritually you have to be able to know why you believe what you believe and you have to be able to back it up with Scripture. The most important thing is that a person has a heartfelt relationship with the Lord. Knowing Scripture is a vital key to not being susceptible to being tossed back and forth by every whim of false Biblical teaching that you may hear. There are many messages, but only one Gospel Message. Know your Bible and why you believe what you believe.

Have you ever heard someone speak of the Bible and you just know that something isn't adding up but you just can't put your finger on what that something is? What did you do when you heard it? Did you pull out your Bible and look it up or did you get on your computer and look it up or did you just let it go? Too often people put off looking it up thinking it is no big deal. It is a big deal my friend. You are a Christian right? We need to speak up when we hear false teachings. We are defenders of the Truth.

Are you rooted
in the Truth?

September 30th

Be careful how you live. The unsaved are constantly observing you to see how you really are, especially if they know that you're a Christian. They want to see if there is anything different about you. Is there any difference between the one who believes in Jesus Christ and calls himself or herself a Christian believer than those of the world? Are you living any differently than the rest of the world? Is your attitude any different than that of the world? How do you respond during times of difficulty? Remember, you're representing Jesus Christ in your actions, your words, your demeanor, your attitude and ultimately in whom you are. This is not to be taken lightly, especially since many are looking to us to determine if the lifestyle of a Christian will make a difference in their own life. The unsaved world is indirectly observing Jesus Christ through you. How does that make you feel? This is definitely a big deal.

I have seen so called Christians act in ways that has brought shame on the name of Jesus Christ. I have seen men come out of strip clubs and I pulled my car over and I asked them what they were doing. They have told me a variety of reasons why they were there including that they were witnessing to the patrons. I told them to quit telling people that they are Christian if they are going to be frequenting places like that. They are only trying to justify their actions by blaming God for their unsavory walk. If you are driving your car in an unlawful way be it speeding or cutting people off and then flipping them off when they honk at you for your thoughtless actions all the while you have a fish emblem or bumper stickers on your car saying you are representing God, do me a favor and take them off of your car because you are giving God and Jesus a black eye by acting that way. Evaluate your driving habits before you decorate your car with Christian emblems. If you claim to be an ambassador of Christ please act accordingly. If you don't you bring shame on all of us, chiefly God Himself.

If you claim to be an Ambassador of Christ, please act like one.

October

October 1st

Be careful of what you put into your mind. Be careful of what you read, what movies you listen to, what television shows you watch, what entertainment you get involved in and what music you listen to. Remember, Lucifer was the angel of music while he resided in Heaven. I personally believe he is using music to bring people down so that he can enslave their souls. We need to guard our hearts and our lives from outside evil influences. We need to pay attention to what our children are getting involved in with all of the different media outlets available today. We need to know what they are listening to and what the musical content is, what games they are playing through video game outlets and what they are bringing home to entertain themselves, where they are surfing while on the internet, etc. They are our responsibility.

We have accepted Jesus Christ as our Personal Lord and Savior. We're the temple of the Holy Spirit. He is living in us. We now carry the Holy Spirit of God within our souls. He isn't living vicariously through us, He is in us. Are we acting like He is in us? Are we paying attention to what we allow into our minds? Our mind is the control center of our emotions, our feelings, our thoughts, our will and who we become. We need to guard our mind and the minds of our family members too. We have been placed over our children and we have been entrusted with them by God. Are you living up to that responsibility?

Once the Holy Spirit comes to live in your body, you will never be the same. You will begin to grow with God, maturing in Him and also in your relationship with Him. The Holy Spirit might convict you to make changes in what you entertain your minds with whereby you can no longer listen to certain music or watch certain show content. Praise God if that's the case. He will let you know. Let Him lead you.

What's in your mind?

October 2nd

     Don't put any expectation on unbelievers whom you know, it's not fair to you or to them. They cannot see what you see. They cannot understand the things of God because their minds have not been renewed by the Holy Spirit. 1 Corinthians 2:14; **"The natural person does not accept the things of the Spirit of God, for they are folly to him, and he is not able to understand them because they are spiritually discerned."** The people of the world do not understand the things of God for their minds are darkened by the prince of lies and the deceiver. You have to be born from above to comprehend the things of God. Pray for the ungodly and show them the love of God. Remember only God saves, not you. Unbelievers may persecute you because they themselves are being manipulated by Satan and his demons. Look beyond what you see and hear.

     In the Gospel of Matthew the religious leaders and the governor's soldiers persecuted Jesus because they had absolutely no spiritual insight into the things of Jesus. There is a supernatural realm where **The Waging War Within** is taking place. Not all is exactly what it seems to the natural eye. We have to learn to think spiritually and to discern the supernatural. Significance has to be placed in what we cannot see instead of what we can see. Our fight is not against what is seen, but what is unseen. Ephesians 6:12; **"For we do not wrestle against flesh and blood, but against the rulers, against the authorities, against the cosmic powers over this present darkness, against the spiritual forces of evil in the heavenly places."**

     Have you ever wondered why there is so much evil in the world? It is because this is the devils realm. The devil is having a field day with the inhabitants of earth. There is rampant evil waging war with the inhabitants of this present darkness. We all need to put on our spiritual armor every day as soon as we realize we are sucking air and that God has given us another opportunity to get it right. We need to pray **Ephesians 6:10-20** each and every day. We need to pray for God's protection over our loved ones also. We are in a war for our very souls and our very existence. Believe it, it's true.

No expectations

October 3rd

Live thankful lives. Be thankful for the little things. Sometimes your blessings are right in front of you, but you miss them. Sometimes the greatest blessings are starring right into your eyes. Don't take anything for granted. God has given every minute of our life. Time is ticking right on bye. We need to have a Spirit of thankfulness. Being thankful and enthusiastic about the things of God is a fantastic strategy for providing yourself with a force field against the devil and his demonic entourage. A Christian that is thankful for everything that God has blessed them with is a Christian that has a right perspective of life. We need to have a grateful heart.

Having an attitude of thankfulness will carry you a long way. Let's look at Luke 17; 11-19; this is the story of Jesus and the 10 Lepers; "**On the way to Jerusalem he was passing along between Samaria and Galilee. And as he entered a village, he was met by ten lepers, who stood at a distance and lifted up their voices, saying, "Jesus, Master, have mercy on us." When he saw them he said to them, "Go and show yourselves to the priests." And as they went they were cleansed. Then one of them, when he saw that he was healed, turned back, praising God with a loud voice; and he fell on his face at Jesus' feet, giving him thanks. Now he was a Samaritan. Then Jesus answered, "Were not ten cleansed? Where are the nine? Was no one found to return and give praise to God except this foreigner?" And he said to him, "Rise and go your way; your faith has made you well.""** A grateful heart will carry you through the marathon of life no matter what you face. Be thankful for your very life. Be thankful for your health and each member within your family. If you find it hard to be thankful then find something good and praise God for it.

The Word speaks on praise. We are not to only give thanks and praise when things are going our way. We are told to praise God in all situations. 1 Thessalonians 5:16-18; "**Rejoice always, pray without ceasing, give thanks in all circumstances; for this is the will of God in Christ Jesus for you.**" Try it next time you have a rough day.

Live thankful lives

October 4th

Give of yourself totally to God and don't expect anything in return. God will provide for you. Give everything you have in your relationship with Jesus. Don't give because you want to be blessed, but give because you want to bless others. Your relationship with God will grow by leaps and bounds when you give in the name of Jesus. Give not with hypocrisy, but give selflessly from the heart. God knows our motives in doing the things that we do. Are we doing things so that we look good to others or are we doing them because we want to bless them?

If you want to know where someone's heart is, all you have to do is take one look at their checkbook. Our monies usually go to things we value and esteem. If cars, then to cars it goes. If homes, then to homes it goes. If boats, then to boats it goes. If clothes, then to clothes it goes. If God, then to God it goes. Be careful that you don't become so preoccupied with things of this world that you miss out on what God truly wants you to do. Be careful these things you want and buy don't become an idol in your life and begin to hinder your relationship with Jesus Christ. Idolatry is anything that is pulling you away from your loved ones and from God. Are there areas of your life that are pulling you away from your loved ones? Are there areas of your life that are pulling you away from God? The First Commandment in Exodus 20:1-3; states; **"And God spoke all these words, saying, "I am the LORD your God, who brought you out of the land of Egypt, out of the house of slavery. "You shall have no other gods before Me.""** Have you made anything in your life more important than God? Don't answer too quickly. Search your heart and your life. God deserves the first fruits of our lives and He deserves to be first in every aspect of our existence.

"Have no other gods before Me."

October 5th

True relationship with God is looking after orphans and widows in their time of distress and hardship. God needs us to carry on the mission He has called us to. He needs our hands and our feet in order for the mission to be fulfilled. He needs our mouths and our eyes. He needs us to spread His Word and His Gospel Message into all the world. He has directed us to do this in the close of the Book of Matthew: Matthew 28:18-20; **"And Jesus came and said to them, "All authority in heaven and on earth has been given to me. Go therefore and make disciples of all nations, baptizing them in the name of the Father and of the Son and of the Holy Spirit, teaching them to observe all that I have commanded you. And behold, I am with you always, to the end of the age."**

God doesn't ask much of us but He needs us to lead others to the Cross of Christ in order for them to spend eternity with Him. We need to be the example of Jesus Christ extended to the world. Let us see the world through the eyes of Christ. Let us hear the world through His ears. Let us walk on earth with His feet. Let us touch the world with His hands. Let the world feel His heart through us. That is what being an Ambassador for Christ is all about. Are you willing to be a true Ambassador for Christ?

Being a Christian in today's times is not an easy task; I am sure that you'll agree with me. If it was an easy thing to do I feel more people would be doing it. It isn't; but the rewards are well worth the sacrifice; eternity with God our Father and His Son Jesus Christ. There are people laying down their lives daily for their beliefs. Some of us may be asked to do just that. It, the second coming of Christ, is drawing near. You can see the writing on the wall. Read the Book of Revelation if you have a doubt as to this statement. We are drawing ever nearer to that glorious day when the Son of God will make His triumphant return. Are you ready? Is your family ready? Have you fulfilled your calling in Matthew 28? All you can do is share the Word with them; you can't force them to accept it. You are only responsible to do your part and then let God do the rest.

Are you doing your part?

October 6th

God is love. The power of love covers a multitude of sins. 1 Peter 4:8; "**Above all, keep loving one another earnestly, since love covers a multitude of sins.**" Love covers many wounds and heals our innermost being. God displayed His love for the world by sending His only begotten Son Jesus Christ to die for the sins of the world. John 3:16; "**For God so loved the world, that he gave his only Son, that whoever believes in him should not perish but have eternal life.**" God displayed sacrificial love. We can love others with the example that Jesus has given us. He is the ultimate example of love. He always thought of His Heavenly Father and others with everything He said and did. He kept both His horizontal and His vertical relationships aligned. Jesus did this with God His Father first and then with the people He came to save. Love is patient, kind, gentle, doesn't keep track of wrongs and exhibits self-control.

The Book of 1 Corinthians, Chapter 13, is known as the "Love Chapter". This Chapter goes through all of the attributes of what love is all about. I can hear some of you fellas now saying "Love is a 4 letter word." I was there myself a few short years ago, but you know what? I finally had to read it in a seminary class and now I am a better man for it. How can you go wrong with God's love? The answer is you can't. It's not of this world, it's of Him. How can you say you love life and not love God? How can you love your kids and your help mate and not love God? You can't. How can you love your very existence and not love God? You can't. They are all gifts from God. God is love my friend. You can't know one without the other.

Love is a 4 letter word,
but what a great word it is.

October 7th

Be careful of busyness. You can hinder your peaceful sense of God while swept up in being busy. We live in such a fast paced world. Don't lose your identity in your work. Our identity needs to be from God and our relationship needs to be with Jesus Christ. God needs to be first and foremost in everything happening in our busy lives. We need to be in right relationship to God our Father and His Son Jesus Christ. Once we prioritize Him as being first in our life, everything else will fall rightly into place.

Be careful of burnout. If you push yourself too much, even in the work of the church and ministry, you might find burnout to become a reality to you. You will find you don't have the energy, the determination and the wanting to go on. You might find that other parts of your life are unmanageable and being negatively affected by all that you are doing for God and others. This is all because you've lost your perspective. While actually thinking you have a good concept of how things are going, suddenly you become worn out, tired and even exhausted. Be watchful of all that you are doing.

We live in a society that is driven. We're driven to produce, to do better and to be the best that we can possibly be. Just like the Army motto, we want to be all that we can be. There is nothing wrong with being a driven person. When you start noticing the negative consequences of deteriorating marriages and shattered relationships with children, you definitely might want to think twice about your priorities. Step back and examine what you are doing and make the necessary changes before the damage to your relationship is irreparable. We are only human.

Loving God is great and we need to be doing things for Him, not to undo our past history, which is covered by The Blood of Christ, but to help out in our church community and the lives of the lost. We need to be a part of not apart from. We all need to be involved in our church. It is not fair that 85% of the body is sitting around doing nothing and the other 15% is doing all of the work. If you are a church slacker or slug, get off of your butt and start to do your part. If you are one of the 15%, thank you for all that you do.

Don't ever be too busy for God

October 8th

Don't place unrealistic expectations on others. Place all of your expectations on God. He alone will never let you down. It isn't fair to another human being to project their expectations onto another. Others were never created to fulfill our intrinsic needs that can only be satisfied by God. Only a relationship with Jesus can fulfill this need to be completely satisfied and loved. God can meet all of our needs through Jesus Christ. Don't ever expect your spouse to meet all of your needs. Don't ever live through your children, expecting them to be everything you are or everything you never amounted to. It isn't fair that they are expected to fulfill this burden placed on them.

Have you ever watched a Little League game or a youth soccer or football game? I watch the games and the reactions of the parents and I honestly want to cry. I see the parents screaming at their kids and the other players. I hear their words and it tears at my heart. I watched my son Kyle play T-ball when he was young and he had a friend named Katie who was also on the team. They were in the outfield when a ball was hit out to where they were assigned to watch the field and they were sitting down on the ground rolling around playing with dandelions. I laughed so hard. The ball was right there and they could have cared less. They were having fun playing together. It was great. Some parents were yelling and freaking out but Katie and Kyle played on. It was hilarious. The point of the matter is, Little League and other sports programs are for kids to have fun. The world isn't going to end because your son or daughter didn't win the game or if they missed a ball hit towards them. Lighten up on the little ones. Let them enjoy life, they are kids. There will be plenty of time for them to stress when life encroaches on them during their adulthood. Let them be kids. Let them laugh and play with the dandelions. They don't need your stress added to the stresses of life which they already face. Relax and let them have fun and laugh while they still can.

Let them laugh

October 9th

Healthy expectations are one thing whereas unrealistic expectations are another thing altogether. Healthy expectations can build others up and unrealistic ones can tear them down. Ask God for discernment in knowing the difference. You never want to break the spirit of another. This is important, as Christians we need to understand this. This should be our goal even in our imperfect spiritual state.

As Christians we're all being pruned, weeded and made more in the image of God on a daily basis. John 15:1-8; "**I am the true vine, and my Father is the Vinedresser. Every branch of mine that does not bear fruit he takes away, and every branch that does bear fruit he prunes, that it may bear more fruit. Already you are clean because of the word that I have spoken to you. Abide in me, and I in you. As the branch cannot bear fruit by itself, unless it abides in the vine, neither can you, unless you abide in me. I am the vine; you are the branches. Whoever abides in me and I in him, he it is that bears much fruit, for apart from me you can do nothing. If anyone does not abide in me he is thrown away like a branch and withers; and the branches are gathered, thrown into the fire, and burned. If you abide in me, and my words abide in you, ask whatever you wish, and it will be done for you. By this my Father is glorified, that you bear much fruit and so prove to be my disciples.**" God is in the pruning business. I thank Him for all He is doing in me. I was a weed filled garden when I started my walk. Just ask Maria, my wife.

When I started my walk I was rough around the edges. People still talk of some of the things I used to say or do when I first came to Christ. One day I was in a Sunday school class and we were speaking on smoking and drinking when Pastor George Cope asked me what I thought. I proudly informed the class that I thought drinking in front of kids was wrong. He asked me about drinking in front of Jesus. I told him that I would have a beer with Jesus and that I was sure He would have one with me. I said we could watch a Green Bay Packer football game and have a few beers together. That was 12 ½ years ago and people still come up to me and say "I remember when you said you would have a beer with Jesus." I ask them to forget that and we all laugh. My thinking has changed since then. Another woman came up to me recently and said "Gregg, I am so proud of you. You have grown so much. I remember when you couldn't pray in choir without swearing." God changes us at His pace. We are all a work in progress. God isn't through with me yet and He isn't through with you either. Praise God.

My friends, we must guard our criticism of others. When we are gossiping of others in the church we are speaking of God's created. When we gossip we are breaking God's heart. My wife Maria works in the Love Center. This is a ministry through Bethany where cloths are given away to the needy along with household items when they are available. There is no charge for these things. The Love Center is a place where the public come to receive these things and where they can be treated with dignity and respect. There are people of different ethnic backgrounds and there are prejudices displayed on occasion. Even among the workers on occasion. I say that they are all God's beloved. I ask the people how they would like someone to speak about their cultural upbringings or their dress or their talk. The truth of the matter is that none of us would like to have people speaking of us behind our backs. If you wouldn't say something to someone's face then don't say it behind their back either. Think before you speak. God hears all people, spoken and unspoken.

When we see someone carrying on in gossip or murmuring, take their hand and ask them to pray for that other person. All the while you are praying for them, you are doing something for their benefit, not their downfall. We need to stop the gossip. The church is a house of prayer, not a house of gossip and destruction. Pray for others, don't gossip about them. If you are guilty of gossip, pray to God that He remove this vile habit from your life. It leads to death and destruction not life and building up of a brother or sister.

Stop the gossip, pray instead!
It's far more productive.

October 10th

Accountability is extremely important in the Christian life. Find another that you can trust and that you respect and ask them to be your accountability partner. These mentors can hold you accountable in your Christian life. We can't do the Christian walk all alone. God never intended for us to be loners. God wants His Church to find strength from others within the body of Christ. You need to establish a couple or a group of solid Christian believers who can hold each other accountable to the Christian Faith. Christianity and being a disciple of Jesus Christ takes refinement, dedication, consistency and support from others. When one member falls, another can lift them up. Ecclesiastes 4:9-12; **"Two are better than one, because they have a good reward for their toil. For if they fall, one will lift up his fellow. But woe to him who is alone when he falls and has not another to lift him up! Again, if two lie together, they keep warm, but how can one keep warm alone? And though a man might prevail against one who is alone, two will withstand him—a threefold cord is not quickly broken."** Just knowing that a Christian friend is a phone call away in time of need can be a comforting thing. The phone can be your lifeline. Sometimes we need guidance, reassurance and direction from a fellow believer. Proverbs 27:17; **"Iron sharpens iron, and one man sharpens another."**

You better believe that God uses others to influence us. This relationship should be reciprocal. It's mutually edifying. Proverbs 8:32-34; **"And now, O sons, listen to me: blessed are those who keep my ways. Hear instruction and be wise, and do not neglect it. Blessed is the one who listens to me, watching daily at my gates, waiting beside my doors."** There is wisdom in Godly counsel. If you call a brother in time of need listen to his words. If you are being reproved, take it to heart and change your ways. Get into the Word. If you are the one reproofing, remember three things: be Spiritual, be gentle yet firm, and be humble. When the reproof is finished, always finish in prayer.

When reproof is finished, pray.

October 11th

Have a vision for your life in God. Do you have one? If you don't have a vision for your life, pray that God will give you one. Pray and work out God's divine destiny in your life. Do this with fear and trembling, as you would your salvation. Malachi 3:16; "**Then those who feared the LORD spoke with one another. The LORD paid attention and heard them, and a book of remembrance was written before him of those who feared the LORD and esteemed his name.**" Fear in this verse doesn't mean being afraid, it means having complete reverence and respect. There are several references to this respect being shown to God. Here are a few more: Jeremiah 5:22, Psalms 90:11, Psalms 119:120, Job 3:25, Jonah 1:16. Look and see if you can find a few more.

To miss the Heavenly calling of God in your life would be a terrible thing. Vision determines destiny. Without a vision the people perish. Lead your life as if you can see the beautiful unfolding of the blessings of God within your life and before long you will. They are right there in front of your eyes. You can reach out and touch them. Open your spiritual eyes and look. Opening your spiritual eyes and having God's vision for you will allow faith to conquer the doubt the enemy might throw your way. With vision, hard work and being led by and empowered with and by the Holy Spirit we can accomplish all things for God. Philippians 4:13; " **I can do all things through him who strengthens me.**" Ask God to breath a vision for your life into existence.

Get a vision for your life
and hang on

October 12th

Perspective is key to everything. We all lose perspective from time to time. God calls me to keep my focus on Him. He always desires to guide us where He would like to take us. Once you take your eyes off God, loss of perspective will come. This is the way it has always been and this is the way it will continue to be. With loss of focus on our higher calling in Jesus Christ our perspective will collapse. The reverse is true when our eyes are on Jesus and the Gospel. God will hold our lives together with His power, love and grace. Even in seemingly difficult times, God will come through and do something beautiful. He's God! All perspective can be maintained when we realize that ultimately God is on the throne above all.

As a Christian, God is living in you. He's working in you and through you. With Him, perspective can never be lost. All perspective can be gained in a twinkling of an eye, with a blast of lightning and at the speed of light. Don't you think that God is faster than the speed of light? Praise Him and Him only. When you give praise to God for the goodness in your life, you're denying the enemy the foothold. The enemy of our souls tries mightily to take our focus off of God. You and I need to remember that all goodness comes from God. We get our sustenance from Him, not the Lotto or whatever else you may have tried to meet your means. God is our provider. Philippians 4:19:1; **"And my God will supply every need of yours according to his riches in glory in Christ Jesus."** We need to keep our focus on God and He will meet our needs.

Take a look at the Book of Exodus and how God provided a vision to His children. Sure God had them wandering for years for their disobedience and whining but He still met their needs, didn't He? They needed to be taken to the woodshed for discipline, but He didn't put them to bed with no dinner, He provided for them. He does it for us today also. Exodus 19:5-6; **"Now therefore, if you will indeed obey my voice and keep my covenant, you shall be my treasured possession among all peoples, for all the earth is mine."** He wants us to keep our eyes on Him alone.

October 13th

Ask God to reveal why you've had the past you've had. He will reveal it. Then you can ask Him to take it and use it for His glory and as a platform to exalt His name forever. He will do it. He will lift you up and take you to places you could never imagine. He will bless you beyond belief. Refresh your mind to think from God's perspective. He longs to take the wreckage of your life to exalt Him in it. He will take the pain and suffering you've experienced and He will exalt Himself through it. He will also exalt Himself through all of the beautiful times in your life.

Give God your past and He might even use it to lead others to Him. He values our testimony in how we came to know Him as our personal Lord and Savior. How He straightened us out and healed our wounds shows the power which He possesses. How He lifted us up out of the pit of this world and places us on His path to righteousness is awesome. How He set our feet on higher ground with Him is a beautiful thing displaying His love for us. How He took us and made us into something special when we often felt worthless shows His heart. The love of God is something beautiful. He has rested His glory upon us. He has given us His anointing! We need to praise Him for His glory! Praise Jesus!

How many of you have felt the sting of drug use and abuse? How many of you battled alcohol and drug addiction? How many of you are now on the path which God has laid out for you? Think about where you have come from and where you are headed. Now give praise for the deliverance which you have experienced. Go ahead and take a few minutes and give Him the praise He rightfully deserves. He didn't have to deliver us from our demons but He did because He loves us that much. Who else would have done that? John 3:16; "**For God so loved the world, that he gave his only Son, that whoever believes in him should not perish but have eternal life.**" God loves us all that much. Thank Him for His love. Don't just take it for granted.

Have you thanked God
for His love today?

October 13th

Ask God to reveal why you've had the past you've had. He will reveal it. Then you can ask Him to take it and use it for His glory and as a platform to exalt His name forever. He will do it. He will lift you up and take you to places you could never imagine. He will bless you beyond belief. Refresh your mind to think from God's perspective. He longs to take the wreckage of your life to exalt Him in it. He will take the pain and suffering you've experienced and He will exalt Himself through it. He also will exalt Himself through all of the beautiful times in your life.

Give God your past and He might even use it to lead others to Him. He values our testimony in how we came to know Him as our personal Lord and Savior. How He straightened us out and healed our wounds shows the power which He possesses. How He lifted us out of the pit of this world and places us on His path to righteousness is awesome. How He set our feet on higher ground with Him is a beautiful thing displaying His love for us. How He took us and made us into something special when we often felt worthless shows His heart. The love of God is something beautiful. He has rested His glory upon us. He has given us His anointing! We need to praise Him for His glory! Praise Jesus!

How many of you have felt the sting of drug use and abuse? How many of you have battled alcohol and drug addiction? How many of you are now on the path which God has laid out for you? Think about where you have come from and where you are headed. Now give praise for the deliverance which you have experienced. Go ahead and take a few minutes and give Him the praise He rightfully deserves. He didn't have to deliver us from our demons but He did because He loves us that much. Who else would have done that? John 3:16; **"For God so loved the world, that he gave his only Son, that whoever believes in him should not perish but have eternal life."** God loves us all that much. Thank Him for His love. Don't just take it for granted.

Have you thanked God
For His love today?

October 14th

Give God your present. You have already given Him your past. Whatever you're doing in your life right now, give it to God. Give Him complete charge of your life. You might rattle a few souls, but who cares. You need to go all the way with God. We don't have any other choice. We do actually but the alternative will only lead us down the path of destruction. But we're not going to make the wrong choice. Go with God, full speed ahead. Go as fast as you can go. Grab onto God and let Him transform your earthly existence. He will challenge you to accomplish the things you never thought you could. Remember that you can accomplish great things through Him. Philippians 4:13; "**I can do all things through him who strengthens me.**" You can accomplish things far greater than you ever fathomed with Christ at your side. Just do all things to His glory.

When you give your life to God, the life that He created, you can't go wrong. He will prosper you wherever you go and in whatever you do as long as you do it for Him. God will help you and lead you in whatever you endeavor as long as you keep your focus on Him. Give the glory to Him, not to yourself. He deserves all praise. What great thing have you accomplished apart from Him? Nothing! The devil is always trying to steal God's thunder by attempting to refocus the glory that belongs to God and placing it on us. We need to maintain a Heavenly perspective. The devil is a dirty ball player. He is a thief and a liar. John 10:10; "**The thief comes only to steal and kill and destroy. I came that they may have life and have it abundantly.**" Live life for God and give Him all of the praise. Keep a healthy focus.

Give the glory to God

October 15th

Soak your life with prayer. Drench your family in prayer and everything you hope and dream of can come true in and through Jesus Christ! He's awesome. Don't rely on your own strength. Trust and rely on God. He's trustworthy. Let Him set your life asail in the mighty wind of the Holy Spirit. Give Him your past, present, and your future along with the future of your family.

God holds everything in the palm of His trustworthy hands. He holds everything together with His super glue. Your future will soar with and through Jesus Christ. It will transcend your mortal self. You will have a supernatural future. The path of God only leads in one direction, down the blessed road. Your future and your family's future will have blessing after blessing when Jesus is placed at the center of your life and when He is exalted within your lives. No power on earth can interfere with God's power. None! Absolutely none!

Don't go into the next minute, let alone the next day, without God being in the center of your life. You will never be sorry and you definitely will never go wrong in your future life excursions. Your valleys will be calmed and your mountaintop experiences will be blessed. You and God equal an army! The path will be made for you, your family and your offspring from generation to generation! Give God your all and see for yourself how the floodgates of blessings will be poured out for you. Give Him your life, your family, your tithe, your talents, etc. If you bless God, He will bless you. Give Him your first fruits all around. He doesn't need our tithes or our talents but we give them as obedience to Him. Malachi 3:10; **"Bring the full tithes into the storehouse, that there may be food in my house. And thereby put me to the test, says the LORD of hosts, if I will not open the windows of heaven for you and pour down for you a blessing until there is no more need."** Just try it.

Give it all to God

DOWN THE VIA DELAROSA TO THE HILL OF GOLGOTHA

When you're facing **The Waging War Within,** your life reflects on Jesus' steps down the Via Delarosa that led to the Hill of Golgotha where He was crucified. What is the Via Delarosa? The Via Dolorosa (Latin for *Way of Grief* or *Way of Suffering*) is a street, in two parts, within the Old City of Jerusalem. It is the path that Jesus walked, carrying his cross, on the way to his crucifixion. Jesus took a long road that was full of pain, suffering and humility and He did it all for us. Nothing that you and I will ever go through in this earthly realm of our existence will ever compare to the road that Jesus took.

In your time of trouble, it should be comforting to know that He experienced severe suffering to the point of being crucified so that we could enjoy eternity with Him and His Father, God. Sometimes we feel like there is no hope. We feel that there is no use in doing anything so we want to give up. We can feel exhausted and completely depleted by the things of this world. Could you imagine what our lives would be like if Jesus said "Forget this man. I'm outta here. I'm not going to do this for them, they won't appreciate it." Life as we know it would be pretty sorry don't you think?

In these times, let's turn our hearts toward God and realize that He walked the roughest road ever imaginable. He knows how to take care of us. Jesus Christ knows how to meet our needs. We need to turn to Him and follow His lead. In His times of turmoil and suffering He turned to His Heavenly Father. We should follow His lead. If it worked for Jesus and He trusted in it, it's good enough for me. Jesus knows the suffering we go through, He walked our path. Remember? He was here for 33 years.

Jesus feels our pain

October 17th

When we're going through a time of immense trial we must regain our focus, no matter what, and get it back onto the Lord Jesus Christ. We have two choices in this case, we can choose to focus on the overwhelming circumstances of our life that we're going through or we can focus on God who can get us through whatever we are going through no matter what. Which one is it going to be? The answer to this for me is a no brainer; I choose to focus on God in every aspect of my life. In my mind I have no other choice.

I believe in my heart that with God all things are possible. The Bible tells me so. Matthew 19:26; **"With man this is impossible, but with God all things are possible."** Because I care for myself I will place my focus on nothing other than Jesus Christ. We all have a choice to make, we can sink into the depths of despair or we can focus and rely on God. Making positive choices is clearly an important aspect of our lives. Why would we ever want to make bad choices that have the possibility of hurting our lives and the lives of others who we care about and possibly even jeopardize our eternity? We would be foolish to rely on the power of anything other than God. Without God, I am nothing. He is everything to me.

When I get in a jam I know I can call upon God for the solution to my dilemma. He has never and will never let me down. I know as long as I walk in the Spirit of God, I will be ok. Galatians 5:16; **"But I say, walk by the Spirit, and you will not gratify the desires of the flesh."** I always pray before I make a big decision. I am not saying I pray for everything I am about to do. I have seen people pray stupidly for every little thing. "God, should I have cornflakes or cheerios for breakfast?" Be for real, please! There are people like that. I know of a lady once who begged everyone for money. She always cried poor. She felt that God would give her employment yet she never applied for a job. If you are in need of a job, ask the Lord to help you find a job - but then be active in actually looking for a job. It is in His power to do so; yet it is highly unlikely that God will cause employers to come looking for you! You have to do your part.

Regain your focus

October 18th

If you and I can allow the Holy Spirit to show us in our minds eye the treacherous road that Jesus took on the Via Delarosa and all that this walk entailed, I'm certain that our faith in Jesus Christ's ability to guide us through difficult times would be greatly enhanced. The significance of His walk down this road and the suffering that He endured in order for us to be saved should weigh on us every time we contemplate doing something unsavory.

After reading and absorbing the path that Jesus took in the Gospel of Matthew, close your eyes and let your mind focus in on Jesus. Ask the Holy Spirit to open your spiritual eyes to the life of Jesus and the road to Golgotha that He walked. When I close my eyes and picture this, I can visualize Him taking this road and carrying the cross that He was about to hang on and which was about to take His life. Could you imagine having to carry the implement of your death? Talk about head games played by the Romans.

Artist after artist have made paintings and sculptures of Jesus on this road over the centuries, however I believe that the Holy Spirit would really like us to get this picture and portrayal of the suffering of Jesus into our mind, heart, soul and spirit. I believe that it is this walk and what took place on the Hill of Golgotha that will allow us as Christians to get through anything that we confront in this life, even if it is death itself. If you haven't seen it, the Mel Gibson movie "The Passion" is probably the most accurate portrayal of the suffering of Christ. I recommend every Christian watch it, however if you are an extremely sensitive person, get counsel from your pastor before you view it. It is very brutal and descriptive. It is not for everyone. Do not let your young children watch it either; it may be too extreme for them. Use your best judgment.

At times God will call us to walk the road of pain and suffering

October 19th

     With Jesus Christ at the center of our lives, we never have to give up. Jesus could have dropped to His knees on the Via Delarosa and refused to move closer to the Hill of Golgotha. He could have had the attitude that He had endured enough and that He wasn't going any further. He could have knelt down, curled up and refused to carry the cross any further. He could have called down a legion of angels and said "Go get them. They're yours." He pressed onward and upward to the Hill of Golgotha where He knew that He must be crucified for the sins of the world. Jesus realized that He had to complete the Father's divine destiny for Him on this road of pain and suffering. Think of this, God could have chosen another way to save humankind. He could have paved the way for salvation through another means. God chose to send Jesus in the form of a man, to suffer and be crucified on the cross for humanity. God wouldn't have chosen this path for Jesus unless it truly signified something for mankind. God the Father knew that we ourselves, on our own road in life, would experience at times intense pain and suffering. He never promised us a soft and cushy life.

     We have examples from Jesus of what to do when we are faced with dilemmas. What did Jesus do? He prayed. That is what we are to do, pray. We should pray always. Pray for wisdom. Pray for the Father's will to be done in your life. Pray for God to deliver you from temptation. Pray for your loved ones to come to know Christ. Pray for a healing to take place in your life. Pray for a job. Pray for whatever it is you need. The thing to do is pray. Luke 21:36; **"But stay awake at all times, praying that you may have strength to escape all these things that are going to take place, and to stand before the Son of Man." Stay awake at all times** means to be spiritually alert. To be made spiritually alert takes prayer. Prayer will enable a believer to avoid being harmed by the daily trials and tribulations, the circumstances and trials of life. We need strength before Christ's return so that we will remain strong and not lose heart. We need God's guidance and provision and this is attained through prayer.

Make Jesus Christ
the center of your life

October 20th

Are you suffering? Are you going through something that you don't think you will be able to make it through? Are you unable to see the other side of the storm? The most important of advice I can give you is Jesus Christ is able to guide you through to the other side. Trust in Him. He was crucified on the Hill of Golgotha for you and me. He is there for you and me to call on. You just finished reading the Gospel of Matthew and you experienced **The Waging War Within** His life. We also have **a Waging War Within** permeating our daily existence. Our salvation and our only avenue of escape from **The Waging War Within** is found in an acceptance of and a relationship with Jesus Christ. Get a vision of who Jesus is and the life He led. This vision of Jesus will transform your life. No preacher, no book (except the Bible), no church, no other earthly person, not you yourself or anybody else will ever be able to take you through your own tumultuous time. Don't put your faith, hope and trust in anything other than Jesus Christ and your personal relationship with Him.

Jesus will deliver us from our trip down our own tumultuous road. Maybe you would like to make a U-turn from the road that you're traveling down in your life. I'm telling you right now that Jesus can be right beside you, and He is, all you have to do is call upon Him. Once you call upon Him, He will come to you in all of His love and glory, to deliver you while you are in the midst of your storm, whichever storm it is. You may be on the wrong road, a road that you never imagined that you would even be on. Jesus longs to deliver you right where you are from whatever hardship you are going through. Nothing is too hopeless that Jesus can't overcome it for you. He's a God of restoration. You think you have it bad. Think of the road that Jesus took and what He experienced for you and me on the Hill of Golgotha. You might be confronting the worst possible situation in your life, Jesus can make a way, not only in this temporal world, but He will also make a way for you to have eternity with Him in Heaven. Just call on Him and feel the peace that surpasses all understanding.

Let Jesus be your guide

October 21st

I don't believe that Jesus doesn't want us to feel pain or suffering. There are many situations and circumstances that come into each one of our lives that cause these intense feelings. Pain and suffering can be a pervasive reality. I believe that Jesus Christ can deliver us right in the middle of our lowest points in life. When we allow Him to take control of the cockpit of our lives, He will never steer us the wrong way. We definitely won't crash with Jesus Christ on our side. We will be victorious in Him. When He carried the cross on the road and up the Hill of Golgotha, He spoke unspoken volumes. God can give us this same power and tenacity that He gave to His Son while He traveled that road. All we have to do is get out of the driver's seat and let Him take the wheel. We have to surrender control.

Surrender isn't always a bad thing and a form and admittance of defeat. In the case of us surrendering our lives to Christ, it isn't an admittance of defeat, it is a total victory. How can you say the surrendering of your will and life to Jesus is a bad thing? It isn't. It is a great thing. The angels in Heaven are rejoicing when one gives his life to the Lord. Luke 15:7; "**I tell you, there will be more joy in heaven over one sinner who repents than over ninety-nine righteous persons who need no repentance.**" Can you imagine the joy when you gave your life to Christ? If you haven't yet surrendered your will and your life to Christ, why not do it now? What's holding you back? What have you got to lose, misery and pain? Why don't you surrender and win.

You have to have to lose
in order to win.

Surrender to win!

October 22nd

     In some cases our pain and suffering will refine us and mold us into the image of Jesus Christ. If we allow our painful experiences, the ones that we've been scarred from, to lead us to the Cross of Christ, then we can't go wrong. If we let these experiences make us bitter, angry, hostile and vindictive individuals, then we're defeated before we even get started. This is a choice we have to make. Are we going to let our pasts dictate our future? If we do, what a waste of a life we will lead. We can make a decision to let our past be history and use our pain to enhance the Kingdom of God. Why let the devil win? Don't give glory to the devil by allowing him to keep throwing up your past to hold you back. When the devil tries to remind you of your past, remind him of his future.

     I'm telling you that you need to get a clear and real vision of who Jesus Christ is in your life. I believe that once you get a glimmer of Jesus and all of the suffering that He did for you and me, you will always prevail through anything and everything that comes your way in life. You are a son or daughter of the Most High. Don't let the devil get the glory for what lies in your future. Pain can either refine us or define us. What's it doing in your life? Are you giving the devil the glory in your life by constantly reminiscing about all of the negative things that have happened to you or are you giving the glory to God for what He has delivered you from? There is a fine line separating the two. Think before you speak. You may be giving the win to the wrong camp.

Pain can either refine us
or it can define us.
Who are you giving the glory to?

This section is your opportunity to explore your personal relationship with Jesus Christ in combating The Waging War Within your life

October 23rd

How has God worked in you through reading this book?

_____

_____

_____

_____

_____

_____

_____

_____

_____

_____

_____

_____

_____

_____

_____

_____

_____

_____

_____

_____

October 24th

What short-term goals do you have in God for your life?

_____

_____

_____

_____

_____

_____

_____

_____

_____

_____

_____

_____

_____

_____

_____

_____

October 25th

What long-term goals do you have for God for your life?

_____

_____

_____

_____

_____

_____

_____

_____

_____

_____

_____

_____

_____

_____

_____

_____

_____

_____

_____

October 26th

What do you think God's divine destiny is for your life?

_____

_____

_____

_____

_____

_____

_____

_____

_____

_____

_____

_____

_____

_____

_____

_____

_____

_____

October 27th

What will you have to do to accomplish God's divine destiny for your life?

_____

_____

_____

_____

_____

_____

_____

_____

_____

_____

_____

_____

_____

_____

_____

_____

_____

_____

_____

_____

October 28th

Are you where you want to be with God spiritually? Why? Why not?

_____

_____

_____

_____

_____

_____

_____

_____

_____

_____

_____

_____

_____

_____

_____

_____

October 29th

Is anything hindering you in your relationship and devotion to God? What is it? Are you willing to change it?

_____

_____

_____

_____

_____

_____

_____

_____

_____

_____

_____

_____

_____

_____

_____

_____

_____

_____

October 30th

Do you sense a calling on your life? What is God speaking to your heart for you to do?

_____

_____

_____

_____

_____

_____

_____

_____

_____

_____

_____

_____

_____

_____

_____

_____

October 31st

Who has God created you to be? Who does God want you to be in Him?

_____

_____

_____

_____

_____

_____

_____

_____

_____

_____

_____

_____

_____

_____

_____

_____

_____

_____

_____

November

November 1st

What do you envision doing with the gifts and abilities that God has given you?

_____

_____

_____

_____

_____

_____

_____

_____

_____

_____

_____

_____

_____

_____

_____

_____

November 2nd

What do you need to change in your life in order to align yourself with the divine destiny that He has given you?

_____

_____

_____

_____

_____

_____

_____

_____

_____

_____

_____

_____

_____

_____

_____

_____

_____

_____

November 3rd

Are you where you want to be with God? If not, why not?

_____

_____

_____

_____

_____

_____

_____

_____

_____

_____

_____

_____

_____

_____

_____

_____

_____

_____

November 4th

What is God doing in your life?

_____

_____

_____

_____

_____

_____

_____

_____

_____

_____

_____

_____

_____

_____

_____

_____

_____

_____

_____

_____

November 5th

Do you feel like you're in **a Waging War Within?** Why? Why not?

_____

_____

_____

_____

_____

_____

_____

_____

_____

_____

_____

_____

_____

_____

_____

_____

_____

_____

November 6th

Do your feelings and thoughts align with the perspectives and insights found in God's Word? Why? Why not?

_____

_____

_____

_____

_____

_____

_____

_____

_____

_____

_____

_____

_____

_____

_____

_____

_____

_____

_____

_____

_____

November 7th

370~ The Waging War Within

Before you die, what do you want to do for God while you are still here on earth?

_____

_____

_____

_____

_____

_____

_____

_____

_____

_____

_____

_____

_____

_____

_____

_____

_____

November 8th

What divine destiny do you want to leave your children and family as it relates to your relationship with God?

_____

_____

_____

_____

_____

_____

_____

_____

_____

_____

_____

_____

_____

_____

_____

_____

_____

_____

_____

_____

November 9th

Who has had the most profound impact in a positive way on your Christian walk? Why?

_____

_____

_____

_____

_____

_____

_____

_____

_____

_____

_____

_____

_____

_____

_____

_____

_____

_____

_____

November 10th

Who has had the most negative impact on your Christian walk? Why?

_____

_____

_____

_____

_____

_____

_____

_____

_____

_____

_____

_____

_____

_____

_____

_____

_____

_____

_____

_____

_____

_____

_____

November 11th

What experiences have had the most profound positive impact on your relationship with

God? Why?

_____

_____

_____

_____

_____

_____

_____

_____

_____

_____

_____

_____

_____

_____

_____

_____

_____

_____

November 12th

What experiences have had the most negative impact on your relationship with God?

Why?_____

_____

_____

_____

_____

_____

_____

_____

_____

_____

_____

_____

_____

_____

_____

_____

_____

_____

_____

_____

_____

November 13th

What do you need to ask God for in prayer and why?

_____

_____

_____

_____

_____

_____

_____

_____

_____

_____

_____

_____

_____

_____

_____

_____

_____

_____

November 14th

Are you involved consistently in a local congregation of believers? If not, why not?

_____

_____

_____

_____

_____

_____

_____

_____

_____

_____

_____

_____

_____

_____

_____

_____

_____

_____

_____

November 15th

Do you feel that you spend quality time with God daily through Bible study, prayer, praise and worship and fellowship with other believers?

November 16th

Do you feel like your cold, lukewarm, warm, hot, or on fire for God? Why?

_____

_____

_____

_____

_____

_____

_____

_____

_____

_____

_____

_____

_____

_____

_____

_____

_____

_____

_____

_____

November 17th

Where do you want to be with God within the next year?, two years?, five years?, ten years?, fifteen years?, or twenty years?

_____

_____

_____

_____

_____

_____

_____

_____

_____

_____

_____

_____

_____

_____

_____

_____

_____

_____

November 18th

Are you satisfied with your relationship with God or do you want more of Him in your life?

November 19th

What do you need to do to make your Christian Life more satisfying and more fulfilling?

_____

_____

_____

_____

_____

_____

_____

_____

_____

_____

_____

_____

_____

_____

_____

_____

_____

_____

_____

_____

November 20th

What do you need to do to strengthen your prayer life and make it more satisfying and more fulfilling?

_____

_____

_____

_____

_____

_____

_____

_____

_____

_____

_____

_____

_____

_____

_____

_____

_____

_____

_____

_____

_____

November 21st

Where is the enemy attacking you most?

_____

_____

_____

_____

_____

_____

_____

_____

_____

_____

_____

_____

_____

_____

_____

_____

_____

_____

_____

November 22nd

What must you do to combat this attack?

_____

_____

_____

_____

_____

_____

_____

_____

_____

_____

_____

_____

_____

_____

_____

_____

_____

_____

_____

_____

November 23rd

Sometimes Godly counsel is necessary. Do you have Godly people, Godly family, pastors or Christian counselors to turn to?

_____

_____

_____

_____

_____

_____

_____

_____

_____

_____

_____

_____

_____

_____

_____

_____

_____

_____

November 24th

Are you willing to allow Jesus Christ by the power of His Holy Spirit to bring you to higher ground in your life? Or are you satisfied with the status quo?

_____

_____

_____

_____

_____

_____

_____

_____

_____

_____

_____

_____

_____

_____

_____

_____

_____

_____

November 25th

Are you surrounding yourself with Godly people, Godly friends and Godly men and women? Why or why not?

_____

_____

_____

_____

_____

_____

_____

_____

_____

_____

_____

_____

_____

_____

_____

_____

_____

_____

_____

_____

November 26th

Are you pursuing the vision that God has for your life?

November 27th

Is sin in your life that needs to be submitted and brought to God to be forgiven?

_____

_____

_____

_____

_____

_____

_____

_____

_____

_____

_____

_____

_____

_____

_____

_____

_____

_____

_____

_____

November 28th

Do you desire to live a holy life before God? Why or why not?

November 29th

Are you willing to pay the price that God requires to follow Him whole heartedly? Why or why not?

_____

_____

_____

_____

_____

_____

_____

_____

_____

_____

_____

_____

_____

_____

_____

_____

_____

_____

November 30th

What gifts and abilities do you think God has given you to use to build up and bless His Church?

_____

_____

_____

_____

_____

_____

_____

_____

_____

_____

_____

_____

_____

_____

_____

_____

_____

_____

_____

December

December 1st

A divine destiny is something that an individual can leave to another generation after they're gone. God has clearly left us a divine destiny through the sacrifice of His only begotten Son Jesus the Christ. Jesus died and rose again after three days, paving the way for us to attain the free gift of eternal salvation through our belief in Him. Jesus Christ opened the doors to Heaven for us. God left the most important divine destiny ever given to humankind throughout all of history. He provided a way for us through His Son Jesus Christ for our eternal security. Jesus left us a divine destiny not of this temporal world, but of an eternal world yet to come. The Holy Bible is a historical God breathed account of the life of Jesus Christ. It documents part of the life of Christ and it gives us a guide of how we are to conduct our life while we are still here on earth. The Bible is an account of creation as well as a historical journal which God left for us. He left us His master blueprint on how to live a Godly life while here on earth.

The Scriptures are more important than all the material possessions you would ever be able to find anywhere on earth. Within the pages of His Holy Scriptures, there exist the hidden treasures of how we are able to receive both salvation and eternal life. The Bible is a message of hope to a lost and dying world which is in desperate need of a redeeming God. If man only read one book in his entire life, the Bible is the Book he should read. The Bible is a gateway to life. It shows us how to live. It guides our life if we would only apply its teachings. The answers to all of life's questions are found within the covers. It keeps us on a path which should be ever narrowing the farther you read into it. Just like a stream, if you narrow it up the force of the water increases. This is what our life does when we tap into the Holy Spirit and apply the Word to our life. God and His Word are the wellsprings in life. We just need to tap into the Source.

Tap into the source.

December 2nd

    I believe that God has given mankind an intrinsic need to leave something of Him for future generations. Our life is temporal. In the Bible it makes it clear that life is but a breath. Genesis 2:7; "**then the LORD God formed the man of dust from the ground and breathed into his nostrils the breath of life, and the man became a living creature.**" God gave us life with His breath. He is the source of all life. Since we are created in the image of God, I believe that God has birthed within us the inherent longing to pass something on to the world and to others after we leave this planet toward our eternal reward. Many quench this need with leaving a monetary gift, with real estate, or with something else monetarily important. These things, gifts if you will, are not important. What is important is the eternal salvation available only through a relationship with God. This is the legacy we should be leaving with and for our loved ones who will be left behind.

    I believe that God always intended for us to leave a divine destiny that will last for eternity. The divine destiny that God intended for us to leave our family members and our offspring is the knowledge of our heartfelt relationship with Jesus Christ. We're promised within the Scriptures of our eternal reward once we accept Jesus Christ as our Personal Lord and Savior. Romans 6:23; "**For the wages of sin is death, but the free gift of God is eternal life through Christ Jesus our Lord.**" This Christian Faith was meant to be passed down from generation to generation, so that all might receive salvation and meet again once we leave our earthly existence. Ephesians 2:6-7; "**and raised us up with him and seated us with him in the heavenly places in Christ Jesus, so that in the coming ages he might show the immeasurable riches of his grace in kindness toward us in Christ Jesus.**" One day, those that have accepted this Gospel Message of Salvation will be Heaven bound with a one way ticket. We just need to believe in Him and repent as we were instructed to do. He loves us and wants to spend eternity with us.

Where are you spending your eternity?

December 3rd

Man through the worldly system that we live in has distorted God's plan in leaving a divine destiny. God intended that our divine destiny be eternal in nature, not temporal. We're called to inculcate our redeeming Christian Faith within our children at all costs. This should be our number one priority throughout our entire lives. Leaving behind our earthly wealth will only provide for those left behind while someone is alive and still remaining on earth. Leaving a spiritually empowered divine destiny will provide a way for all of eternity. This is what's really important. Leaving behind money and wealth according to earthly standards often times just leads to court battles and provisions that only last for a short period of time. Eternity in Heaven with Our Lord and Savior is an everlasting gift. That is what really matters isn't it?

Have you started to pass down your eternal divine destiny to others? Do your children and family know that you have an unwavering faith in Jesus Christ? Do they see this by the example that you lead in your life and how you conduct all of your affairs while you are still here? Do you live your life while no one else sees you in the same manner as you do when you are visible to all? Are you leading a double life known only to your family? Are you a hypocrite? It is never too late to start preparing the way of living out your Christianity in such a way that it translates down to future generations within your family. Why don't you start today?

Live a spiritually empowered divine destiny

December 4th

When we reflect on all that Jesus Christ has done for us, we cannot help but to have an insatiable gratitude to Him. He has provided a way for our salvation. We're written in the Lambs Book of Life with Heaven as our divine destiny! Revelation 21:27; "**But nothing unclean will ever enter it, nor anyone who does what is detestable or false, but only those who are written in the Lamb's book of life.**" How can we go wrong? We really can't. Thanks be to God!

We're called to run our Christian race with everything we have. With all that is in us. With every ounce of blood, sweat and tears that we can muster. We are to run it with the entire fabric of our beings and with every DNA molecule that we possess. In other words we're required to give God our everything! He will settle for nothing less than our all. Hebrews 12:1-2; "**Therefore, since we are surrounded by so great a cloud of witnesses, let us also lay aside every weight, and sin which clings so closely, and let us run with endurance the race that is set before us, looking to Jesus, the founder and perfecter of our faith, who for the joy that was set before him endured the cross, despising the shame, and is seated at the right hand of the throne of God.**"

Our approach to running this race and leaving a divine destiny of faith for others requires us to actually live out our Christianity. We need to walk the walk and not just talk the talk. We need to be authentic, real and have a Christianity that is working in our lives from the inside out. We cannot be living a life of duplicity and fakeness before the world. If we're going to preach this message then we have to be living it out for real, in the real world. Not perfectly, but authentically. We need to run the race by following the rules laid out in the Word. Those rules govern our life as the rules of competition govern the athletes performing in the Olympics. There are judges watching over the athletes and the games and we have The Judge watching over us, God. Are you performing by the rules? He's watching over you and me. We need to pray for the strength to run a good race.

Run a good race.

December 5th

      Every December we reflect on the birth of Jesus Christ and all that He has given us in Him. We are so blessed to know Him and to have a relationship with Him. Annually we're given the opportunity as a family, as individuals, as a community and as a society within the United States of America to celebrate the birth of Jesus Christ. How powerful and blessed we are to belong to our Society and Country. Just think of how much God has blessed America! God sent His Son, Jesus Christ, and He has blessed us as a Nation. This is a powerful divine destiny that God has undoubtedly blessed us with. We need to make certain that this divine destiny is passed on from generation to generation within our families.

      What is the best gift that you have ever received at Christmas or any other time in your life? Did you answer Jesus or was your answer something else? Be honest now. What was the first thing that came to your mind? If it wasn't Jesus, why wasn't it? I believe a lot of people take their gift of salvation for granted. I am not judging, I am making an observation. We must reflect on all that we have and remember that we have nothing without God in our life. Have you ever seen an armored truck in a funeral procession? I haven't either. I have a friend that tells me now that you can get coffins that have locking drawers where the family can put money and other possessions in them so that they go with the departed. Is that sad or what? It just goes to show the selfishness of some people. He says that it is being done to prevent the fighting of the surviving members of the family. I guess you really can take it with you now. I would rather store up my treasures in Heaven. Matthew 6:20; "**Lay up for yourselves treasures in heaven, where neither moth nor rust destroys and where thieves do not break in and steal.**"

Live out your divine destiny

December 6th

      God has given us and our country a divine destiny of freedom in Him. We need to pass the importance of this on to our children and grandchildren. We have to let them see how walking with the Lord Jesus Christ has transformed our lives and let them know that all of the blessings are available for them to grab onto also. We need to let them inculcate within their own lives and the lives of their children the value of getting involved in a local Christian Church and incorporating the things of God within their lives. What more powerful divine destiny can you leave someone other than the powerful legacy of Jesus Christ?

      December is a time of blessing that we, as a nation, have an opportunity to reflect on the birth of Jesus Christ! The coming of our Savior, Jesus Christ, lying in a manger as baby is a time to remember and thank Him for all that He has blessed us with and how He continues to bless us even today. This is the divine destiny that God has left for all future generations. How astounding! How perplexing! How magnificent! God chose to send His Only Begotten Son to earth in the form of an infant to save all of mankind. We have a divine destiny beyond belief from God! What are you doing with your gift? Are you using all that He has given you in a selfish or a selfless manner? Are you passing it on at every opportunity? Are you hording it? Think about it.

      If you passed a total stranger on the street and you saw that he was hungry and you had money in your pocket, would you feed him? If it was a child and he was shoeless would you give him a pair of shoes? If it was cold and rainy outside and you had an extra coat in your car would you offer it to them? Really? Would you? Every time you see one of these aforementioned situations and you just put a blind eye to it you are doing the same to God. We are all His children and whatever you do to the least of these you do to Him. The Word says so. Matthew 25:40; "**Truly, I say to you, as you did it to one of the least of these my brothers, you did it to me.**" We must start treating people as Christ would. If you change one life for the better you changed an entire generation. Let's start.

Change a generation

December 7th

       As we go to our local churches this December in remembrance of the Birth of Jesus Christ, let's reflect how fortunate we are to live in a society that values the things of God. We may complain that God is being taken out of everything, this may seem like it is happening, but we can still attend church without repercussions. This may not be the case in several other parts of the world so we must be grateful for this blessing. We're fortunate to have the freedom of worship, unlike so many other countries. I believe that we as Americans have been blessed with so much, and with all of this, God expects more of us. Luke 12:48; **"Everyone to whom much was given, of him much will be required, and from him to whom they entrusted much, they will demand the more."** In order for us to be continuously blessed we must pass on the blessings to another.

       God wants us to reach out to others in His name with all of the grace and blessings He has given us. He would like our hands to be an extension of His hands to the hurting people within our world. He desires the divine destiny of love that He's left us to be translated into an authentic relationship with Him that has the power to change the world. He desires that our relationship with Him be not just be a form of Godliness, but He desires us to walk in His power. God has given us a divine destiny of; love, mercy, salvation, power and relationship. It is a gift given to us that is to be given away to another.

       We are called Christ's Ambassadors for a reason my friends, the reason is that we are to be His hands and feet while we are still sucking air. We have been given the command to go out and spread the Word. Are you doing that? Matthew 28:18-20; **"All authority in heaven and on earth has been given to me. Go therefore and make disciples of all nations, baptizing them in the name of the Father and of the Son and of the Holy Spirit, teaching them to observe all that I have commanded you. And behold, I am with you always, to the end of the age."** This is the season to give as you have been given.

Try it, you'll like it.

December 8th

The divine destiny that God has bestowed upon the United States of America is vast. American's have more opportunity and freedom than any other people group on the world map. We're a country of blessing, but with blessing comes responsibility and privilege. Luke 12:48; **"Everyone to whom much was given, of him much will be required, and from him to whom they entrusted much, they will demand the more."** Another thing is that we have been given so much but are we giving back in return? I see us as a very blessed but spoiled people. Luke 12: 47-48; **"And that servant who knew his master's will but did not get ready or act according to his will, will receive a severe beating. But the one who did not know, and did what deserved a beating, will receive a light beating."** If you are a Christian and you are reading this, you have been told that you are to give freely of the blessings bestowed upon you. If you were never told this, you just read it so count yourself informed.

This past Christmas we once again had the opportunity of worshipping Jesus in the church we attend with our families. Once again we had the opportunity to celebrate the birth of Jesus Christ in a free country. We lifted our hands to Jesus Christ with full reverence in worship and song. Our praise should have been loud and proud of the God we serve. We should be unashamed of our Christianity. We need to realize and embrace the divine destiny that God has given us. I have such a gratitude in my heart to Jesus, because I truly have realized the divine destiny of love that He has freely given to us through His Son Jesus Christ.

We cannot worship the almighty dollar and God at the same time. Matthew 6:19-24; **"Do not lay up for yourselves treasures on earth, where moth and rust destroy and where thieves break in and steal, but lay up for yourselves treasures in heaven, where neither moth nor rust destroys and where thieves do not break in and steal. For where your treasure is, there your heart will be also. The eye is the lamp of the body. So, if your eye is healthy, your whole body will be full of light, but if your eye is bad, your whole body will be full of darkness. If then the light in you is darkness, how great is the darkness! No one can serve two masters, for either he will hate the one and love the other, or he will be devoted to the one and despise the other. You cannot serve God and money."** If you have your focus on you and what you have been given and how you can get more, then you need a check-up from the neck up. You need to take a long hard look at yourself in the mirror and reevaluate your sense of priorities. You and I would have nothing if it weren't for God. We are nothing without Him.

We are all creations made by the Creator. We are made in His image. Genesis 1:27; **"So God created man in his own image, in the image of God he created him; male and female he created them."** It was not mere happenstance that we are as we are. God made you and me just the way we are. We were not created to be selfish. We were made to take care of each other. Sin entered the world in the Garden of Eden and the sin and selfishness all started. God sent Jesus as a lamb to set the example for us to follow and what did we do? We killed the Lamb of God. He came first as a lamb and next He is coming as a lion. Revelation Chapter 5 juxtaposes Jesus Christ as both the Lion of Judah and The Lamb of God. He is both my friends. We need to get our heads right so we don't stand before God as a selfish and greedy person. Our time is running out.

1 Corinthians 15:10; "But by the grace of God I am what I am." God made Paul as referenced here as he was and He made us as we are. We need to act towards all as He would have us act; with love and compassion. Paul was a persecutor of Christians and he changed

and started to show love and compassion. If Paul can change so can we. We are a blessed people. We have so much to offer. Ask yourself what God would have you do and do it. It's not too late. You're still sucking air aren't you? Well get moving.

What are you waiting for?

Get moving!!

December 9th

All I desire to do is to pass the divine destiny which God has given to me on to my children and also on to the world in which we live. I have so much gratitude to God that He has brought me to a point of spiritual enlightenment to realize and grasp all that I have in Him. The blinders have not only been lifted, but the Holy Spirit has helped me to see Jesus more clearly than ever before in my life. All I want to do is share God's revelation with the world. He has given me a divine destiny of uncompromising love. I long to inculcate a heightened passion for the things of God with others I come into contact with. I want to do this on a daily basis with everyone. Don't you? If not, why not?

Have you ever heard anyone say they can't go witnessing because they are too shy? How does that make you feel? I want to say first off that "Can't means won't." Next I want to say "Why would they be too shy if the words won't be yours, they will be from the Holy Spirit?" Imagine if the one who gave us the Word was too shy. Where would you be right now? We can't be selfish with the Word. We need to get outside of our comfort zone. We need to stretch ourselves. Get out there and share the greatest blessing you have ever been given!

We've been given a divine destiny of love. Share it!

December 10th

My family had the opportunity last year to participate in the Christmas production at the church which we attend, Bethany Assembly of God in Agawam, MA. What a blessing for the entire family. My wife, my children and I all were actively involved. God moved within our family in a powerful way. I was so thankful to God for giving our family the opportunity to be together in these Christmas performances. God opened my spiritual eyes to all the blessings that I have through Him. As I watched my children and my wife actively engage in this aspect of ministry I myself was ministered to by the Holy Spirit. My heart was comforted and I had a peace that only comes from God. If you have a relationship with God you know what I mean. Philippians 4:7; **"And the peace of God, which surpasses all understanding, will guard your hearts and your minds in Christ Jesus."**

I prayed throughout these performances and thanked God for giving us as a family the gifts and abilities to participate in these church ministries. I was ministering to others by my involvement, but I was also being ministered to by the Holy Spirit. As I looked toward the manger scene I was so thankful to God for all that He has done in my life and the lives of my family. God showed me through these experiences the awesome divine destiny I'm leaving my children. I'm leaving them memories of an earthly father that was in love with his Heavenly Father, Jesus Christ. There is nothing more important than passing on this Godly divine destiny of relationship with Jesus Christ.

Embrace God's love!

It is His gift to you.

December 11th

I remember while in college I had to do an exercise that has stayed with me up until now. I often reflect on this exercise. The class had to ask themselves and answer the question, "What do I want others to remember of me after I'm dead?" The second half of the exercise was that we had to think and share with the class what we wanted written on our "headstone at our grave." The goal of this lesson was to make you think how you wanted to live life while alive here on earth. How would you want others to remember you? What would you want written on your headstone? This all ties into the divine destiny that you would desire to leave behind to your children, your grandchildren, your loved ones and others that knew you. I think that this is a profound exercise because it gets you to really think about your faith is Jesus Christ.

I used to say I wanted "You don't get out alive" written on mine. The truth is that I would want "He was God's servant" written on mine. I strive night and day to be a servant of God. I know I can never undo the devastation and destruction I have left in the wake of my earlier life. I have had a profound change of heart and I have made many changes in my life thanks to my relationship with my Lord and Savior Jesus Christ and the mighty men of God which I embrace as true friends and brothers in the Lord today.

We are all going to die one day; that is a gimme. What are you leaving behind as your legacy? When you pass on and stand before God, is He going to say "Well done my good and faithful servant." Or is He going to say "What were you thinking?" We are all going to be held accountable for our actions. He will forgive our trespasses if we are truly repentant of them. Have you asked forgiveness for your past? Are you serving Him to the best of your abilities today? Can your walk be a bit straighter? Are you living a life that would have God saying "Good job?"

How do you want
to be remembered?

December 12th

Leaving a divine destiny is a powerful thing to think about. It's powerful because it signifies how you lived your life. Living and leaving a divine destiny is our opportunity to pass on our Christian values to our future generations. Our children and grandchildren will be watching us to see how we live. They're watching how we act, what we say, and how much we love Jesus Christ. They're watching to see if there is authenticity in our faith in Jesus or if it is just an act. They have today's world telling them many different messages, so it is really up to us to train up a child in the ways of the Lord. Proverbs 22:6; **"Train up a child in the way he should go; even when he is old he will not depart from it."** The Waging War Within is taking place within their inner selves just as it is within us and our lives. This divine destiny is of critical importance because of the potentiality of it impacting generation after generation. This is huge.

Look at the legacy left by Paul, the former Saul of Tarsus. Saul was a tormenter and killer of Christians and look at the change God had on his life other than just changing his name to Paul. He had a dynamic change of heart. He gave his life for Christ. We may not have been Saul's in our prior lives but the change is nonetheless just as important and impacting. There are people out there in your past who know what you were like before you came to Christ and how He has changed your heart and life. Have you shared the change He has made in you? Don't be ashamed of your past; embrace it; it is what has brought you to the reforming grace of God. You are no longer who you were. You are a new creation in Christ. 2 Corinthians 5:17; **"Therefore, if anyone is in Christ, he is a new creation. The old has passed away; behold, the new has come."** Ezekiel 36:26; **"And I will give you a new heart, and a new spirit I will put within you. And I will remove the heart of stone from your flesh and give you a heart of flesh."** You are now a son or daughter of the Most High God. Praise Him! Thank you Lord.

Praise Him!

December 13th

It's critical that we allow the Holy Spirit to penetrate our lives so that He can show us how to live while here on earth. We need Him to show us how to survive this battle called **The Waging War Within.** We have to allow God to show us how to pass this knowledge on to our children. We must demonstrate how to create a firm foundation for ourselves within our Christian Faith and how our children can live out their divine destiny which God has for them within their own lives.

For us to pass on our Christian Faith, we ourselves have to be living our faith and truly carrying it out in our daily lives. We have to pray for God to empower us and to work in and through us and also within the parenting of our children. We have to rely and trust in God to give us wisdom and discernment in raising children in our Christian Faith. Making our Christian Faith a rock solid part of our family heritage is a critical part of being able to pass on the divine destiny to our next generation. Christianity needs to become the very fabric that our family is made of. This means that Jesus Christ needs to be the central focus of our lives. Are you praying for this? As long as you're breathing, you still have an obligation to pass on the love and knowledge of Christ. Matthew 28:19-20; **"Go therefore and make disciples of all nations, baptizing them in the name of the Father and of the Son and of the Holy Spirit, teaching them to observe all that I have commanded you."** It was a command, not a suggestion or invitation to decline.

Christianity needs to be a rock solid part of our family heritage.

December 14th

       Jesus Christ has passed on His Holy Scriptures and all that they entail as His Divine Destiny on to the entire world. I am only able to walk in Him because He gave us His Holy Word which my Christian faith is built upon. If I didn't have the Bible, I would be utterly lost in how to carry out my Christian walk. God's Word is His Divine Destiny for me as well as for you. Now it is up to us to convey our faith in Jesus Christ to our children and to our siblings, parents, and ultimately to the entire world in which I live. God has given us the responsibility of touching the world for Him.

       When we're gone and our children are left behind we want them to be able to carry on the torch of our Christian faith within their lives and to inculcate their faith with their own children. This takes much prayer, and most importantly, it takes living a constant and a consistent Christian lifestyle. We need to be sure of that which we are sure of. Are you sure of your belief in Jesus Christ? Are you sure of your eternity? Do you know The Word? Have you shared it with your immediate family? Do you want to see your loved ones saved? Of course you do. Gather up boldness and share your faith. God will give you boldness that will surprise you.

       Moses was a stutterer and yet he brought God's chosen out of Egypt. David was a runt yet he slew a giant. Esther was a Jew and she had the boldness to stand up to a king. Jesus was as meek as a lamb and He saved the world. God can and will do great and mighty things with the most unlikely people. He has done it before and He will do it again. Just pray for boldness and He will provide it. He hears the prayers of His people. James 5:16; **"Therefore, confess your sins to one another and pray for one another, that you may be healed. The prayer of a righteous person has great power as it is working."** Pray my friends. Pray.

Pray always!

December 15th

    Reflect daily on the divine destiny that Jesus Christ has left you and your family. Don't just reflect on this as Christmas is approaching, focus on it throughout the entire year. Keep the vision of what you have in and through Jesus Christ on a daily basis. An individual relationship with Jesus Christ is a must. How powerful it is to reflect on all that we have as Christians. We have; our church, our church family, Godly leadership at church, the Bible, ministries that we're involved in, salvation, redemption, the Holy Spirit, God the Father and most importantly, our personal relationship with Jesus Christ. We also have an opportunity daily to pass on the gift of salvation to those with whom we come into contact with. Why be selfish? We need to share.

    We need to let this divine destiny of Jesus Christ flow through us to those within our families and to those we associate with, both saved and unsaved. We need to allow God to work in the hearts of man just as He did in ours. It is only God who can save, not man. Isaiah 43:11; **"I, I am the LORD, and besides me there is no savior."** We can present the truth and live it out in our daily lives, but it is ultimately God that saves people. Don't ever try and play God. Let God do the work of salvation in someone's heart. He does this by the working of His Holy Spirit. He is the Savior, not you or I. We just need to be willing to do our part, the presenting of Him and His Word; the rest is up to the individual we present it to. It is between them and God. We need to be willing servants for Him.

Are you willing
to be a servant to Him?

December 16th

Can you get a vision of Jesus Christ laying down His life for you and me on the Cross of Calvary? Can you envision Jesus Christ; being tried, taunted, and persecuted, Jesus being beaten and flogged, having a thorn of crowns placed on His head and beaten some more, Christ being spat on and forced to carry the implement of His own death through the very streets that only a few days earlier carried the people who praised and worshipped Him and now turned on Him, Him being crucified for you and me and ultimately speared in the side to insure His death? When you truly let this sink into your mind and heart it's unbelievably powerful. It's life changing and moving.

God loves you and me so very much. He knew before the foundation of the world that He would leave us this divine destiny of love. He knew He would be sacrificing His Son so that we could be saved from an eternity in Hell. Shouldn't we to, as a result of this love He left us, leave a divine destiny to our loved ones and the world in which we live? Of course we should. It is the gift that keeps on giving. It should be every one win one. If we all accepted this concept of every one win one, just imagine how beautiful the world could be. We all need to get the Word out before it is too late. We all need to get out and do our part for the Kingdom. Let's get busy.

Every one win one.

December 17th

  I believe that God would have us to remember His love for us on a daily basis. Imagine our children and grandchildren thinking of us when we're gone to be with the Lord. We want our children to think of us as Godly men and women. We want our children to think of us as Godly men and women who are sold out for Jesus Christ. I want my children to remember me; as a man of prayer, as a man that reads the Bible, as a man that not only attended church but was actively involved in ministry, as a man who loved others and ultimately placed Jesus Christ first in his life. I would like to be remembered as a man with a spiritually empowered divine destiny. It is most crucial, especially in this ever changing world culture, that we accept this destiny given to us by our Lord and Savior Jesus Christ. We need to embrace it.

  Do you want to leave your children and others a divine destiny? The question to answer is the following. While you were alive did people see Jesus Christ through you; in your communications with them and others, things you did, the way you loved others, in your speech, work, rest, and overall in how you lived life? Did you act as an Ambassador of Christ should? If not, it is not too late to start. As long as you aren't taking the dirt nap, it's not too late. Start studying the Word and apply what you read to your life and your walk.

  Remember my friends; Jesus started His ministry at 30 years of age. What do you think He was doing those first 30 years? He was studying the Word so that He could live it out for us. His ministry was only 3 years. Imagine that; in 3 short years He changed the world. Just think of what you can do with the time you have left remaining.

What are you doing with your time?

December 18th

As we wait for Christmas to approach this December 25th, let's renew our faith in Jesus Christ. Let's thank God for everything that He has given us, especially all the blessings that come with and through His Son Jesus Christ. Let's thank God for Jesus' birth, life, death and resurrection this Christmas shall we? We have so much to be thankful for every day, let alone at Christmas where we celebrate the birth of our Savior. God wants us to live every day as if it's Christmas. Let's see Christmas for what it truly represents; the birth of Jesus Christ. Let's be thankful that He's taking us through **The Waging War Within** our lives. He's leading us, guiding us, and ultimately blessing us throughout our lives. We may find difficult times ahead, but our personal relationship with God will take us through these times. We need to be grateful for all things, both good and bad. The Word tells us this.

- [Eph. 5:20] **Giving thanks always for all things** unto God and the Father in the name of our Lord Jesus Christ;

- [1 Thess. 5:18] **In everything give thanks**: for this is the will of God in Christ Jesus concerning you.

- [Col. 3:17] And **whatsoever ye do** in word or deed, do all in the name of the Lord Jesus, **giving thanks to God** and the Father by him.

- [Heb. 13:15] By him therefore let us **offer the sacrifice of praise to God continually**, that is, the fruit of our lips **giving thanks to his name**.

We must learn to see the blessings in whatever form they may come. Have you ever heard the statement said that the calamity you face may be a blessing in disguise? There is wisdom in that statement. We need to find the blessing. For the child of God, who is walking in the light, all things are blessings, even though they often appear in disguise. Romans 8:28; **"And we know that for those who love God all things work together for good, for those who are called according to his purpose."** Are you a whiner or a thankful servant? There are enough thumb suckers in the world; God needs workers who see Him in all things. Are you a Truth seeker or a Truth talker? Do you talk or walk in the Word?

Have you ever been to a funeral service and heard people ask; "Why was he taken? He was such a good man." Or have you ever wondered why a child was called to be with God when they had their whole life before them? Listen to this verse; Isaiah 57:1-2; **"The righteous man perishes, and no one lays it to heart; devout men are taken away, while no one understands. For the righteous man is taken away from calamity; he enters into peace; they rest in their beds who walk in their uprightness."** Blessings come in disguise. We need to remember that God is in charge and we need to focus on Him and His divine providence. If He notices the fall of each little sparrow, He certainly cares about His children and each little problem they have. He wants to be the absolute center of our life and all of our thoughts. Have you made Him the center of yours?

December 19th

Think of what God the Father left in terms of a divine destiny for us through Jesus Christ. He bridged the gap for mankind to have a personal relationship with Jesus Christ, His dearly treasured Son. God the Father made a way for sinful human beings to find a way to live forever in His Heavenly Home. God the Father parted with His Son, in order to draw all men unto Himself. Without Jesus' birth, life, death and resurrection mankind would never have the ability to experience salvation from all of their sins. We will all someday be transported to Heaven for our heavenly reward. What will your reward be? God the Father delivered us from **The Waging War Within,** which has the capacity to conform us to the things of this world, instead of the things of Jesus Christ. Our testimony in Jesus Christ wouldn't ever be, if God the Father never sent His Son to earth for us and our salvation. Have you ever thought of that?

We need to get our eye off of the almighty I. We must focus our attention on Him. He is the reason for our being. God is our provider. Psalm 23:1; **"The LORD is my shepherd; I shall not want."** Whatever we need He provides. This does not include our wants. There is a difference between a need and a want. We need to search our hearts and our motives to see just what it is we are longing for. Jesus is to be our all and all. Have you ever talked to an evolutionist? I have and they seem so convinced in the theory of evolution. I asked them the question; "If we evolved from monkeys, then why are there still monkeys?" They had no answer. It is like the bumper stickers "Now even Darwin is convinced there is a God", and another, "God is dead" Nietzsche. "Nietzsche is dead" God. I don't know what your theology is. I believe in God. I believe in the Big Bang Theory also, God said it and Bang!! It was done. Amen.

The Big Bang Theory?
God said it and Bang!! It was done!

December 20th

Thank God for the divine destiny of the Holy Spirits power to operate both in and through our lives. The Holy Spirit has the ministering ability to empower us to live out our Christian Faith. The Holy Spirit has the capacity to convict us when we're going off the trail which God would have us to take in our lives. What would we ever do without the divine destiny of the Trinity; the Father, the Son and the Holy Spirit being carried out in our human existence? My life would be meaningless without God. I cannot imagine living without having God in my life. Can you? He's given us so much. How could we ever turn away from these treasures of Heaven?

God has also given us the gift of being protected by His mighty angels and His blood covering. All of these riches can be found in and through Him. Let's open our eyes America, look around and see how He's blessed us both as a nation and as a people. We have a freedom to worship our God and to live out our Christian Faith. God has given us a freedom to operate in His power anywhere we live in this, the most blessed of nations. We have the opportunity to allow God to flow freely in our country and in our individual hearts! Are we taking this freedom for granted and being selfish with it or are we making the most of it? God could take back these blessings if He so chose to do so. He gives and He takes away. Job 1:21; "**Naked I came from my mother's womb, and naked shall I return. The LORD gave, and the LORD has taken away; blessed be the name of the LORD.**" He is God. We are not to be selfish with the gifts of God. We are to use them to better the Kingdom of God. Are you using yours for the Kingdom or yourself?

Use your gifts to enhance
the Kingdom of God

December 21st

How about the divine destiny of being baptized in the name of Jesus? How about the divine destiny of being able to accept communion and remember the blessing that God the Father has given us through His Son Jesus Christ? How about the divine destiny of being able to go to the altar asking God for forgiveness, healing and restoration and then being granted the same? How about the divine destiny of Him being able to restore us and mend our brokenness? How about the divine destiny of calling some to be pastors, evangelist, teachers, missionaries, prophets and ministers of the Gospel of Jesus Christ? Let's open our eyes, church, and realize the divine destiny that we have in the truth of Jesus Christ and His Church. We are so abundantly blessed that I feel we are spoiled in it all.

Have you ever been to a third world country? Have you ever personally experienced poverty? Our poorest in America is still rich to the majority of the world. Are you aware of that? Yet we are probably the most morally bankrupt people on the face of the planet. We have so much yet we have so little. We are rich in material things and so broke morally at the same time. This is so sad. Luke 12:48; **"Everyone to whom much was given, of him much will be required, and from him to whom they entrusted much, they will demand the more."** We have a responsibility to use the things with which we have been blessed with in a responsible way, the way in which God entrusted us with using them. If we are not doing that we will have to account for their usage. We need to be wise with all that we have been given. Are you being wise?

**Let's open our eyes and grasp
what we have in Jesus
Christ**

December 22nd

      Some men and women of God have taken hold of the divine destiny that God has given them. These Godly Christians have started incredible ministries throughout the world because they have grasped the magnitude of the divine destiny that God has given us in Jesus Christ. Christian colleges, universities and theological seminaries have been started due to that divine destiny which God has bestowed on us through Jesus Christ. Many now secular colleges and universities started at their inception with founders that were Christian men and women. Men and women have been saved by the Lord Jesus Christ at huge Christian gatherings that fill entire sports stadiums. Worldwide Christian organizations have been started with individuals that have grasped the divine destiny that Jesus Christ has left freely for all. What vision has God given you? He has left you personally a divine destiny. What are you going to do with it? Hopefully you will reach out to the world with the compassion of Jesus Christ.

      When you look at Billy Graham, what do you think? He's no different than you or me. The difference is that he grasped the things of God and he used them to their fullest. We are all promised that the things that Christ did we could do and even more. Did you know that? John 14:12-14; **"Truly, truly, I say to you, whoever believes in me will also do the works that I do; and greater works than these will he do, because I am going to the Father. Whatever you ask in my name, this I will do, that the Father may be glorified in the Son. If you ask me anything in my name, I will do it."** We have the power of potential. If we use our full potential, we will have all of the power that God promised us. We are what's holding us back. We are sometimes our worst enemies. If you want to be effective in ministry, He has already promised you that you can do it like Jesus did and even more. Develop your faith and see for yourself the potential you have within. Step out in faith my brother or sister and see the wonder of God unfold in your life.

Grab all that God has
in store for you

December 23rd

Have you been blessed with Godly men, women and children in your family? If you have, consider yourself blessed. This was part of God's divine destiny for you. Someone who prays to God has already grasped some of what God's divine destiny is for His church. I can recall my Grandfather quietly, and sometimes audibly, kneeling beside his bed in prayer every night. He would also pray every morning, all the while kneeling beside his bedside. He would have his cross in his hands as he was praying to God. You see, he grasped what God the Father has given to the world through the gift of His Son Jesus Christ. I could see and hear my grandfather pray for his family, others, and the world in which he lived. He was a man of faith. Watching my grandfather pray as a boy was a legacy left by my grandfather which has stayed with me even to this day. I will never forget the wonderful memories that I have of my grandfather praying in the quietness of his room. I'll cherish the memories he left me until I meet him again in God's Heavenly Kingdom.

What are the memories you are leaving behind? Are they peaceful memories? Are they Godly memories? If not, you have time to change. I know through personal experience that if you have unforgiveness in your heart towards someone, you will not have peace in your life. John 20:23; **"If you forgive the sins of anyone, they are forgiven; if you withhold forgiveness from anyone, it is withheld."** We need to forgive in order for us to be forgiven. Psalms 103:12; **"As far as the east is from the west, so far does he remove our transgressions from us."** Ephesians 4:32; **"Be kind to one another, tenderhearted, forgiving one another, as God in Christ forgave you."** Mark 11:25; **"And whenever you stand praying, forgive, if you have anything against anyone, so that your Father also who is in heaven may forgive you your trespasses."** If you follow through on the forgiveness my friend, you will experience a peace that is just incredible in nature. It will be the ultimate release. What have you got to lose? You can't pray fully if you are harboring anything against another. It isn't possible.

Forgive.
What have you
got to lose?

December 24th

    With God's divine destiny at work in our lives we cannot go wrong. We will succeed in all we do because we're holding onto the things of God and our most precious Christian Faith. Some have received all kinds of riches, monetary gains and worldly legacies within their lives, only to find out that wealth doesn't satisfy the soul. Money cannot and doesn't buy happiness or fulfillment. If you lose your focus and confuse your priorities, money can bring you away from the things that God wants you to see in Jesus Christ. Many people have stored up their treasures here on earth, but they are spiritually lost by not having God in their lives. They're searching for spirituality and a deeper meaning to life. They realize that they're missing something in life and they can't quite figure it out what it is. Have you ever had the feeling that something's missing and you can't quite put your finger on what it is? There are people out there that you know personally who are searching for that something. They're missing a personal relationship with Jesus Christ and no one has shared Him with them. This personal relationship with Jesus Christ is the only thing that can bring about total fulfillment. God longs to fill the incompleteness of your soul with Him. Try to remember what life felt like without Him.

    This is the perfect day to share God with someone you know. Can you imagine how great a gift you can give someone this day of all days? It is Christmas Eve and you can give someone the personal relationship which they have been missing their whole life. You have the opportunity to introduce someone to Jesus Christ, the Savior of the World. You can do this on the eve of the celebration of His Birth. What a gift. Well, what are you waiting for? Go out and do it.

Give someone the gift
that keeps on giving

December 25th

Merry Christmas! Christmas, the celebration of the birth of Jesus Christ is taking place today. Praise God! Let us reflect, give honor and all glory to the One that has allowed us to live another year by His grace, mercy and love. God has given us life and He has given us the opportunity of having and experiencing another Christmas with our family and friends. How blessed we are as Christians living here in the United States of America. We have the freedom of celebrating Christmas, the birth of Jesus Christ. Let's rejoice with the heavenly angels for the birth of Jesus Christ. Let us gather in our local assembly of worshippers to celebrate this Holy Day when the Savior came into the world to save the lost. Can't you picture little baby Jesus in a manger, with Mary, Joseph and the three wise men looking on? I ask God to never let us to forget the significance of the coming of Jesus Christ to this earth, to our families, and ultimately to our individual lives.

The Gospels of Matthew and Luke record the birth of Jesus. I encourage you to read them. When you read them, think of how you would have reacted if you were either Mary or Joseph. There are so many possible reactions that could have happened but they didn't. Why? It was a God thing. God had orchestrated the perfect symphony. He had it all planned out and it culminated with the birth of the Savior of Mankind entering the world as a tiny little bundle of joy. Now think of all that He came to do and the reason for which He came. Talk about a Christmas present; He was the ultimate gift for all mankind. Are you grateful this Holiday season? Have you taken Christ out of Christmas? It's not too late to put Him back. Don't say "Happy Holidays", say "Merry Christmas" and mean it. I do. You can't make me say anything else. He is the reason for the season after all.

Remember the reason
for the season!

December 26ᵗʰ

Let us pray that Jesus Christ will combat **The Waging War Within** our lives and allow us to fulfill the destiny which He has given us. Ask Him to give us the strength so that we will be the witness that He has called us to be. We can be that witness if we will just do our part. He is waiting for us to take up the yoke. If the world doesn't experience the saving power of Christ through us, who will God use? He desires to use us in order to reach the world around us. We need to ask ourselves how He would have us touch our world for Him. Let's pray that God, by the power of the Holy Spirit, would empower us to live a life of witnessing for Him. A destiny has no value if the world culture steals it, ruins it, and ultimately diminishes its worth. Let's pray that God would allow us to be men and women of integrity so that we could carry out His destiny in the world in which we live. This divine destiny is God's reason for creating us.

He commanded us to witness. Matthew 28:19-20; "**Go therefore and make disciples of all nations, baptizing them in the name of the Father and of the Son and of the Holy Spirit, teaching them to observe all that I have commanded you.**" When was the last time you went out and witnessed? It isn't scary once you do it. All you have to do is open your mouth and He will give you the words to use. Just open your mouth. It's like anything else in life; it's the fear of the unknown. That is why Christ gave us the Helper, the Holy Spirit. Acts 2:17; "**And in the last days it shall be, God declares, that I will pour out my Spirit on all flesh.**" We have the Helper promised by God. His purpose is to assist in the work of the Father. He is here to help build the Kingdom. We have His assistance if we only would ask for it. Have you asked for it?

Ask for His assistance

December 27th

One of the crucial aspects of **The Waging War Within** is to convey to the following generations of Christian believers that we're in a spiritual war that requires us to learn how to fight spiritually. The following generations need to realize that in-order to live a strong and successful Christian life; we need to be spiritually equipped with the understanding of how to fight spiritual combat. Our lives will be radically enhanced spiritually once we drop to our knees in humility and meekness, allowing God to go forth with His Holy Spirit and His Angelic Host to fight on our behalf. Christians will win the war while on their knees in prayer. It's critical to convey the truths which Jesus has given us. Just as Jesus displayed when He went off by Himself to pray, we should be doing this also. We should model our lives after Jesus' life. He knew firsthand the power of prayer. He displayed the example of humbling Himself before the Father.

Spiritual warfare is no joke my friends. You must be prayed up before you engage the enemy. You cannot bring a knife to a gunfight; if you do, you're an idiot. You will be taken out for sure. God has given us spiritual armor for a reason. Ephesians 6: 10-18; **"Finally, be strong in the Lord and in the strength of his might. Put on the whole armor of God, that you may be able to stand against the schemes of the devil. For we do not wrestle against flesh and blood, but against the rulers, against the authorities, against the cosmic powers over this present darkness, against the spiritual forces of evil in the heavenly places. Therefore take up the whole armor of God, that you may be able to withstand in the evil day, and having done all, to stand firm. Stand therefore, having fastened on the belt of truth, and having put on the breastplate of righteousness, and, as shoes for your feet, having put on the readiness given by the gospel of peace. In all circumstances take up the shield of faith, with which you can extinguish all the flaming darts of the evil one; and take the helmet of salvation, and the sword of the Spirit, which is the word of God, praying at all times in the Spirit, with all prayer and supplication."** Don your armor my friends for we are in a battle.

We are in a battle.
It's a spiritual war.

December 28th

      Jesus has left us a destiny of peace. Despite the conflicts that are happening on the world scene and the tumultuous world that we live in, we have peace in God. God's peace transcends understanding. Philippians 4:7; **"And the peace of God, which surpasses all understanding, will guard your hearts and your minds in Christ Jesus."** It defies logic and flies in the face of reason. It comes by faith. Romans 10:17; **"So faith comes from hearing, and hearing through the word of Christ."** We need faith. In order to get faith we need God. In order to get God, someone needs to open their mouth and tell us about Him. It's a cycle my friends. Someone takes a step in faith and shares the Word and then you come to know Christ. Then you study the Word and then you take a step of faith and share and so on and so on. In the midst of **The Waging War Within** we can have comfort and peace with the empowerment of the Holy Spirit. Even in the most difficult times God has promised to give us His peace; a peace not of this present world, but a peace from God.

      God can comfort us in all situations and circumstances that we find ourselves in. The Holy Spirit is the Comforter that can give us a real peace in the midst of the storms of life. God gives peace not as this world gives peace; His peace is a peace from above. The world cannot conjure up a peace that is like the one from above. God's peace is authentic and it comes by placing your faith in Him. This Christmas season, we want to look at little baby Jesus lying in a manger and reflect on the peace that He has given us, despite all of the things that are going on around us. We need to concentrate on His peace; the peace that surpasses all understanding. We need to take our focus off of us and our circumstances and reflect on Him. When we reflect on ourselves and our circumstances, we are giving the devil a foothold in our lives. When we reflect on our circumstances, we start the pity party and thumb sucking. We need to get our thumbs out of our mouths and we need to get busy with the work that He would have us do. We can't let the enemy of our souls win **The Waging War Within.**

Don't let the enemy win!

December 29th

  God has given us self-control. Despite **The Waging War Within** happening within us and all around us, He has given us the ability through Him to maintain our composure in all circumstances. We can maintain a steadiness and control within our lives that is fully consistent with the Word of God. We don't have to let the anxieties of this life pervade, conquer and get us down. We can conquer all things through Jesus Christ our Lord and Savior. Philippians 4:13; "**I can do all things through him who strengthens me.**" That means that when the world is doing its best day and night to try to get you to conform to the immoral ways of it, that you are able to stand strong knowing that God has got your back. He can and does give you strength to stand in the face of adversity that you would never possess on your own. Nothing is or will be too difficult for us to get through with God on our side.

  We can rise above the cares and stresses of this world with our faith intact through the strength that God has given to us. With the power of the Holy Spirit indwelling within us we can maintain our tongue when we're angry or distressed. The tongue is small yet extremely powerful. James devotes an entire chapter on the tongue. Read James chapter 3 for a better idea on the power of the tongue. We can call upon God to help us in our time of troubles and need. He will respond immediately once called. We have to allow Him to enter our lives, work on our behalf, and minister to us by and through the power of the Holy Spirit.

**The power of the
tongue is incredible.
It can build up or tear down.**

December 30th

God has left us a destiny of joy and freedom. We have the freedom to worship and praise Him within our hearts, our lives, our minds, our souls and our spirits; we also have the freedom to reject Him all at the same time. When we worship and praise the Lord we experience a joy that transcends all human understanding. Through faith in the midst of even devastating news, we can lift our hands to our Lord and Savior Jesus Christ singing and praising with a genuine joy that comes only from within. Our spirits are set free from the bondages of this world that would hold us captive if we allowed it to happen. God has given us the ability to make choices. We're not puppets that He controls; we all have free will. We can use this freewill to follow the things of this world or we can use this freewill to follow the things of God. We can choose the direction in life we're going to take and what road we're going to go down. It's a matter of decision that only we can make.

Have you ever contemplated doing something and then you got a check in your spirit telling you not to do it but you went ahead and did it anyway? We all have. How did it make you feel when you went against what the Holy Spirit was telling you to do? Pretty crummy huh? I never paid much attention to that feeling before coming to Christ. Now when I get that check in the spirit I heed its warning. It is usually preventing me from doing something that will have long term regrets. That check in the spirit is a blessing. We all need to heed the warning given to us by the Holy Spirit. We have a conscience which knows right from wrong. The Holy Spirit is building off of that.

I hate feeling guilty. That is how I feel when I don't heed the warnings given to me by the Holy Spirit. I feel like a naughty boy. What I hate worse is when God takes me to the woodshed. Ouch!! There is nothing worse than getting the Holy Smack down. When God gives you a stinger, you don't ever want a repeat performance. Trust me on that one. We just need to trust and obey our spirit checks.

Trust and obey your
Spiritual instincts.

December 31st

  God has left us a destiny of power. With His power comes responsibility. We have power in Jesus Christ to overcome everything this world can throw at us. Every obstacle that comes our way to impede, block, or thwart our growth in Jesus Christ can be hurdled with the power that we find with God. Nothing can penetrate the destiny of God's power and authority here on earth. He's the Supreme Being who's created the entire universe. His power is unlimited and unquenchable. He will not stop until He accomplishes what He has set out to do here on earth.

  When we're living in right relationship with God, we have the power that exists within God. He empowers us with the power of His Holy Spirit. The Holy Spirit empowers us from the inside out. He can be seen outwardly in our lives as long as we're allowing Him to operate on us inwardly. The work that we do for the Kingdom is delivered through the power of the Holy Spirit.

  When we allow the power of the Holy Spirit to manifest Himself through us, we are allowing the work of God to be witnessed by all. We are Gods Ambassadors after all. We are all serving as examples of God to the world. It is up to us whether we are going to be good examples or bad examples. We can either give God a smile or a black eye by our actions. What we need to do is act as if God is walking with us every hour of every day and we will be thinking of all of our actions before we commit to them. Let's think before we speak or act. Let's live out God's destiny for our lives. Let's be all that He has us here to be.

We can overcome all things with
Jesus Christ as our Lord.

Conclusion

Our hearts desire and prayer is that this devotional would be used by God to bring those that know Jesus Christ as their Personal Lord and Savior into a deeper relationship with Him. I also pray that those that have not accepted Jesus Christ as their Personal Lord and Savior would accept Him into their hearts and lives.

For those that have accepted Jesus and those that haven't, my prayer is that God would use this book to touch lives for Him, in His way, in His power, and in His time, by the power of the Holy Spirit. My prayer is that God would use this book as a tool and a vehicle in which He can work through to bring people from all over the world into His Saving Grace.

My final prayer is that God would empower you through Jesus Christ to find every spiritual dynamic you need in Him to not only fight, but win **The Waging War Within.**

You can accept Jesus Christ right now as your Personal Lord and Savior if you haven't already done so. By accepting Jesus Christ as your Personal Lord and Savior, you will be able to conquer death, hell, and the grave. You will be saved and Jesus Christ, by the power of His Holy Spirit, will come to live in your life with all of His power and glory. God will transform you, bringing you into right relationship with Him. You will be a new creation in Jesus Christ, your name will be written in the Lamb's Book of Life and Heaven will be your eternal reward. There is no other name under heaven, except for the name of Jesus Christ, whereby we must be saved. Acts 4:12; **"Salvation is found in no one else, for there is no other name under heaven given to men by which we must be saved."**

You can repeat the following to God through Jesus Christ His Son if you wish to accept Him as your Personal Lord and Savior.

"Dear Jesus Christ- I accept you into my heart and life. I pray that you would come into my life and save me from all of my sins. I accept you as my Personal Lord and Savior. I know that when I pray this prayer of salvation that you will come to live in me and you will start to transform my life in a powerful way. Thank you Jesus and now I pray that you would lead me, guide me in that path of righteousness for your names sake for the rest of my days here on earth. I ask this in Jesus' Holy name, Amen."

You have now accepted Jesus Christ as your Personal Lord and Savior and you're now born again into His Kingdom. You no longer belong to this world but have accepted our Heavenly Father into your heart and life. Find yourself a solid Bible believing church where you can grow in the Lord and your personal relationship with Him. You just made the most important decision of your life my friend. The angels in heaven rejoice when another soul comes to accept Jesus as their Personal Lord and Savior. I pray God uses you mightily for the building of His Kingdom. I pray blessings upon you and yours.

About the Authors

Gregg Joseph Kretschmer currently resides in the town of Agawam, MA. Gregg was born in Kenosha, WI. and is a veteran of the Armed Forces. Gregg is a graduate student attending Gordon-Conwell Theological Seminary where he is working towards his Masters of Divinity degree. Gregg attends Bethany Assembly of God in Agawam where he is currently the Director of Men's Ministry. Gregg has a heart to see men become the men of God that they have been called to be. Gregg is currently leading men in the Champions of Honor plan started by former Secret Service Agent Chuck Brewster. Gregg has attained all three tiers in the plan and is passing on his zeal for men, to men who want to be all that they have been called to be, the priests of their home, work place, church, and community. Gregg is also working towards his licensing and credentialing through the Assemblies of God. Gregg has been on numerous missions carrying out God's plan to other nations through building schools for Latin American Child Care. Gregg is married and he has a son.

Jason Christian Ravizza, M.Ed., C.A.G.S., also resides in the town of Agawam, MA. Jason was born in Hartford Connecticut. Jason is licensed; as a mental health counselor, a teacher, a school adjustment counselor/social worker, an assistant principal and a principal in the state of Massachusetts. Jason attained his Bachelors of Science and Masters of Education from Springfield College and his Certificate of Advanced Graduate Studies in Educational Administration from the University of Massachusetts at Amherst. Jason has worked within mental health agencies and clinics, at lock-up residential facilities, within the hospital setting, within public schools, in private practice, as adjunct faculty on the college level, as a supervisor within the fields of mental health and education, and as a Christian Counselor. Jason has served as a youth leader and has been involved in work with the youth, young adults and adults within his local church and the Body of Jesus Christ. Jason is married and has three children.

Bibliography

Barker, Kenneth, Gen. Ed. *The NIV Study Bible.* Grand Rapids, MI: Zondervan, 1995Crossway Bibles.

The ESV Study Bible, English Standard Version. Wheaton, Illinois 60187: Good News Publishers. (2007).